The Eggs, Beans and Crumpets of the Drones Club are a rum lot, but kindly. Ask Barmy Fotheringay-Phipps why his stories have never been collected and it's a fair wager that he'll gaze at the ceiling and think of the case of Pongo Twistleton-Twistleton, and he'll ponder the question deeply before failing to reply. Freddie Widgeon wouldn't know the answer either—but it's the favorite in the Derby against a milk-float pony that he'll pour you a double snifter and slap you on the back instead. They're like that, up at the Drones Club.

But now these strong silent types have decided to tell all—and so you can discover what really happened during the Great Peke Crisis, what was the deep secret of the Beef Trust, and why Bramley is so bracing. You'll find the results as lively as a Boat Race Night party—and what better host for the festivities than P. G. Wodehouse.

P. G. WODEHOUSE

TALES FROM THE
DRONES CLUB

INTERNATIONAL POLYGONICS, LTD.
NEW YORK CITY

TALES FROM THE DRONES CLUB

Copyright © by the Trustees of the Wodehouse Estate, 1982.
Published by arrangement with the Trustees and A.P. Watt Ltd.
Wodehouse biographical sketch copyright © by D.R. Bensen, 1991.
Cover illustration copyright © by Jeff Fisher, 1991.

The following appeared in the hardbound edition:

Library of Congress Cataloging-in-Publication Data

Wodehouse, P. G. (Pelham Grenville), 1881-1975
    Tales from the drones club / P. G. Wodehouse
    p. cm
    Originally published: London : Hutchinson, 1982
    ISBN 1-55882-088-4
    1. Men—England—London—Societies and clubs—Fiction. I.
Title.
PR6045.053A6 1991a
823'.912—dc20   91-8386 CIP

Library of Congress Catalog No. 92-70415
ISBN 1-55882-118-X

Printed in the United States of America
First IPL printing April 1991
First paperback printing April 1992
10 9 8 7 6 5 4 3 2

CONTENTS

1
FATE

It was the hour of the morning snifter, and a little group of Eggs and Beans and Crumpets had assembled in the smoking room of the Drones Club to do a bit of inhaling. There had been a party of sorts overnight, and the general disposition of the company was towards a restful and somewhat glassy-eyed silence. This was broken at length by one of the Crumpets.

'Old Freddie's back,' he observed.

Some moments elapsed before any of those present felt equal to commenting on this statement. Then a Bean spoke.

'Freddie Who?'

'Freddie Widgeon.'

'Back where?'

'Back here.'

'I mean, back from what spot?'

'New York.'

'I didn't know Freddie had been to New York.'

'Well, you can take it from me he has. Or else how,' argued the Crumpet, 'could he have got back?'

The Bean considered the point.

'Something in that,' he agreed. 'What sort of a time did he have?'

'Not so good. He lost the girl he loved.'

'I wish I had a quid for every girl Freddie Widgeon has loved and lost,' sighed an Egg wistfully. 'If I had, I shouldn't be touching you for a fiver.'

'You aren't,' said the Crumpet.

The Bean frowned. His head was hurting him, and he considered that the conversation was becoming sordid.

'How did he lose his girl?'

'Because of the suitcase.'

'What suitcase?'

'The suitcase he carried for the other girl.'

'What other girl?'

'The one he carried the suitcase for.'

The Bean frowned again.

'A bit complex, all this, isn't it?' he said. 'Hardly the sort of stuff, I mean, to spring on personal friends who were up a trifle late last night.'

'It isn't really,' the Crumpet assured him. 'Not when you know the facts. The way old Freddie told me the story it was as limpid as dammit. And what he thinks – and what I think, too – is that it just shows what toys we are in the hands of Fate, if you know what I mean. I mean to say, it's no good worrying and trying to look ahead and plan and scheme and weigh your every action, if you follow me, because you never can tell when doing such-and-such won't make so-and-so happen – while, on the other hand, if you do so-and-so it may just as easily lead to such-and-such.'

A pale-faced Egg with heavy circles under his eyes rose at this point and excused himself. He said his head had begun to throb again and he proposed to step round to the chemist on the corner for another of his dark brown pick-me-ups.

'I mean to say,' resumed the Crumpet, 'if Freddie – with the best motives in the world – hadn't carried that suitcase for that girl, he might at this moment be walking up the aisle with a gardenia in his buttonhole and Mavis Peasemarch, only daughter of the fifth Earl of Bodsham, on his arm.'

The Bean demurred. He refused to admit the possibility of such a thing, even if Freddie Widgeon had sworn off suitcases for life.

'Old Bodders would never have allowed Mavis to marry a bird of Freddie's calibre. He would think him worldly and frivolous. I don't know if you are personally acquainted with the Bod, but I may tell you that my people once lugged me to a weekend at his place and not only were we scooped in and shanghaied to church twice on the Sunday, regardless of age or sex, but on the Monday morning at eight o'clock – eight, mark you – there were family prayers in the dining-room. There you have old Bodders in a nutshell. Freddie's a good chap, but he can't have stood a dog's chance from the start.'

'On the contrary,' said the Crumpet warmly. 'He made his presence felt right from the beginning to an almost unbelievable extent, and actually clicked as early as the fourth day out.'

'Were Bodders and Mavis on the boat, then?'

'They certainly were. All the way over.'

'And Bodders, you say, actually approved of Freddie?'

'He couldn't have been more all over him, Freddie tells me, if Freddie had been a Pan-Anglican Congress. What you overlook is that Bodsham – living, as he does, all the year round in the country – knew nothing of Freddie except that one of his uncles was his old schoolfriend, Lord Blicester, and another of his uncles was actually a

Bishop. Taking a line through them, he undoubtedly regarded Freddie as a pretty hot potato.'

The Bean seemed shaken, but he put another point.

'What about Mavis, then?'

'What about her?'

'I should have thought Freddie would have been the last bloke she would have considered hitching up with. I've seen her in action down at Peasemarch, and you can take it from me that she is very far from being one of the boys. You needn't let it get about, of course, but that girl, to my certain knowledge, plays the organ in the local church and may often be seen taking soup to the deserving villagers with many a gracious word.'

The Crumpet had his answer to this, too.

'She knew nothing of Freddie, either. She liked his quiet, saintly manner and considered that he had a soul. At any rate, I can assure you that everything went like a breeze. Helped by the fact that the sea was calm and that there was a dashed fine moon every night, old Freddie shoved his nose past the judge's box at 10.45 p.m. on the fourth day out. And when next morning he informed old Bodsham that he had now a son to comfort his declining years, there was not a discordant note. The old boy said that he could wish no better husband for his daughter than a steady, respectable young fellow like Freddie, and they arrived in New York a happy and united family.

The only thing in the nature of a flaw that Freddie found in New York, he tells me, was the fact that the populace, to judge from the daily papers, didn't seem to be so ideally happy in its love-life as he was. What I mean to say, he wanted smiling faces about him, so to speak, and it looked to him as if everybody in the place were cutting up their wives and hiding them in sacks in the Jersey marshes or else putting detectives on to them to secure the necessary evidence.

It saddened him, he tells me, when he opened his illustrated tabloid of a morning, to have to try to eat eggs and bacon while gazing at a photograph of Mae Belle McGinnis, taken when she was not looking her best because Mr McGinnis had just settled some domestic dispute with the meat-axe.

Also, there seemed to him far too much of all that stuff about Sugar Daddies being Discovered In Love Nest As Blizzard Grips City.

However, when you are the guest of a great nation, you have to take the rough with the smooth. And there appears to be no doubt that, despite all the marital unrest around him, Freddie at this juncture was indisputably in the pink. I've never been engaged myself, so I know nothing of the symptoms at first hand, but Freddie tells me that the way it takes a fellow is to make him feel as if he were floating on a fleecy cloud, high up in the air, and only touching the ground at odd spots.

Most of the time, he says, he just hovered over New York like some winged thing. But occasionally he would come down and emerge from the ether, and on one of these rare occasions he found himself wandering in the neighbourhood of Seventy-Second Street, somewhere on the West Side.

And just in front of him was a girl lugging a dashed great heavy suitcase.

Now, I want you to follow me very closely here. This is where Freddie stands or falls. He was pretty eloquent at this point, when he told me the story: and, as far as I am concerned, I may say fearlessly that I dismiss him without a stain on his character. I consider his motives to have been pure to the last drop.

One of the things that being engaged does to you, you must remember, is to fill you to the gills with a sort of knightly chivalry. So Freddie tells me. You go about the place like a Boy Scout, pouncing out on passers-by and doing acts of kindness to them. Three times that day Freddie had chased seedy-looking birds up side streets and forced cash on them. He had patted four small boys on the head and asked them if they meant to be President some day. He had beamed benevolently on the citizenry till his cheeks ached. And he was still full of the milk of human kindness and longing to assist some less fortunate fellow-traveller along the road of Life, when he saw this girl in front of him, staggering under the weight of the suitcase.

Now, although the impulse to help her with her burden was intense, he tells me that, if she had been a pretty girl, he would have resisted it. His sense of loyalty to Mavis was so great that he was right off pretty girls. They were the only persons he had excluded from his beaming operations. Towards them, in spite of all that milk of human kindness, he had been consistently aloof and austere. The cold face. The unwobbly eye. Something seemed to tell him that Mavis would prefer it so.

But this girl before him was not pretty. She was distinctly plain. Even ugly. She looked as if she might be a stenographer selected for some business magnate by his wife out of a number of competing applicants. And, such being so, he did not hesitate. Already the suitcase seemed to be giving the poor little thing a crick in the back, and it was as if he heard Mavis's voice in his ear, whispering: 'Go to it!'

He ambled up like a courtly mustang.

'Excuse me,' he said. 'May I help you with that apparatus of yours?'

The girl gave him a keen look through her spectacles, and either thought he was thoroughly to be trusted, or didn't. At any rate, she passed over the bag.

'And now where?' asked Freddie.

The girl said she lived in Sixty-Ninth Street, and Freddie right-hoed, and they set off. And presently they came to a brown stone building, in which she had Flat B on the fourth floor.

Well, of course, you may say that, having deposited female and suitcase at their destination, old Freddie should have uttered a brief, courteous 'Pip-pip!' and legged it. And very possibly you are right. But consider the facts. The flat, as I have indicated, was four flights up. There was no lift, so he had had to hoof it up all those stairs. It was a warm day. And the suitcase appeared to be packed with sheet-iron or something.

I mean to say, by the time he had reached Journey's End, he was in sore need of a spot of repose. So, rightly or wrongly, he didn't biff off, but sort of collapsed into a chair and sat there restoring his tissues.

The girl, meanwhile, prattled in friendly vein. As far as Freddie can recall her remarks, her name was Myra Jennings. She was employed in the office of a wholesale silk importer. She had just come back from the country. The photograph over the sideboard was her mother's, who lived in Waterbury, Connecticut. The girlfriend with whom she shared the flat was away on her vacation. And all that sort of thing, don't you know. I mean, pleasant gossip from the home.

She had just begun to tell him that, though she yielded to no one in her admiration for Ronald Colman, she couldn't help saying that William Powell had a sort of something that kind of seemed to place him sort of even higher in a girl's estimation, when there occurred one of those interruptions which, I understand, are always happening in New York.

If you're a native, you hardly notice them. You just look over your shoulder and say 'Oh, ah?' and go on trying to get Los Angeles on the radio.

But Freddie, being new to the place, was a little startled. Because you see, what happened was that just as they were sitting there, chatting of this and that, there was a sudden crash. The door of the hallway which opened on to the landing outside was burst open. And in surged an extraordinarily hefty bloke with a big moustache. He wore a bowler hat. Behind him came a couple of other birds, also hefty and similarly bowler-hatted.

'Ah!' said Bloke A, in a satisfied sort of voice.

Freddie did a bit of gaping. He was a good deal on the nonplussed side. He supposed, as his head began to clear, that this was one of those cases of Bandits Break Into Home and Rob Two.

'Seems to me,' said the Bloke, addressing his associate Blokes, 'this case is open and shut.'

The other two nodded.

'That's right,' said one.

'Open and shut,' said the other.

'Yes,' said the Bloke, summing up. 'That's about what it is. Open *and* shut.'

Miss Jennings, who had been dusting the photograph of her mother, now appeared to notice for the first time that she had visitors. She spoke as follows:

'What in the world do you think you're doing?'

The Bloke lit a cigar. So did his associates. Two cigars.

'That's all right, Mrs Silvers,' he said.

'Sure it's all right,' said the other two.

'You boys are witnesses,' said the Bloke.

'Sure, we're witnesses,' said the other two.

'You can give evidence that we found Mrs Silvers alone in her apartment with this pie-faced cluck.'

'Sure, we can give evidence that we found her alone in her apartment with this pie-faced cluck.'

'Then that's all right,' said the Bloke contentedly. 'That is all her husband will want to know. It makes the thing open and shut.'

And it came home to Freddie with a sickening thud that these fellows were not, as he had supposed, a hold-up gang, but detectives. He ought to have recognized them from the start, he tells me, by the bowler hats. What had misled him was the fact that at the outset they weren't smoking cigars. When they started smoking cigars, the scales fell from his eyes.

He gulped a bit. In fact, he gulped rather more than a bit. He realized now what his mistaken sense of knightly chivalry had made him stumble into. The soup, no less. With the best intentions, meaning only to scatter light and sweetness on every side, he had become a Sugar Daddy Surprised In Love Nest.

The female of the species, however, appeared unwilling to take this thing lying down. Her chin was up, her shoulders were squared, she had both feet on the ground, and she looked the troupe steadily in the eye through her spectacles.

'Just for fun,' she said, 'tell me where you fellows think you are?'

'Where do we think we are?' said the Bloke. 'That's all right where we think we are. We're in Flat 4A. And you're Mrs Silvers. And I'm from the Alert Detective Agency. And I'm acting under instructions from your husband. Laugh that off!'

'I will,' said the girl. 'I'm not Mrs Silvers. I haven't a husband. And this isn't Flat A, it's Flat B.'

The Bloke gasped. He reminded Freddie of his Uncle Joseph, the time he swallowed the bad oyster. The same visible emotion.

'Don't tell me we've busted into the wrong flat?' he said, pleadingly.

'That's just what I am telling you.'

'The wrong flat?'

'The wrong flat.'

There was a pause.

'I'll tell you what it is,' said one of the assistant Blokes, a pretty acute chap, quick on the uptake. 'We've been and busted into the wrong flat.'

'That's it,' said the other. 'The wrong flat.'

Well, they were very decent about it, Freddie tells me. They didn't take off their hats, and they went on smoking their cigars, but they paid for the door. And presently the party broke up, the Bloke protesting to the last that this was the first mistake he had made in twenty years.

Having had a hearty laugh with the Jennings over the whole amusing episode, Freddie hopped into a taxi and started off for Forty-Sixth Street, for he was lunching with old Bodsham and Mavis at the Ritz-Carlton and was a bit late already. All the way down there, he was chuckling to himself at the thought of what a capital story he had to tell them. Put him one up, he thought it would.

You see, if there was a snag in the whole-hearted joy of being engaged to Mavis Peasemarch, it was the fact that, when in the society of herself and father, he occasionally found the going a bit sticky as regarded conversation.

Freddie, as you know, is a bird who, when the conditions are right, can be the life and soul of the party. Shoot a few stiffish cocktails into him and give him his head in the matter of sprightly anecdotes and the riper kind of limerick, and he will hold you spellbound. But, cut off from these resources, he frequently found himself a trifle tongue-tied when taking a bite with old Bodsham.

And, as no fellow likes to feel that his future father-in-law is beginning to regard him as a loony deaf-mute, he welcomed the opportunity of showing himself a gay and gifted raconteur.

If the story of his morning's adventure, told as he proposed to tell it, didn't have the old boy hiccoughing and wiping the tears from his eyes, he would be jolly well dashed.

And the same applied to Mavis.

'Capital! Capital! Ah, Van Sprunt, this is my son-in-law-to-be, Frederick Widgeon. A most entertaining young fellow. Get him to tell you his story about the detectives in the wrong flat. You'll die laughing. We all think very highly of Frederick Widgeon.'

And all that sort of thing, I mean. What? I mean to say, you follow his reasoning.

Well, he didn't get a chance to spring the story over the melon and powdered ginger, because old Bodsham was rather holding the floor a bit on the subject of iniquitous Socialist attacks on the House of Lords. Then, with the *côtelettes* and mashed, Mavis started to haul up her slacks about the Soul of America. In fact, it wasn't till the coffee had arrived that he secured a genuine opening.

'I say,' said Freddie, catching the Speaker's eye at this juncture, 'a most awfully funny thing happened to me this morning. Make you scream. You'll burst your corsets.'

And, lighting a carefree cigarette, he embarked upon the narrative.

He told it well. Looking back, he says, he can't remember when he has ever done more justice to a yarn, squeezed the last drop of juice out of it with a firmer hand, if you know what I mean. The grave, intent faces of his audience, he tells me, only spurred him on to further efforts. He approved of their self-restraint. He realized that they realized that a story like this was not the sort of story to fritter away with giggles. You saved yourself up for the big howl at the finish.

And then suddenly – he couldn't tell just when – there stole over him a sort of feeling that the *conte* wasn't getting across quite so big as he had hoped. There seemed to him to be a certain definite something in the atmosphere. You know how it is when you strike a cold audience. Old Bodsham was looking a little like a codfish with something on its mind, and there was an odd kind of expression in Mavis's eye.

When he had finished, there was a longish silence. Mavis looked at old Bodsham. Old Bodsham looked at Mavis.

'I don't quite understand, Frederick,' said Mavis at length. 'You say this girl was a stranger?'

'Why, yes,' said Freddie.

'And you accosted her in the street?'

'Why, yes,' said Freddie.

'Oh?' said Mavis.

'I was sorry for her,' said Freddie.

'Oh?' said Mavis.

'In fact, you might say that my heart bled for her.'

'Oh?' said Mavis.

Old Bodsham let his breath go in a sort of whistling sigh.

'Is it your practice, may I ask,' he said, 'to scrape acquaintance in the public streets with young persons of the opposite sex?'

'You must remember, father,' said Mavis, in a voice which would have had an Esquimau slapping his ribs and calling for the steam-heat, 'that this girl was probably very pretty. So many of these New York girls are. That would, of course, explain Frederick's behaviour.'

'She wasn't!' yipped Freddie. 'She was a gargoyle.'

'Oh?' said Mavis.

'Spectacled to bursting-point and utterly lacking in feminine allure.'

'Oh?' said Mavis.

'And when I saw her frail form bowed down by that dashed great suitcase ... I should have thought,' said Freddie, injured, 'that, having learned the salient facts, you would have fawned on me for my big-hearted chivalry.'

'Oh?' said Mavis.

There was another silence.

'I must be going, father,' said Mavis. 'I have some shopping to do.'

'Shall I come with you?' said Freddie.

'I would prefer to be alone,' said Mavis.

'I must be going,' said old Bodsham. 'I have some thinking to do.'

'Thinking?' said Freddie.

'Thinking,' said old Bodsham. 'Some serious thinking. Some extremely serious thinking. Some very serious thinking indeed.'

'We will leave Frederick to finish his cigarette,' said Mavis.

'Yes,' said old Bodsham. 'We will leave Frederick to finish his cigarette.'

'But listen,' bleated Freddie. 'I give you my honest word she looked like something employed by the Government for scaring crows in the cornfields of Minnesota.'

'Oh?' said Mavis.

'Oh?' said old Bodsham.

'Come, father,' said Mavis.

And old Freddie found himself alone, and not feeling so frightfully good.

Now, it was Freddie's practice – and a very prudent practice, too – to

carry on his person, concealed in his hip pocket, a small but serviceable flask full of the true, the blushful Hippocrene. Friends whom he
had made since his arrival in New York had advocated this policy,
pointing out that you never knew when it would come in useful. His
first act, accordingly, after the two Vice-Presidents of the Knickerbocker Ice Company had left him and he had begun to thaw out a bit,
was to produce this flask and take a quick, sharp snort.

The effect was instantaneous. His numbed brain began to work.
And presently, after a couple more swift ones, he saw daylight.

The whole nub of the thing, he perceived clearly, was the personal
appearance of the girl Jennings. In the matter of her loved one's acts
of chivalry towards damsels in distress, a fiancée holds certain
definite views. If the damsels he assists are plain, he is a good chap
and deserves credit. If they are pretty, he is a low hound who jolly
well gets his ring and letters back by the first post.

Obviously, then, his only course was to return to Sixty-Ninth
Street, dig up the Jennings, and parade her before Mavis. Her mere
appearance, he was convinced, would clear him completely.

Of course, the thing would have to be done delicately. I mean to
say, you can't just go to a comparatively strange female and ask her to
trot round to see a friend of yours so that the latter can ascertain at
first hand what a repellently unattractive girl she is. But Freddie,
now full of the juice, fancied he could work it all right. All it wanted
was just a little tact.

'Yoicks!' said Freddie to himself. 'Hark for'ard!' And, in his
opinion, that about summed it up.

It was a lovely afternoon as Freddie got into his taxi outside the Ritz
and tooled off up town. Alighting at Sixty-Ninth Street, he braced
himself with a visible effort and started the long climb up the four
flights of stairs. And presently he was outside the door of Flat 4B and
tootling on the bell.

Nothing happened. He tootled again. He knocked. He even went
so far as to kick the door. But there were no signs of human occu-
pation, and after a bit he was reluctantly forced to the conclusion that
the Jennings was out.

Freddie had not foreseen this possibility, and he leaned against the
wall for a space, thinking out his next move. He had just come to the
conclusion that the only thing to do was to edge away for the nonce
and have another pop later on, when a door opposite opened and a
female appeared.

'Hullo,' said this bird.

'Hullo,' said Freddie.

He spoke, he tells me, a little doubtfully, for a glance had shown him that this woman was not at all the kind of whom Mavis would have approved. A different species altogether. Her eyes were blue and totally free from spectacles. Her teeth were white and even. Her hair was a beautiful gold.

Judging by her costume, she seemed to be a late riser. The hour was 3.30, but she had not yet progressed beyond the negligee and slippers stage. That negligee, moreover, was a soft pink in colour and was decorated throughout with a series of fowls of some kind. Love-birds, Freddie tells me he thinks they were. And a man who is engaged to be married and who, already, is not any too popular with the bride-to-be, shrinks – automatically, as it were – from blue-eyed, golden-haired females in pink negligees picked out with ultramarine lovebirds.

However, a fellow has to be civil. So, having said 'Hullo!' he threw in a reserved, gentlemanly sort of smile for good measure.

He assures me that it was merely one of those aloof smiles which the Honorary Secretary of a Bible Class would have given the elderly aunt of a promising pupil: but it had the effect of encouraging the contents of the negligee to further conversation.

'Looking for someone?' she asked.

'Why, yes,' said Freddie. 'I suppose you couldn't tell me when Miss Jennings will be in?'

'Miss Who?'

'Jennings.'

'What name?'

'Jennings.'

'How do you spell it?'

'Oh, much in the usual way, I expect. Start off with a J and then a good many 'n's and 'g's and things.'

'Miss Jennings, did you say?'

'That's right. Jennings.'

'I'll tell you something,' said the female frankly. 'I've never seen any Miss Jennings. I've never heard of any Miss Jennings. I don't know who she is. She means literally nothing in my life. And I'll tell you something else. I've been breaking my back for half an hour trying to open my living room window, and do you think I can do it? No, sir! What do you advise?'

'Leave it shut,' said Freddie.

'But it's so warm. The weather, I mean.'

'It *is* warm,' agreed Freddie.

'I'm just stifling. Yes, sir. That's what I am. Stifling in my tracks.'

At this point, undoubtedly, old Freddie should have said 'Oh?' or

'Well, best o' luck!' or something on that order, and buzzed off. But once a fellow drops into the habit of doing acts of kindness, he tells me, it's dashed difficult to pull up. The thing becomes second nature.

So now, instead of hoofing it, he unshipped another of those polished smiles of his, and asked if there was anything he could do.

'Well, it's a shame to trouble you . . .'

'Not at all.'

'I hate to impose on you . . .'

'Not – a – tall,' said Freddie, becoming more *preux* every moment. 'Only too pleased.'

And he trotted after her into the flat.

'There it is,' said the female. 'The window, I mean.'

Freddie surveyed it carefully. He went over and gave it a shake. It certainly seemed pretty tightly stuck.

'The way they build these joints nowadays,' observed the female, with a certain amount of severity, 'the windows either won't open at all or else they drop out altogether.'

'Well, that's Life, isn't it,' said Freddie.

The thing didn't look any too good to him, but he buckled to like a man, and for some moments nothing was to be heard in the room but his tense breathing.

'How are you getting on?' asked the female.

'I've a sort of rummy buzzing in my head,' said Freddie. 'You don't think it's apoplexy or something?'

'I'd take a rest if I was you,' said his hostess. 'You look warm.'

'I *am* warm,' said Freddie.

'Take your coat off.'

'May I? Thanks.'

'Your collar, too, if you like.'

'Thanks.'

The removal of the upholstery made Freddie feel a little better.

'I once knew a man who opened a window in a Pullman car,' said the female.

'No, really?' said Freddie.

'Ah, what a man!' sighed the female wistfully. 'They don't make 'em like that nowadays.'

I don't suppose she actually intended anything in the way of a slur or innuendo, if you know what I mean, but Freddie tells me he felt a bit stung. It was as if his manly spirit had been challenged. Setting his teeth, he charged forward and had another go.

'Try pulling it down from the top,' said the female.

Freddie tried pulling it down from the top, but nothing happened.

'Try wiggling it sideways,' said the female.

Freddie tried wiggling it sideways, but his efforts were null and void.

'Have a drink,' said the female.

This seemed to old Freddie by miles the best suggestion yet. He sank into a chair and let his tongue hang out. And presently a brimming glass stole into his hand, and he quaffed deeply.

'That's some stuff I brought away from home,' said the female.

'From where?' said Freddie.

'Home.'

'But isn't this your home?'

'Well, it is now. But I used to live in Utica. Mr Silvers made this stuff. About the only good thing he ever did. Mr Silvers, I mean.'

Freddie pondered a bit.

'Mr Silvers? Don't I seem to know that name?'

'I wish I didn't,' said the female. 'There was a palooka, if you want one.'

'A what?'

'A palooka. Mr Silvers. Slice him where you like, he was still boloney.'

The rather generous nature of the fluid he was absorbing was making Freddie feel a bit clouded.

'I don't altogether follow this. Who is Mr Silvers?'

'Ed Silvers. My husband. And is he jealous? Ask me!'

'Ask who?'

'Ask *me*.'

'Ask you what?'

'I'm telling you. I left him flat, because he didn't have no ideals.'

'Who didn't?'

'Mr Silvers.'

'Your husband?'

'That's right.'

'Ah!' said Freddie. 'Now we've got it straight.'

He quaffed again. The foundation of the beverage manufactured by Mr Silvers seemed to be neat vitriol, but, once you had got used to the top of your head going up and down like the lid of a kettle with boiling water in it, the effects were far from unpleasant. Mr Silvers may not have had ideals, but he unquestionably knew what to do when you handed him a still and a potato.

'He made me very unhappy,' said the female.

'Who did?'

'Mr Silvers.'

'Mr Silvers made you unhappy?'

'You're dern tooting Mr Silvers made me unhappy. Entertaining his low suspicions.'

Freddie was shocked.

'Did Mr Silvers entertain low suspicions?'

'He certainly did.'

'Mr Ed Silvers?'

'That's right.'

'I bet that made you unhappy.'

'You never said a truer word.'

'You poor little thing,' said Freddie. 'You poor little Mrs Silvers.'

'Mrs Ed Silvers.'

'You poor little Mrs Ed Silvers. I never heard anything so dashed monstrous in my life. May I pat your hand?'

'You bet your lavender spats you may pat my hand.'

'I will,' said Freddie, and did so.

He even went further. He squeezed her hand. His whole attitude towards her, he tells me, was that of a brother towards a suffering sister.

And at this moment the door flew open, and a number of large objects crashed in. Without any warning the air had suddenly become full of bowler hats.

Freddie, gazing upon them, was conscious of an odd feeling. You know that feeling you sometimes feel of feeling you're feeling that something has happened which has happened before. I believe doctors explain it by saying that the two halves of the brain aren't working strictly on the up-and-up. Anyway, that was how Freddie felt at this point. He felt he had seen those bowler hats before – perhaps in some previous existence.

'What ho!' he said. 'Callers, what?'

And then his brain seemed to clear – or the two halves clicked together, or something – and he recognized the Bloke who had interrupted his *tête-à-tête* with Miss Myra Jennings that morning.

Now, the last time Freddie had seen this Bloke, the latter had been bathed in confusion. You pictured his embarrassment. He was now looking far cheerier. He had the air of a bloke in a bowler hat who has won through to his objective.

'We're in, boys,' he said.

The two subsidiary Blokes nodded briefly. One of them said: 'Sure, we're in.' The other said: 'Hot dog!'

The head Bloke scrutinized Freddie closely.

'Well, I'm darned!' he exclaimed. 'If it isn't you again! Boys,' he said, a note of respect creeping into his voice, 'take a good slant at this guy. Eye him reverently. The swiftest worker in New York. Mark how he flits from spot to spot. You can't go anywhere without finding him. And he hasn't even got a bicycle.'

Freddie saw that it was time to draw himself up to his full height and put these fellows in their place. He endeavoured to do so, but something seemed to prevent him.

'Let me explain,' he said.

The Bloke sneered visibly.

'Are you going to tell us we are in the wrong flat again?'

'My answer to that,' said Freddie, 'is yes – and no.'

'What do you mean, yes and no? This is Flat 4A.'

'True,' said Freddie. 'That point I yield. This *is* Flat 4A. But I assure you, on the word of an English gentleman, that this lady is a complete stranger to me.'

'Stranger?'

'A complete and total stranger.'

'Oh?' said the Bloke. 'Then what's she doing sitting in your lap?'

And Freddie, with acute astonishment, perceived that this was indeed so. At what point in their conversation it had occurred, he could not have said, but Mrs Ed Silvers was undeniably nestling on the spot indicated. It was this, he saw now, which had prevented him a moment ago drawing himself up to his full height.

'By Jove!' he said. 'She is, isn't she?'

'She certainly is.'

'Well, well!' said Freddie. 'Well, well, well!'

You could have knocked him down with a feather, and he said as much.

Mrs Silvers spoke.

'Listen,' she said. 'As Heaven is my witness I never saw this man before.'

'Then what's he doing here?'

'Opening the window.'

'It's shut.'

'I know it's shut.'

'Open *and* shut,' said the Bloke. 'Like this case. Eh, boys?'

'Ah!' said one of the boys.

'Uh-huh,' said the other.

The Bloke eyed Mrs Silvers severely.

'You ought to be ashamed of yourself, lady,' he said. 'Such goings-on. I'm shocked. That's what I am. Shocked. And the boys are shocked, too.'

Freddie was able to rise now, for the female had ceased to roost. He got up, and would have towered above the Bloke, only it so happened that the latter was about six inches taller.

'You are aspersing a woman's name,' he said.

'Eh?'

'Don't attempt to evade the issue,' said Freddie, giving him a haughty glance. 'You are aspersing a woman's name, and – what makes it worse – you are doing it in a bowler hat. Take off that hat,' said Freddie.

The Bloke stared at him blankly. He was probably on the point of explaining that detectives' hats don't take off, when Freddie – injudiciously, in my opinion – got him in the right eye with one of the nicest wallops you could wish to see.

And after that, Freddie tells me, things got a bit mixed. He is conscious of having done his best, but he thinks he must have had rather the worse of the exchanges, because some little time later he became aware that he was in a prison cell and that one of his ears had swollen to the proportions of a medium-sized cauliflower. Also the black eye and the bees swarming in the head.

And scarcely had he coughed up the fifty dollars to the Clerk of the Court next morning when, coming out into the open and buying a paper, he found the entire events of the previous afternoon splashed over half a column of the very periodical which, he knew, old Bodsham was in the habit of reading with his morning Java and egg.

And, to show you how overwrought the poor chap must have been, Freddie had actually omitted to take the elementary precaution of giving a false name. He had even gone to the extraordinary length of revealing his middle one – which, though I don't think we should hold it against him, is Fotheringay.

Well, that finished it. Rightly or wrongly, Freddie decided not to wait for the full returns. There was a boat starting back for England that night, and he leaped aboard it without having ascertained from a personal interview what old Bodsham and Mavis thought of the episode. He is a pretty intuitive chap, Freddie, and he was content to guess.

So now he's back, and more or less soured and morose. He was saying some pretty harsh things about Woman this morning, some very harsh things.

And I happen to know that, as the boat docked at Southampton, an extraordinarily pretty girl standing beside him stumbled and dropped her vanity bag. And Freddie, instead of springing to her aid, just folded his arms and looked away with a sombre frown. He says that damsels in distress from now on must seek elsewhere for custom, because he has retired from business.

This fact, he tells me, cannot be too widely known.

2
TRIED IN THE FURNACE

The annual smoking-concert of the Drones Club had just come to an end, and it was the unanimous verdict of the little group assembled in the bar for a last quick one that the gem of the evening had been item number six on the programme, the knockabout cross-talk act of Cyril ('Barmy') Fotheringay-Phipps and Reginald ('Pongo') Twistleton-Twistleton. Both Cyril, in the red beard, and Reginald, in the more effective green whiskers, had shown themselves, it was agreed, at the very peak of their form. With sparkling repartee and vigorous by-play they had gripped the audience from the start.

'In fact,' said an Egg, 'it struck me that they were even better than last year. Their art seemed to have deepened somehow.'

A thoughtful Crumpet nodded.

'I noticed the same thing. The fact is, they passed through a soul-testing experience not long ago and it has left its mark upon them. It also dashed nearly wrecked the act. I don't know if any of you fellows are aware of it, but at one time they had definitely decided to scratch the fixture and not give a performance at all.'

'What!'

'Absolutely. They were within a toucher of failing to keep faith with their public. Bad blood had sprung up between them. Also pique and strained relations. They were not on speaking terms.'

His hearers were frankly incredulous. They pointed out that the friendship between the two artistes had always been a byword or whatever you called it. A well-read Egg summed it up by saying that they were like Thingummy and what's-his-name.

'Nevertheless,' insisted the Crumpet, 'what I am telling you is straight, official stuff. Two weeks ago, if Barmy had said to Pongo: "Who was that lady I saw you coming down the street with?" Pongo would not have replied: "That was no lady, that was my wife" – he would simply have raised his eyebrows coldly and turned away in a marked manner.'

It was a woman, of course (proceeded the Crumpet) who came between them. Angelica Briscoe was her name, and she was the daughter of the Rev. P. P. Briscoe, who vetted the souls of the local peasantry at a place called Maiden Eggesford down in Somersetshire. This hamlet is about half a dozen miles from the well-known resort, Bridmouth-on-Sea, and it was in the establishment of the Messrs Thorpe and Widgery, the popular grocers of that town, that Barmy and Pongo first set eyes on the girl.

They had gone to Bridmouth partly for a splash of golf, but principally to be alone and away from distractions, so that they would be able to concentrate on the rehearsing and building-up of this cross-talk act which we have just witnessed. And on the morning of which I speak they had strolled into the Thorpe and Widgery emporium to lay in a few little odds and ends, and there, putting in a bid for five pounds of streaky bacon, was a girl so lovely that they congealed in their tracks. And, as they stood staring, she said to the bloke behind the counter:

'That's the lot. Send them to Miss Angelica Briscoe, The Vicarage, Maiden Eggesford.'

She then pushed off, and Barmy and Pongo, feeling rather as if they had been struck by lightning, bought some sardines and a segment of certified butter in an overwrought sort of way and went out.

They were both pretty quiet for the rest of the day, and after dinner that night Pongo said to Barmy: 'I say, Barmy.'

And Barmy said: 'Hullo?'

And Pongo said: 'I say, Barmy, it's a bally nuisance, but I'll have to buzz up to London for a day or two. I've suddenly remembered some spots of business that call for my personal attention. You won't mind my leaving you?'

Barmy could scarcely conceal his braceness. Within two minutes of seeing that girl, he had made up his mind that somehow or other he must repair to Maiden Eggesford and get to know her, and the problem which had been vexing him all day had been what to do with the body – viz. Pongo's.

'Not a bit,' he said.

'I'll be back as soon as I can.'

'Don't hurry,' said Barmy heartily. 'As a matter of fact, a few days' lay-off will do the act all the good in the world. Any pro will tell you that the worst thing possible is to over-rehearse. Stay away as long as you like.'

So next morning – it was a Saturday – Pongo climbed on to a train, and in the afternoon Barmy collected his baggage and pushed off to the Goose and Grasshopper at Maiden Eggesford. And, having booked a room there and toddled into the saloon bar for a refresher with the lovelight in his eyes, the first thing he saw was Pongo chatting across the counter with the barmaid.

Neither was much bucked. A touch of constraint about sums it up.

'Hullo!' said Barmy.

'Hullo!' said Pongo.

'You here?'

'Yes. You here?'

'Yes.'

'Oh.'

There was a bit of a silence.

'So you didn't go to London?' said Barmy.

'No,' said Pongo.

'Oh,' said Barmy.

'And you didn't stick on at Bridmouth?' said Pongo.

'No,' said Barmy.

'Oh,' said Pongo.

There was some more silence.

'You came here, I see,' said Pongo.

'Yes,' said Barmy. 'I see *you* came here.'

'Yes,' said Pongo. 'An odd coincidence.'

'Very odd.'

'Well, skin off your nose,' said Pongo.

'Fluff in your latchkey,' said Barmy.

He drained his glass and tried to exhibit a light-hearted non-chalance, but his mood was sombre. He was a chap who could put two and two together and sift and weigh the evidence and all that sort of thing, and it was plain to him that love had brought Pongo also to this hamlet, and he resented the fact. Indeed, it was at this instant, he tells me, that there came to him the first nebulous idea of oiling out of that cross-talk act of theirs. The thought of having to ask a beastly, butting-in blighter like Reginald Twistleton-Twistleton if he was fond of mutton broth and being compelled to hit him over the head with a rolled-up umbrella when he replied 'No, Mutt and Jeff,' somehow seemed to revolt his finest feelings.

Conversation rather languished after this, and presently Pongo excused himself in a somewhat stiff manner and went upstairs to his room. And it was while Barmy was standing at the counter listening in a distrait kind of way to the barmaid telling him what cucumber did to her digestive organs that a fellow in plus fours entered the bar and Barmy saw that he was wearing the tie of his old school.

Well, you know how it is when you're in some public spot and a stranger comes in wearing the old school tie. You shove a hasty hand over your own and start to sidle out before the chap can spot it and grab you and start gassing. And Barmy was just doing this when the barmaid uttered these sensational words: 'Good evening, Mr Briscoe.'

Barmy stood spellbound. He turned to the barmaid and spoke in a hushed whisper.

'Did you say "Briscoe"?'

'Yes, sir.'

'From the Vicarage?'

'Yes, sir.'

Barmy quivered like a jelly. The thought that he had had the amazing luck to find in the brother of the girl he loved an old school-mate made him feel boneless. After all, he felt, as he took his hand away from his tie, there is no bond like that of the old school. If you meet one of the dear old school in a public spot, he meant to say, why, you go straight up to him and start fraternizing.

He made a beeline for the chap's table.

'I say,' he said, 'I see you're wearing a . . .'

The chap's hand had shot up to his tie with a sort of nervous gesture, but he evidently realized that the time had gone by for pro-tective measures. He smiled a bit wryly.

'Have a drink,' he said.

'I've got one, thanks,' said Barmy. 'I'll bring it along to your table, shall I? Such a treat meeting someone from the dear old place, what?'

'Oh, rather.'

'I think I'd have been a bit after your time, wouldn't I?' said Barmy, for the fellow was well stricken in years – twenty-eight, if a day. 'Fotheringay-Phipps is more or less my name. Yours is Briscoe, what?'

'Yes.'

Barmy swallowed a couple of times.

'Er . . . Ah . . . Um . . . I think I saw your sister yesterday in Brid-mouth,' he said, blushing prettily.

So scarlet, indeed, did his countenance become that the other regarded him narrowly, and Barmy knew that he had guessed his secret.

'You saw her in Bridmouth yesterday, eh?'

'Yes.'

'And now you're here.'

'Er – yes.'

'Well, well,' said the chap, drawing his breath in rather thought-fully.

There was a pause, during which Barmy's vascular motors contin-ued to do their bit.

'You must meet her,' said the chap.

'I should like to,' said Barmy. 'I only saw her for a moment buying streaky bacon, but she seemed a charming girl.'

'Oh, she is.'

'I scarcely noticed her, of course, but rather attractive she struck me as.'

'Quite.'

'I gave her the merest glance, you understand, but I should say at a venture that she has a great white soul. In fact,' said Barmy, losing his grip altogether, 'you wouldn't be far out in describing her as divine.'

'You must certainly meet her,' said the chap. Then he shook his head. 'No, it wouldn't be any good.'

'Why not?' bleated Barmy.

'Well, I'll tell you,' said the chap. 'You know what girls are. They have their little enthusiasms and it hurts them when people scoff at them. Being a parson's daughter, Angelica is wrapped up at present in the annual village School Treat. I can see at a glance the sort of fellow you are – witty, mordant, ironical. You would get off one of your devastating epigrams at the expense of the School Treat, and, while she might laugh at the wit, she would be deeply wounded by the satire.'

'But I wouldn't dream . . .'

'Ah, but if you didn't, if you spoke approvingly of the School Treat, what then? The next thing that would happen would be that she would be asking you to help her run it. And that would bore you stiff.'

Barmy shook from stem to stern. This was better even than he had hoped.

'You don't mean she would let me help her with the School Treat?'

'Why, you wouldn't do it, would you?'

'I should enjoy it above all things.'

'Well, if that's the way you feel, the matter can easily be arranged. She will be here any moment now to pick me up in her car.'

And, sure enough, not two minutes later there floated through the open window a silvery voice, urging the fellow, who seemed to answer to the name of 'Fathead,' to come out quick, because the voice did not intend to remain there all night.

So the fellow took Barmy out, and there was the girl, sitting in a two-seater. He introduced Barmy. The girl beamed. Barmy beamed. The fellow said that Barmy was anxious to come and help with the School Treat. The girl beamed again. Barmy beamed again. And presently the car drove off, the girl's last words being a reminder that the binge started at two sharp on the Monday.

That night, as they dined together, Barmy and Pongo put in their usual spot of rehearsing. It was their practice to mould and shape the act during meals, as they found that mastication seemed to sharpen their intellect. But tonight it would have been plain to an observant spectator that their hearts were not in it. There was an unmistakable coolness between them. Pongo said he had an aunt who complained of rheumatism, and Barmy said, Well, who wouldn't? And Barmy said his father could not meet his creditors, and Pongo said, Did he want to? But the old fire and sparkle were absent. And they had relapsed into a moody silence when the door opened and the barmaid pushed her head in.

'Miss Briscoe has just sent over a message, Mr Phipps,' said the barmaid. 'She says she would like you to be there a little earlier than two, if you can manage it. One-fifteen, if possible, because there's always so much to do.'

'Oh, right,' said Barmy, a bit rattled, for he had heard the sharp hiss of his companion's in-drawn breath.

'I'll tell her,' said the barmaid.

She withdrew, and Barmy found Pongo's eyes resting on him like a couple of blobs of vitriol.

'What's all this?' asked Pongo.

Barmy tried to be airy.

'Oh, it's nothing. Just the local School Treat. The vicar's daughter here – a Miss Briscoe – seems anxious that I should drop round on Monday and help her run it.'

Pongo started to grind his teeth, but he had a chunk of potato in his mouth at the moment and was hampered. But he gripped the table till his knuckles stood out white under the strain.

'Have you been sneaking round behind my back and inflicting your beastly society on Miss Briscoe?' he demanded.

'I do not like your tone, Reginald.'

'Never mind about my tone. I'll attend to my tone. Of all the bally low hounds that ever stepped you are the lowest. So this is what the friendship of years amounts to, is it? You crawl in here and try to cut me out with the girl I love.'

'Well dash it . . .'

'That is quite enough.'

'But, dash it . . .'

'I wish to hear no more.'

'But, dash it, I love her, too. It's not my fault if you happen to love her, too, is it? I mean to say, if a fellow loves a girl and another fellow loves her, too, you can't expect the fellow who loves the girl to edge out because he happens to be acquainted with the fellow who loves her, too. When it comes to Love, a chap has got to look out for his own interests, hasn't he? You didn't find Romeo or any of those chaps easing away from the girl just to oblige a pal, did you? Certainly not. So I don't see...'

'Please!' said Pongo.

A silence fell.

'Might I trouble you to pass the mustard, Fotheringay-Phipps,' said Pongo coldly.

'Certainly, Twistleton-Twistleton,' replied Barmy, with equal hauteur.

It is always unpleasant not to be on speaking terms with an old friend. To be cooped up alone in a mouldy village pub with an old friend with whom one has ceased to converse is simply rotten. And this is especially so if the day happens to be a Sunday.

Maiden Eggesford, like so many of our rural hamlets, is not at its best and brightest on a Sunday. When you have walked down the main street and looked at the Jubilee Watering-Trough, there is nothing much to do except go home and then come out again and walk down the main street once more and take another look at the Jubilee Watering-Trough. It will give you some rough idea of the state to which Barmy Fotheringay-Phipps had been reduced by the end of the next day when I tell you that the sound of the church bells ringing for evensong brought him out of the Goose and Grasshopper as if he had heard a fire engine. The thought that at last something was going to happen in Maiden Eggesford in which the Jubilee Watering-Trough *motif* was not stressed, stirred him strangely. He was in his pew in three jumps. And as the service got under way he began to feel curious emotions going on in his bosom.

There is something about evening church in a village in the summertime that affects the most hard-boiled. They had left the door open, and through it came the scent of lime trees and wallflowers and the distant hum of bees fooling about. And gradually there poured over Barmy a wave of sentiment. As he sat and listened to the First Lesson he became a changed man.

The Lesson was one of those chapters of the Old Testament all about how Abimelech begat Jazzbo and Jazzbo begat Zachariah. And, what with the beauty of the words and the peace of his surroundings, Barmy suddenly began to become conscious of a great remorse.

He had not done the square thing, he told himself, by dear old Pongo. Here was a chap, notoriously one of the best, as sound an egg as ever donned a heliotrope sock, and he was deliberately chiselling him out of the girl he loved. He was doing the dirty on a fellow whom he had been pally with since their Eton jacket days – a bloke who time and again had shared with him his last bar of almond rock. Was this right? Was this just? Would Abimelech have behaved like that to Jazzbo or – for the matter of that – Jazzbo to Zachariah? The answer, he could not disguise it from himself, was in the negative.

It was a different, stronger Barmy, a changed, chastened Cyril Fotheringay-Phipps, who left the sacred edifice at the conclusion of the vicar's fifty-minute sermon. He had made the great decision. It would play the dickens with his heart and probably render the rest of his life a blank, but nevertheless he would retire from the unseemly struggle and give the girl up to Pongo.

That night, as they cold-suppered together, Barmy cleared his throat and looked across at Pongo with a sad, sweet smile.

'Pongo,' he said.

The other glanced distantly up from his baked potato.

'There is something you wish to say to me, Fotheringay-Phipps?'

'Yes,' said Barmy. 'A short while ago I sent a note to Miss Briscoe, informing her that I shall not be attending the School Treat and mentioning that you will be there in my stead. Take her, Pongo, old man. She is yours. I scratch my nomination.'

Pongo stared. His whole manner changed. It was as if he had been a Trappist monk who had suddenly decided to give Trappism a miss and become one of the boys again.

'But, dash it, this is noble!'

'No, no.'

'But it is! It's . . . well, dash it, I hardly know what to say.'

'I hope you will be very, very happy.'

'Thanks, old man.'

'Very, very, very happy.'

'Rather! I should say so. And I'll tell you one thing. In the years to come there will always be a knife and fork for you at our little home. The children shall be taught to call you Uncle Barmy.'

'Thanks,' said Barmy. 'Thanks.'

'Not at all,' said Pongo. 'Not at all.'

At this moment, the barmaid entered with a note for Barmy. He read it and crumpled it up.

'From Her?' asked Pongo.

'Yes.'

'Saying she quite understands, and so forth?'

'Yes.'

Pongo ate a piece of cheese in a meditative manner. He seemed to be pursuing some train of thought.

'I should think,' he said, 'that a fellow who married a clergyman's daughter would get the ceremony performed at cut rates, wouldn't he?'

'Probably.'

'If not absolutely on the nod?'

'I shouldn't wonder.'

'Not,' said Pongo, 'that I am influenced by any consideration like that, of course. My love is pure and flamelike, with no taint of dross. Still, in times like these, every little helps.'

'Quite,' said Barmy. 'Quite.'

He found it hard to control his voice. He had lied to his friend about that note. What Angelica Briscoe had really said in it was that it was quite all right if he wanted to edge out of the School Treat, but that she would require him to take the Village Mothers for their Annual Outing on the same day. There had to be some responsible person with them, and the curate had sprained his ankle tripping over a footstool in the vestry.

Barmy could read between the lines. He saw what this meant. His fatal fascination had done its deadly work, and the girl had become infatuated with him. No other explanation would fit the facts. It was absurd to suppose that she would lightly have selected him for this extraordinarily important assignment. Obviously it was the big event of the village year. Anyone would do to mess about at the School Treat, but Angelica Briscoe would place in charge of the Mothers' Annual Outing only a man she trusted . . . respected . . . loved.

He sighed. What must be, he felt, must be. He had done his conscientious best to retire in favour of his friend, but Fate had been too strong.

I found it a little difficult (said the Crumpet) to elicit from Barmy exactly what occurred at the annual outing of the Village Mothers of Maiden Eggesford. When telling me the story, he had the air of a man whose old wound is troubling him. It was not, indeed, till the fourth cocktail that he became really communicative. And then, speaking with a kind of stony look in his eye, he gave me a fairly comprehensive account. But even then each word seemed to hurt him in some tender spot.

The proceedings would appear to have opened in a quiet and orderly manner. Sixteen females of advanced years assembled in a motor coach, and the expedition was seen off from the Vicarage door by the Rev. P. P. Briscoe in person. Under his eye, Barmy tells me, the Beauty Chorus was demure and docile. It was a treat to listen to their murmured responses. As nice and respectable a bunch of

mothers, Barmy says, as he had ever struck. His only apprehension at
this point, he tells me, was lest the afternoon's proceedings might
possibly be a trifle stodgy. He feared a touch of ennui.

He needn't have worried. There was no ennui.

The human cargo, as I say, had started out in a spirit of demure-
ness and docility. But it was amazing what a difference a mere fifty
yards of the high road made to these Mothers. No sooner were they
out of sight of the Vicarage than they began to effervesce to an almost
unbelievable extent. The first intimation Barmy had that the binge
was going to be run on lines other than those which he had anticipated, was when a very stout Mother in a pink bonnet and a dress
covered with bugles suddenly picked off a passing cyclist with a
well-directed tomato, causing him to skid into a ditch. Upon
which, all sixteen mothers laughed like fiends in hell, and it was
plain that they considered that the proceedings had now been
formally opened.

Of course, looking back at it now in a calmer spirit, Barmy tells me
that he can realize that there is much to be said in pallation of the
exuberance of these ghastly female pimples. When you are shut up all
the year round in a place like Maiden Eggesford, with nothing to do
but wash underclothing and attend Divine Service, you naturally
incline to let yourself go a bit at times of festival and holiday. But at
the moment he did not think of this, and his spiritual agony was
pretty pronounced.

If there's one thing Barmy hates it's being conspicuous, and conspicuous is precisely what a fellow cannot fail to be when he's in a
motor coach with sixteen women of mature ages who alternate
between singing ribald songs and hurling volleys of homely chaff at
passers-by. In this connection, he tells me, he is thinking particularly
of a Mother in spectacles and a Homburg hat, which she had pinched
from the driver of the vehicle, whose prose style appeared to have
been modelled on that of Rabelais.

It was a more than usually penetrating sally on the part of this
female which at length led him to venture a protest.

'I say! I mean, I say. I say, dash it, you know. I mean, dash it,' said
Barmy, feeling, even as he spoke, that the rebuke had not been
phrased as neatly as he could have wished.

Still, lame though it had been, it caused a sensation which can only
be described as profound. Mother looked at Mother. Eyebrows were
raised, breath drawn in censoriously.

'Young man,' said the Mother in the pink bonnet, who seemed to
have elected herself forewoman, 'kindly keep your remarks to
yourself.'

Another Mother said: 'The idea!' and a third described him as a kill-joy.

'We don't want none of *your* impudence,' said the one in the pink bonnet.

'Ah!' agreed the others.

'A slip of a boy like that!' said the Mother in the Homburg hat, and there was a general laugh, as if the meeting considered that the point had been well taken.

Barmy subsided. He was wishing that he had yielded to the advice of his family and become a curate after coming down from the University. Curates are specially trained to handle this sort of situation. A tough, hard-boiled curate, spitting out of the corner of his mouth, would soon have subdued these mothers, he reflected. He would have played on them as on a stringed instrument – or, rather, as on sixteen stringed instruments. But Barmy, never having taken orders, was helpless.

So helpless, indeed, that when he suddenly discovered that they were heading for Bridmouth-on-Sea he felt that there was nothing he could do about it. From the vicar's own lips he had had it officially that the programme was that the expedition should drive to the neighbouring village of Bottsford Mortimer, where there were the ruins of an old abbey, replete with interest; lunch among these ruins; visit the local museum (founded and presented to the village by the late Sir Wandesbury Pott, J.P.); and, after filling in with a bit of knitting, return home. And now the whole trend of the party appeared to be towards the Amusement Park on the Bridmouth pier. And, though Barmy's whole soul shuddered at the thought of these sixteen Bacchantes let loose in an Amusement Park, he hadn't the nerve to say a word.

It was at about this point, he tells me, that a vision rose before him of Pongo happily loafing through the summer afternoon amidst the placid joys of the School Treat.

Of what happened at the Amusement Park Barmy asked me to be content with the sketchiest of outlines. He said that even now he could not bear to let his memory dwell upon it. He confessed himself perplexed by the psychology of the thing. These mothers, he said, must have had mothers of their own and at those mothers' knees must have learned years ago the difference between right and wrong, and yet ... Well, what he was thinking of particularly, he said, was what occurred on the Bump the Bumps apparatus. He refused to specify exactly, but he said that there was one woman in a puce mantle who definitely seemed to be living for pleasure alone.

It was a little unpleasantness with the proprietor of this concern that eventually led to the expedition leaving the Amusement Park and going down to the beach. Some purely technical point of finance, I understand – he claiming that a Mother in bombazine had had eleven rides and only paid once. It resulted in Barmy getting lugged into the brawl and rather roughly handled – which was particularly unfortunate, because the bombazined Mother explained on their way down to the beach that the whole thing had been due to a misunderstanding. In actual fact, what had really happened was that she had had twelve rides and paid twice.

However, he was so glad to get his little troupe out of the place that he counted an eye well blacked as the price of deliverance, and his spirits, he tells me, had definitely risen when suddenly the sixteen mothers gave a simultaneous whoop and made for a sailing-boat which was waiting to be hired, sweeping him along with them. And the next moment they were off across the bay, bowling along before a nippy breeze which, naturally, cheesed it abruptly as soon as it had landed them far enough away from shore to make things interesting for the unfortunate blighter who had to take to the oars.

This, of course, was poor old Barmy. There was a man in charge of the boat, but he, though but a rough, untutored salt, had enough sense not to let himself in for a job like rowing this Noah's Ark home. Barmy did put it up to him tentatively, but the fellow said that he had to attend to the steering, and when Barmy said that he, Barmy, knew how to steer, the fellow said that he, the fellow, could not entrust a valuable boat to an amateur. After which, he lit his pipe and lolled back in the stern sheets with rather the air of an ancient Roman banqueter making himself cosy among the cushions. And Barmy, attaching himself to a couple of oars of about the size of those served out to galley-slaves in the old trireme days, started to put his back into it.

For a chap who hadn't rowed anything except a light canoe since he was up at Oxford, he considers he did dashed well, especially when you take into account the fact that he was much hampered by the Mothers. They would insist on singing that thing about 'Give yourself a pat on the back,' and, apart from the fact that Barmy considered that something on the lines of the Volga Boat Song would have been far more fitting, it was a tune it was pretty hard to keep time to. Seven times he caught crabs, and seven times those sixteen Mothers stopped singing and guffawed like one Mother. All in all, a most painful experience. Add the fact that the first thing the females did on hitting the old Homeland again was to get up an informal dance on the sands and that the ride home in the quiet evenfall was more or less a repetition of the journey out, and you will agree with me that Barmy, as he eventually tottered into the saloon bar of the Goose and Grasshopper, had earned the frothing tankard which he now proceeded to order.

He had just sucked it down and was signalling for another, when the door of the saloon bar opened and in came Pongo.

If Barmy had been less preoccupied with his own troubles he would have seen that Pongo was in poorish shape. His collar was torn, his hair dishevelled. There were streaks of chocolate down his face and half a jam sandwich attached to the back of his coat. And so moved was he at seeing Barmy that he started ticking him off before he had so much as ordered a gin and ginger.

'A nice thing you let me in for!' said Pongo. 'A jolly job you shoved off on me!'

Barmy was feeling a little better after his ingurgitations, and he was able to speak.

'What are you talking about?'

'I am talking about School Treats,' replied Pongo, with an intense bitterness. 'I am talking about seas of children, all with sticky hands, who rubbed those hands on me. I am talking... Oh, it's no good your gaping like a diseased fish, Fotheringay-Phipps. You know dashed well that you planned the whole thing. Your cunning fiend's brain formulated the entire devilish scheme. You engineered the bally outrage for your own foul purposes, to queer me with Angelica. You thought that when a girl sees a man blindfolded and smacked with rolled-up newspapers by smelly children she can never feel the same to him again. Ha!' said Pongo, at last ordering his gin and ginger.

Barmy was stunned, of course, by this violent attack, but he retained enough of the nice sense of propriety of the Fotheringay-Phippses to realize that this discussion could not be continued in public. Already the barmaid's ears had begun to work loose at the roots as she pricked them up.

'I don't know what the dickens you're talking about,' he said, 'but bring your drink up to my room and we'll go into the matter there. We cannot bandy a woman's name in a saloon bar.'

'Who's bandying a woman's name?'

'You are. You bandied it only half a second ago. If you don't call what you said bandying, there are finer-minded men who do.'

So they went upstairs, and Barmy shut the door.

'Now, then,' he said. 'What's all this drivel?'

'I've told you.'

'Tell me again.'

'I will.'

'Right ho. One moment.'

Barmy went to the door and opened it sharply. There came the un-mistakable sound of a barmaid falling downstairs. He closed the door again.

'Now, then,' he said.

Pongo drained his gin and ginger.

'Of all the dirty tricks one man ever played on another,' he began, 'your sneaking out of that School Treat and letting me in for it is one which the verdict of history will undoubtedly rank the dirtiest. I can read you now like a book, Fotheringay-Phipps. Your motive is crystal clear to me. You knew at what a disadvantage a man appears at a School Treat, and you saw to it that I and not you should be the poor mutt to get smeared with chocolate and sloshed with newspapers before the eyes of Angelica Briscoe. And I believed you when you handed me all that drip about yielding your claim and what not. My gosh!'

For an instant, as he heard these words, stupefaction rendered Barmy speechless. Then he found his tongue. His generous soul was seething with indignation at the thought of how his altruism, his great sacrifice, had been misinterpreted.

'What absolute rot!' he cried. 'I never heard such bilge in my life. My motives in sending you to that School Treat instead of me were unmixedly chivalrous. I did it simply and solely to enable you to ingratiate yourself with the girl, not reflecting that it was out of the question that she should ever love a pop-eyed, pimply-faced poop like you.'

Pongo started.

'Pop-eyed?'

'Pop-eyed was what I said.'

'Pimply-faced?'

'Pimply-faced was the term I employed.'

'Poop?'

'Poop was the expression with which I concluded. If you want to know the real obstacle in the way of any wooing you may do now or in the years to come, Twistleton-Twistleton, it is this – that you entirely lack sex-appeal and look like nothing on earth. A girl of the sweet, sensitive nature of Angelica Briscoe does not have to see you smeared with chocolate to recoil from you with loathing. She does it automatically, and she does it on her head.'

'Is that so?'

'That is so.'

'Oh? Well, let me inform you that in spite of what has happened, in spite of the fact that she has seen me at my worst, there is something within me that tells me that Angelica Briscoe loves me and will one day be mine.'

'Mine, you mean. I can read the message in a girl's shy, drooping eyes, Twistleton-Twistleton, and I am prepared to give you odds of eleven to four that before the year is out I shall be walking down the aisle with Angelica Fotheringay-Phipps on my arm. I will go further. Thirty-three to eight.'

'What in?'

'Tenners.'

'Done.'

It was at this moment that the door opened.

'Excuse me, gentlemen,' said the barmaid.

The two rivals glared at the intruder. She was a well-nourished girl with a kind face. She was rubbing her left leg, which appeared to be paining her. The staircases are steep at the Goose and Grasshopper.

'You'll excuse me muscling in like this, gentlemen,' said the barmaid, or words to that effect, 'but I happened inadvertently to overhear your conversation, and I feel it my duty to put you straight on an important point of fact. Gentlemen, all bets are off. Miss Angelica Briscoe is already engaged to be married.'

You can readily conceive the effect of this announcement. Pongo biffed down into the only chair, and Barmy staggered against the wash-hand stand.

'What!' said Pongo.

'What!' said Barmy.

The barmaid turned to Barmy.

'Yes, sir. To the gentleman you were talking to in the bar the afternoon you arrived.'

Her initial observation had made Barmy feel as if he had been punched in the wind by sixteen Mothers, but at this addendum he was able to pull himself together a bit.

'Don't be an ass, my dear old barmaid,' he said. 'That was Miss Briscoe's brother.'

'No, sir.'

'But his name was Briscoe, and you told me he was at the Vicarage.'

'Yes, sir. He spends a good deal of his time at the Vicarage, being the young lady's second cousin, and engaged to her since last Christmas!'

Barmy eyed her sternly. He was deeply moved.

'Why did you not inform me of this earlier, you chump of a barmaid? With your gift for listening at doors you must long since have become aware that this gentleman here and myself were deeply enamoured of Miss Briscoe. And yet you kept these facts under your hat, causing us to waste our time and experience the utmost alarm and despondency. Do you realize, barmaid, that, had you spoken sooner, my friend here would not have been subjected to nameless indignities at the School Treat...'

'Yes, sir. It was the School Treat that Mr Briscoe was so bent on not having to go to, which he would have had to have done, Miss Angelica insisting. He had a terrible time there last year, poor gentleman. He was telling me about it. And that was why he asked me as a particular favour not to mention that he was engaged to Miss Briscoe, because he said that, if he played his cards properly and a little secrecy and silence were observed in the proper quarters, there was a mug staying at the inn that he thought he could get to go instead of him. It would have done you good, sir, to have seen the way his face lit up as he said it. He's a very nice gentleman, Mr Briscoe, and we're all very fond of him. Well, I mustn't stay talking here, sir. I've got my bar to see to.'

She withdrew, and for some minutes there was silence in the room. It was Barmy who was the first to break it.

'After all, we still have our Art,' said Barmy.

He crossed the room and patted Pongo on the shoulder.

'Of course, it's a nasty shock, old man...'

Pongo had raised his face from his hands and was fumbling for his cigarette case. There was a look in his eyes as if he had just wakened from a dream.

'Well, *is* it?' he said. 'You've got to look at these things from every angle. Is a girl who can deliberately allow a man to go through the horrors of a School Treat worth bothering about?'

Barmy started.

'I never thought of that. Or a girl, for that matter, who could callously throw a fellow to the Village Mothers.'

'Remind me some time to tell you about a game called "Is Mr Smith At Home?" where you put your head in a sack and the younger generation jab you with sticks.'

'And don't let me forget to tell you about that Mother in the puce mantle on the Bump the Bumps.'

'There was a kid called Horace...'

'There was a Mother in a Homburg hat...'

'The fact is,' said Pongo, 'we have allowed ourselves to lose our sober judgment over a girl whose idea of a mate is a mere "Hey, you," to be ordered hither and thither at her will, and who will unleash the juvenile population of her native village upon him without so much as a pang of pity – in a word, a parson's daughter. If you want to know the secret of a happy and successful life, Barmy, old man, it is this: Keep away from parsons' daughters.'

'Right away,' agreed Barmy. 'How do you react to hiring a car and pushing off to the metropolis at once?'

'I am all for it. And if we're to give of our best on the evening of the eleventh *prox.* we ought to start rehearsing again immediately.'

'We certainly ought.'

'We haven't any too much time, as it is.'

'We certainly haven't. I've got an aunt who complains of rheumatism.'

'Well, who wouldn't? My father can't meet his creditors.'

'Does he want to? My uncle Joe's in very low water just now.'

'Too bad. What's he doing?'

'Teaching swimming. Listen, Pongo,' said Barmy, 'I've been thinking. You take the green whiskers this year.'

'No, no.'

'Yes, really. I mean it. If I've said it to myself once, I've said it a hundred times – good old Pongo simply must have the green whiskers this year.'

'Barmy!'

'Pongo!'

They clasped hands. Tried in the furnace, their friendship had emerged strong and true. Cyril Fotheringay-Phipps and Reginald Twistleton-Twistleton were themselves again.

3

TROUBLE DOWN AT TUDSLEIGH

Two Eggs and a couple of Beans were having a leisurely spot in the smoking room of the Drones Club, when a Crumpet came in and asked if anybody present wished to buy a practically new copy of Tennyson's poems. His manner, as he spoke, suggested that he had little hope that business would result. Nor did it. The two Beans and one of the Eggs said No. The other Egg merely gave a short, sardonic laugh.

The Crumpet hastened to put himself right with the company.

'It isn't mine. It belongs to Freddie Widgeon.'

The senior of the two Beans drew his breath in sharply, genuinely shocked.

'You aren't telling us that Freddie Widgeon bought a Tennyson?'

The junior Bean said that this confirmed a suspicion which had long been stealing over him. Poor old Freddie was breaking up.

'Not at all,' said the Crumpet. 'He had the most excellent motives. The whole thing was a strategic move, and in my opinion a jolly fine strategic move. He did it to boost his stock with the girl.'

'What girl?'

'April Carroway. She lived at a place called Tudsleigh down in Worcestershire. Freddie went there for the fishing, and the day he left London he happened to run into his uncle, Lord Blicester, and the latter, learning that he was to be in those parts, told him on no account to omit to look in at Tudsleigh Court and slap his old friend, Lady Carroway, on the back. So Freddie called there on the afternoon of his arrival, to get the thing over: and as he was passing through the garden on his way out he suddenly heard a girl's voice proceeding from the interior of a summerhouse. And so musical was it that he edged a bit closer and shot a glance through the window. And, as he did so, he reeled and came within a toucher of falling.

From where he stood he could see the girl plainly, and she was, he tells me, the absolute ultimate word, the last bubbling cry. She could not have looked better to him if he had drawn up the specifications personally. He was stunned. He had had no idea that there was anything like this on the premises. There and then he abandoned his scheme of spending the next two weeks fishing: for day by day in every way, he realized, he must haunt Tudsleigh Court from now on like a resident spectre.

He had now recovered sufficiently for his senses to function once more, and he gathered that what the girl was doing was reading some species of poetry aloud to a small, grave female kid with green eyes and a turned-up nose who sat at her side. And the idea came to him that it would be a pretty sound scheme if he could find out what this bilge was. For, of course, when it comes to wooing, it's simply half the battle to get a line on the adored object's favourite literature. Ascertain what it is and mug it up and decant an excerpt or two in her presence, and before you can say 'What ho!' she is looking on you as a kindred soul and is all over you.

And it was at this point that he had a nice little slice of luck. The girl suddenly stopped reading: and, placing the volume face-down on her lap, sat gazing dreamily nor'-nor'-east for a space, as I believe girls frequently do when they strike a particularly juicy bit half-way through a poem. And the next moment Freddie was haring off to the local post-office to wire to London for a *Collected Works of Alfred, Lord Tennyson*. He was rather relieved, he tells me, because, girls being what they are, it might quite easily have been Shelley or even Browning.

Well, Freddie lost no time in putting into operation his scheme of becoming the leading pest of Tudsleigh Court. On the following afternoon he called there again, met Lady Carroway once more, and was introduced to this girl, April, and to the green-eyed kid, who, he learned, was her young sister Prudence. So far, so good. But just as he was starting to direct at April a respectfully volcanic look which would give her some rough kind of preliminary intimation that here came old Colonel Romeo in person, his hostess went on to say something which sounded like 'Captain Bradbury,' and he perceived with a nasty shock that he was not the only visitor. Seated in a chair with a cup of tea in one hand and half a muffin in the other was an extraordinarily large and beefy bird in tweeds.

'Captain Bradbury, Mr Widgeon,' said Lady Carroway. 'Captain Bradbury is in the Indian Army. He is home on leave and has taken a house up the river.'

'Oh?' said Freddie, rather intimating by his manner that this was just the dirty sort of trick he would have imagined the other would have played.

'Mr Widgeon is the nephew of my old friend, Lord Blicester.'

'Ah?' said Captain Bradbury, hiding with a ham-like hand a yawn that seemed to signify that Freddie's foul antecedents were of little interest to him. It was plain that this was not going to be one of those sudden friendships. Captain Bradbury was obviously feeling that a world fit for heroes to live in should contain the irreducible minimum of Widgeons: while, as for Freddie, the last person he wanted hanging about the place at this highly critical point in his affairs was a richly tanned military man with deep-set eyes and a natty moustache.

However, he quickly rallied from his momentary agitation. Once that volume of Tennyson came, he felt, he would pretty soon put this bird where he belonged. A natty moustache is not everything. Nor is rich tan. And the same may be said of deep-set eyes. What bungs a fellow over with a refined and poetical girl is Soul. And in the course of the next few days Freddie expected to have soul enough for six. He exerted himself, accordingly, to be the life of the party, and so successful were his efforts that, as they were leaving, Captain Bradbury drew him aside and gave him the sort of look he would have given a Pathan discovered pinching the old regiment's rifles out on the North-West Frontier. And it was only now that Freddie really began to appreciate the other's physique. He had had no notion that they were making the soldiery so large nowadays.

'Tell me, Pridgeon...'

'Widgeon,' said Freddie, to keep the records straight.

'Tell me, Widgeon, are you making a long stay in these parts?'

'Oh, yes. Fairly longish.'

'I shouldn't.'

'You wouldn't?'

'Not if I were you.'

'But I like the scenery.'

'If you got both eyes bunged up, you wouldn't be able to see the scenery.'

'Why should I get both eyes bunged up?'

'You might.'

'But why?'

'I don't know. You just might. These things happen. Well, good evening, Widgeon,' said Captain Bradbury and hopped into his two-seater like a performing elephant alighting on an upturned barrel. And Freddie made his way to the Blue Lion in Tudsleigh village, where he had established his headquarters.

*

It would be idle to deny that this little chat gave Frederick Widgeon food for thought. He brooded on it over his steak and French fried that night, and was still brooding on it long after he had slid between the sheets and should have been in a restful sleep. And when morning brought its eggs and bacon and coffee he began to brood on it again.

He's a pretty astute sort of chap, Freddie, and he had not failed to sense the threatening note in the Captain's remarks. And he was somewhat dubious as to what to do for the best. You see, it was the first time anything of this sort had happened to him. I suppose, all in all, Freddie Widgeon has been in love at first sight with possibly twenty-seven girls in the course of his career: but hitherto everything had been what you might call plain sailing. I mean, he would flutter round for a few days and then the girl, incensed by some floater on his part or possibly merely unable to stand the sight of him any longer, would throw him out on his left ear, and that would be that. Everything pleasant and agreeable and orderly, as you might say. But this was different. Here he had come up against a new element, the jealous rival, and it was beginning to look not so good.

It was the sight of Tennyson's poems that turned the scale. The volume had arrived early on the previous day, and already he had mugged up two-thirds of the 'Lady of Shalott.' And the thought that, if he were to oil out now, all this frightful sweat would be so much dead loss, decided the issue. That afternoon he called once more at Tudsleigh Court, prepared to proceed with the matter along the lines originally laid out. And picture his astonishment and delight when he discovered that Captain Bradbury was not among those present.

There are very few advantages about having a military man as a rival in your wooing, but one of these is that every now and then such a military man has to pop up to London to see the blokes at the War Office. This Captain Bradbury had done today, and it was amazing what a difference his absence made. A gay confidence seemed to fill Freddie as he sat there wolfing buttered toast. He had finished the 'Lady of Shalott' that morning and was stuffed to the tonsils with good material. It was only a question of time, he felt, before some chance remark would uncork him and give him the cue to do his stuff.

And presently it came. Lady Carroway, withdrawing to write letters, paused at the door to ask April if she had any message for her Uncle Lancelot.

'Give him my love,' said April, 'and say I hope he likes Bournemouth.'

The door closed. Freddie coughed.

'He's moved, then?' he said.

'I beg your pardon?'

'Just a spot of persiflage. Lancelot, you know. Tennyson, you know. You remember in the "Lady of Shalott" Lancelot was putting in most of his time at Camelot.'

The girl stared at him, dropping a slice of bread-and-butter in her emotion.

'You don't mean to say you read Tennyson, Mr Widgeon?'

'Me?' said Freddie. 'Tennyson? Read Tennyson? Me read Tennyson? Well, well, well! Bless my soul! Why, I know him by heart – some of him.'

'So do I! "Break, break, break, on your cold grey stones, oh Sea..."'

'Quite. Or take the "Lady of Shalott".'

'"I hold it truth with him who sings..."'

'So do I, absolutely. And then, again, there's the "Lady of Shalott." Dashed extraordinary that you should like Tennyson, too.'

'I think he's wonderful.'

'What a lad! That "Lady of Shalott!" Some spin on the ball there.'

'It's so absurd, the way people sneer at him nowadays.'

'The silly bounders. Don't know what's good for them.'

'He's my favourite poet.'

'Mine, too. Any bird who could write the "Lady of Shalott" gets the cigar or coconut, according to choice, as far as I'm concerned.'

They gazed at one another emotionally.

'Well, I'd never have thought it,' said April.

'Why not?'

'I mean, you gave me the impression of being ... well, rather the dancing, nightclub sort of man.'

'What! Me? Nightclubs? Good gosh! Why, my idea of a happy evening is to curl up with Tennyson's latest.'

'Don't you love "Locksley Hall"?'

'Oh, rather. And the "Lady of Shalott".'

'And "Maud"?'

'Aces,' said Freddie. 'And the "Lady of Shalott".'

'How fond you seem of the "Lady of Shalott"!'

'Oh, I am.'

'So am I, of course. The river here always reminds me so much of that poem.'

'Why, of course it does!' said Freddie. 'I've been trying to think all the time why it seemed so dashed familiar. And, talking of the river, I suppose you wouldn't care for a row up it tomorrow?'

The girl looked doubtful.

'Tomorrow?'

'My idea was to hire a boat, sling in a bit of chicken and ham and a Tennyson...'

'But I had promised to go to Birmingham tomorrow with Captain Bradbury to help him choose a fishing rod. Still, I suppose, really, any other day would do for that, wouldn't it?'

'Exactly.'

'We could go later on.'

'Positively,' said Freddie. 'A good deal later on. Much later on. In fact the best plan would be to leave it quite open. One o'clock tomorrow, then, at the Town Bridge? Right. Fine. Splendid. Topping. I'll be there with my hair in a braid.'

All through the rest of the day Freddie was right in the pink. Walked on air, you might say. But towards nightfall, as he sat in the bar of the Blue Lion, sucking down whisky and splash and working his way through 'Locksley Hall,' a shadow fell athwart the table and, looking up, he perceived Captain Bradbury.

'Good evening, Widgeon,' said Captain Bradbury.

There is only one word, Freddie tells me, to describe the gallant C's aspect at this juncture. It was sinister. His eyebrows had met across the top of his nose, his chin was sticking out from ten to fourteen inches, and he stood there flexing the muscles of his arms, making the while a low sound like the rumbling of an only partially extinct volcano. The impression Freddie received was that at any moment molten lava might issue from the man's mouth, and he wasn't absolutely sure that he liked the look of things.

However, he tried to be as bright as possible.

'Ah, Bradbury!' he replied, with a lilting laugh.

Captain Bradbury's right eyebrow had now become so closely entangled with his left that there seemed no hope of ever extricating it without the aid of powerful machinery.

'I understand that you called at Tudsleigh Court today.'

'Oh, rather. We missed you, of course, but, nevertheless, a pleasant time was had by all.'

'So I gathered. Miss Carroway tells me that you have invited her to picnic up the river with you tomorrow.'

'That's right. Up the river. The exact spot.'

'You will, of course, send her a note informing her that you are unable to go, as you have been unexpectedly called back to London.'

'But nobody's called me back to London.'

'Yes, they have. I have.'

Freddie tried to draw himself up. A dashed difficult thing to do, of course, when you're sitting down, and he didn't make much of a job of it.

'I fail to understand you, Bradbury.'

'Let me make it clearer,' said the Captain. 'There is an excellent train in the mornings at twelve fifteen. You will catch it tomorrow.'

'Oh, yes?'

'I shall call here at one o'clock. If I find that you have not gone, I shall . . . Did I ever happen to mention that I won the Heavyweight Boxing Championship of India last year?'

Freddie swallowed a little thoughtfully.

'You did?'

'Yes.'

Freddie pulled himself together.

'The Amateur Championship?'

'Of course.'

'I used to go in quite a lot for amateur boxing,' said Freddie with a little yawn. 'But I got bored with it. Not enough competition. Too little excitement. So I took on pros. But I found them so extraordinarily brittle that I chucked the whole thing. That was when Bulldog Whacker had to go to hospital for two months after one of our bouts. I collect old china now.'

Brave words, of course, but he watched his visitor depart with emotions that were not too fearfully bright. In fact, he tells me, he actually toyed for a moment with the thought that there might be a lot to be said for that twelve-fifteen train.

It was but a passing weakness. The thought of April Carroway soon strengthened him once more. He had invited her to this picnic, and he intended to keep the tryst even if it meant having to run like a rabbit every time Captain Bradbury hove in sight. After all, he reflected, it was most improbable that a big heavy fellow like that would be able to catch him.

His frame of mind, in short, was precisely that of the old Crusading Widgeons when they heard that the Paynim had been sighted in the offing.

The next day, accordingly, found Freddie seated in a hired row-boat at the landing-stage by the Town Bridge. It was a lovely summer morning with all the fixings, such as blue skies, silver wavelets, birds, bees, gentle breezes and what not. He had stowed the luncheon-basket in the stern, and was whiling away the time of waiting by brushing up his 'Lady of Shalott,' when a voice spoke from the steps. He looked up and perceived the kid Prudence gazing down at him with her grave, green eyes.

'Oh, hullo,' he said.

'Hullo,' said the child.

Since his entry to Tudsleigh Court, Prudence Carroway had meant little or nothing in Freddie's life. He had seen her around, of course, and had beamed at her in a benevolent sort of way, it being his invariable policy to beam benevolently at all relatives and connections of the adored object, but he had scarcely given her a thought. As always on these occasions, his whole attention had been earmarked for the adored one. So now his attitude was rather that of a bloke who wonders to what he is indebted for the honour of this visit.

'Nice day,' he said, tentatively.

'Yes,' said the kid. 'I came to tell you that April can't come.'

The sun, which had been shining with exceptional brilliance, seemed to Freddie to slip out of sight like a diving-duck.

'You don't mean that!'

'Yes, I do.'

'Can't come?'

'No. She told me to tell you she's awfully sorry, but some friends of Mother's have phoned that they are passing through and would like lunch, so she's got to stay on and help cope with them.'

'Oh, gosh!'

'So she wants you to take me instead, and she's going to try to come on afterwards. I told her we would lunch near Griggs's Ferry.'

Something of the inky blackness seemed to Freddie to pass from the sky. It was a jar, of course, but still, if the girl was going to join him later . . . And, as for having this kid along, well, even that had its bright side. He could see that it would be by no means a bad move to play the hearty host to the young blighter. Reports of the lavishness of his hospitality and the suavity of his demeanour would get round to April and might do him quite a bit of good. It is a recognized fact that a lover is never wasting his time when he lushes up the little sister.

'All right,' he said. 'Hop in.'

So the kid hopped, and they shoved off. There wasn't anything much in the nature of intellectual conversation for the first ten minutes or so, because there was a fairish amount of traffic on the river at this point and the kid, who had established herself at the steering apparatus, seemed to have a rather sketchy notion of the procedure. As she explained to Freddie after they had gone about half-way through a passing barge, she always forgot which of the ropes it was that you pulled when you wanted to go to the right. However, the luck of the Widgeons saw them through and eventually they came, still afloat, to the unfrequented upper portions of the stream. Here in some mysterious way the rudder fell off, and after that it was all much easier. And it was at this point that the kid, having no longer anything to occupy herself with, reached out and picked up the book.

'Hullo! Are you reading Tennyson?'

'I was before we started, and I shall doubtless dip into him again later on. You will generally find me having a pop at the bard under advisement when I get a spare five minutes.'

'You don't mean to say you like him?'

'Of course I do. Who doesn't?'

'I don't. April's been making me read him, and I think he's soppy.'

'He is not soppy at all. Dashed beautiful.'

'But don't you think his girls are awful blisters?'

Apart from his old crony, the Lady of Shalott, Freddie had not yet made the acquaintance of any of the women in Tennyson's poems, but he felt very strongly that if they were good enough for April Carroway they were good enough for a green-eyed child with freckles all over her nose, and he said as much, rather severely.

'Tennyson's heroines,' said Freddie, 'are jolly fine specimens of pure, sweet womanhood, so get that into your nut, you soulless kid. If you behaved like a Tennyson heroine, you would be doing well.'

'Which of them?'

'Any of them. Pick 'em where you like. You can't go wrong. How much further to this Ferry place?'

'It's round the next bend.'

It was naturally with something of a pang that Freddie tied the boat up at their destination. Not only was this Griggs's Ferry a lovely spot, it was in addition completely deserted. There was a small house through the trees, but it showed no signs of occupancy. The only living thing for miles around appeared to be an elderly horse which was taking a snack on the river bank. In other words, if only April had been here and the kid hadn't, they would have been alone together with no human eye to intrude upon their sacred solitude. They could have read Tennyson to each other till they were blue in the face, and not a squawk from a soul.

A saddening thought, of course. Still, as the row had given him a nice appetite, he soon dismissed these wistful yearnings and started unpacking the luncheon basket. And at the end of about twenty minutes, during which period nothing had broken the stillness but the sound of champing jaws, he felt that it would not be amiss to chat with his little guest.

'Had enough?' he asked.

'No,' said the kid. 'But there isn't any more.'

'You seem to tuck away your food all right.'

'The girls at school used to call me Teresa the Tapeworm,' said the kid with a touch of pride.

It suddenly struck Freddie as a little odd that with July only half over this child should be at large. The summer holidays, as he remembered it, always used to start round about the first of August.

'Why aren't you at school now?'

'I was bunked last month.'

'Really?' said Freddie, interested. 'They gave you the push, did they? What for?'

'Shooting pigs.'

'Shooting pigs?'

'With a bow and arrow. One pig, that is to say. Percival. He belonged to Miss Maitland, the headmistress. Do you ever pretend to be people in books?'

'Never. And don't stray from the point at issue. I want to get to the bottom of this thing about the pig.'

'I'm not straying from the point at issue. I was playing William Tell.'

'The old apple-knocker, you mean?'

'The man who shot an apple off his son's head. I tried to get one of the girls to put the apple on her head, but she wouldn't, so I went down to the pigsty and put it on Percival's. And the silly goop shook it off and started to eat it just as I was shooting, which spoiled my aim and I got him on the left ear. He was rather vexed about it. So was Miss Maitland. Especially as I was supposed to be in disgrace at the time, because I had set the dormitory on fire the night before.'

Freddie blinked a bit.

'You set the dormitory on fire?'

'Yes.'

'Any special reason, or just a passing whim?'

'I was playing Florence Nightingale.'

'Florence Nightingale?'

'The Lady with the Lamp. I dropped the lamp.'

'Tell me,' said Freddie. 'This Miss Maitland of yours. What colour is her hair?'

'Grey.'

'I thought as much. And now, if you don't mind, switch off the childish prattle for the nonce. I feel a restful sleep creeping over me.'

'My uncle Joe says that people who sleep after lunch have got fatty degeneration of the heart.'

'Your Uncle Joe is an ass,' said Freddie.

★

How long it was before Freddie awoke, he could not have said. But when he did the first thing that impressed itself upon him was that the kid was no longer in sight, and this worried him a bit. I mean to say, a child who, on her own showing, plugged pigs with arrows and set fire to dormitories was not a child he was frightfully keen on having roaming about the countryside at a time when he was supposed to be more or less in charge of her. He got up, feeling somewhat perturbed, and started walking about and bellowing her name.

Rather a chump it made him feel, he tells me, because a fellow all by himself on the bank of a river shouting, 'Prudence! Prudence!' is apt to give a false impression to any passer-by who may hear him. However, he didn't have to bother about that long, for at this point, happening to glance at the river, he saw her body floating in it.

'Oh, dash it!' said Freddie.

Well, I mean, you couldn't say it was pleasant for him. It put him in what you might call an invidious position. Here he was, supposed to be looking after this kid, and when he got home April Carroway would ask him if he had had a jolly day and he would reply: 'Topping, thanks, except that young Prudence went and got drowned, regretted by all except possibly Miss Maitland.' It wouldn't go well, and he could see it wouldn't go well, so on the chance of a last-minute rescue he dived in. And he was considerably surprised, on arriving at what he had supposed to be a drowning child, to discover that it was merely the outer husk. In other words, what was floating there was not the kid in person but only her frock. And why a frock that had had a kid in it should suddenly have become a kidless frock was a problem beyond him.

Another problem, which presented itself as he sloshed ashore once more, was what the dickens he was going to do now. The sun had gone in and a rather nippy breeze was blowing, and it looked to him as if only a complete change of costume could save him from pneumonia. And as he stood there wondering where this change of costume was to come from he caught sight of that house through the trees.

Now, in normal circs. Freddie would never dream of calling on a bird to whom he had never been introduced and touching him for a suit of clothes. He's scrupulously rigid on points like that and has been known to go smokeless through an entire night at the theatre rather than ask a stranger for a match. But this was a special case. He didn't hesitate. A quick burst across country, and he was at the front door, rapping the knocker and calling 'I say!' And when at the end of about three minutes nobody had appeared he came rather shrewdly to the conclusion that the place must be deserted.

Well, this, of course, fitted in quite neatly with his plans. He much preferred to nip in and help himself rather than explain everything at length to someone who might very easily be one of those goops who are not quick at grasping situations. Observing that the door was not locked, accordingly he pushed in and toddled up the stairs to the bedroom on the first floor.

Everything was fine. There was a cupboard by the bed, and in it an assortment of clothes which left him a wide choice. He fished out a neat creation in checked tweed, located a shirt, a tie, and a sweater in the chest of drawers and, stripping off his wet things, began to dress.

As he did so, he continued to muse on this mystery of the child Prudence. He wondered what Sherlock Holmes would have made of it, or Lord Peter Wimsey, for that matter. The one thing certain was that the moment he was clothed he must buzz out and scour the countryside for her. So with all possible speed he donned the shirt, the tie, and the sweater, and had just put on a pair of roomy but serviceable shoes when his eye, roving aimlessly about the apartment, fell upon a photograph on the mantelpiece.

It represented a young man of powerful physique seated in a chair in flimsy garments. On his face was a rather noble expression, on his lap a massive silver cup, and on his hands boxing-gloves. And in spite of the noble expression he had no difficulty in recognizing the face as that of his formidable acquaintance, Captain Bradbury.

And at this moment, just as he had realized that Fate, after being tolerably rough with him all day, had put the lid on it by leading him into his rival's lair, he heard a sound of footsteps in the garden below. And, leaping to the window, he found his worst fears confirmed. The Captain, looking larger and tougher than ever, was coming up the gravel path to the front door. And that door, Freddie remembered with considerable emotion, he had left open.

Well, Freddie, as you know, has never been the dreamy meditative type. I would describe him as essentially the man of action. And he acted now as never before. He tells me he doubts if a chamois of the Alps, unless at the end of a most intensive spell of training, could have got down those stairs quicker than he did. He says the whole thing rather resembled an effort on the part of one of those Indian fakirs who bung their astral bodies about all over the place, going into thin air in Bombay and reassembling the parts two minutes later in Darjeeling. The result being that he reached the front door just as Captain Bradbury was coming in, and slammed it in his face. A hoarse cry, seeping through the woodwork, caused him to shoot both bolts and prop a small chair against the lower panel.

And he was just congratulating himself on having done all that man could do and handled a difficult situation with energy and tact, when a sort of scrabbling noise to the southwest came to his ears, and he realized with a sickening sinking of the heart what it means to be up against one of these Indian Army strategists, trained from early youth to do the dirty on the lawless tribes of the North-West Frontier. With consummate military skill, Captain Bradbury, his advance checked at the front door, was trying to outflank him by oozing in through the sitting-room window.

However, most fortunately it happened that whoever washed and brushed up this house had left a mop in the hall. It was a good outsize mop, and Freddie whisked it up in his stride and shot into the sitting room. He arrived just in time to see a leg coming over the sill. Then a face came into view, and Freddie tells me that the eyes into which he found himself gazing have kept him awake at night ever since.

For an instant, they froze him stiff, like a snake's. Then reason returned to her throne and, recovering himself with a strong effort, he rammed the mop home, sending his adversary base over apex into a bed of nasturtiums. This done, he shut the window and bolted it.

You might have thought that with a pane of glass in between them Captain Bradbury's glare would have lost in volume. This, Freddie tells me, was not the case. As he had now recognized his assailant, it had become considerably more above proof. It scorched Freddie like a death ray.

But the interchange of glances did not last long. These Indian Army men do not look, they act. And it has been well said of them that, while you may sometimes lay them a temporary stymie, you cannot baffle them permanently. The Captain suddenly turned and began to gallop round the corner of the house. It was plainly his intention to resume the attack from another and a less well-guarded quarter. This, I believe, is a common manœuvre on the North-West Frontier. You get your Afghan shading his eyes and looking out over the *maidan*, and then you sneak up the *pahar* behind him and catch him bending.

This decided Freddie. He simply couldn't go on indefinitely, leaping from spot to spot, endeavouring with a mere mop to stem the advance of a foe as resolute as this Bradbury. The time had come for a strategic retreat. Not ten seconds, accordingly, after the other had disappeared, he was wrenching the front door open.

He was taking a risk, of course. There was the possibility that he might be walking into an ambush. But all seemed well. The Captain had apparently genuinely gone round to the back, and Freddie reached the gate with the comfortable feeling that in another couple of seconds he would be out in the open and in a position to leg it away from the danger zone.

All's well that ends well, felt Freddie.

It was at this juncture that he found that he had no trousers on.

I need scarcely enlarge upon the agony of spirit which this discovery caused poor old Freddie. Apart from being the soul of modesty, he is a chap who prides himself on always being well and suitably dressed for both town and country. In a costume which would have excited remark at the Four Arts Ball in Paris, he writhed with shame and embarrassment. And he was just saying: 'This is the end!' when what should he see before him but a two-seater car, which he recognized as the property of his late host.

And in the car was a large rug.

It altered the whole aspect of affairs. From neck to waist, you will recall, Freddie was adequately, if not neatly, clad. The garments which he had borrowed from Captain Bradbury were a good deal too large, but at least they covered the person. In a car with that rug over his lap his outward appearance would be virtually that of the Well-Dressed Man.

He did not hesitate. He had never pinched a car before, but he did it now with all the smoothness of a seasoned professional. Springing into the driving seat, he tucked the rug about his knees, trod on the self-starter, and was off.

His plans were all neatly shaped. It was his intention to make straight for the Blue Lion. Arrived there, a swift dash would take him through the lobby and up the stairs to his room, where no fewer than seven pairs of trousers awaited his choice. And as the lobby was usually deserted except for the growing boy who cleaned the knives and boots, a lad who could be relied on merely to give a cheery guffaw and then dismiss the matter from his mind, he anticipated no further trouble.

But you never know. You form your schemes and run them over in your mind and you can't see a flaw in them, and then something happens out of a blue sky which dishes them completely. Scarcely had Freddie got half a mile down the road when a girlish figure leaped out of some bushes at the side, waving its arms, and he saw that it was April Carroway.

If you had told Freddie only a few hours before that a time would come when he would not be pleased to see April Carroway, he would have laughed derisively. But it was without pleasure that he looked upon her now. Nor, as he stopped the car and was enabled to make a closer inspection of the girl, did it seem as if she were pleased to see him. Why this should be so he could not imagine, but beyond a question she was not looking chummy. Her face was set, and there was an odd, stony expression in her eyes.

'Oh, hullo!' said Freddie. 'So you got away from your lunch party all right.'

'Yes.'

Freddie braced himself to break the bad news. The whole subject of the kid Prudence and her mysterious disappearance was one on which he would have preferred not to touch, but obviously it had to be done. I mean, you can't go about the place mislaying girls' sisters and just not mention it. He coughed.

'I say,' he said, 'a rather rummy thing has occurred. Odd, you might call it. With the best intentions in the world, I seem to have lost your sister Prudence.'

'So I gathered. Well, I've found her.'

'Eh?'

At this moment, a disembodied voice suddenly came from inside one of the bushes, causing Freddie to shoot a full two inches out of his seat. He tells me he remembered a similar experience having happened to Moses in the Wilderness, and he wondered if the prophet had taken it as big as he had done.

'I'm in here!'

Freddie gaped.

'Was that Prudence?' he gurgled.

'That was Prudence,' said April coldly.

'But what's she doing there?'

'She is obliged to remain in those bushes, because she has nothing on.'

'Nothing on? No particular engagements, you mean?'

'I mean no clothes. The horse kicked hers into the river.'

Freddie blinked. He could make nothing of this.

'A horse kicked the clothes off her?'

'It didn't kick them off me,' said the voice. 'They were lying on the bank in a neat bundle. Miss Maitland always taught us to be neat with our clothes. You see, I was playing Lady Godiva, as you advised me to.'

Freddie clutched at his brow. He might have known, he told himself, that the moment he dropped off for a few minutes refreshing sleep this ghastly kid would be up to something frightful. And he might also have known, he reflected, that she would put the blame on him. He had studied Woman, and he knew that when Woman gets into a tight place her first act is to shovel the blame off on to the nearest male.

'When did I ever advise you to play Lady Godiva?'

'You told me I couldn't go wrong in imitating any of Tennyson's heroines.'

'You appear to have encouraged her and excited her imagination,' said April, giving him a look which, while it was of a different calibre from Captain Bradbury's, was almost as unpleasant to run up against. 'I can't blame the poor child for being carried away.'

Freddie did another spot of brow-clutching. No wooer, he knew, makes any real progress with the girl he loves by encouraging her young sister to ride horses about the countryside in the nude.

'But, dash it...'

'Well, we need not go into that now. The point is that she is in those bushes with only a small piece of sacking over her, and is likely to catch cold. Perhaps you will be kind enough to drive her home?'

'Oh, rather. Of course. Certainly.'

'And put that rug over her,' said April Carroway. 'It may save her from a bad chill.'

The world reeled about Freddie. The voice of a donkey braying in a neighbouring meadow seemed like the mocking laughter of demons. The summer breeze was still murmuring through the tree-tops and birds still twittered in the hedgerows, but he did not hear them.

He swallowed a couple of times.

'I'm sorry...'

April Carroway was staring at him incredulously. It was as if she could not believe her ears.

'You don't mean to say that you refuse to give up your rug to a child who is sneezing already?'

'I'm sorry...'

'Do you realize...'

'I'm sorry... Cannot relinquish rug... Rheumatism... Bad... In the knee-joints... Doctor's orders...'

'Mr Widgeon,' said April Carroway imperiously, 'give me that rug immediately!'

An infinite sadness came into Frederick Widgeon's eyes. He gave the girl one long, sorrowful look – a look in which remorse, apology, and a lifelong devotion were nicely blended. Then, without a word, he put the clutch in and drove on, out into the sunset.

Somewhere on the outskirts of Wibbleton-in-the-Vale, when the dusk was falling and the air was fragrant with the evening dew, he managed to sneak a pair of trousers from a scarecrow in a field. Clad in these, he drove to London. He is now living down in the suburbs somewhere, trying to grow a beard in order to foil possible pursuit from Captain Bradbury.

And what he told me to say was that, if anybody cares to have an only slightly soiled copy of the works of Alfred, Lord Tennyson, at a sacrifice price, he is in the market. Not only has he taken an odd dislike to this particular poet, but he had a letter from April Carroway this morning, the contents of which have solidified his conviction that the volume to which I allude is of no further use to owner.

4
THE AMAZING HAT MYSTERY

A Bean was in a nursing home with a broken leg as the result of trying to drive his sports-model Poppenheim through the Marble Arch instead of round it, and a kindly Crumpet had looked in to give him the gossip of the town. He found him playing halma with the nurse, and he sat down on the bed and took a grape, and the Bean asked what was going on in the great world.

'Well,' said the Crumpet, taking another grape, 'the finest minds in the Drones are still wrestling with the Great Hat Mystery.'

'What's that?'

'You don't mean you haven't heard about it?'

'Not a word.'

The Crumpet was astounded. He swallowed two grapes at once in his surprise.

'Why, London's seething with it. The general consensus of opinion is that it has something to do with the Fourth Dimension. You know how things do. I mean to say, something rummy occurs and you consult some big-brained bird and he wags his head and says "Ah! The Fourth Dimension!" Extraordinary nobody's told you about the Great Hat Mystery.'

'You're the first visitor I've had. What is it, anyway? What hat?'

'Well, there were two hats. Reading from left to right, Percy Wimbolt's and Nelson Cork's.'

The Bean nodded intelligently.

'I see what you mean. Percy had one, and Nelson had the other.'

'Exactly. Two hats in all. Top hats.'

'What was mysterious about them?'

'Why, Elizabeth Bottsworth and Diana Punter said they didn't fit.'

'Well, hats don't sometimes.'

'But these came from Bodmin's.'

The Bean shot up in bed.

'What?'

'You mustn't excite the patient,' said the nurse, who up to this point had taken no part in the conversation.

'But dash it, nurse,' cried the Bean, 'you can't have caught what he said. If we are to give credence to his story, Percy Wimbolt and Nelson Cork bought a couple of hats at Bodmin's – at *Bodmin's*, I'll trouble you – and they didn't fit. It isn't possible.'

He spoke with strong emotion, and the Crumpet nodded understandingly. People can say what they please about the modern young man believing in nothing nowadays, but there is one thing every right-minded young man believes in, and that is the infallibility of Bodmin's hats. It is one of the eternal verities. Once admit that it is possible for a Bodmin hat not to fit, and you leave the door open for Doubt, Schism, and Chaos generally.

'That's exactly how Percy and Nelson felt, and it was for that reason that they were compelled to take the strong line they did with E. Bottsworth and D. Punter.'

'They took a strong line, did they?'

'A very strong line.'

'Won't you tell us the whole story from the beginning?' said the nurse.

'Right ho,' said the Crumpet, taking a grape. 'It'll make your head swim.'

'So mysterious?'

'So absolutely dashed uncanny from start to finish.'

You must know, to begin with, my dear old nurse (said the Crumpet), that these two blokes, Percy Wimbolt and Nelson Cork, are fellows who have to exercise the most watchful care about their lids, because they are so situated that in their case there can be none of that business of just charging into any old hattery and grabbing the first thing in sight. Percy is one of those large, stout, outsize chaps with a head like a watermelon, while Nelson is built more on the lines of a minor jockey and has a head like a peanut.

You will readily appreciate, therefore, that it requires an artist's hand to fit them properly, and that is why they have always gone to Bodmin. I have heard Percy say that his trust in Bodmin is like the unspotted faith of a young curate in his Bishop and I have no doubt that Nelson would have said the same, if he had thought of it.

It was at Bodmin's door that they ran into each other on the morning when my story begins.

'Hullo,' said Percy. 'You come to buy a hat?'

'Yes,' said Nelson. 'You come to buy a hat?'

'Yes.' Percy glanced cautiously about him, saw that he was alone (except for Nelson, of course) and unobserved, and drew closer and lowered his voice. 'There's a reason!'

'That's rummy,' said Nelson. He, also, spoke in a hushed tone. 'I have a special reason, too.'

Percy looked warily about him again, and lowered his voice another notch.

'Nelson,' he said, 'you know Elizabeth Bottsworth?'

'Intimately,' said Nelson.

'Rather a sound young potato, what?'

'Very much so.'

'Pretty.'

'I've often noticed it.'

'Me, too. She is so small, so sweet, so dainty, so lively, so viv—, what's-the-word? – that a fellow wouldn't be far out in calling her an angel in human shape.'

'Aren't all angels in human shape?'

'Are they?' said Percy, who was a bit foggy on angels. 'Well, be that as it may,' he went on, his cheeks suffused to a certain extent, 'I love that girl, Nelson, and she's coming with me to the first day of Ascot, and I'm relying on this new hat of mine to do just that extra bit that's needed in the way of making her reciprocate my passion. Having only met her so far at country houses, I've never yet flashed upon her in a topper.'

Nelson Cork was staring.

'Well, if that isn't the most remarkable coincidence I ever came across in my puff!' he exclaimed, amazed. 'I'm buying my new hat for exactly the same reason.'

A convulsive start shook Percy's massive frame. His eyes bulged.

'To fascinate Elizabeth Bottsworth?' he cried, beginning to writhe.

'No, no,' said Nelson, soothingly. 'Of course not. Elizabeth and I have always been great friends, but nothing more. What I meant was that I, like you, am counting on this forthcoming topper of mine to put me across with the girl I love.'

Percy stopped writhing.

'Who is she?' he asked, interested.

'Diana Punter, the niece of my godmother, old Ma Punter. It's an odd thing, I've known her all my life – brought up as kids together and so forth – but it's only recently that passion has burgeoned. I now worship that girl, Percy, from the top of her head to the soles of her divine feet.'

Percy looked dubious.

'That's a pretty longish distance, isn't it? Diana Punter is one of my closest friends, and a charming girl in every respect, but isn't she a bit tall for you, old man?'

'My dear chap, that's just what I admire so much about her, her superb statuesqueness. More like a Greek goddess than anything I've

struck for years. Besides, she isn't any taller for me than you are for
Elizabeth Bottsworth.'

'True,' admitted Percy.

'And, anyway, I love her, blast it, and I don't propose to argue the
point. I love her, I love her, I love her, and we are lunching together
the first day of Ascot.'

'At Ascot?'

'No. She isn't keen on racing, so I shall have to give Ascot a miss.'

'That's Love,' said Percy, awed.

'The binge will take place at my godmother's house in Berkeley
Square, and it won't be long after that, I feel, before you see an interesting announcement in the *Morning Post*.'

Percy extended his hand. Nelson grasped it warmly.

'These new hats are pretty well bound to do the trick, I should say,
wouldn't you?'

'Infallibly. Where girls are concerned, there is nothing that brings
home the gravy like a well-fitting topper.'

'Bodmin must extend himself as never before,' said Percy.

'He certainly must,' said Nelson.

They entered the shop. And Bodmin, having measured them with
his own hands, promised that two of his very finest efforts should be
at their respective addresses in the course of the next few days.

Now, Percy Wimbolt isn't a chap you would suspect of having
nerves, but there is no doubt that in the interval which elapsed before
Bodmin was scheduled to deliver he got pretty twittery. He kept
having awful visions of some great disaster happening to his new hat:
and, as things turned out, these visions came jolly near being ful-
filled. It has made Percy feel that he is psychic.

What occurred was this. Owing to these jitters of his, he hadn't
been sleeping any too well, and on the morning before Ascot he was
up as early as ten-thirty, and he went to his sitting room window to
see what sort of a day it was, and the sight he beheld from that
window absolutely froze the blood in his veins.

For there below him, strutting up and down the pavement, were
a uniformed little blighter whom he recognized as Bodmin's errand-
boy and an equally foul kid in mufti. And balanced on each child's
loathsome head was a top hat. Against the railings were leaning a
couple of cardboard hatboxes.

Now, considering that Percy had only just woken from a dream in
which he had been standing outside the Guildhall in his new hat,
receiving the Freedom of the City from the Lord Mayor, and the
Lord Mayor had suddenly taken a terrific swipe at the hat with his

mace, knocking it into hash, you might have supposed that he would
have been hardened to anything. But he wasn't. His reaction was
terrific. There was a moment of sort of paralysis, during which he
was telling himself that he had always suspected this beastly little boy
of Bodmin's of having a low and frivolous outlook and being temperamentally unfitted for his high office: and then he came alive with a
jerk and let out probably the juiciest yell the neighbourhood had
heard for years.

It stopped the striplings like a high-powered shell. One moment,
they had been swanking up and down in a mincing and affected sort
of way: the next, the second kid had legged it like a streak and
Bodmin's boy was shoving the hats back in the boxes and trying to do
it quickly enough to enable him to be elsewhere when Percy should
arrive.

And in this he was successful. By the time Percy had got to the
front door and opened it, there was nothing to be seen but a hatbox
standing on the steps. He took it up to his flat and removed the
contents with a gingerly and reverent hand, holding his breath for
fear the nap should have got rubbed the wrong way or a dent of any
nature been made in the gleaming surface; but apparently all was
well. Bodmin's boy might sink to taking hats out of their boxes and
fooling about with them, but at least he hadn't gone to the last awful
extreme of dropping them.

The lid was O.K. absolutely: and on the following morning Percy,
having spent the interval polishing it with stout, assembled the boots,
the spats, the trousers, the coat, the flowered waistcoat, the collar,
the shirt, the quiet grey tie, and the good old gardenia, and set off in a
taxi for the house where Elizabeth was staying. And presently he was
ringing the bell and being told she would be down in a minute, and
eventually down she came, looking perfectly marvellous.

'What ho, what ho!' said Percy.

'Hullo, Percy,' said Elizabeth.

Now, naturally, up to this moment Percy had been standing with
bared head. At this point, he put the hat on. He wanted her to get the
full effect suddenly in a good light. And very strategic, too. I mean to
say, it would have been the act of a juggins to have waited till they
were in the taxi, because in a taxi all toppers look much alike.

So Percy popped the hat on his head with a meaning glance and
stood waiting for the uncontrollable round of applause.

And instead of clapping her little hands in girlish ecstasy and doing
Spring dances round him, this young Bottsworth gave a sort of
gurgling scream not unlike a coloratura soprano choking on a
fishbone.

Then she blinked and became calmer.

'It's all right,' she said. 'The momentary weakness has passed. Tell me, Percy, when do you open?'

'Open?' said Percy, not having the remotest.

'On the Halls. Aren't you going to sing comic songs on the Music Halls?'

Percy's perplexity deepened.

'Me? No. How? Why? What do you mean?'

'I thought that hat must be part of the make-up and that you were trying it on the dog. I couldn't think of any other reason why you should wear one six sizes too small.'

Percy gasped.

'You aren't suggesting this hat doesn't fit me?'

'It doesn't fit you by a mile.'

'But it's a Bodmin.'

'Call it that if you like. I call it a public outrage.'

Percy was appalled. I mean, naturally. A nice thing for a chap to give his heart to a girl and then find her talking in this hideous, flippant way of sacred subjects.

Then it occurred to him that, living all the time in the country, she might not have learned to appreciate the holy significance of the name Bodmin.

'Listen,' he said gently. 'Let me explain. This hat was made by Bodmin, the world-famous hatter of Vigo Street. He measured me in person and guaranteed a fit.'

'And I nearly had one.'

'And if Bodmin guarantees that a hat shall fit,' proceeded Percy, trying to fight against a sickening sort of feeling that he had been all wrong about this girl, 'it fits. I mean, saying a Bodmin hat doesn't fit is like saying ... well, I can't think of anything awful enough.'

'That hat's awful enough. It's like something out of a two-reel comedy. Pure Chas. Chaplin. I know a joke's a joke, Percy, and I'm as fond of a laugh as anyone, but there is such a thing as cruelty to animals. Imagine the feelings of the horses at Ascot when they see that hat.'

Poets and other literary blokes talk a lot about falling in love at first sight, but it's equally possible to fall out of love just as quickly. One moment, this girl was the be-all and the end-all, as you might say, of Percy Wimbolt's life. The next, she was just a regrettable young blister with whom he wished to hold no further communication. He could stand a good deal from the sex. Insults directed at himself left him unmoved. But he was not prepared to countenance destructive criticism of a Bodmin hat.

'Possibly,' he said, coldly, 'you would prefer to go to this bally race-meeting alone?'

'You bet I'm going alone. You don't suppose I mean to be seen in broad daylight in the paddock at Ascot with a hat like that?'

Percy stepped back and bowed formally.

'Drive on, driver,' he said to the driver, and the driver drove on.

Now, you would say that that was rummy enough. A full-sized mystery in itself, you might call it. But wait. Mark the sequel. You haven't heard anything yet.

We now turn to Nelson Cork. Shortly before one-thirty, Nelson had shoved over to Berkeley Square and had lunch with his godmother and Diana Punter, and Diana's manner and deportment had been absolutely all that could have been desired. In fact, so chummy had she been over the cutlets and fruit salad that it seemed to Nelson that, if she was like this now, imagination boggled at the thought of how utterly all over him she would be when he sprang his new hat on her.

So when the meal was concluded and coffee had been drunk and old Lady Punter had gone up to her boudoir with a digestive tablet and a sex-novel, he thought it would be a sound move to invite her to come for a stroll along Bond Street. There was the chance, of course, that she would fall into his arms right in the middle of the pavement: but if that happened, he told himself, they could always get into a cab. So he mooted the saunter, and she checked up, and presently they started off.

And you will scarcely believe this, but they hadn't gone more than half-way along Bruton Street when she suddenly stopped and looked at him in an odd manner.

'I don't want to be personal, Nelson,' she said, 'but really I do think you ought to take the trouble to get measured for your hats.'

If a gas main had exploded beneath Nelson's feet, he could hardly have been more taken aback.

'M-m-m-m . . .' He gasped. He could scarcely believe that he had heard right.

'It's the only way with a head like yours. I know it's a temptation for a lazy man to go into a shop and just take whatever is offered him, but the result is so sloppy. That thing you're wearing now looks like an extinguisher.'

Nelson was telling himself that he must be strong.

'Are you endeavouring to intimate that this hat doesn't fit?'

'Can't you feel that it doesn't fit?'

'But it's a Bodmin.'

'I don't know what you mean. It's just an ordinary silk hat.'

'Not at all. It's a Bodmin.'

'I don't know what you are talking about.'

'The point I am trying to drive home,' said Nelson stiffly, 'is that this hat was constructed under the personal auspices of Jno. Bodmin of Vigo Street.'

'Well, it's too big.'

'It is not too big.'

'I say it is too big.'

'And I say a Bodmin hat cannot be too big.'

'Well, I've got eyes, and I say it is.'

Nelson controlled himself with an effort.

'I would be the last person,' he said, 'to criticize your eyesight, but on the present occasion you will permit me to say that it has let you down with a considerable bump. Myopia is indicated. Allow me,' said Nelson, hot under the collar, but still dignified, 'to tell you something about Jno. Bodmin, as the name appears new to you. Jno. is the last of a long line of Bodmins, all of whom have made hats assiduously for the nobility and gentry all their lives. Hats are in Jno. Bodmin's blood.'

'I don't . . .'

Nelson held up a restraining hand.

'Over the door of his emporium in Vigo Street the passer-by may read a significant legend. It runs: "Bespoke Hatter To The Royal Family." That means, in simple language adapted to the lay intelligence, that if the King wants a new topper he simply ankles round to Bodmin's and says: "Good morning, Bodmin, we want a topper." He does not ask if it will fit. He takes it for granted that it will fit. He has bespoken Jno. Bodmin, and he trusts him blindly. You don't suppose His Gracious Majesty would bespeak a hatter whose hats did not fit. The whole essence of being a hatter is to make hats that fit, and it is to this end that Jno. Bodmin has strained every nerve for years. And that is why I say again – simply and without heat – This hat is a Bodmin.'

Diana was beginning to get a bit peeved. The blood of the Punters is hot, and very little is required to steam it up. She tapped Bruton Street with a testy foot.

'You always were an obstinate, pig-headed little fiend, Nelson, even as a child. I tell you once more, for the last time, that that hat is too big. If it were not for the fact that I can see a pair of boots and part of a pair of trousers, I should not know that there was a human being under it. I don't care how much you argue, I still think you ought to be ashamed of yourself for coming out in the thing. Even if you didn't mind for your own sake, you might have considered the feelings of the pedestrians and traffic.'

Nelson quivered.

'You do, do you?'

'Yes, I do.'

'Oh, you do?'

'I said I did. Didn't you hear me? No, I suppose you could hardly be expected to, with an enormous great hat coming down over your ears.'

'You say this hat comes down over my ears?'

'Right over your ears. It's a mystery to me why you think it worth while to deny it.'

I fear that what follows does not show Nelson Cork in the role of a parfait gentil knight, but in extenuation of his behaviour I must remind you that he and Diana Punter had been brought up as children together, and a dispute between a couple who have shared the same nursery is always liable to degenerate into an exchange of personalities and innuendos. What starts as an academic discussion on hats turns only too swiftly into a raking-up of old sores and a grand parade of family skeletons.

It was so in this case. At the word 'mystery,' Nelson uttered a nasty laugh.

'A mystery, eh? As much a mystery, I suppose, as why your uncle George suddenly left England in the year 1920 without stopping to pack up?'

Diana's eyes flashed. Her foot struck the pavement another shrewd wallop.

'Uncle George,' she said haughtily, 'went abroad for his health.'

'You bet he did,' retorted Nelson. 'He knew what was good for him.'

'Anyway, he wouldn't have worn a hat like that.'

'Where they would have put him if he hadn't been off like a scalded kitten, he wouldn't have worn a hat at all.'

A small groove was now beginning to appear in the paving stone on which Diana Punter stood.

'Well, Uncle George escaped one thing by going abroad, at any rate,' she said. 'He missed the big scandal about your Aunt Clarissa in 1922.'

Nelson clenched his fists.

'The jury gave Aunt Clarissa the benefit of the doubt,' he said hoarsely.

'Well, we all know what that means. It was accompanied, if you recollect, by some very strong remarks from the Bench.'

There was a pause.

'I may be wrong,' said Nelson, 'but I should have thought it ill beseemed a girl whose brother Cyril was warned off the Turf in 1924 to haul up her slacks about other people's Aunt Clarissas.'

'Passing lightly over my brother Cyril in 1924,' rejoined Diana, 'what price your cousin Fred in 1927?'

They glared at one another in silence for a space, each realizing with a pang that the supply of erring relatives had now given out. Diana was still pawing the paving stone, and Nelson was wondering what on earth he could ever have seen in a girl who, in addition to talking subversive drivel about hats, was eight feet tall and ungainly, to boot.

'While as for your brother-in-law's niece's sister-in-law Muriel . . .' began Diana, suddenly brightening.

Nelson checked her with a gesture.

'I prefer not to continue this discussion,' he said, frigidly.

'It is no pleasure to me,' replied Diana, with equal coldness, 'to have to listen to your vapid gibberings. That's the worst of a man who wears his hat over his mouth – he will talk through it.'

'I bid you a very hearty good afternoon, Miss Punter,' said Nelson.

He strode off without a backward glance.

Now, one advantage of having a row with a girl in Bruton Street is that the Drones is only just round the corner, so that you can pop in and restore the old nervous system with the minimum of trouble. Nelson was round there in what practically amounted to a trice, and the first person he saw was Percy, hunched up over a double and splash.

'Hullo,' said Percy.

'Hullo,' said Nelson.

There was a silence, broken only by the sound of Nelson ordering a mixed vermouth. Percy continued to stare before him like a man who has drained the wine-cup of life to its lees, only to discover a dead mouse at the bottom.

'Nelson,' he said at length, 'what are your views on the Modern Girl?'

'I think she's a mess.'

'I thoroughly agree with you,' said Percy. 'Of course, Diana Punter is a rare exception, but, apart from Diana, I wouldn't give you twopence for the Modern Girl. She lacks depth and reverence and has no sense of what is fitting. Hats, for example.'

'Exactly. But what do you mean Diana Punter is an exception? She's one of the ringleaders – the spearhead of the movement, if you like to put it that way. Think,' said Nelson, sipping his vermouth, 'of all the unpleasant qualities of the Modern Girl, add them up, double them, and what have you got? Diana Punter. Let me tell you what took place between me and this Punter only a few minutes ago.'

'No,' said Percy. 'Let me tell you what transpired between me and Elizabeth Bottsworth this morning. Nelson, old man, she said my hat – my Bodmin hat – was too small.'

'You don't mean that?'

'Those were her very words.'

'Well, I'm dashed. Listen. Diana Punter told me my equally Bodmin hat was too large.'

They stared at one another.

'It's the Spirit of something,' said Nelson. 'I don't know what, quite, but of something. You see it on all sides. Something very serious has gone wrong with girls nowadays. There is lawlessness and licence abroad.'

'And here in England, too.'

'Well, naturally, you silly ass,' said Nelson, with some asperity. 'When I said abroad, I didn't mean abroad, I meant abroad.'

He mused for a moment.

'I must say, though,' he continued, 'I am surprised at what you tell me about Elizabeth Bottsworth, and am inclined to think there must have been some mistake. I have always been a warm admirer of Elizabeth.'

'And I have always thought Diana one of the best, and I find it hard to believe that she should have shown up in such a dubious light as you suggest. Probably there was a misunderstanding of some kind.'

'Well, I ticked her off properly, anyway.'

Percy Wimbolt shook his head.

'You shouldn't have done that, Nelson. You may have wounded her feelings. In my case, of course, I had no alternative but to be pretty crisp with Elizabeth.'

Nelson Cork clicked his tongue.

'A pity,' he said. 'Elizabeth is sensitive.'

'So is Diana.'

'Not so sensitive as Elizabeth.'

'I should say, at a venture, about five times as sensitive as Elizabeth. However, we must not quarrel about a point like that, old man. The fact that emerges is that we seem both to have been dashed badly treated. I think I shall toddle home and take an aspirin.'

'Me, too.'

They went off to the cloakroom, where their hats were, and Percy put his on.

'Surely,' he said, 'nobody but a half-witted little pipsqueak who can't see straight would say this was too small?'

'It isn't a bit too small,' said Nelson. 'And take a look at this one. Am I not right in supposing that only a female giantess with straws in her hair and astigmatism in both eyes could say it was too large?'

'It's a lovely fit.'

And the cloakroom waiter, a knowledgeable chap of the name of Robinson, said the same.

'So there you are,' said Nelson.

'Ah, well,' said Percy.

They left the club, and parted at the top of Dover Street.

Now, though he had not said so in so many words, Nelson Cork's heart had bled for Percy Wimbolt. He knew the other's fine sensibilities and he could guess how deeply they must have been gashed by this unfortunate breaking-off of diplomatic relations with the girl he loved. For, whatever might have happened, however sorely he might have been wounded, the way Nelson Cork looked at it was that Percy loved Elizabeth Bottsworth in spite of everything. What was required here, felt Nelson, was a tactful mediator – a kindly, sensible friend of both parties who would hitch up his socks and plunge in and heal the breach.

So the moment he had got rid of Percy outside the club he hared round to the house where Elizabeth was staying and was lucky enough to catch her on the front door steps. For, naturally, Elizabeth hadn't gone off to Ascot by herself. Directly Percy was out of sight, she had told the taxi-man to drive her home, and she had been occupying the interval since the painful scene in thinking of things she wished she had said to him and taking her hostess's dog for a run – a Pekinese called Clarkson.

She seemed very pleased to see Nelson, and started to prattle of this and that, her whole demeanour that of a girl who, after having been compelled to associate for a while with the Underworld, has at last found a kindred soul. And the more he listened, the more he wanted to go on listening. And the more he looked at her, the more he felt that a lifetime spent in gazing at Elizabeth Bottsworth would be a lifetime dashed well spent.

There was something about the girl's exquisite petiteness and fragility that appealed to Nelson Cork's depths. After having wasted so much time looking at a female Carnera like Diana Punter, it was a genuine treat to him to be privileged to feast the eyes on one so small and dainty. And, what with one thing and another, he found the most extraordinary difficulty in lugging Percy into the conversation.

They strolled along, chatting. And, mark you, Elizabeth Bottsworth was a girl a fellow could chat with without getting a crick in the

neck from goggling up at her, the way you had to do when you took
the air with Diana Punter. Nelson realized now that talking to Diana
Punter had been like trying to exchange thoughts with a flagpole
sitter. He was surprised that this had never occurred to him before.

'You know, you're looking perfectly ripping, Elizabeth,' he said.

'How funny!' said the girl. 'I was just going to say the same thing
about you.'

'Not really?'

'Yes, I was. After some of the gargoyles I've seen today – Percy
Wimbolt is an example that springs to the mind – it's such a relief to
be with a man who really knows how to turn himself out.'

Now that the Percy *motif* had been introduced, it should have been
a simple task for Nelson to turn the talk to the subject of his absent
friend. But somehow he didn't. Instead, he just simpered a bit and
said: 'Oh, no, I say, really, do you mean that?'

'I do, indeed,' said Elizabeth earnestly. 'It's your hat, principally, I
think. I don't know why it is, but ever since a child I have been intensely sensitive to hats, and it has always been a pleasure to me to
remember that at the age of five I dropped a pot of jam out of the
nursery window on to my Uncle Alexander when he came to visit us
in a deer-stalker cap with ear-flaps, as worn by Sherlock Holmes. I
consider the hat the final test of a man. Now, yours is perfect. I never
saw such a beautiful fit. I can't tell you how much I admire that hat. It
gives you quite an ambassadorial look.'

Nelson Cork drew a deep breath. He was tingling from head to
foot. It was as if the scales had fallen from his eyes and a new life
begun for him.

'I say,' he said, trembling with emotion, 'I wonder if you would
mind if I pressed your little hand?'

'Do,' said Elizabeth cordially.

'I will,' said Nelson, and did so. 'And now,' he went on, clinging to
the fin like glue and hiccoughing a bit, 'how about buzzing off somewhere for a quiet cup of tea? I have a feeling that we have much to say
to one another.'

It is odd how often it happens in this world that when there are two
chaps and one chap's heart is bleeding for the other chap you find that
all the while the second chap's heart is bleeding just as much for the
first chap. Both bleeding, I mean to say, not only one. It was so in the
case of Nelson Cork and Percy Wimbolt. The moment he had left
Nelson, Percy charged straight off in search of Diana Punter with the
intention of putting everything right with a few well-chosen words.

Because what he felt was that, though at the actual moment of

going to press pique might be putting Nelson off Diana, this would
pass off and love come into its own again. All that was required, he
considered, was a suave go-between, a genial mutual pal who would
pour oil on the troubled w's and generally fix things up.

He found Diana walking round and round Berkeley Square with
her chin up, breathing tensely through the nostrils. He drew up
alongside and what-hoed, and as she beheld him the cold, hard gleam
in her eyes changed to a light of cordiality. She appeared charmed to
see him and at once embarked on an animated conversation. And
with every word she spoke his conviction deepened that of all the
ways of passing a summer afternoon there were none fruitier than
having a friendly hike with Diana Punter.

And it was not only her talk that enchanted him. He was equally
fascinated by that wonderful physique of hers. When he considered
that he had actually wasted several valuable minutes that day conversing with a young shrimp like Elizabeth Bottsworth, he could have
kicked himself.

Here, he reflected, as they walked round the square, was a girl
whose ear was more or less on a level with a fellow's mouth, so that
such observations as he might make were enabled to get from point to
point with the least possible delay. Talking to Elizabeth Bottsworth
had always been like bellowing down a well in the hope of attracting
the attention of one of the smaller infusoria at the bottom. It surprised him that he had been so long in coming to this conclusion.

He was awakened from this reverie by hearing his companion utter
the name of Nelson Cork.

'I beg your pardon?' he said.

'I was saying,' said Diana, 'that Nelson Cork is a wretched little
undersized blob who, if he were not too lazy to work, would long
since have signed up with some good troupe of midgets.'

'Oh, would you say that?'

'I would say more than that,' said Diana firmly. 'I tell you, Percy,
that what makes life so ghastly for girls, what causes girls to get grey
hair and go into convents, is the fact that it is not always possible for
them to avoid being seen in public with men like Nelson Cork. I trust
I am not uncharitable. I try to view these things in a broad-minded
way, saying to myself that if a man looks like something that has come
out from under a flat stone it is his misfortune rather than his fault
and that he is more to be pitied than censured. But on one thing I do
insist, that such a man does not wantonly aggravate the natural
unpleasantness of his appearance by prancing about London in a hat
that reaches down to his ankles. I cannot and will not endure being
escorted along Bruton Street by a sort of human bacillus the brim of

whose hat bumps on the pavement with every step he takes. What I have always said and what I shall always say is that the hat is the acid test. A man who cannot buy the right-sized hat is a man one could never like or trust. Your hat, now, Percy, is exactly right. I have seen a good many hats in my time, but I really do not think that I have ever come across a more perfect specimen of all that a hat should be. Not too large, not too small, fitting snugly to the head like the skin on a sausage. And you have just the kind of head that a silk hat shows off. It gives you a sort of look ... how shall I describe it? ... it conveys the idea of a master of men. Leonine is the word I want. There is something about the way it rests on the brow and the almost imperceptible tilt towards the southeast ...'

Percy Wimbolt was quivering like an Oriental muscle-dancer. Soft music seemed to be playing from the direction of Hay Hill, and Berkeley Square had begun to skip round him on one foot.

He drew a deep breath.

'I say,' he said, 'stop me if you've heard this before, but what I feel we ought to do at this juncture is to dash off somewhere where it's quiet and there aren't so many houses dancing the "Blue Danube" and shove some tea into ourselves. And over the pot and muffins I shall have something very important to say to you.'

'So that,' concluded the Crumpet, taking a grape, 'is how the thing stands; and, in a sense, of course, you could say that it is a satisfactory ending.

'The announcement of Elizabeth's engagement to Nelson Cork appeared in the Press on the same day as that of Diana's projected hitching up with Percy Wimbolt: and it is pleasant that the happy couples should be so well matched as regards size.

'I mean to say, there will be none of that business of a six-foot girl tripping down the aisle with a five-foot-four man, or a six-foot-two man trying to keep step along the sacred edifice with a four-foot-three girl. This is always good for a laugh from the ringside pews, but it does not make for wedded bliss.

'No, as far as the principals are concerned, we may say that all has ended well. But that doesn't seem to me the important point. What seems to me the important point is this extraordinary, baffling mystery of those hats.'

'Absolutely,' said the Bean.

'I mean to say, if Percy's hat really didn't fit, as Elizabeth Bottsworth contended, why should it have registered as a winner with Diana Punter?'

'Absolutely,' said the Bean.

'And, conversely, if Nelson's hat was the total loss which Diana Punter considered it, why, only a brief while later, was it going like a breeze with Elizabeth Bottsworth?'

'Absolutely,' said the Bean.

'The whole thing is utterly inscrutable.'

It was at this point that the nurse gave signs of wishing to catch the Speaker's eye.

'Shall I tell you what I think?'

'Say on, my dear young pillow-smoother.'

'I believe Bodmin's boy must have got those hats mixed. When he was putting them back in the boxes, I mean.'

The Crumpet shook his head, and took a grape.

'And then at the club they got the right ones again.'

The Crumpet smiled indulgently.

'Ingenious,' he said, taking a grape. 'Quite ingenious. But a little far-fetched. No, I prefer to think the whole thing, as I say, has something to do with the Fourth Dimension. I am convinced that that is the true explanation, if our minds could only grasp it.'

'Absolutely,' said the Bean.

5

GOODBYE TO ALL CATS

As the club kitten sauntered into the smoking room of the Drones Club and greeted those present with a friendly miauw, Freddie Widgeon, who had been sitting in a corner with his head between his hands, rose stiffly.

'I had supposed,' he said, in a cold, level voice, 'that this was a quiet retreat for gentlemen. As I perceive that it is a blasted zoo, I will withdraw.'

And he left the room in a marked manner.

There was a good deal of surprise, not unmixed with consternation.

'What's the trouble?' asked an Egg, concerned. Such exhibitions of the naked emotions are rare at the Drones. 'Have they had a row?'

A Crumpet, always well-informed, shook his head.

'Freddie has had no personal breach with this particular kitten,' he said. 'It is simply that since that weekend at Matcham Scratchings he can't stand the sight of a cat.'

'Matcham what?'

'Scratchings. The ancestral home of Dahlia Prenderby in Oxfordshire.'

'I met Dahlia Prenderby once,' said the Egg. 'I thought she seemed a nice girl.'

'Freddie thought so, too. He loved her madly.'

'And lost her, of course?'

'Absolutely.'

'Do you know,' said a thoughtful Bean, 'I'll bet that if all the girls Freddie Widgeon has loved and lost were placed end to end – not that I suppose one could do it – they would reach half-way down Piccadilly.'

'Further than that,' said the Egg. 'Some of them were pretty tall. What beats me is why he ever bothers to love them. They always turn him down in the end. He might just as well never begin. Better, in fact, because in the time saved he could be reading some good book.'

'I think the trouble with Freddie,' said the Crumpet, 'is that he always gets off to a flying start. He's a good-looking sort of chap who dances well and can wiggle his ears, and the girl is dazzled for the moment, and this encourages him. From what he tells me, he appears to have gone very big with this Prenderby girl at the outset. So much so, indeed, that when she invited him down to Matcham Scratchings he had already bought his copy of *What Every Young Bridegroom Ought To Know*.'

'Rummy, these old country-house names,' mused the Bean. 'Why Scratchings, I wonder?'

'Freddie wondered, too, till he got to the place. Then he tells me he felt it was absolutely the *mot juste*. This girl Dahlia's family, you see, was one of those animal-loving families, and the house, he tells me, was just a frothing maelstrom of dumb chums. As far as the eye could reach, there were dogs scratching themselves and cats scratching the furniture. I believe, though he never met it socially, there was even a tame chimpanzee somewhere on the premises, no doubt scratching away as assiduously as the rest of them. You get these conditions here and there in the depths of the country, and this Matcham place was well away from the centre of things, being about six miles from the nearest station.

'It was at this station that Dahlia Prenderby met Freddie in her two-seater, and on the way to the house there occurred a conversation which I consider significant – showing, as it does, the cordial relations existing between the young couple at that point in the proceedings. I mean, it was only later that the bitter awakening and all that sort of thing popped up.

'I do want you to be a success, Freddie,' said the girl, after talking a while of this and that. 'Some of the men I've asked down here have been such awful flops. The great thing is to make a good impression on Father.'

'I will,' said Freddie.

'He can be a little difficult at times.'

'Lead me to him,' said Freddie. 'That's all I ask. Lead me to him.'

'The trouble is, he doesn't much like young men.'

'He'll like me.'

'He will, will he?'

'Rather!'

'What makes you think that?'

'I'm a dashed fascinating chap.'

'Oh, you are?'

'Yes, I am.'

'You are, are you?'

'Rather!'

Upon which, she gave him a sort of push and he gave her a sort of push, and she giggled and he laughed like a paper bag bursting, and she gave him a kind of shove and he gave her a kind of shove, and she said 'You *are* a silly ass!' and he said 'What ho!' All of which shows you, I mean to say, the stage they had got to by this time. Nothing definitely settled, of course, but Love obviously beginning to burgeon in the girl's heart.

Well, naturally, Freddie gave a good deal of thought during the drive to this father of whom the girl had spoken so feelingly, and he resolved that he would not fail her. The way he would suck up to the old dad would be nobody's business. He proposed to exert upon him the full force of his magnetic personality, and looked forward to registering a very substantial hit.

Which being so, I need scarcely tell you, knowing Freddie as you do, that his first act on entering Sir Mortimer Prenderby's orbit was to make the scaliest kind of floater, hitting him on the back of the neck with a tortoiseshell cat not ten minutes after his arrival.

His train having been a bit late, there was no time on reaching the house for any stately receptions or any of that 'Welcome to Meadowsweet Hall' stuff. The girl simply shot him up to his room and told him to dress like a streak, because dinner was in a quarter of an hour, and then buzzed off to don the soup and fish herself. And Freddie was just going well when, looking round for his shirt, which he had left on the bed, he saw a large tortoiseshell cat standing on it, kneading it with its paws.

Well, you know how a fellow feels about his shirt-front. For an instant, Freddie stood spellbound. Then with a hoarse cry he bounded forward, scooped up the animal, and, carrying it out on to the balcony, flung it into the void. And an elderly gentleman, coming round the corner at this moment, received a direct hit on the back of his neck.

'Hell!' cried the elderly gentleman.

A head popped out of a window.

'Whatever is the matter, Mortimer?'

'It's raining cats.'

'Nonsense. It's a lovely evening,' said the head, and disappeared.

Freddie thought an apology would be in order.

'I say,' he said.

The old gentleman looked in every direction of the compass, and finally located Freddie on his balcony.

'I say,' said Freddie, 'I'm awfully sorry you got that nasty buffet. It was me.'

'It was not you. It was a cat.'

'I know. I threw the cat.'

'Why?'

'Well . . .'

'Dam' fool.'

'I'm sorry,' said Freddie.

'Go to blazes,' said the old gentleman.

Freddie backed into the room, and the incident closed.

Freddie is a pretty slippy dresser, as a rule, but this episode had shaken him, and he not only lost a collar-stud but made a mess of the first two ties. The result was that the gong went while he was still in his shirt-sleeves: and on emerging from his boudoir he was informed by a footman that the gang were already nuzzling their *bouillon* in the dining room. He pushed straight there, accordingly, and sank into a chair beside his hostess just in time to dead-heat with the final spoonful.

Awkward, of course, but he was feeling in pretty good form owing to the pleasantness of the thought that he was shoving his knees under the same board as the girl Dahlia: so, having nodded to his host, who was glaring at him from the head of the table, as much as to say that all would be explained in God's good time, he shot his cuffs and started to make sparkling conversation to Lady Prenderby.

'Charming place you have here, what?'

Lady Prenderby said that the local scenery was generally admired. She was one of those tall, rangy, Queen Elizabeth sort of women, with tight lips and cold, blancmangey eyes. Freddie didn't like her looks much, but he was feeling, as I say, fairly fizzy, so he carried on with a bright zip.

'Pretty good hunting country, I should think?'

'I believe there is a good deal of hunting near here, yes.'

'I thought as much,' said Freddie. 'Ah, that's the stuff, is it not? A cracking gallop across good country with a jolly fine kill at the end of it, what, what? Hark fo'ard, yoicks, tally-ho, I mean to say, and all that sort of thing.'

Lady Prenderby shivered austerely.

'I fear I cannot share your enthusiasm,' she said. 'I have the strongest possible objection to hunting. I have always set my face against it, as against all similar brutalizing blood-sports.'

This was a nasty jar for poor old Freddie, who had been relying on the topic to carry him nicely through at least a couple of courses. It silenced him for the nonce. And as he paused to collect his faculties, his host, who had now been glowering for six and a half minutes practically without cessation, put a hand in front of his mouth and addressed the girl Dahlia across the table. Freddie thinks he was under the impression that he was speaking in a guarded whisper, but, as a matter of fact, the words boomed through the air as if he had been a costermonger calling attention to his Brussels sprouts.

'Dahlia!'

'Yes, Father?'

'Who's that ugly feller?'

'Hush!'

'What do you mean, hush? Who is he?'

'Mr Widgeon.'

'Mr Who?'

'Widgeon.'

'I wish you would articulate clearly and not mumble,' said Sir Mortimer fretfully. 'It sound to me just like "Widgeon." Who asked him here?'

'I did.'

'Why?'

'He's a friend of mine.'

'Well, he looks a pretty frightful young slab of damnation to me. What I'd call a criminal face.'

'Hush!'

'Why do you keep saying "Hush"? Must be a lunatic, too. Throws cats at people.'

'Please, Father!'

'Don't say "Please, Father!" No sense in it. I tell you he does throw cats at people. He threw one at me. Half-witted, I'd call him – if that. Besides being the most offensive-looking young toad I've ever seen on the premises. How long's he staying?'

'Till Monday.'

'My God! And today's only Friday!' bellowed Sir Mortimer Prenderby.

It was an unpleasant situation for Freddie, of course, and I'm bound to admit he didn't carry it off particularly well. What he ought to have done, obviously, was to have plunged into an easy flow of small talk: but all he could think of was to ask Lady Prenderby if she was fond of shooting. Lady Prenderby having replied that, owing to being deficient in the savage instincts and wanton blood-lust that went to make up a callous and cold-hearted murderess, she was not, he relapsed into silence with his lower jaw hanging down.

All in all, he wasn't so dashed sorry when dinner came to an end.

As he and Sir Mortimer were the only men at the table, most of the seats having been filled by a covey of mildewed females whom he had classified under the general heading of Aunts, it seemed to Freddie that the moment had now arrived when they would be able to get together once more, under happier conditions than those of their last meeting, and start to learn to appreciate one another's true worth. He looked forward to a cosy *tête-à-tête* over the port, in the course of which he would smooth over that cat incident and generally do all that lay within his power to revise the unfavourable opinion of him which the other must have formed.

But apparently Sir Mortimer had his own idea of the duties and obligations of a host. Instead of clustering round Freddie with decanters, he simply gave him a long, lingering look of distaste and shot out of the french window into the garden. A moment later, his head reappeared and he uttered the words: 'You and your dam' cats!' Then the night swallowed him again.

Freddie was a good deal perplexed. All this was new stuff to him. He had been in and out of a number of country houses in his time, but this was the first occasion on which he had ever been left flat at the conclusion of the evening meal, and he wasn't quite sure how to handle the situation. He was still wondering, when Sir Mortimer's head came into view again and its owner, after giving him another of those long, lingering looks, said: 'Cats, forsooth!' and disappeared once more.

Freddie was now definitely piqued. It was all very well, he felt, Dahlia Prenderby telling him to make himself solid with her father, but how can you make yourself solid with a fellow who doesn't stay put for a couple of consecutive seconds? If it was Sir Mortimer's intention to spend the remainder of the night flashing past like a merry-go-round, there seemed little hope of anything amounting to a genuine *rapprochement*. It was a relief to his feelings when there suddenly appeared from nowhere his old acquaintance the tortoise-shell cat. It seemed to offer to him a means of working off his spleen.

Taking from Lady Prenderby's plate, accordingly, the remains of a banana, he plugged the animal neatly at a range of two yards. It yowled and withdrew. And a moment later, there was Sir Mortimer again.

'Did you kick that cat?' said Sir Mortimer.

Freddie had half a mind to ask this old disease if he thought he was a man or a jack-in-the-box, but the breeding of the Widgeons restrained him.

'No,' he said, 'I did not kick that cat.'

'You must have done something to it to make it come charging out at forty miles an hour.'

'I merely offered the animal a piece of fruit.'

'Do it again and see what happens to you.'

'Lovely evening,' said Freddie, changing the subject.

'No, it's not, you silly ass,' said Sir Mortimer. Freddie rose. His nerve, I fancy, was a little shaken.

'I shall join the ladies,' he said, with dignity.

'God help them!' replied Sir Mortimer Prenderby in a voice instinct with the deepest feeling, and vanished once more.

Freddie's mood, as he made for the drawing room, was thoughtful. I don't say he has much sense, but he's got enough to know when he is and when he isn't going with a bang. Tonight, he realized, he had been very far from going in such a manner. It was not, that is to say, as the Idol of Matcham Scratchings that he would enter the drawing room, but rather as a young fellow who had made an unfortunate first impression and would have to do a lot of heavy ingratiating before he could regard himself as really popular in the home.

He must bustle about, he felt, and make up leeway. And, knowing that what counts with these old-style females who have lived in the country all their lives is the exhibition of those little politenesses and attentions which were all the go in Queen Victoria's time, his first action, on entering, was to make a dive for one of the aunts who seemed to be trying to find a place to put her coffee cup.

'Permit me,' said Freddie, suave to the eyebrows.

And bounding forward with the feeling that this was the stuff to give them, he barged right into a cat.

'Oh, sorry,' he said, backing and bringing down his heel on another cat.

'I say, most frightfully sorry,' he said.

And, tottering to a chair, he sank heavily on to a third cat.

Well, he was up and about again in a jiffy, of course, but it was too late. There was the usual not-at-all-ing and don't-mention-it-ing, but he could read between the lines. Lady Prenderby's eyes had rested on his for only a brief instant, but it had been enough. His standing with her, he perceived, was now approximately what King Herod's would have been at an Israelite Mothers Social Saturday Afternoon.

The girl Dahlia during these exchanges had been sitting on a sofa at the end of the room, turning the pages of a weekly paper, and the sight of her drew Freddie like a magnet. Her womanly sympathy was just what he felt he could do with at this juncture. Treading with infinite caution, he crossed to where she sat: and, having scanned the terrain narrowly for cats, sank down on the sofa at her side. And conceive his agony of spirit when he discovered that womanly sympathy had been turned off at the main. The girl was like a chunk of ice cream with spikes all over it.

'Please do not trouble to explain,' she said coldly, in answer to his opening words. 'I quite understand that there are people who have this odd dislike of animals.'

'But, dash it . . .' cried Freddie, waving his arm in a frenzied sort of way. 'Oh, I say, sorry,' he added, as his fist sloshed another of the menagerie in the short ribs.

Dahlia caught the animal as it flew through the air.

'I think perhaps you had better take Augustus, Mother,' she said. 'He seems to be annoying Mr Widgeon.'

'Quite,' said Lady Prenderby. 'He will be safer with me.'

'But, dash it . . .' bleated Freddie.

Dahlia Prenderby drew in her breath sharply.

'How true it is,' she said, 'that one never really knows a man till after one has seen him in one's own home.'

'What do you mean by that?'

'Oh, nothing,' said Dahlia Prenderby.

She rose and moved to the piano, where she proceeded to sing old Breton folksongs in a distant manner, leaving Freddie to make out as best he could with a family album containing faded photographs with 'Aunt Emmy bathing at Llandudno, 1893', and 'This is Cousin George at the fancy-dress ball' written under them.

And so the long, quiet, peaceful home evening wore on, till eventually Lady Prenderby mercifully blew the whistle and he was at liberty to sneak off to his bedroom.

You might have supposed that Freddie's thoughts, as he toddled upstairs with his candle, would have dwelt exclusively on the girl Dahlia. This, however, was not so. He did give her obvious shirtiness a certain measure of attention, of course, but what really filled his mind was the soothing reflection that at long last his path and that of the animal kingdom of Matcham Scratchings had now divided. He, so to speak, was taking the high road while they, as it were, would take the low road. For whatever might be the conditions prevailing in the dining room, the drawing room, and the rest of the house, his bedroom, he felt, must surely be a haven totally free from cats of all descriptions.

Remembering, however, that unfortunate episode before dinner, he went down on all fours and subjected the various nooks and crannies to a close examination. His eye could detect no cats. Relieved, he rose to his feet with a gay song on his lips: and he hadn't got much beyond the first couple of bars when a voice behind him suddenly started taking the bass: and, turning, he perceived on the bed a fine Alsatian dog.

Freddie looked at the dog. The dog looked at Freddie. The situation was one fraught with embarrassment. A glance at the animal was enough to convince him that it had got an entirely wrong angle on the position of affairs and was regarding him purely in the light of an intrusive stranger who had muscled in on its private sleeping quarters. Its manner was plainly resentful. It fixed Freddie with a cold, yellow eye and curled its upper lip slightly, the better to display a long, white tooth. It also twitched its nose and gave a *sotto-voce* imitation of distant thunder.

Freddie did not know quite what avenue to explore. It was impossible to climb between the sheets with a thing like that on the counterpane. To spend the night in a chair, on the other hand, would have been foreign to his policy. He did what I consider the most statesmanlike thing by sidling out on to the balcony and squinting along the wall of the house to see if there wasn't a lighted window hard by, behind which might lurk somebody who would rally round with aid and comfort.

There was a lighted window only a short distance away, so he shoved his head out as far as it would stretch, and said: 'I say!' There being no response, he repeated: 'I say!'

And, finally, to drive his point home, he added: 'I say! I say! I say!'

This time he got results. The head of Lady Prenderby suddenly protruded from the window.

'Who,' she inquired, 'is making that abominable noise?'

It was not precisely the attitude Freddie had hoped for, but he could take the rough with the smooth.

'It's me. Widgeon, Frederick.'

'Must you sing on your balcony, Mr Widgeon?'

'I wasn't singing. I was saying "I say".'

'What were you saying?'

'"I say".'

'You say what?'

'I say I was saying "I say." Kind of a heart-cry, if you know what I mean. The fact is, there's a dog in my room.'

'What sort of dog?'

'A whacking great Alsatian.'

'Ah, that would be Wilhelm. Good night, Mr Widgeon.'

The window closed. Freddie let out a heart-stricken yip.

'But I say!'

The window reopened.

'Really, Mr Widgeon!'

'But what am I to do?'

'Do?'

'About this whacking great Alsatian!'

Lady Prenderby seemed to consider.

'No sweet biscuits,' she said. 'And when the maid brings you your tea in the morning please do not give him sugar. Simply a little milk in the saucer. He is on a diet. Good night, Mr Widgeon.'

Freddie was now pretty well nonplussed. No matter what his hostess might say about this beastly dog being on a diet, he was convinced from its manner that its medical adviser had not forbidden it Widgeons, and once more he bent his brain to the task of ascertaining what to do next.

There were several possible methods of procedure. His balcony being not so very far from the ground, he could, if he pleased, jump down and pass a health-giving night in the nasturtium bed. Or he might curl up on the floor. Or he might get out of the room and doss downstairs somewhere.

This last scheme seemed about the best. The only obstacle in the way of its fulfilment was the fact that, when he started for the door, his room-mate would probably think he was a burglar about to loot silver from a lonely country house and pin him. Still, it had to be risked, and a moment later he might have been observed tiptoeing across the carpet with all the caution of a slack-wire artist who isn't any too sure he remembers the correct steps.

Well, it was a near thing. At the instant when he started, the dog seemed occupied with something that looked like a cushion on the bed. It was licking this object in a thoughtful way, and paid no attention to Freddie till he was half-way across No Man's Land. Then it suddenly did a sort of sitting high-jump in his direction, and two seconds later Freddie, with a draughty feeling about the seat of his trouserings, was on top of a wardrobe, with the dog underneath looking up. He tells me that if he ever moved quicker in his life it was only on the occasion when, a lad of fourteen, he was discovered by his uncle, Lord Blicester, smoking one of the latter's cigars in the library: and he rather thinks he must have clipped at least a fifth of a second off the record then set up.

It looked to him now as if his sleeping arrangements for the night had been settled for him. And the thought of having to roost on top of a wardrobe at the whim of a dog was pretty dashed offensive to his proud spirit, as you may well imagine. However, as you cannot reason with Alsatians, it seemed the only thing to be done: and he was trying to make himself as comfortable as a sharp piece of wood sticking into the fleshy part of his leg would permit, when there was a snuffling noise in the passage and through the door came an object which in the dim light he was at first not able to identify. It looked something like a pen-wiper and something like a piece of a hearthrug. A second and keener inspection revealed it as a Pekingese puppy.

The uncertainty which Freddie had felt as to the newcomer's status was shared, it appeared, by the Alsatian: for after raising its eyebrows in a puzzled manner it rose and advanced inquiringly. In a tentative way it put out a paw and rolled the intruder over. Then, advancing again, it lowered its nose and sniffed.

It was a course of action against which its best friends would have advised it. These Pekes are tough eggs, especially when, as in this case, female. They look the world in the eye, and are swift to resent familiarity. There was a sort of explosion, and the next moment the Alsatian was shooting out of the room with its tail between its legs, hotly pursued. Freddie could hear the noise of battle rolling away along the passage, and it was music to his ears. Something on these lines was precisely what that Alsatian had been asking for, and now it had got it.

Presently, the Peke returned, dashing the beads of perspiration from its forehead, and came and sat down under the wardrobe, wagging a stumpy tail. And Freddie, feeling that the All Clear had been blown and that he was now at liberty to descend, did so.

His first move was to shut the door, his second to fraternize with his preserver. Freddie is a chap who believes in giving credit where credit is due, and it seemed to him that this Peke had shown itself an ornament of its species. He spared no effort, accordingly, to entertain it. He lay down on the floor and let it lick his face two hundred and thirty-three times. He tickled it under the left ear, the right ear, and at the base of the tail, in the order named. He also scratched its stomach.

All these attentions the animal received with cordiality and marked gratification: and as it seemed still in pleasure-seeking mood and had plainly come to look upon him as the official Master of the Revels, Freddie, feeling that he could not disappoint it but must play the host no matter what the cost to himself, took off his tie and handed it over. He would not have done it for everybody, he says, but where this life-saving Peke was concerned the sky was the limit.

Well, the tie went like a breeze. It was a success from the start. The Peke chewed it and chased it and got entangled in it and dragged it about the room, and was just starting to shake it from side to side when an unfortunate thing happened. Misjudging its distance, it banged its head a nasty wallop against the leg of the bed.

There is nothing of the Red Indian at the stake about a puppy in circumstances like this. A moment later, Freddie's blood was chilled by a series of fearful shrieks that seemed to ring through the night like the dying cries of the party of the second part to a first-class murder. It amazed him that a mere Peke, and a juvenile Peke at that, should

have been capable of producing such an uproar. He says that a
baronet, stabbed in the back with a paper-knife in his library, could
not have made half such a row.

Eventually, the agony seemed to abate. Quite suddenly, as if
nothing had happened, the Peke stopped yelling and with an amused
smile started to play with the tie again. And at the same moment there
was a sound of whispering outside, and then a knock at the door.

'Hullo?' said Freddie.

'It is I, sir. Biggleswade.'

'Who's Biggleswade?'

'The butler, sir.'

'What do you want?'

'Her ladyship wishes me to remove the dog which you are tortur-
ing.'

There was more whispering.

'Her ladyship also desires me to say that she will be reporting the
affair in the morning to the Society for the Prevention of Cruelty to
Animals.'

There was another spot of whispering.

'Her ladyship further instructs me to add that, should you prove
recalcitrant, I am to strike you over the head with the poker.'

Well, you can't say this was pleasant for poor old Freddie, and he
didn't think so himself. He opened the door, to perceive without, a
group consisting of Lady Prenderby, her daughter Dahlia, a few
assorted aunts, and the butler, with poker. And he says he met
Dahlia's eyes and they went through him like a knife.

'Let me explain...' he began.

'Spare us the details,' said Lady Prenderby with a shiver. She
scooped up the Peke and felt it for broken bones.

'But listen...'

'Good night, Mr Widgeon.'

The aunts said good night, too, and so did the butler. The girl
Dahlia preserved a revolted silence.

'But, honestly, it was nothing, really. It banged its head against the
bed...'

'What did he say?' asked one of the aunts, who was a little hard of
hearing.

'He says he banged the poor creature's head against the bed,' said
Lady Prenderby.

'Dreadful!' said the aunt.

'Hideous!' said a second aunt.

A third aunt opened up another line of thought. She said that with
men like Freddie in the house, was anyone safe? She mooted the

possibility of them all being murdered in their beds. And though Freddie offered to give her a written guarantee that he hadn't the slightest intention of going anywhere near her bed, the idea seemed to make a deep impression.

'Biggleswade,' said Lady Prenderby.

'M'lady?'

'You will remain in this passage for the remainder of the night with your poker.'

'Very good, m'lady.'

'Should this man attempt to leave his room, you will strike him smartly over the head.'

'Just so, m'lady.'

'But, listen . . .' said Freddie.

'Good night, Mr Widgeon.'

The mob scene broke up. Soon the passage was empty save for Biggleswade the butler, who had begun to pace up and down, halting every now and then to flick the air with his poker as if testing the lissomness of his wrist muscles and satisfying himself that they were in a condition to ensure the right amount of follow-through.

The spectacle he presented was so unpleasant that Freddie withdrew into his room and shut the door. His bosom, as you may imagine, was surging with distressing emotions. That look which Dahlia Prenderby had given him had churned him up to no little extent. He realized that he had a lot of tense thinking to do, and to assist thought he sat down on the bed.

Or rather, to be accurate, on the dead cat which was lying on the bed. It was this cat which the Alsatian had been licking just before the final breach in his relations with Freddie – the object, if you remember, which the latter had supposed to be a cushion.

He leaped up as if the corpse, instead of being cold, had been piping hot. He stared down, hoping against hope that the animal was merely in some sort of coma. But a glance told him that it had made the great change. He had never seen a deader cat. After life's fitful fever it slept well.

You wouldn't be far out in saying that poor old Freddie was now appalled. Already his reputation in this house was at zero, his name mud. On all sides he was looked upon as Widgeon the Amateur Vivisectionist. This final disaster could not but put the tin hat on it. Before, he had had a faint hope that in the morning, when calmer moods would prevail, he might be able to explain that matter of the Peke. But who was going to listen to him if he were discovered with a dead cat on his person?

And then the thought came to him that it might be possible not to

be discovered with it on his person. He had only to nip downstairs
and deposit the remains in the drawing room or somewhere and suspicion might not fall upon him. After all, in a super-catted house like
this, cats must always be dying like flies all over the place. A housemaid would find the animal in the morning and report to GHQ that
the cat strength of the establishment had been reduced by one, and
there would be a bit of tut-tutting and perhaps a silent tear or two,
and then the thing would be forgotten.

The thought gave him new life. All briskness and efficiency, he
picked up the body by the tail and was just about to dash out of the
room when, with a silent groan, he remembered Biggleswade.

He peeped out. It might be that the butler, once the eye of auth-
ority had been removed, had departed to get the remainder of his
beauty-sleep. But no. Service and Fidelity were evidently the watch-
words at Matcham Scratchings. There the fellow was, still practising
half-arm shots with the poker. Freddie closed the door.

And, as he did so, he suddenly thought of the window. There lay
the solution. Here he had been, fooling about with doors and
thinking in terms of drawing rooms, and all the while there was the
balcony staring him in the face. All he had to do was to shoot the body
out into the silent night, and let gardeners, not housemaids, discover
it.

He hurried out. It was a moment for swift action. He raised his
burden. He swung it to and fro, working up steam. Then he let it go,
and from the dark garden there came suddenly the cry of a strong
man in his anger.

'Who threw that cat?'

It was the voice of his host, Sir Mortimer Prenderby.

'Show me the man who threw that cat!' he thundered.

Windows flew up. Heads came out. Freddie sank to the floor of the
balcony and rolled against the wall.

'Whatever is the matter, Mortimer?'

'Let me get at the man who hit me in the eye with a cat.'

'A cat?' Lady Prenderby's voice sounded perplexed. 'Are you
sure?'

'Sure? What do you mean sure? Of course I'm sure. I was just
dropping off to sleep in my hammock, when suddenly a great beastly
cat came whizzing through the air and caught me properly in the
eyeball. It's a nice thing. A man can't sleep in hammocks in his own
garden without people pelting him with cats. I insist on the blood of
the man who threw that cat.'

'Where did it come from?'

'Must have come from that balcony there.'

'Mr Widgeon's balcony,' said Lady Prenderby in an acid voice. 'As I might have guessed.'

Sir Mortimer uttered a cry.

'So might I have guessed! Widgeon, of course! That ugly feller. He's been throwing cats all the evening. I've got a nasty sore place on the back of my neck where he hit me with one before dinner. Somebody come and open the front door. I want my heavy cane, the one with the carved ivory handle. Or a horsewhip will do.'

'Wait, Mortimer,' said Lady Prenderby. 'Do nothing rash. The man is evidently a very dangerous lunatic. I will send Biggleswade to overpower him. He has the kitchen poker.'

Little (said the Crumpet) remains to be told. At 2.15 that morning a sombre figure in dress clothes without a tie limped into the little railway station of Lower Smattering on the Wissel, some six miles from Matcham Scratchings. At 3.47 it departed Londonwards on the up milk-train. It was Frederick Widgeon. He had a broken heart and blisters on both heels. And in that broken heart was that loathing for all cats of which you recently saw so signal a manifestation. I am revealing no secrets when I tell you that Freddie Widgeon is permanently through with cats. From now on, they cross his path at their peril.

6
THE LUCK OF THE STIFFHAMS

The bar of the Drones Club was packed to bursting point. The word had gone round that Pongo Twistleton was standing free drinks, and a man who does that at the Drones can always rely on a full house and the sympathy of the audience. Eggs jostled Crumpets, Crumpets elbowed Beans, and the air was vibrant with the agonized cries of strong men who see their cocktails in danger of being upset.

A couple of Eggs, their thirst slaked, detached themselves from the crowd and made for the deserted smoking room. They were both morning-coated, spatted and gardeniaed, for like most of those present they had just come from the Stiffham-Spettisbury wedding reception.

For a while they sat in thoughtful silence. In addition to their more recent potations, they had tucked fairly freely into the nuptial champagne provided by the bride's father, the Earl of Wivelscombe. At length the first Egg spoke.

'Oofy Prosser's as sore as a gumboil,' he said.

'Who is?' asked the second Egg, opening his eyes.

'Oofy Prosser.'

'As sore as a what?'

'A gumboil. It's his money that young Pongo is spending out there. Oofy gave him a hundred to eight that Adolphus Stiffham would never marry Geraldine Spettisbury and Pongo collected the cash the moment the parson had said "Wilt though, Adolphus?" and the All Right flag had gone up.'

'And Oofy's sore about losing?'

'Naturally. He thought he had the event sewn up. At the time when he made the bet, it looked as if Stiffy hadn't an earthly. Consider the facts. Except for about a couple of hundred a year, the only money Stiffy had in the world was his salary as secretary to old Wivelscombe. And then he lost even that meagre pittance. One morning, happening to stroll into the yew alley at the ancestral seat and finding the young couple locked in a close embrace, the aged parent unlimbered his right leg and kicked Stiffy eleven feet, two inches – a record for the midland counties. He then lugged Geraldine back to the house, shut her up in her room, handing Stiffy a cheque in lieu of a month's notice, and told him that if he was within a mile of the premises at the expiration of ten minutes dogs would be set upon him. You can't say the outlook was promising for Stiffy, and I am not surprised that Oofy regarded the bet as money for jam.'

'How did it come unstuck?'

'Nobody knows.'

'Yes, they do,' said a fresh young voice. It was a Crumpet who, unperceived, had left the throng about the human drinking-fountain and joined them in their solitude. 'I do, for one. I had it straight from Stiffy's own lips, and it has proved to me that what a fellow needs in this world is luck. Without luck, Stiffy would never have made a large fortune in New York.'

'He didn't,' said the first Egg.

'He did.'

'He couldn't have. How could Stiffy have been in New York? He once went to Le Touquet for Whitsun and was so seasick that he swore he would never set foot on a boat again. And you can't get to New York, I happen to know, without taking a boat. So your story breaks down.'

'My story jolly well does not break down,' said the Crumpet warmly, 'because Stiffy beyond question did go to New York not a week after the painful episode in the yew alley.

'It was love that nerved him to the ordeal. Geraldine got him on the phone at the club and told him that the only thing for him to do was to go to America and make his fortune, and Stiffy went. And after he had been there about a fortnight he made the acquaintance of a very decent sort of chap with eyes a bit close together and a rather rummy way of talking out of the southwest corner of his mouth, and this bird took him off to a place where a lot of similar blokes were playing a local game they have over there called craps.'

You conduct this pastime, apparently, with dice, though what you aim to do with them remained a mystery to Stiffy from start to finish. However, when one of the blokes was preparing to heave the dice and another bloke offered to bet anybody ten that he wouldn't make it, he felt the old Stiffham sporting blood stir in his veins. After all, he reasoned, ten dollars wasn't so much to lose, and a little flutter helped to pass the time and make the evening interesting. So he booked the bet – to discover a moment later that what the chap had really meant was ten thousand.

Stiffy freely confesses that this was a nasty moment. It was too late to back out now, and he watched the proceedings with a bulging eye,

fully cognizant of the fact that all that stood between him and a very
sticky finish was the luck of the Stiffhams.

It held, of course. Half a minute later, the chap was paying up like
a gentleman, and with ten thousand dollars in his pocket Stiffy
decided that this was a good thing and should be pushed along. And
the upshot of the whole affair was that about an hour afterwards he
found himself in the open spaces in possession of a sum amounting to
around thirty thousand quid.

He was a good beal bucked, of course, and I don't blame him.
There he was, you see, set up for life and in a position to return to old
Wivelscombe riding on a camel laden with gold and precious stones
and demand the hand of his daughter. Pretty soft it all looked to old
Stiffy at this juncture.

Next day, he bunged the stuff into a bank, and at nightfall left his
hotel and started out to celebrate.

Now, as I have no doubt you know, when Stiffy celebrates, he celebrates. Exactly how and where he did it on this occasion, I couldn't
tell you. He is a bit vague about it himself. He seems to have collected
a gang of sorts, for he can distinctly recall, he tells me, that from the
very inception of the affair he did not lack for friends: and they
apparently roamed hither and thither, getting matier all the time, and
the next thing he remembers is waking up in the back premises of
some sort of pub or hostelry with nothing on his person except a five-
cent stamp, two balloons, three champagne corks, and a rattle.

This evidence of a well-spent evening pleased him a good deal. He
popped the balloons, rattled the rattle for a while, and then, feeling
that he had better collect a little loose cash for the day's expenses,
toddled off to his bank to draw a cheque.

And conceive his emotion when, arriving there, he found that the
bank had closed its doors. There they were, both of them, shut as
tight as oysters. Too late, he remembered now having read in the
papers that this sort of thing was happening all the time in New York.

For some minutes he stood staring, while everything seemed to go
black. Then he tottered back to his hotel and sank into a chair in the
lobby, to think things over.

Bim, obviously, had gone his chance of ever marrying the daughter
of the haughty Earl of Wivelscombe. That project could be washed
right out. And for some time he remained mourning over this fact.

It was only quite a while later that there came into his mind a
sudden thought, and for the first time since this hideous disaster had
occurred he felt a little better.

With his last hope of wedding Geraldine gone, he told himself, there was nothing now to prevent him writing that strong letter to her father.

For weeks and weeks, you see, Stiffy had been yearning to write an absolute stinker to old Wivelscombe, telling him exactly what he thought of him. And naturally as long as there had been any chance of the other relenting and allowing the marriage to come off such a stinker did not fall within the sphere of practical politics. But now that he had nothing to lose he could go ahead and give of his best. He felt in his pocket to see if the five-cent stamp was still there. Then he raced to the writing-table and seized pen and paper.

I don't know if you have ever had dealings with Stiffy in his capacity of a writer of stinkers. I have. I was with him once when he composed a four-page effort to Oofy Prosser in reply to Oofy's communication declining to lend him a tenner. It was real, ripe stuff, without a dull line, and I was proud to call the author my friend.

Well, on this occasion, he tells me, he absolutely surpassed himself. It was as if he was inspired. Sheet after sheet he covered, each sheet filled with burning thoughts. He left no aspect of Lord Wivelscombe untouched. He stated in the most precise detail exactly what he felt about the old blighter's habits, manners, face, ties, trousers, morals, method of drinking soup, ditto of chewing moustache, and a hundred more such matters. To a single pimple on the other's nose, he tells me he devoted as much as six lines. Then, addressing the envelope, he attached the five-cent stamp and posted the letter personally in the box by the reception desk.

And, being by the reception desk and happening to note standing behind it the manager of the hotel, he thought that this was a good opportunity of putting him abreast of the position of affairs.

'I say,' said Stiffy.

'Sir?' said the manager.

'Tell me, my dear old hotel manager,' said Stiffy, 'you know that room of mine with bath?'

'I know it well,' said the manager.

'What do you get paid for it?'

'Six dollars a day.'

Stiffy broke the bad news gently.

'Not by me you don't,' he said. 'Because I haven't a penny in the world.'

'Eh?' said the manager, not looking any too chirpy.

'No,' said Stiffy. 'Not a penny. My bank's gone bust.'

'Which bank is that?'

'The Inter-State Superlative.'

The manager seemed surprised.

'It's the first I've heard of it. We bank there ourselves.'

'Meaning by "we" you and the wife and the tots?'

'Meaning this hotel.'

'I'm sorry,' said Stiffy, genuinely moved, for they had treated him with marked civility. 'But there it is. I was down there just now and the institution had closed its doors.'

'Didn't you expect it to on a Sunday?' asked the manager.

Stiffy gaped. 'On a what?'

'On a Sunday.'

'Is today Sunday?'

'It is.'

'Then what became of Saturday?' asked Stiffy, amazed.

'We had it all right,' said the manager. 'Quite a nice Saturday.'

And Stiffy realized that, what with this and what with that, he must have slept right through Saturday. And he also realized – and, as he did so, he paled visibly – that he had just written the supreme stinker of all time to old Wivelscombe and that it had been posted beyond recall.

Yes, that was the position. He, Stiffy, had written him, Wivelscombe, a letter which would make him, Wivelscombe, reject him, Stiffy, as a suitor for his daughter's hand even if he, Stiffy, had all the money in the world and proposed to hand it over to him, Wivelscombe, as a personal present. Pretty rotten for him, Stiffy, you will admit.

It was a crisis that called for rapid thinking, and that was just what he gave it. For some little time he obtained no results. Then something clicked in his brain.

'Hotel manager,' he said.

'Sir?' said the manager.

'If you posted a letter to England, when would it get there?'

'Much,' said the manager, 'would depend on when you posted it.'

'I dropped it in the box just now.'

The manager consulted a list of sailings.

'It will go by the *Senator J. Freylinghusen Botts* on Tuesday.'

'So shall I,' said Stiffy.

He had seen the way out. He had been secretary to old Wivelscombe long enough to know the procedure as regarded the arrival of letters at the family seat. The postman shot them into the box at the front door, and Gascoigne, the butler, hoiked them out and placed them on the breakfast table in the morning room, to be opened by the addressee when he or she came down to shove his or her nose in the trough.

It would be a simple task to get to the house, lurk in the shrubbery

outside the morning room and, when Gascoigne had completed his
duties, to nip in through the french windows and snitch the fatal
papers. It was simply a matter of buzzing over to England by the
same boat on which the letter travelled.

On the Tuesday, accordingly, those assembled to give the *Senator
J. Freylinghusen Botts* a send-off might have observed a young man
with a set, resolute face striding up the gang-plank, and I daresay
some of them did.

I don't suppose you want to hear all about Stiffy's trip across. The
salient point is that he did get across. He landed at Liverpool in due
season and hit London towards the evenfall, at an hour when the last
train for Upton Snodsbury, which is the station for Wivelscombe
Court, had left. It seemed to him that his best plan was to hire a car
and put up at Worcester for the night. This he did, leaving orders
that he was to be called at six sharp in the morning.

Well, you know what it's like when you've got anything on your mind
similar to what Stiffy had on his. You sleep fitfully. You rise with
dawn. It wasn't six-thirty when he started out for the Court, and it
couldn't have been much more than seven when he found himself
standing on the old familiar lawn. And, as there wasn't a chance of
the postman blowing in before eight-fifteen at the earliest, he thought
he might as well take a stroll to keep the circulation brisk.

I have never been up as early as seven myself, but Stiffy tells me
that it is quite a pleasant hour to be abroad. You get Nature in its
pristine freshness and all that sort of thing. The dew was still on the
grass, the sun was shining nicely, and there were a goodish few birds
tootling away in the shrubberies. All dashed pleasant, no doubt, for
those who like these things. Stiffy did. The general effect of it all, he
says, was to make him feel not a little romantic. I mean to say, the old
spot, the scene of his great love, and so on and so forth. At any rate,
he tells me that his bosom swelled, and I see no reason to disbelieve
him.

And little by little, as the dew glistened and the sun shone and the
birds tootled, there crept over him a feeling that in the existing circs.
there was only one thing for a red-blooded young lover to do, viz.
trickle round underneath Geraldine's window and bung gravel at it.
This would result in her popping her head out, and then he would
blow a silent kiss and she would blow a silent kiss and he would tell
her in the language of the eyes that his heart was still hers and what
not. A very jolly method of passing the time of waiting, felt Stiffy,
and he collected a fistful of mud and pebbles and let it go with a will.

Now, slinging gravel at windows is a tricky business. If you're in form, fine. But if you haven't done it for a goodish time your aim is likely to suffer. This is what happened to Stiffy.

He had drawn a bead on his loved one's window, but instead of landing there the entire consignment went several feet to the left and sloshed up against the next one – that of the room in which Ferdinand James Delamere, sixth Earl of Wivelscombe, was sleeping.

At least, he wasn't sleeping, because it so happened that on the previous night he had taken the chair at the annual dinner of the Loyal Sons of Worcestershire and, despite doctor's orders, had done himself so well that he had woken early with that strange, jumpy feeling which always came to him the morning after this particular banquet. He was in the sort of overwrought state when a fly treading a little too heavily on the carpet is enough to make a man think he's one of the extras in *All Quiet On The Western Front.*

The effect, therefore, of about a quarter of a pound of mixed solids on the window-pane was to bring him leaping out of bed as if a skewer had suddenly come through the mattress. He reached the window in two jumps, and was just in time to see his late employee, Adolphus Stiffham, disappearing into the bushes. For Stiffy, observing that he had nearly cracked the wrong window, and remembering whose that window was, had not loitered.

Now, I want you to follow me very closely here, while I explain why old Wivelscombe took the view of the matter which he did. You see, the way he looked at it, his visitor could not possibly be Adolphus Stiffham in the flesh. He had studied human nature pretty closely and he knew that a man who has been kicked eleven feet, two inches does not willingly return to the spot where the incident occurred. He was aware, moreover, that Stiffy had gone to America. Furthermore, he was, as I say, in a highly nervous condition as the upshot or aftermath of the banquet of the Society of the Loyal Sons of Worcestershire. The result was that a moment later he was charging into Geraldine's room with consternation and concern written on every feature.

'Why, Father,' said Geraldine, sitting up in bed, 'what's the matter? You look as if you had seen a ghost.'

'I have seen a ghost.'

'The White Lady of Wivelscombe?'

'No, the Pink Secretary of Wivelscombe. I give you my word, Geraldine, that not two minutes ago I heard a sort of uncanny tapping on my window and I looked out and there was the wraith of that young fathead, Adolphus Stiffham.'

'What do you mean, that young fathead, Adolphus Stiffham?'

demanded Geraldine with a womanly warmth which became her
well. 'Where do you get that young fathead stuff? You are speaking
of the man I love.'

'Well, you had better dashed well stop loving him,' rejoined her
father with equal heat, 'because he has passed beyond the veil.'

'Are you sure it was his ghost?'

'Of course it was his ghost. Do you think I don't know a ghost
when I see one? I've been psychic all my life. All my family have been
psychic. My mother was a Ballindalloch of Portknockie and used to
see her friends in winding-sheets. It got her disliked in the county.
Besides, you told me Stiffham was in America. Obviously what has
happened is that somewhere out in those great open spaces the
unhappy half-wit has handed in his dinner pail.'

Geraldine faced him with burning eyes.

'And whose fault was it that he went to America? Yours.'

'Eh? What do you mean, dash it? I never asked him to go to
America.'

'He went there as the direct result of your hard-heartedness and
inhumanity. And now, I suppose, he has been shot by gangsters, like
everybody else in America. Was there a bullet wound in his
forehead?'

'I couldn't tell you. He got away too quick. Just smiled a hideous
sort of smile and seemed to melt into the bushes. Phew!' said Lord
Wivelscombe. 'I'm going down to get a bite of breakfast. I need
coffee. Strong, hot coffee with a kick in it. Put on a dressing-gown
and come along.'

'I shall do nothing of the kind,' said Geraldine coldly. 'Breakfast,
forsooth! It would choke me. I shall remain up here and try to get
Adolphus on the ouija board.'

Stiffy, meanwhile, after removing some twigs from his hair and
brushing a few of the local beetles off his face, had come cautiously
out of the bushes and made his way snakily to the french windows of
the morning room. A glance at his watch had told him that at any
moment now the postman would be arriving. And, sure enough, he
had not been there more than about two minutes when the door of the
morning room opened and the butler came in and placed a bundle of
correspondence beside Lord Wivelscombe's plate. He then
withdrew, and Stiffy, abandoning the role of snake, gave a spirited
impersonation of a pouncing leopard. He was in through the
windows in a matter of one and three-fifth seconds. It took him
perhaps another second to locate and pouch the letter. And he was
just about to buzz off, which would have taken him possibly another

second and a quarter, when he heard a footstep outside.

There was no time for the smooth getaway. Already the door was beginning to open. With considerable presence of mind Stiffy revised his whole plan of campaign at a moment's notice and shot silently under the table.

And there for a while the matter rested.

As far as Stiffy could gather from the look of the legs moving about in his vicinity, it was the butler who had returned, presumably with coffee and foodstuffs. He could just see the lower section of a pair of striped trousers, as worn by butlers.

Then the door opened once more, this time to admit a.pair of pyjamaed legs terminating in bedroom slippers, and reason told him that this must be old Wivelscombe. When the pyjamas passed from his view to appear again under the table within a couple of inches of his nose, their owner having sunk heavily into a chair, he knew that he had been right, and he is not ashamed to confess that he was conscious of a certain qualm. Seeing at such close range the foot which had once landed so forcefully on his trouser seat was, he tells me, an unnerving experience.

A bit of dialogue now unshipped itself in the upper regions. The butler started it.

'Good morning, m'lord. Shall I assist your lordship to a little eggs and bacon?'

The table shook as the aged peer shuddered strongly.

'Don't try to be funny, Gascoigne. There is a time to speak of eggs and a time not to speak of eggs. At the moment, I would prefer to try to forget that there are such things in the world. What you can bring me – and dashed quick, too – is a very hot, very strong cup of coffee, liberally laced with old brandy, and a very dry slice of toast.'

The butler coughed in rather an unpleasant and censorious manner.

'Did your lordship exceed last night?'

'Certainly not.'

'Did your lordship imbibe champagne?'

'The merest spot.'

'A bottle?'

'It may have been a bottle.'

'Two bottles?'

'Yes. Possibly two bottles.'

The butler coughed again.

'I shall inform Doctor Spelvin.'

'Don't be a cad, Gascoigne.'

'He has expressly forbidden your lordship champagne.'

'Tchah!'

'I need scarcely remind your lordship that champagne brings your lordship out in spots.'

Old Wivelscombe barked querulously.

'I wish to goodness you wouldn't stand there babbling about champagne. It is a word that I do not wish to have mentioned in my presence.'

'Very good, m'lord,' said the butler stiffly. 'Your coffee, m'lord. The dry toast is at your lordship's elbow.'

There was a pause. From the sloshing sound which broke out above him at this point, Stiffy deduced that old Wivelscombe was drinking the coffee. The theory was borne out by the fact that when he spoke again it was in a stronger voice.

'It's no good your looking like that, Gascoigne. After all, what's an occasional binge? It's a poor heart that never rejoices.'

'At your lordship's age, all binges are highly injudicious.'

'What do you mean, my age? A man is as old as he feels.'

'Very good, m'lord.'

'Where you go wrong, Gascoigne – where you make your bloomer is in assuming that I have a hangover this morning. Nothing could be further from the truth. I feel like a two-year-old. Look at my hand. Steady as a rock.'

Apparently, at this point, old Wivelscombe ventured on a physical demonstration. A napkin came fluttering down on the floor.

'Very wobbly, m'lord.'

'Nothing of the kind,' said old Wivelscombe testily. 'I dropped that napkin on purpose, just to show you how easily I could pick it up. See, Gascoigne. I will now pick up the napkin.'

But he didn't. He stooped down and his fingers touched the thing, but as they did so he suddenly found himself looking into Stiffy's bulging eyes. There was an embarrassing pause for a moment: then his face shot up out of sight and Stiffy heard him gulp.

'Gascoigne!'

'M'lord?'

'Gascoigne, there's a ghost under the table.'

'Very good, m'lord.'

'What do you mean. "Very good, m'lord"? Don't stand there saying "Very good, m'lord." Do something about it, man, do something about it.'

'I beg your lordship's pardon, but I cannot comprehend just what it is that your lordship desires me to do.'

'Why, shoo it out.'

'Really, m'lord!'

THE LUCK OF THE STIFFHAMS

Old Wivelscombe's voice grew tense.

'Gascoigne, do you hear me telling you that the room is overrun with ghosts?'

'Yes, m'lord.'

'Don't you believe me?'

'No, m'lord.'

'Well, look for yourself. I tell you it's there. The dashed thing's been following me about all the morning. Lift the cloth, Gascoigne, and take a dekko.'

'Very good, m'lord, if your lordship insists. But I do not anticipate that I shall be able to observe the spectre to which your lordship alludes.'

He did, of course. The first thing that met his eyes was young Stiffy. But by this time Stiffy, who, chump though he is, can act on occasion with a good deal of rugged sense, was holding the forefinger of his left hand to his lips and stretching out the other hand with a fiver in it.

The butler scooped the fiver and straightened himself.

'Well, Gascoigne?'

'The light under the table is a little uncertain, m'lord. I will take another look.'

He bent down once more, and Stiffy repeated business with fiver.

'No, m'lord. There is nothing there.'

'No spectres, Gascoigne?'

'No spectres, m'lord.'

Old Wivelscombe groaned in a hollow sort of way, and there was the sound of a chair being pushed back.

'I shall go for a brisk walk, Gascoigne.'

'Very good, m'lord.'

'You're sure you saw nothing?'

'Quite sure, m'lord.'

'Not the late Adolphus Stiffham?'

'No, m'lord.'

The door closed behind old Wivelscombe, and Stiffy crawled out.

'Good morning, Gascoigne.'

'Good morning, sir.'

'I expect I gave you a start, Gascoigne?'

'I must confess to a momentary sensation of surprise, sir. I had supposed that you were in the United States of Northern America.'

'It's a long story,' said Stiffy, 'but the nub of it is that I must see Lady Geraldine immediately. Is she in her room?'

'I cannot speak from first-hand observation, sir, but I am inclined to fancy that her ladyship has not yet descended. Would you desire me to announce you, sir?'

'No, thanks. I'll find my way up.'

So up Stiffy buzzed, and presently he was sitting on Gerladine's bed, gazing into her eyes and holding her little hand in his. The exact words of their conversation Stiffy did not reveal to me, but no doubt he opened with a brief explanation of his presence and then they spoke of things which young lovers do speak about when they get together for a chat after long separation. At any rate, he tells me that they were more or less absorbed when the door handle rattled. He had just time to make a leap for a convenient cupboard as old Wivelscombe came in. There was a moment when the eyes of the two men met. And then Stiffy was in the cupboard among Geraldine's summer frocks.

Old Wivelscombe was gulping a bit.

'Geraldine,' he said, 'you see before you a haunted man.'

'Do I Father?'

'You certainly do. When I went down to breakfast, guess what? There beneath the table was the phantasm of that fat-... of that excellent young fellow, Adolphus Stiffham, whom I always liked though he may have drawn wrong conclusions from my surface manner,' said old Wivelscombe, raising his voice slightly. 'He was staring at me with just that same idiot-... with precisely that same frank, winning expression on his face that I remember so well.'

'What did you do?'

'I requested Gascoigne to check up my facts. So Gascoigne took a look. But the apparition was invisible to him.'

'Was it?'

'It was. I gather that it is also invisible to you. For I assure you, on the word of a Worcestershire Wivelscombe, that as I entered this room I distinctly observed the spectre nip into that cupboard over there.'

'Nonsense.'

'It isn't nonsense.'

'That cupboard there?'

'That very cupboard.'

'I'll go and look.'

'Take care it doesn't bite you,' said Lord Wivelscombe anxiously.

The cupboard door opened, and Geraldine peeped in.

'No,' she said. 'There's nothing there.'

Old Wivelscombe unleashed another of those hollow groans of his.

'Of course you wouldn't see it. It's meant for me. A nice thing this is going to be, trying to run an estate with a beastly great ghost popping in and out all the time. Concentration will become impossible.'

Geraldine laid a soothing hand on his quivering shoulder.

'I don't think it is going to be as bad as that, father. I think I see what has happened. In my opinion, this thing has been sent to you as a warning."'

'A warning?'

'Yes. I have read of such cases. It sometimes happens that the apparition of an entity . . . let us call him A or B . . .'

'Whichever you prefer.'

'The apparition of an entity, A or B, will occasionally appear not after but before the entity has crossed the great divide. The object of this is to impress on the mind of the individual observing the phenomenon . . . shall we call him C . . .?'

'By all means.'

'. . . to impress on the mind of the individual, C, that, unless steps are taken promptly through the proper channels, the entity will pass over. It is, as it were, a cautionary projection of a distant personality.'

Lord Wivelscombe raised his head from his hands.

'You mean, then, that you think that that blasted . . . that that delightful lad, Adolphus Stiffham, on whom I have always looked more as a son than anything, is still alive?'

'For the moment, yes.'

'Tell me,' said Lord Wivelscombe, 'how do we keep him that way?'

Geraldine reflected.

'I think the best plan is for me to cable him today to return at once as you are now prepared to give your full consent to our marriage.'

Lord Wivelscombe sat for a moment in thought.

'You consider that the best plan?'

'I do.'

'What's the next best?'

'There is no other.'

'You mean that, unless I want to be haunted for the rest of my life, I've got to have that – er – him for a son-in-law?'

'I do.'

Lord Wivelscombe looked once more at the cupboard. Then he spoke with what a close observer might have thought a slightly exaggerated heartiness.

'Charmed!' he said. 'Delighted. Capital. Splendid. Only too pleased.'

And that (concluded the Crumpet) is the inner history of the Stiffham-Spettisbury wedding which we have just seen solemnized at St George's, Hanover Square. And you can understand now what I meant when I said that what a man needs in this world is not virtue, character, steadiness, and nobility of mind – or I should have done better myself – but luck. It was his faith in the Luck of the Stiffhams that led young Pongo Twistleton-Twistleton to take the short end from Oofy Prosser against all the ruling of the form-book, and I honour him for it and am delighted that he has cleaned up.

7

NOBLESSE OBLIGE

On the usually unruffled brow of the Bean who had just entered the smoking room of the Drones Club there was a furrow of perplexity. He crossed pensively to the settee in the corner and addressed the group of Eggs and Crumpets assembled there.

'I say,' he said, 'in re Freddie Widgeon, do any of you chaps happen to know if he's gone off his rocker?'

An Egg asked what made him think so.

'Well, he's out in the bar, drinking Lizard's Breaths...'

'Nothing unbalanced about that.'

'No, but his manner is strange. It so happens that at the seminary where he and I were educated they are getting up a fund for some new racquets courts, and when I tackled Freddie just now and said that he ought to chip in and rally round the dear old school, he replied that he was fed to the tonsils with dear old schools and never wished to hear anyone talk about dear old schools again.'

'Rummy,' agreed the Egg.

'He then gave a hideous laugh and added that, if anybody was interested in his plans, he was going to join the Foreign Legion, that Cohort of the Damned in which broken men may toil and die and, dying, forget.'

'Beau Widgeon?' said the Egg, impressed. 'What ho!'

A Crumpet shook his head.

'You won't catch Freddie joining any Foreign Legion, once he gets on to the fact that it means missing his morning cup of tea. All the same, I can understand his feeling a bit upset at the moment, poor old blighter. Tragedy has come into his life. He's just lost the only girl in the world.'

'Well, he ought to be used to that by this time.'

'Yes. But he also got touched for his only tenner in the world, and on top of that his uncle, old Blicester, has cut his allowance in half.'

'Ah,' said the Egg understandingly.

'It was at Cannes that it all happened,' proceeded the Crumpet. 'Old Blicester had been ordered there by his doctor, and he offered to take Freddie along, paying all expenses. A glittering prospect, of course, for there are few juicier spots than the South of France during the summer season: nevertheless, I warned the poor fish not to go. I told him no good could come of it, pointing out the unexampled opportunities he would have of making some sort of a bloomer and alienating the old boy, if cooped up with him at a foreign resort for a matter of six weeks. But he merely blushed prettily and said that, while nobody was more alive to that possibility than himself, he was jolly well going to go, because this girl was at Cannes.'

'Who was this girl?'

'I forget her name. Drusilla something. Never met her myself. He described her to me, and I received the impression of a sort of blend of Tallulah Bankhead and a policewoman. Fascinating exterior, I mean to say, but full of ideas at variance with the spirit of modern progress. Apparently she sprang from a long line of Bishops and Archdeacons and what not, and was strongly opposed to all forms of gambling, smoking, and cocktail drinking. And Freddie had made an excellent first impression on her owing to the fact that he never gambled, never smoked, and looked on cocktails as the curse of the age.'

'Freddie?' said the Egg, startled.

'That was what he had told her, and I consider it a justifiable stratagem. I mean to say, if you don't kid the delicately nurtured along a bit in the initial stages, where are you?'

'True,' said the Egg.

Well, that is how matters stood when Freddie arrived at Cannes, and as he sauntered along the Croisette on the fourth or fifth day of his visit I don't suppose there was a happier bloke in all that gay throng. The sun was shining, the sea was blue, the girl had promised to have tea with him that afternoon at the Casino, and he knew he was looking absolutely his best. Always a natty dresser, today he had eclipsed himself. The glistening trousers, the spotless shirt, the form-fitting blue coat ... all these combined to present an intoxicating picture. And this picture he had topped off with a superb tie which he had contrived to pinch overnight from his uncle's effects. Gold and lavender in its general colour scheme, with a red stripe thrown in for good measure. Lots of fellows, he tells me, couldn't have carried it off, but it made him look positively godlike.

Well, when I tell you that he hadn't been out on the Croisette ten minutes before a French bloke came up and offered him five hundred francs to judge a Peasant Mothers Baby Competition down by the harbour, where they were having some sort of local fête or jamboree in honour of a saint whose name has escaped me, you will admit that he must have looked pretty impressive. These knowledgeable Gauls don't waste their money on tramps.

Now, you might have thought that as old Blicester, the world's greatest exponent of the one-way pocket, consistently refused to slip him so much as a franc for current expenses, Freddie would have jumped at this chance of making a bit. But it so happened that he had recently wired to a staunch pal in London for a tenner and had received intimation that the sum would be arriving by that afternoon's post. He had no need, accordingly, for the gold the chap was dangling before his eyes. However, he was pleased by the compliment, and said he would most certainly look in, if he could, and lend the binge the prestige of his presence, and they parted on cordial terms.

It was almost immediately after this that the bird in the shabby reach-me-downs accosted him.

His watch having told him that the afternoon post would be in any minute now, Freddie, in his perambulations, had not moved very far from the Carlton, which was the hotel where he and his uncle and also the girl were stopping, and he was manœuvring up and down about opposite it when a voice at his elbow, speaking in that sort of surprised and joyful manner in which one addresses an old friend encountered in a foreign spot, said: 'Why, hullo!'

And, turning, he perceived the above-mentioned bird in the reach-me-downs as described. A tallish, thinnish chap.

'Well, well, well!' said the bird.

Freddie goggled at him. As far as memory served, he didn't know the blighter from Adam.

'Hullo,' he said, playing for time.

'Fancy running into you,' said the chap.

'Ah,' said Freddie.

'It's a long time since we met.'

'Absolutely,' said Freddie, the persp. beginning to start out a bit on the brow. Because if there's one thing that makes a man feel a chump it is this business of meeting ancient cronies and not being able to put a name to them.

'I don't suppose you see any of the old crowd now?' said the chap.

'Not many,' said Freddie.

'They scatter.'

'They do scatter.'

'I came across Smith a few weeks ago.'

'Oh, yes?'

'T. T. Smith, I mean.'

'Oh, T. T. Smith?'

'Yes. Not J. B. I hear J. B.'s gone to the Malay States. T. T.'s in some sort of agency business. Rather prosperous.'

'That's good.'

'You seem to be doing pretty well, yourself.'

'Oh, fairly.'

'Well, I'm not surprised,' said the chap. 'One always knew you would, even at school.'

The word, Freddie tells me, was like a lifebelt. He grabbed at it. So this was a fellow he had known at school. That narrowed it down a lot. Surely now, he felt, the old brain would begin to function. Then he took another look at the chap, and the momentary exhilaration ebbed. He had not known him from Adam, and he still did not know him from Adam. The situation had thus become more awkward than ever, because the odds were that in the end this fellow was going to turn out to be someone he had shared a study with and ought to be falling on the neck of and swopping reminiscences of the time when old Boko Jervis brought the white rabbit into chapel and what not.

'Yes,' said the chap. 'Even then one could tell that you were bound to go up and up. Gosh, how I used to admire you at the dear old school. You were my hero.'

'What!' yipped Freddie. He hadn't the foggiest that he had been anyone's hero at school. His career there hadn't been so dashed distinguished as all that. He had scraped into the cricket team in his last year, true: but even so he couldn't imagine any of his contemporaries looking up to him much.

'You were,' said the chap. 'I thought you a marvel.'

'No, really?' said Freddie, suffused with coy blushes. 'Well, well, well, fancy that. Have a cigarette?'

'Thanks,' said the chap. 'But what I really want is a meal. I'm right on my uppers. We aren't all like you, you see. While you've been going up and up, some of us have been going down and down. If I don't get a meal today, I don't know what I shall do.'

Freddie tells me the thing came on him as a complete surprise. You might have supposed that a wary bird like him, who has been a member of this club since he came down from Oxford, would have known better, but he insists that he had absolutely no suspicion that a touch was in the air till it suddenly hit him like this. And his first impulse, he says, was to mumble something at the back of his throat and slide off.

And he was just going to when a sudden surge of generous emotion swept over him. Could he let a fellow down who had not only been at school with him but who, when at school, had looked upon him as a hero? Imposs., felt Freddie. There had been six hundred and forty-seven chaps at the old school. Was he to hand the callous mitten to the only one of those six hundred and forty-seven who had admired him? Absolutely out of the q., was Freddie's verdict. A *mille* was the dickens of a sum of money, of course – at the present rate of exhange a bit more than a tenner – but it would have to be found somehow. Noblesse oblige, he meant to say.

And just when the fervour was at its height he recollected this cheque which was arriving by the afternoon post. In the stress of emotion it had quite slipped his mind.

'By Jove!' he said. 'Yes, I can fix you up. Suppose we meet at the Casino a couple of hours from now.'

'God bless you,' said the chap.

'Not at all,' said Freddie.

It was with mixed feelings that he went into the hotel to see if the post had come. On the one hand, there was the solemn anguish of parting with a tenner which he had earmarked for quite a different end. On the other, there was the quiet chestiness induced by the realization that here he had been jogging along through the world, not thinking such a frightful lot of himself, and all the while in the background was this bloke treasuring his memory and saying to himself: 'Ah, if we could all be like Freddie Widgeon!' Cheap at a tenner, he told himself, the sensation of spiritual yeastiness which this reflection gave him.

All the same, he wished the chap could have done with five, because there was a bookie in London to whom he had owed a fiver for some months now and recent correspondence had shown that this hell-hound was on the verge of becoming a bit unpleasant. Until this episode had occurred, he had fully intended to send the man thirty bob or so, to sweeten him. Now, of course, this was out of the question. The entire sum must go unbroken to this old school-fellow whose name he wished he could remember.

Spivis? . . . Brent? . . . Jerningham? . . . Fosway? . . .

No.

Brewster? . . . Goggs? . . . Bootle? . . . Finsbury? . . .

No.

He gave it up and went to the desk. The letter was there, and in it the cheque. The very decent johnnie behind the counter cashed it for him without a murmur, and he was just gathering up the loot when somebody behind him said 'Ah!'

Now, in the word 'Ah!' you might say that there is nothing really to fill a fellow with a nameless dread. Nevertheless, that is what this 'Ah!' filled Freddie with. For he had recognized the voice. It was none other than that of the bookie to whom he owed the fiver. That is the trouble about Cannes in August – it becomes very mixed. You get your Freddie Widgeons there – splendid chaps who were worshipped by their schoolmates – and you also get men like this bookie. All sorts, if you follow me, from the highest to the lowest.

From the very moment when he turned and gazed into the fellow's steely eyes, Freddie tells me he hadn't a hope. But he did his best.

'Hullo, Mr McIntosh!' he said. 'You here? Well, well, well! Ha, ha!'

'Yes,' said the bookie.

'I never thought I should run into you in these parts.'

'You have,' the bookie assured him.

'Come down here for a nice holiday, what? Taking a perfect rest, eh? Going to bask in the lovely sunshine and put all thoughts of business completely out of your head, yes?'

'Well, not quite all,' said the bookie, producing the little black book. 'Now, let me see, Mr Widgeon... Ah, yes, five pounds on Marmalade to cop in the second at Ally Pally. Should have won by the form-book, but ran third. Well, that's Life, isn't it? I think it comes to a little more than four hundred and fifty francs, really, but we'll call it four-fifty. One doesn't want any haggling among friends.'

'I'm awfully sorry,' said Freddie. 'Some other time, what? I can't manage it just at the moment. I haven't any money.'

'No?'

'I mean to say, I want this for a poor man.'

'So do I,' said the bookie.

And the upshot and outcome, of course, was that poor old Freddie had to brass up. You can't appeal to a bookie's better feelings, because he hasn't any. He pushed over the four hundred and fifty.

'Oh, very well,' he said. 'Here you are. And let me tell you, Mr McIntosh, that the curse of the Widgeons goes with it.'

'Right,' said the bookie.

So there Freddie was with five hundred and fifty francs in his kick, and needing a thousand.

I must say I wouldn't have blamed him if, in these circs., he had decided to give a miss to the old schoolfriend. Allowing fifty francs for lushing up the girl Drusilla at the tea-table, he would in that case have had a cool five hundred with which to plunge into the variegated pleasures of Cannes in the summertime. A very nice sum, indeed.

But, though tempted, he was strong. This old admirer of his – Muttlebury?... Jukes?... Ferguson?... Braithwaite?... – had said that he needed a *mille*, and a *mille* he must have.

But how to raise the other five hundred? That was the prob.

For some moments he toyed with mad schemes like trying to borrow it from his uncle. Then it suddenly flashed upon him that the sum he required was the exact amount which the intelligent Gaul had offered him if he would come down to the jamboree by the harbour and judge the Peasant Mothers Baby Competition.

Now, Freddie's views on babies are well defined. He is prepared to cope with them singly, if all avenues of escape are blocked and there is a nurse or mother standing by to lend aid in case of sudden hiccoughs, retchings, or nauseas. Under such conditions he has even been known to offer his watch to one related by ties of blood in order that the little stranger might listen to the tick-tick. But it would be paltering with the truth to say that he likes babies. They give him, he says, a sort of grey feeling. He resents their cold stare and the supercilious and up-stage way in which they dribble out of the corner of their mouths on seeing him. Eyeing them, he is conscious of doubts as to whether Man can really be Nature's last word.

This being so, you will readily understand that, even for so stupendous a fee as five hundred francs, he shrank from being closeted with a whole platoon of the little brutes. And I think it is greatly to his credit that after only the shortest of internal struggles he set his teeth, clenched his fists, and made for the harbour with a steady step. How different it would all have been, he felt wistfully, if he were being called upon to judge a contest of Bathing Belles.

There was the possibility, of course, that in the interval since he had met the intelligent Gaul the post of judge would have been filled. But no. The fellow welcomed him with open arms and led him joyfully into a sort of marquee place crowded with as tough-looking a bunch of mothers and as hard-boiled a gaggle of issue as anybody could wish to see. He made a short speech in French which was much too rapid for Freddie to follow, and the mothers all applauded, and the babies all yelled, and then he was conducted along the line, with all the mothers glaring at him in an intimidating way, as much as to warn him that if he dared give the prize to anybody else's offspring he had jolly well better look out for himself. Dashed unpleasant, the whole thing, Freddie tells me, and I see his view-point.

He kept his head, however. This was the first time he had ever been let in for anything of this nature, but a sort of instinct told him to adopt the policy followed by all experienced judges at these affairs – viz. to ignore the babies absolutely and concentrate entirely on the mothers. So many points for ferocity of demeanour, that is to say, and so many for possibility of knife concealed in stocking, and so on and so forth. You ask any curate how he works the gaff at the annual Baby Competition in his village, and he will tell you that these, broadly, are the lines on which he goes.

There were, it seemed, to be three prizes, and about the first one there could be no question at all. It went automatically to a heavy-weight mother with beetling eyebrows who looked as if she had just come from doing a spot of knitting at the foot of the guillotine. Just to see those eyebrows, Freddie tells me, was to hear the heads dropping into the basket, and he had no hesitation, as I say, in declaring her progeny the big winner.

The second and third prizes were a bit more difficult, but after some consideration he awarded them to two other female pluguglies with suspicious bulges in their stockings. This done, he sidled up to the intelligent Gaul to receive his wage, doing his best not to listen to the angry mutterings from the losers which were already beginning to rumble through the air.

The brand of English which this bird affected was not of the best, and it took Freddie some moments to get his drift. When he did, he reeled and came very near clutching for support at the other's beard. Because what the Gaul was endeavouring to communicate was the fact that, so far from being paid five hundred francs for his services, Freddie was expected to cough up that sum.

It was an old Cannes custom, the man explained, for some rich visiting milord to take on the providing of the prizes on this occasion, his reward being the compliment implied in the invitation.

He said that when he had perceived Freddie promenading himself on the Croisette he had been so struck by his appearance of the most elegant and his altogether of a superbness so unparalleled that he had picked him without another look at the field.

Well, dashed gratifying, of course, from one point of view and a handsome tribute to the way Freddie had got himself up that day: but it was not long before he was looking in a tentative sort of manner at the nearest exit. And I think that, had that exit been just a shade closer, he would have put his fortune to the test, to win or lose it all.

But to edge out and leg it would have taken that ten seconds or so which make all the difference. Those mothers would have been on his very heels, and the prospect of sprinting along the streets of Cannes under such conditions was too much for him. Quite possibly he might have shown a flash of speed sufficient to shake off their chal-lenge, but it would have been a very close thing, with nothing in it for the first hundred yards or so, and he could not have failed to make himself conspicuous.

So, with a heavy sigh, he forked out the five h., and tottered into the open. So sombre was his mood that he scarcely heard the mutter-ings of the disappointed losers, who were now calling him an *espèce de*

something and hinting rather broadly in the local *patois* that he had
been fixed.

And the thing that weighed so heavily upon him was the thought
that, unless some miracle occurred, he would now be forced to let
down his old chum Bulstrode, Waters, Parsloe, Bingley, Murgatroyd, or whatever the blighter's name might be.

He had told the fellow to meet him outside the Casino – which in
summer at Cannes is, of course, the Palm Beach at the far end of the
Croisette – so he directed his steps thither. And jolly halting steps
they were, he tells me. The urge to give the school-chum his *mille* had
now become with Frederick Widgeon a regular obsession. He felt
that his honour was involved. And he shuddered at the thought of the
meeting that lay before him. Up the chap would come frisking, with
his hand outstretched and the light of expectation in his eyes, and
what would ensue? The miss-in-baulk.

He groaned in spirit. He could see the other's pained and disillus-
ioned look. He could hear him saying to himself: 'This is not the old
Widgeon form. The boy I admired so much in the dear old days of
school would not have foozled a small loan like this. A pretty serious
change for the worse there must have been in Frederick W. since the
time when we used to sport together in the shade of the old cloisters.'
The thought was agony.

All the way along the Croisette he pondered deeply. To the gay
throng around him he paid no attention. There were girls within a
biscuit-throw in bathing-suits which began at the base of the spine
and ended about two inches lower down, but he did not give them so
much as a glance. His whole being was absorbed in this reverie of his.

By the time he reached the Casino, he had made up his mind. Vis-
ionary, chimerical though the idea would have seemed to anybody
who knew the latter and his views on parting with cash, he had
resolved to make the attempt to borrow a thousand francs from his
uncle. With this end, therefore, he proceeded to the Baccarat rooms.
The other, he knew, was always to be found at this hour seated at one
of the three-louis chemmy tables. For, definite though the Earl of Blicester's creed was on the subject of his nephew gambling, he himself
enjoyed a modest flutter.

He found the old boy, as expected, hunched up over the green
cloth. At the moment of Freddie's arrival he was just scooping in
three pink counters with a holy light of exaltation on his face. For
there was nothing spacious and sensational about Lord Blicester's
methods of play. He was not one of those punters you read about in
the paper who rook the Greek Syndicate of three million francs in
an evening. If he came out one-and-sixpence ahead of the game, he

considered his day well spent.

It looked to Freddie, examining the counters in front of his relative, as if the moment were propitious for a touch. There must have been fully five bobs' worth of them, which meant that the other had struck one of those big winning streaks which come to all gamblers sooner or later. His mood, accordingly, ought to be sunny.

'I say, uncle,' he said, sidling up.

'Get to hell out of here,' replied Lord Blicester, not half so sunny as might have been expected. 'Banco!' he cried, and a second later was gathering in another sixty francs.

'I say, uncle . . .'

'Well, what is it?'

'I say, uncle, will you lend me . . .'

'No.'

'I only want . . .'

'Well, you won't get it.'

'It's not for myself . . .'

'Go to blazes,' said old Blicester.

Freddie receded. Though he had never really expected any solid results, his heart was pretty well bowed down with weight of care. He had shot his bolt. His last source of supply had proved a washout.

He looked at his watch. About now, the old schoolmate would be approaching the tryst. He would be walking – so firm would be his faith in his hero – with elastic steps. Possibly he would even be humming some gay air. Had he a stick? Freddie could not remember. But if he had he would be twirling it.

And then would come the meeting . . . the confession of failure . . . the harsh awakening and the brutal shattering of dreams. . . .

It was at this moment that he was roused from his meditations by the one word in the French language capable of bringing him back to the world.

'*Un mille.*'

It was the voice of the croupier, chanting his litany.

'*Cinquante louis à la banque. Un banco de mille.*'

I can't do the dialect, you understand, but what he meant was that somebody holding the bank had run it up to a thousand francs. And Freddie, waking with a start, perceived that a pile of assorted counters, presumably amounting to that sum, now lay in the centre of the board.

Well, a thousand francs isn't much, of course, to the nibs at the big tables, but among the three-louis-minimum lizards if you run a bank up to a *mille* you make a pretty big sensation. There was quite a crowd round the table now, and over their heads Freddie could see that pile of counters, and it seemed to smile up at him.

For an instant he hesitated, while his past life seemed to flit before him as if he had been a drowning man. Then he heard a voice croak '*Banco!*' and there seemed something oddly familiar about it, and he suddenly realized that it was his own. He had taken the plunge.

It was a pretty agonizing moment for old Freddie, as you may well imagine. I mean to say, he had bancoed this fellow, whoever he was, and if he happened to lose the *coup* all he would have to offer him would be fifty francs and his apologies. There would, he could not conceal it from himself, be the devil of a row. What exactly, he wondered, did they do to you at these French Casinos if you lost and couldn't pay up? Something sticky, beyond a question. Hardly the guillotine, perhaps, and possibly not even Devil's Island. But something nasty, undoubtedly. With a dim recollection of a movie he had once seen, he pictured himself in the middle of a hollow square formed by punters and croupiers with the managing director of the place snipping off his coat buttons.

Or was it trouser buttons? No, in a mixed company like this it would hardly be trouser buttons. Still, even coat buttons would be bad enough.

And, if the moment was agonizing for Freddie, it was scarcely less so for his uncle, Lord Blicester. It was his bank which had been running up to such impressive proportions, and he was now faced with the problem of whether to take a chance on doubling his loot or to pass the hand.

Lord Blicester was a man who, when in the feverish atmosphere of the gaming rooms, believed in small profits and quick returns. He was accustomed to start his bank at the minimum, run it twice with his heart in his mouth, and then pass. But on the present occasion he had been carried away to such an extent that he had worked the kitty up to a solid *mille*. It was a fearful sum to risk losing. On the other hand, suppose he didn't lose? Someone in the crowd outside his line of vision had said 'Banco!' and with a bit of luck he might be two *mille* up instead of one, just like that.

What to do? It was a man's crossroads.

In the end, he decided to take the big chance. And it was as the croupier pushed the cards along the table and the crowd opened up a bit to let the challenger get at them that he recognized in the individual leaning forward his nephew Frederick.

'Brzzgh!' gasped Lord Blicester. 'Gor! Woosh!'

What he meant was that the deal was off because the young hound who had just come into the picture was his late sister's son Frederick Fotheringay Widgeon, who had never had a penny except what he allowed him and certainly hadn't a hundredth part of the sum necessary for cashing in if he lost. But he hadn't made himself clear enough. The next moment, with infinite emotion, Freddie was chucking down a nine and the croupier was pushing all old Blicester's hard-earned at him.

It was as he was gathering it up that he caught the old boy's eye. The effect of it was to cause him to spill a hundred-franc counter, two louis counters, and a five-franc counter. And he had just straightened himself after picking these up, when a voice spoke.

'Good afternoon, Mr Widgeon,' said the girl Drusilla.

'Oh, ah,' said Freddie.

You couldn't say it was a frightfully bright remark, but he considers it was dashed good going to utter even as much as that. In the matter of eyes, he tells me, there was not much to choose between this girl's and his uncle's. Their gazes differed in quality, it is true, because, whereas old Blicester's had been piping hot and had expressed hate, fury and the desire to skin, the girl Drusilla's was right off the ice and conveyed a sort of sick disillusionment and a loathing contempt. But as to which he would rather have met on a dark night down a lonely alley, Freddie couldn't have told you.

'You appear to have been lucky,' said this Drusilla.

'Oh, ah,' said Freddie.

He looked quickly away, and ran up against old Blicester's eye again. Then he looked back and caught Drusilla's. The whole situation, he tells me, was extraordinarily like that of an African explorer who, endeavouring to ignore one of the local serpents, finds himself exchanging glances with a man-eating tiger.

The girl was now wrinkling her nose as if a particularly foul brand of poison-gas had begun to permeate the Casino and she was standing nearest it.

'I must confess I am a little surprised,' she said, 'because I was under the impression that you had told me that you never gambled.'

'Oh, ah,' said Freddie.

'If I remember rightly, you described gambling as a cancer in the body politic.'

'Oh, ah,' said Freddie.

She took a final sniff, as if she had been hoping against hope that he was not a main sewer and was now reluctantly compelled to realize that he was.

'I am afraid I shall not be able to come to tea this afternoon. Goodbye, Mr Widgeon.'

'Oh, ah,' said Freddie.

He watched her go, knowing that she was going out of his life and that any chance of the scent of orange-blossoms and the amble up the aisle with the organ playing 'O perfect Love' was now blue round the edges; and it was as if there was a dull weight pressing on him.

And then he found that there was a dull weight pressing on him, viz. that of all the counters he was loaded down with. And it was at this point that it dawned upon him that, though he had in prospect an interview with old Blicester which would undoubtedly lower all previous records, and though a life's romance had gone phut, he was at least in a position to satisfy the noblesse oblige of the Widgeons.

So he tottered to the cashier's desk and changed the stuff into a pink note, and then he tottered out of the Casino, and was tottering down the steps when he perceived the schoolfriend in the immediate offing, looking bright and expectant.

'Here I am,' said the schoolfriend.

'Oh, ah,' said Freddie.

And with a supreme gesture of resignation he pressed the *mille* into the man's hand.

There was never any doubt about the chap taking it. He took it like a trout sucking down a may-fly and shoved it away in a pocket at the back of his costume. But what was odd was that he seemed stupefied. His eyes grew round, his jaw fell, and he stared at Freddie in awe-struck amazement.

'I say,' he said, 'don't think I'm raising any objections or anything of that sort, because I'm not. I am heart and soul in this scheme of giving me a *mille*. But it's an awful lot, isn't it? I don't mind telling you that what I had been sketching out as more or less the sum that was going to change hands was something in the nature of fifty francs.'

Freddie was a bit surprised too. He couldn't make this out.

'But you said you had to have a *mille*.'

'And a meal is just what I'm going to have,' replied the chap, en-thusiastically. 'I haven't had a bite to eat since breakfast.'

Freddie was stunned. He isn't what you would call a quick thinker, but he was beginning to see that there had been a confusion of ideas.

'Do you mean to tell me,' he cried, 'that when you said a *mille* what you meant was a meal?'

'I don't suppose anyone ever meant a meal more,' said the chap. He stood awhile in thought. 'Hors d'œuvres, I think, to start with,' he went on, passing his tongue meditatively over his lips. 'Then perhaps a touch of clear soup, followed by some fish of the country and a good steak *minute* with fried potatoes and a salad. Cheese, of course, and the usual etceteras, and then coffee, liqueur, and a cigar to wind up with. Yes, you may certainly take it as official that I intend to have a meal. Ah, yes, and I was forgetting. A bot of some nice, dry wine to wash things down. Yes, yes, yes, to be sure. You see this stomach?' he said, patting it. 'Here stands a stomach that is scheduled in about a quarter of an hour to get the surprise of its young life.'

Freddie saw it all now, and the irony of the situation seemed to hit him like a bit of lead-piping on the base of the skull. Just because of this footling business of having words in one language which meant something quite different in another language – a thing which could so easily have been prevented by the responsible heads of the French and English nations getting together across a round table and coming to some sensible arrangement – here he was deeper in the soup than he had ever been in the whole course of his career.

He tells me he chafed, and I don't blame him. Anybody would have chafed in the circs. For about half a minute he had half a mind to leap at the chap and wrench the *mille* out of him and substitute for it the fifty francs which he had been anticipating.

Then the old noblesse oblige spirit awoke once more. He might be in the soup, he might be a financial wreck, he might be faced with a *tête-à-tête* with his uncle, Lord Blicester, in the course of which the testy old man would in all probability endeavour to bite a piece out of the fleshy part of his leg, but at least he had done the fine, square thing. He had not let down a fellow who had admired him at school.

The chap had begun to speak again. At first, all he said was a brief word or two revising that passage in his previous address which had dealt with steak *minute*. A steak *minute*, he told Freddie, had among its obvious merits one fault – to wit, that it was not as filling as it might be. A more prudent move, he considered, and he called on Freddie to endorse this view, would be a couple of chump chops. Then he turned from that subject.

'Well, it was certainly a bit of luck running into you, Postlethwaits,' he said.

Freddie was a trifle stymied.

'Postlethwaite?' he said. 'How do you mean, Postlethwaite?'

The chap seemed surprised.

'How do you mean, how do I mean Postlethwaite?'

'I mean, why Postlethwaite? How has this Postlethwaite stuff crept in?'

'But, Postlethwaite, your name's Postlethwaite.'

'My name's Widgeon.'

'Widgeon?'

'Widgeon.'

'*Not* Postlethwaite?'

'Certainly not.'

The chap uttered an indulgent laugh.

'Ha, ha. Still the same old jovial, merry, kidding Postlethwaite, I see.'

'I'm not the same old jovial, merry, kidding Postlethwaite,' said Freddie, with heat. 'I never was the jovial, merry, kidding Postlethwaite.'

The chap stared.

'You aren't the Postlethwaite I used to admire so much at dear old Bingleton?'

'I've never been near dear old Bingleton in my life.'

'But you're wearing an Old Bingletonian tie.'

Freddie reeled.

'Is this beastly thing an Old Bingletonian tie? It's one I sneaked from my uncle.'

The chap laughed heartily.

'Well, of all the absurd mix-ups! You look like Postlethwaite and you're wearing an OB tie. Naturally, I thought you *were* Postlethwaite. And all the time we were thinking of a couple of other fellows! Well, well, well! However, it's all worked out for the best, what? Goodbye,' he added hastily, and was round the corner like a streak.

Freddie looked after him dully. He was totting up in his mind the final returns. On the debit side, he had lost Drusilla whatever-her-name-was. He had alienated his uncle, old Blicester. He was down a tenner. And, scaliest thought of all, he hadn't been anybody's hero at school.

On the credit side, he had fifty francs.

At the Palm Beach Casino at Cannes you can get five Martini cocktails for fifty francs. Freddie went and had them.

Then, wiping his lips with the napkin provided by the management, he strode from the bar to face the hopeless dawn.

8

UNCLE FRED FLITS BY

In order that they might enjoy their after-luncheon coffee in peace, the Crumpet had taken the guest whom he was entertaining at the Drones Club to the smaller and less frequented of the two smoking rooms. In the other, he explained, though the conversation always touched an exceptionally high level of brilliance, there was apt to be a good deal of sugar thrown about.

The guest said he understood.

'Young blood, eh?'

'That's right. Young blood.'

'And animal spirits.'

'And animal, as you say, spirits,' agreed the Crumpet. 'We get a fairish amount of those here.'

'The complaint, however, is not, I observe, universal.'

'Eh?'

The other drew his host's attention to the doorway, where a young man in form-fitting tweeds had just appeared. The aspect of this young man was haggard. His eyes glared wildly and he sucked at an empty cigarette holder. If he had a mind, there was something on it. When the Crumpet called to him to come and join the party, he merely shook his head in a distraught sort of way and disappeared, looking like a character out of a Greek tragedy pursued by the Fates.

The Crumpet sighed.

'Poor old Pongo!'

'Pongo?'

'That was Pongo Twistleton. He's all broken up about his Uncle Fred.'

'Dead?'

'No such luck. Coming up to London again tomorrow. Pongo had a wire this morning.'

'And that upsets him?'

'Naturally. After what happened last time.'

'What was that?'

'Ah!' said the Crumpet.

'What happened last time?'

'You may well ask.'
'I do ask.'
'Ah!' said the Crumpet.

Poor old Pongo (said the Crumpet) has often discussed his Uncle
Fred with me, and if there weren't tears in his eyes when he did so, I
don't know a tear in the eye when I see one. In round numbers the
Earl of Ickenham, of Ickenham Hall, Ickenham, Hants, he lives in
the country most of the year, but from time to time has a nasty way of
slipping his collar and getting loose and descending upon Pongo at
his flat in the Albany. And every time he does so, the unhappy young
blighter is subjected to some soul-testing experience. Because the
trouble with his uncle is that, though sixty if a day, he becomes on
arriving in the metropolis as young as he feels – which is, apparently,
a youngish twenty-two. I don't know if you happen to know what the
word 'excesses' means, but those are what Pongo's Uncle Fred from
the country, when in London, invariably commits.

It wouldn't so much matter, mind you, if he would confine his activities to the club premises. We're pretty broad-minded here, and if
you stop short of smashing the piano, there isn't much that you can
do at the Drones that will cause the raised eyebrow and the sharp
intake of breath. The snag is that he will insist on lugging Pongo out
in the open and there, right in the public eye, proceeding to step
high, wide and plentiful.

So when, on the occasion to which I allude, he stood pink and
genial on Pongo's hearthrug, bulging with Pongo's lunch and
wreathed in the smoke of one of Pongo's cigars, and said: 'And now,
my boy, for a pleasant and instructive afternoon,' you will readily
understand why the unfortunate young clam gazed at him as he
would have gazed at two-penn'orth of dynamite, had he discovered it
lighting up in his presence.

'A what?' he said, giving at the knees and paling beneath the tan a
bit.

'A pleasant and instructive afternoon,' repeated Lord Ickenham,
rolling the words round his tongue. 'I propose that you place yourself
in my hands and leave the programme entirely to me.'

Now, owing to Pongo's circumstances being such as to necessitate
his getting into the aged relative's ribs at intervals and shaking him
down for an occasional much-needed tenner or what not, he isn't in a
position to use the iron hand with the old buster. But at these words
he displayed a manly firmness.

'You aren't going to get me to the dog races again.'
'No, no.'

'You remember what happened last June.'

'Quite,' said Lord Ickenham, 'quite. Though I still think that a wiser magistrate would have been content with a mere reprimand.'

'And I won't – '

'Certainly not. Nothing of that kind at all. What I propose to do this afternoon is to take you to visit the home of your ancestors.'

Pongo did not get this.

'I thought Ickenham was the home of my ancestors.'

'It is one of the homes of your ancestors. They also resided rather nearer the heart of things, at a place called Mitching Hill.'

'Down in the suburbs, do you mean?'

'The neighbourhood is now suburban, true. It is many years since the meadows where I sported as a child were sold and cut up into building lots. But when I was a boy Mitching Hill was open country. It was a vast, rolling estate belonging to your great-uncle, Marmaduke, a man with whiskers of a nature which you with your pure mind would scarcely credit, and I have long felt a sentimental urge to see what the hell the old place looks like now. Perfectly foul, I expect. Still, I think we should make the pious pilgrimage.'

Pongo absolutely-ed heartily. He was all for the scheme. A great weight seemed to have rolled off his mind. The way he looked at it was that even an uncle within a short jump of the looney bin couldn't very well get into much trouble in a suburb. I mean, you know what suburbs are. They don't, as it were, offer the scope. One follows his reasoning, of course.

'Fine!' he said. 'Splendid! Topping!'

'Then put on your hat and rompers, my boy,' said Lord Ickenham, 'and let us be off. I fancy one gets there by omnibuses and things.'

Well, Pongo hadn't expected much in the way of mental uplift from the sight of Mitching Hill, and he didn't get it. Alighting from the bus, he tells me, you found yourself in the middle of rows and rows of semidetached villas, all looking exactly alike, and you went on and you came to more semidetached villas, and those all looked exactly alike, too. Nevertheless, he did not repine. It was one of those early spring days which suddenly change to mid-winter and he had come out without his overcoat, and it looked like rain and he hadn't an umbrella, but despite this his mood was one of sober ecstasy. The hours were passing and his uncle had not yet made a goat of himself. At the dog races the other had been in the hands of the constabulary in the first ten minutes.

It began to seem to Pongo that with any luck he might be able to keep the old blister pottering harmlessly about here till nightfall, when he could shoot a bit of dinner into him and put him to bed. And as Lord Ickenham had specifically stated that his wife, Pongo's Aunt Jane, had expressed her intention of scalping him with a blunt knife if he wasn't back at the Hall by lunch time on the morrow, it really looked as if he might get through this visit without perpetrating a single major outrage on the public weal. It is rather interesting to note that as he thought this Pongo smiled, because it was the last time he smiled that day.

All this while, I should mention, Lord Ickenham had been stopping at intervals like a pointing dog and saying that it must have been just about here that he plugged the gardener in the trousers seat with his bow and arrow and that over there he had been sick after his first cigar, and he now paused in front of a villa which for some unknown reason called itself The Cedars. His face was tender and wistful.

'On this very spot, if I am not mistaken,' he said, heaving a bit of a sigh, 'on this very spot, fifty years ago come Lammas Eve, I ... Oh, blast it!'

The concluding remark had been caused by the fact that the rain, which had held off until now, suddenly began to buzz down like a shower-bath. With no further words, they leaped into the porch of the villa and there took shelter, exchanging glances with a grey parrot which hung in a cage in the window.

Not that you could really call it shelter. They were protected from above all right, but the moisture was now falling with a sort of swivel action, whipping in through the sides of the porch and tickling them up properly. And it was just after Pongo had turned up his collar and was huddling against the door that the door gave way. From the fact that a female of general-servant aspect was standing there he gathered that his uncle must have rung the bell.

This female wore a long mackintosh, and Lord Ickenham beamed upon her with a fairish spot of suavity.

'Good afternoon,' he said.

The female said good afternoon.

'The Cedars?'

The female said yes, it was The Cedars.

'Are the old folks at home?'

The female said there was nobody at home.

'Ah? Well, never mind. I have come,' said Lord Ickenham, edging in, 'to clip the parrot's claws. My assistant, Mr Walkinshaw, who applies the anæsthetic,' he added, indicating Pongo with a gesture.

'Are you from the bird shop?'

'A very happy guess.'

'Nobody told me you were coming.'

'They keep things from you, do they? ' said Lord Ickenham, sympathetically. 'Too bad.'

Continuing to edge, he had got into the parlour by now, Pongo following in a sort of dream and the female following Pongo.

'Well, I suppose it's all right,' she said. 'I was just going out. It's my afternoon.'

'Go out,' said Lord Ickenham cordially. 'By all means go out. We will leave everything in order.'

And presently the female, though still a bit on the dubious side, pushed off, and Lord Ickenham lit the gas fire and drew a chair up.

'So here we are, my boy,' he said. 'A little tact, a little address, and here we are, snug and cosy and not catching our deaths of cold. You'll never go far wrong if you leave things to me.'

'But, dash it, we can't stop here,' said Pongo.

Lord Ickenham raised his eyebrows.

'Not stop here? Are you suggesting that we go out into that rain? My dear lad, you are not aware of the grave issues involved. This morning, as I was leaving home, I had a rather painful disagreement with your aunt. She said the weather was treacherous and wished me to take my woolly muffler. I replied that the weather was not treacherous and that I would be dashed if I took my woolly muffler. Eventually, by the exercise of an iron will, I had my way, and I ask you, my dear boy, to envisage what will happen if I return with a cold in the head. I shall sink to the level of a fifth-class power. Next time I came to London, it would be with a liver pad and a respirator. No! I shall remain here, toasting my toes at this really excellent fire. I had no idea that a gas fire radiated such warmth. I feel all in a glow.'

So did Pongo. His brow was wet with honest sweat. He is reading for the Bar, and while he would be the first to admit that he hasn't yet got a complete toe-hold on the Law of Great Britain he had a sort of notion that oiling into a perfect stranger's semidetached villa on the pretext of pruning the parrot was a tort or misdemeanour, if not actual barratry or soccage in fief or something like that. And apart from the legal aspect of the matter there was the embarrassment of the thing. Nobody is more of a whale on correctness and not doing what's not done than Pongo, and the situation in which he now found himself caused him to chew the lower lip and, as I say, perspire a goodish deal.

'But suppose the blighter who owns this ghastly house comes back?' he asked. 'Talking of envisaging things, try that one over on your pianola.'

And, sure enough, as he spoke, the front door bell rang.

'There!' said Pongo.

'Don't say "There!" my boy,' said Lord Ickenham reprovingly. 'It's the sort of thing your aunt says. I see no reason for alarm. Obviously this is some casual caller. A ratepayer would have used his latchkey. Glance cautiously out of the window and see if you can see anybody.'

'It's a pink chap,' said Pongo, having done so.

'How pink?'

'Pretty pink.'

'Well, there you are, then. I told you so. It can't be the big chief. The sort of fellows who own houses like this are pale and sallow, owing to working in offices all day. Go and see what he wants.'

'You go and see what he wants.'

'We'll both go and see what he wants,' said Lord Ickenham.

So they went and opened the front door, and there, as Pongo had said, was a pink chap. A small young pink chap, a bit moist about the shoulder-blades.

'Pardon me,' said this pink chap, 'is Mr Roddis in?'

'No,' said Pongo.

'Yes,' said Lord Ickenham. 'Don't be silly, Douglas – of course I'm in. I am Mr Roddis,' he said to the pink chap. 'This, such as he is, is my son Douglas. And you?'

'Name of Robinson.'

'What about it?'

'My name's Robinson.'

'Oh, *your* name's Robinson? Now we've got it straight. Delighted to see you, Mr Robinson. Come right in and take your boots off.'

They all trickled back to the parlour, Lord Ickenham pointing out objects of interest by the wayside to the chap, Pongo gulping for air a bit and trying to get himself abreast of this new twist in the scenario. His heart was becoming more and more bowed down with weight of woe. He hadn't liked being Mr Walkinshaw, the anæsthetist, and he didn't like it any better being Roddis Junior. In brief, he feared the worst. It was only too plain to him by now that his uncle had got it thoroughly up his nose and had settled down to one of his big afternoons, and he was asking himself, as he had so often asked himself before, what would the harvest be?

Arrived in the parlour, the pink chap proceeded to stand on one leg and look coy.

'Is Julia here?' he asked, simpering a bit, Pongo says.

'Is she?' said Lord Ickenham to Pongo.

'No,' said Pongo.

'No,' said Lord Ickenham.

'She wired me she was coming here today.'

'Ah, then we shall have a bridge four.'

The pink chap stood on the other leg.

'I don't suppose you've ever met Julia. Bit of trouble in the family, she gave me to understand.'

'It is often the way.'

'The Julia I mean is your niece Julia Parker. Or, rather, your wife's niece Julia Parker.

'Any niece of my wife is a niece of mine,' said Lord Ickenham heartily. 'We share and share alike.'

'Julia and I want to get married.'

'Well, go ahead.'

'But they won't let us.'

'Who won't?'

'Her mother and father. And Uncle Charlie Parker and Uncle Henry Parker and the rest of them. They don't think I'm good enough.'

'The morality of the modern young man is notoriously lax.'

'Class enough, I mean. They're a haughty lot.'

'What makes them haughty? Are they earls?'

'No, they aren't earls.'

'Then why the devil,' said Lord Ickenham warmly, 'are they haughty? Only earls have a right to be haughty. Earls are hot stuff. When you get an earl, you've got something.'

'Besides, we've had words. Me and her father. One thing led to another, and in the end I called him a perishing old – Coo!' said the pink chap, breaking off suddenly.

He had been standing by the window, and he now leaped lissomely into the middle of the room, causing Pongo, whose nervous system was by this time definitely down among the wines and spirits and who hadn't been expecting this *adagio* stuff, to bite his tongue with some severity.

'They're on the doorstep! Julia and her mother and father. I didn't know they were all coming.'

'You do not wish to meet them?'

'No, I don't!'

'Then duck behind the settee, Mr Robinson,' said Lord Ickenham, and the pink chap, weighing the advice and finding it good, did so. And as he disappeared the door bell rang.

Once more, Lord Ickenham led Pongo out into the hall.

'I say!' said Pongo, and a close observer might have noted that he was quivering like an aspen.

'Say on, my dear boy.'

'I mean to say, what?'

'What?'

'You aren't going to let these bounders in, are you?'

'Certainly,' said Lord Ickenham. 'We Roddises keep open house. And as they are presumably aware that Mr Roddis has no son, I think we had better return to the old layout. You are the local vet, my boy, come to minister to my parrot. When I return, I should like to find you by the cage, staring at the bird in a scientific manner. Tap your teeth from time to time with a pencil and try to smell of iodoform. It will help to add conviction.'

So Pongo shifted back to the parrot's cage and stared so earnestly that it was only when a voice said 'Well!' that he became aware that there was anybody in the room. Turning, he perceived that Hampshire's leading curse had come back, bringing the gang.

It consisted of a stern, thin, middle-aged woman, a middle-aged man and a girl.

You can generally accept Pongo's estimate of girls, and when he says that this one was a pippin one knows that he uses the term in its most exact sense. She was about nineteen, he thinks, and she wore a black beret, a dark green leather coat, a shortish tweed skirt, silk stockings and high-heeled shoes. Her eyes were large and lustrous and her face like a dewy rosebud at daybreak on a June morning. So Pongo tells me. Not that I suppose he has ever seen a rosebud at daybreak on a June morning, because it's generally as much as you can do to lug him out of bed in time for nine-thirty breakfast. Still, one gets the idea.

'Well,' said the woman, 'you don't know who I am, I'll be bound. I'm Laura's sister Connie. This is Claude, my husband. And this is my daughter Julia. Is Laura in?'

'I regret to say, no,' said Lord Ickenham.

The woman was looking at him as if he didn't come up to her specifications.

'I thought you were younger,' she said.

'Younger than what?' said Lord Ickenham.

'Younger than you are.'

'You can't be younger than you are, worse luck,' said Lord Ickenham. 'Still, one does one's best, and I am bound to say that of recent years I have made a pretty good go of it.'

The woman caught sight of Pongo, and he didn't seem to please her, either.

'Who's that?'

'The local vet, clustering round my parrot.'

'I can't talk in front of him.'

'It is quite all right,' Lord Ickenham assured her. 'The poor fellow is stone deaf.'

And with an imperious gesture at Pongo, as much as to bid him stare less at girls and more at parrots, he got the company seated.

'Now, then,' he said.

There was silence for a moment, then a sort of muffled sob, which Pongo thinks proceeded from the girl. He couldn't see, of course, because his back was turned and he was looking at the parrot, which looked back at him – most offensively, he says, as parrots will, using one eye only for the purpose. It also asked him to have a nut.

The woman came into action again.

'Although,' she said, 'Laura never did me the honour to invite me to her wedding, for which reason I have not communicated with her for five years, necessity compels me to cross her threshold today. There comes a time when differences must be forgotten and relatives must stand shoulder to shoulder.'

'I see what you mean,' said Lord Ickenham. 'Like the boys of the old brigade.'

'What I say is, let bygones be bygones. I would not have intruded on you, but needs must. I disregard the past and appeal to your sense of pity.'

The thing began to look to Pongo like a touch, and he is convinced that the parrot thought so, too, for it winked and cleared its throat. But they were both wrong. The woman went on.

'I want you and Laura to take Julia into your home for a week or so, until I can make other arrangements for her. Julia is studying the piano, and she sits for her examination in two weeks' time, so until then she must remain in London. The trouble is, she has fallen in love. Or thinks she has.'

'I know I have,' said Julia.

Her voice was so attractive that Pongo was compelled to slew round and take another look at her. Her eyes, he says, were shining like twin stars and there was a sort of Soul's Awakening expression on her face, and what the dickens there was in a pink chap like the pink chap, who even as pink chaps go wasn't much of a pink chap, to make her look like that, was frankly, Pongo says, more than he could understand. The thing baffled him. He sought in vain for a solution.

'Yesterday, Claude and I arrived in London from our Bexhill home to give Julia a pleasant surprise. We stayed, naturally, in the boarding-house where she has been living for the past six weeks. And what do you think we discovered?'

'Insects.'

'Not insects. A letter. From a young man. I found to my horror that a young man of whom I knew nothing was arranging to marry my daughter. I sent for him immediately, and found him to be quite impossible. He jellies eels!'

'Does what?'

'He is an assistant at a jellied eel shop.'

'But surely,' said Lord Ickenham, 'that speaks well for him. The capacity to jelly an eel seems to me to argue intelligence of a high order. It isn't everybody who can do it, by any means. I know if someone came to me and said "Jelly this eel!" I should be nonplussed. And so, or I am very much mistaken, would Ramsay MacDonald and Winston Churchill.'

The woman did not seem to see eye to eye.

'Tchah!' she said. 'What do you suppose my husband's brother Charlie Parker would say if I allowed his niece to marry a man who jellies eels?'

'Ah!' said Claude, who, before we go any further, was a tall, drooping bird with a red soup-strainer moustache.

'Or my husband's brother, Henry Parker.'

'Ah!' said Claude. 'Or Cousin Alf Robbins, for that matter.'

'Exactly. Cousin Alfred would die of shame.'

The girl Julia hiccoughed passionately, so much so that Pongo says it was all he could do to stop himself nipping across and taking her hand in his and patting it.

'I've told you a hundred times, mother, that Wilberforce is only jellying eels till he finds something better.'

'What is better than an eel?' asked Lord Ickenham, who had been following this discussion with the close attention it deserved. 'For jellying purposes, I mean.'

'He is ambitious. It won't be long,' said the girl, 'before Wilberforce suddenly rises in the world.'

She never spoke a truer word. At this very moment, up he came from behind the settee like a leaping salmon.

'Julia!' he cried.

'Wilby!' yipped the girl.

And Pongo says he never saw anything more sickening in his life than the way she flung herself into the blighter's arms and clung there like the ivy on the old garden wall. It wasn't that he had anything specific against the pink chap, but this girl had made a deep impression on him and he resented her glueing herself to another in this manner.

Julia's mother, after just that brief moment which a woman needs in which to recover from her natural surprise at seeing eel-jelliers pop up from behind sofas, got moving and plucked her away like a referee breaking a couple of welterweights.

'Julia Parker,' she said, 'I'm ashamed of you!'

'So am I,' said Claude.

'I blush for you.'

'Me, too,' said Claude. 'Hugging and kissing a man who called your father a perishing old bottle-nosed Gawd-help-us.'

'I think,' said Lord Ickenham, shoving his oar in, 'that before proceeding any further we ought to go into that point. If he called you a perishing old bottle-nosed Gawd-help-us, it seems to me that the first thing to do is to decide whether he was right, and frankly, in my opinion . . .'

'Wilberforce will apologize.'

'Certainly I'll apologize. It isn't fair to hold a remark passed in the heat of the moment against a chap . . .'

'Mr Robinson,' said the woman, 'you know perfectly well that whatever remarks you may have seen fit to pass don't matter one way or the other. If you were listening to what I was saying you will understand . . .'

'Oh, I know, I know. Uncle Charlie Parker and Uncle Henry Parker and Cousin Alf Robbins and all that. Pack of snobs!'

'What!'

'Haughty, stuck-up snobs. Them and their class distinctions. Think themselves everybody just because they've got money. I'd like to know how they got it.'

'What do you mean by that?'

'Never mind what I mean.'

'If you are insinuating – '

'Well, of course, you know, Connie,' said Lord Ickenham mildly, 'he's quite right. You can't get away from that.'

I don't know if you have ever seen a bull-terrier embarking on a scrap with an Airedale and just as it was getting down nicely to its work suddenly having an unexpected Kerry Blue sneak up behind it and bite it in the rear quarters. When this happens, it lets go of the Airedale and swivels round and fixes the butting-in animal with a pretty nasty eye. It was exactly the same with the woman Connie when Lord Ickenham spoke these words.

'What!'

'I was only wondering if you had forgotten how Charlie Parker made his pile.'

'What are you talking about?'

'I know it is painful,' said Lord Ickenham, 'and one doesn't mention it as a rule, but, as we are on the subject, you must admit that lending money at two hundred and fifty per cent interest is not done in the best circles. The judge, if you remember, said so at the trial.'

'I never knew that!' cried the girl Julia.

'Ah,' said Lord Ickenham. 'You kept it from the child? Quite right, quite right.'

'It's a lie!'

'And when Henry Parker had all that fuss with the bank it was touch and go they didn't send him to prison. Between ourselves, Connie, has a bank official, even a brother of your husband, any right to sneak fifty pounds from the till in order to put it on a hundred to one shot for the Grand National? Not quite playing the game, Connie. Not the straight bat. Henry, I grant you, won five thousand of the best and never looked back afterwards, but, though we applaud his judgment of form, we must surely look askance at his financial methods. As for Cousin Alf Robbins . . .'

The woman was making rummy stuttering sounds. Pongo tells me he once had a Pommery Seven which used to express itself in much the same way if you tried to get it to take a hill on high. A sort of mixture of gurgles and explosions.

'There is not a word of truth in this,' she gasped at length, having managed to get the vocal cords disentangled. 'Not a single word. I think you must have gone mad.'

Lord Ickenham shrugged his shoulders.

'Have it your own way, Connie. I was only going to say that, while the jury were probably compelled on the evidence submitted to them to give Cousin Alf Robbins the benefit of the doubt when charged with smuggling dope, everybody knew that he had been doing it for years. I am not blaming him, mind you. If a man can smuggle cocaine and get away with it, good luck to him, say I. The only point I am trying to make is that we are hardly a family that can afford to put on dog and sneer at honest suitors for our daughters' hands. Speaking for myself, I consider that we are very lucky to have the chance of marrying even into eel-jellying circles.'

'So do I,' said Julia firmly.

'You don't believe what this man is saying?'

'I believe every word.'

'So do I,' said the pink chap.

The woman snorted. She seemed overwrought.

'Well,' she said, 'goodness knows I have never liked Laura, but I would never have wished her a husband like you!'

'Husband?' said Lord Ickenham, puzzled. 'What gives you the impression that Laura and I are married?'

There was a weighty silence, during which the parrot threw out a general invitation to the company to join it in a nut. Then the girl

Julia spoke.

'You'll have to let me marry Wilberforce now,' she said. 'He knows too much about us.'

'I was rather thinking that myself,' said Lord Ickenham. 'Seal his lips, I say.'

'You wouldn't mind marrying into a low family, would you darling?' asked the girl, with a touch of anxiety.

'No family could be too low for me, dearest, if it was yours,' said the pink chap.

'After all, we needn't see them.'

'That's right.'

'It isn't one's relations that matter: it's oneselves.'

'That's right, too.'

'Wilby!'

'Julia!'

They repeated the old ivy on the garden wall act. Pongo says he didn't like it any better than the first time, but his distaste wasn't in it with the woman Connie's.

'And what, may I ask,' she said, 'do you propose to marry on?'

This seemed to cast a damper. They came apart. They looked at each other. The girl looked at the pink chap, and the pink chap looked at the girl. You could see that a jarring note had been struck.

'Wilberforce is going to be a very rich man some day.'

'Some day!'

'If I had a hundred pounds,' said the pink chap, 'I could buy a half-share in one of the best milk walks in South London tomorrow.'

'If!' said the woman.

'Ah!' said Claude.

'Where are you going to get it?'

'Ah!' said Claude.

'Where,' repeated the woman, plainly pleased with the snappy crack and loath to let it ride without an encore, 'are you going to get it?'

'That,' said Claude, 'is the point. Where are you going to get a hundred pounds?'

'Why, bless my soul,' said Lord Ickenham jovially, 'from me, of course. Where else?'

And before Pongo's bulging eyes he fished out from the recesses of his costume a crackling bundle of notes and handed it over. And the agony of realizing that the old bounder had had all that stuff on him all this time and that he hadn't touched him for so much as a tithe of it was so keen, Pongo says, that before he knew what he was doing he had let out a sharp, whinnying cry which rang through the room like the yowl of a stepped-on puppy.

'Ah,' said Lord Ickenham. 'The vet wishes to speak to me. Yes, vet?'

This seemed to puzzle the cerise bloke a bit.

'I thought you said this chap was your son.'

'If I had a son,' said Lord Ickenham, a little hurt, 'he would be a good deal better-looking than that. No, this is the local veterinary surgeon. I may have said I *looked* on him as a son. Perhaps that was what confused you.'

He shifted across to Pongo and twiddled his hands inquiringly. Pongo gaped at him, and it was not until one of the hands caught him smartly in the lower ribs that he remembered he was deaf and started to twiddle back. Considering that he wasn't supposed to be dumb, I can't see why he should have twiddled, but no doubt there are moments when twiddling is about all a fellow feels himself equal to. For what seemed to him at least ten hours Pongo had been undergoing great mental stress, and one can't blame him for not being chatty. Anyway, be that as it may, he twiddled.

'I cannot quite understand what he says,' announced Lord Ickenham at length, 'because he sprained a finger this morning and that makes him stammer. But I gather that he wishes to have a word with me in private. Possibly my parrot has got something the matter with it which he is reluctant to mention even in sign language in front of a young unmarried girl. You know what parrots are. We will step outside.'

'*We* will step outside,' said Wilberforce.

'Yes,' said the girl Julia. 'I feel like a walk.'

'And you?' said Lord Ickenham to the woman Connie, who was looking like a female Napoleon at Moscow. 'Do you join the hikers?'

'I shall remain and make myself a cup of tea. You will not grudge us a cup of tea, I hope?'

'Far from it,' said Lord Ickenham cordially. 'This is Liberty Hall. Stick around and mop it up till your eyes bubble.'

Outside, the girl, looking more like a dewy rosebud than ever, fawned on the old buster pretty considerably.

'I don't know how to thank you!' she said. And the pink chap said he didn't, either.

'Not at all, my dear, not at all,' said Lord Ickenham.

'I think you're simply wonderful.'

'No, no.'

'You are. Perfectly marvellous.'

'Tut, tut,' said Lord Ickenham. 'Don't give the matter another thought.'

He kissed her on both cheeks, the chin, the forehead, the right
eyebrow, and the tip of the nose, Pongo looking on the while in a
baffled and discontented manner. Everybody seemed to be kissing
this girl except him.

Eventually the degrading spectacle ceased and the girl and the pink
chap shoved off, and Pongo was enabled to take up the matter of that
hundred quid.

'Where,' he asked, 'did you get all that money?'

'Now, where did I?' mused Lord Ickenham. 'I know your aunt
gave it to me for some purpose. But what? To pay some bill or other, I
rather fancy.'

This cheered Pongo up slightly.

'She'll give you the devil when you get back,' he said, with not a
little relish. 'I wouldn't be in your shoes for something. When you
tell Aunt Jane,' he said, with confidence, for he knew his Aunt Jane's
emotional nature, 'that you slipped her entire roll to a girl, and
explain, as you will have to explain, that she was an extraordinarily
pretty girl – a girl, in fine, who looked like something out of a beauty
chorus of the better sort, I should think she would pluck down one of
the ancestral battleaxes from the wall and jolly well strike you on the
mazzard.'

'Have no anxiety, my dear boy,' said Lord Ickenham. 'It is like
your kind heart to be so concerned, but have no anxiety. I shall tell
her that I was compelled to give the money to you to enable you to
buy back some compromising letters from a Spanish *demi-mondaine*.
She will scarcely be able to blame me for rescuing a fondly loved
nephew from the clutches of an adventuress. It may be that she will
feel a little vexed with you for a while, and that you may have to allow
a certain time to elaspe before you visit Ickenham again, but then I
shan't be wanting you at Ickenham till the ratting season starts, so all
is well.'

At this moment, there came toddling up to the gate of The Cedars a
large red-faced man. He was just going in when Lord Ickenham
hailed him.

'Mr Roddis?'

'Hey?'

'Am I addressing Mr Roddis?'

'That's me.'

'I am Mr J. G. Bulstrode from down the road,' said Lord
Ickenham. 'This is my sister's husband's brother, Percy Frensham,
in the lard and imported-butter business.'

The red-faced bird said he was pleased to meet them. He asked
Pongo if things were brisk in the lard and imported-butter business,

and Pongo said they were all right, and the red-faced bird said he was glad to hear it.

'We have never met, Mr Roddis,' said Lord Ickenham, 'but I think it would be only neighbourly to inform you that a short while ago I observed two suspicious-looking persons in your house.'

'In my house? How on earth did they get there?'

'No doubt through a window at the back. They looked to me like cat burglars. If you creep up, you may be able to see them.'

The red-faced bird crept, and came back not exactly foaming at the mouth but with the air of a man who for two pins would so foam.

'You're perfectly right. They're sitting in my parlour as cool as dammit, swigging my tea and buttered toast.'

'I thought as much.'

'And they've opened a pot of my raspberry jam.'

'Ah, then you will be able to catch them red-handed. I should fetch a policeman.'

'I will. Thank you, Mr Bulstrode.'

'Only too glad to have been able to render you this little service, Mr Roddis,' said Lord Ickenham. 'Well, I must be moving along. I have an appointment. Pleasant after the rain, is it not? Come, Percy.'

He lugged Pongo off.

'So that,' he said, with satisfaction, 'is that. On these visits of mine to the metropolis, my boy, I always make it my aim, if possible, to spread sweetness and light. I look about me, even in a foul hole like Mitching Hill, and I ask myself – How can I leave this foul hole a better and happier foul hole than I found it? And if I see a chance, I grab it. Here is our omnibus. Spring aboard, my boy, and on our way home we will be sketching out rough plans for the evening. If the old Leicester Grill is still in existence, we might look in there. It must be fully thirty-five years since I was last thrown out of the Leicester Grill. I wonder who is the bouncer there now.'

Such (concluded the Crumpet) is Pongo Twistleton's Uncle Fred from the country, and you will have gathered by now a rough notion of why it is that when a telegram comes announcing his impending arrival in the great city Pongo blenches to the core and calls for a couple of quick ones.

The whole situation, Pongo says, is very complex. Looking at it from one angle, it is fine that the man lives in the country most of the year. If he didn't, he would have him in his midst all the time. On the other hand, by living in the country he generates, as it were, a store of loopiness which expends itself with frightful violence on his rare visits to the centre of things.

What it boils down to is this – Is it better to have a loopy uncle whose loopiness is perpetually on tap but spread out thin, so to speak, or one who lies low in distant Hants for three hundred and sixty days in the year and does himself proud in London for the other five? Dashed moot, of course, and Pongo has never been able to make up his mind on the point.

Naturally, the ideal thing would be if someone would chain the old hound up permanently and keep him from Jan. One to Dec. Thirty-one where he wouldn't do any harm – viz. among the spuds and tenantry. But this, Pongo admits, is a Utopian dream. Nobody could work harder to that end than his Aunt Jane, and she has never been able to manage it.

9
THE MASKED TROUBADOUR

A young man came out of the Drones Club and paused on the steps to light a cigarette. As he did so, there popped up – apparently through the pavement, for there had been no sign of him in the street a moment before – a seedy individual who touched his hat and smiled ingratiatingly. The young man seemed to undergo a brief inward struggle – then he felt in his pocket, pressed a coin into the outstretched palm, and passed on.

It was a pretty, heart-warming little scene, the sort of thing you see in full-page pictures in the Christmas numbers, but the only emotion it excited in the bosoms of the two Beans who had witnessed it from the window of the smoking room was amazement.

'Well, stap my vitals,' said the first Bean. 'If I hadn't seen it with my own eyes I wouldn't have believed it.'

'Nor me,' said the second Bean.

'Believed what?' asked a Crumpet, who had come up behind them.

The two Beans turned to him as one Bean and spoke in alternate lines, like a Greek chorus.

'Freddie Widgeon – '

' – was outside there a moment ago – '

' – and a chap came up and touched his hat – '

' – and then he touched Freddie.'

'And Freddie, though he was on the steps at the time – '

' – and so had only to leap backwards in order to win to safety – '

' – stood there and let the deal go through.'

The Crumpet clicked his tongue.

'What sort of a looking chap was he? Small and a bit greasy?'

'Quite fairly greasy.'

'I thought as much,' said the Crumpet. 'I know the bird. He's a fellow named·Waterbury, a pianist by profession. He's a sort of pensioner of Freddie's. Freddie is always slipping him money – here a tanner, there a bob.'

The astonishment of the two Beans deepened.

'But Freddie's broke,' said the senior Bean.

'True,' said the Crumpet. 'He can ill spare these bobs and tanners, but that old noblesse oblige spirit of his has cropped up again. He feels that he must allow himself to be touched, because this greasy bird has a claim on him. He saved his life.'

'The greasy bird saved Freddie's life?'

'No. Freddie saved the greasy bird's life.'

'Then Freddie ought to be touching the greasy bird.'

'Not according to the code of the Widgeons.' The Crumpet sighed. 'Poor old Freddie – it's a shame, this constant drain on his meagre resources, after all he's been through.'

'What's he been through?' asked the junior Bean.

'You would not be far out,' replied the Crumpet gravely, 'if you said that he had been through the furnace.'

At the time when this story opens (said the Crumpet) Freddie was feeling a bit low. His heart had just been broken, and that always pulls him down. He had loved Dahlia Prenderby with every fibre of his being, and she had handed him the horse's laugh. He was, therefore, as you may suppose, in no mood for social gaiety: and when he got a note from his uncle, old Blicester, asking him to lunch at the Ritz, his first impulse was to refuse.

But as Lord Blicester was the source from which proceeded his quarterly allowance, he couldn't do that, of course. The old boy's invitations were commands. So he turned up at the eating-house and was sitting in the lobby, thinking long, sad thoughts of Dahlia Prenderby, when his host walked in.

'Ha, Frederick,' he said, having eased his topper and umbrella off on to a member of the staff. 'Glad you were able to come. I want to have a serious talk with you. I've been thinking a lot about you lately.'

'Have you, uncle?' said Freddie, touched.

'Yes,' said old Blicester. 'Wondering why you were such a blasted young blot on the escutcheon and trying to figure out some way of stopping you being the world's worst ass and pest. And I think I've found the solution. It would ease the situation very much, in my opinion, if you got married. Don't puff like that. What the devil are you puffing for?'

'I was sighing, uncle.'

'Well, don't. Good God! I thought you'd got asthma. Yes,' said Lord Blicester, 'I believe that if you were married and settled down, things might brighten considerably all round. I've known bigger ... well, no, scarcely that, perhaps ... I've known very nearly as big fools as you improve out of all recognition by marriage. And here is what I wanted to talk to you about. You will, no doubt, have been wondering why I am buying you a lunch in an infernally expensive place like this. I will tell you. My old friend, Lady Pinfold, is joining us in a few minutes with her daughter Dora. I have decided that she is the girl you shall marry. Excellent family, plenty of money of her own, and sense enough for two – which is just the right amount. So mind you make yourself attractive, if that is humanly possible, to Dora Pinfold.'

A weary, mirthless smile twisted Freddie's lips.

'All this – ' he began.

'And let me give you a warning. She is not one of your fast modern girls, so bear in mind when conversing with her that you are not in the smoking room of the Drones Club. Only carefully selected stories, and no limericks whatsoever.'

'All this – ' began Freddie again.

'Don't drink anything at lunch. She is strict in her views about that. And, talking of lunch, when the waiter comes round with the menu, don't lose your head. Keep an eye on the prices in the right-hand column.'

'All this,' said Freddie at last, getting a word in, 'is very kind of you, uncle, and I appreciate it. Your intentions are good. But I cannot marry this girl.'

Old Blicester nodded intelligently.

'I see what you mean. You feel it would be a shabby trick to play on any nice girl. True. There is much in what you say. But somebody has got to suffer in this world. You can't make an omelette without breaking eggs. So never mind the ethics of the thing. You go ahead and fascinate her, or I'll . . . Sh. Here they come.'

He got up and started to stump forward to greet a stout, elderly woman who was navigating through the doorway, and Freddie, following, suddenly halted in his tracks and nearly took a toss. He was looking at the girl floating along in the wake of the stout woman. In a blinding flash of revelation he saw that he had been all wrong in supposing that he had loved Dahlia Prenderby and all the other girls who had turned him down. Just boyish infatuations, he could see now. This was his soulmate. There was none like her, none. Freddie, as you know, always falls in love at first sight, and he had done so on this occasion, with a wallop.

His knees were wobbling under him as he went in to lunch, and he was glad to be able to sit down and take the weight off them.

The girl seemed to like him. Girls always do like Freddie at first. It is when the gruelling test of having him in their hair for several weeks comes that they throw in the towel. Over the fish and chips he and this Dora Pinfold fraternized like billy-o. True, it was mostly a case of her telling him about her dreams and ideals and him saying 'Oh, ah' and 'Oh, absolutely,' but that did not alter the fact that the going was good.

So much so that with the cheese Freddie, while not actually pressing her hand, was leaning over towards her at an angle of forty-five and saying why shouldn't they lap up their coffee quick at the conclusion of the meal and go and see a picture or something. And she said she would have loved it, only she had to be in Notting Hill at a quarter to three.

'I'm interested in a sort of Mission there,' she said.

'Great Scott!' said Freddie. 'Cocoa and good works, do you mean?'

'Yes. We are giving an entertainment this afternoon, to the mothers.'

Freddie nearly choked over his Camembert. A terrific idea had come to him.

If, he reflected, he was going to meet this girl again only at dinners and dances – the usual social round, I mean to say – all she would ever get to know about him was that he had a good appetite and india-rubber legs. Whereas, if he started frequenting Notting Hill in her company, he would be able to flash his deeper self on her. He could be suave, courteous, the *preux chevalier*, and shower her with those little attentions which make a girl sit up and say to herself: 'What ho!'

'I say,' he said, 'couldn't I come along?'

'Oh, it would bore you.'

'Not a bit. I could hover round and shove the old dears into their seats and so on. I'm good at that. I've been an usher at dozens of weddings.'

The girl reflected.

'I'll tell you what you can do, if you really want to help,' she said. 'We are a little short of talent. Can you sing?'

'Rather!'

'Then will you sing?'

'Absolutely.'

'That would be awfully kind of you. Any old song will do.'

'I shall sing,' said Freddie, directing at her a glance which he rather thinks – though he is not sure – made her blush in modest confusion, 'a number entitled, "When the Silver of the Moonlight Meets the Lovelight in Your Eyes."'

So directly lunch was over, off they popped, old Blicester beaming on Freddie and very nearly slapping him on the back – and no wonder, for his work had unquestionably been good – and as the clocks were striking three-thirty Freddie was up on the platform with the Vicar and a Union Jack behind him, the girl Dora at the piano at his side, and about two hundred Notting Hill mothers in front of him, letting it go like a Crosby.

He was a riot. Those mothers, he tells me, just sat back and ate it up. He did two songs, and they wanted a third. He did a third, and they wanted an encore. He did an encore, and they started whistling through their fingers till he came on and bowed. And when he came on and bowed, they insisted on a speech. And it was at this point, as he himself realizes now, that Freddie lost his cool judgment. He allowed himself to be carried away by the intoxication of the moment and went too far.

Briefly, what happened was that in a few cordial words he invited all those present to be his guests at a binge to be held in the mission hall that day week.

'Mothers,' said Freddie, 'this is on me. I shall expect you to the last mother. And if any mothers here have mothers of their own, I hope they will bring them along. There will be no stint. Buns and cocoa will flow like water. I thank you one and all.'

And it was only when he got home, still blinking from the bright light which he had encountered in the girl Dora's eyes as they met his and still half deafened by the rousing cheers which had greeted his remarks, that he remembered that all he had in the world was one pound, three shillings and fourpence.

Well, you can't entertain a multitude of mothers in slap-up style on one pound, three and fourpence, so it was obvious that he would be obliged to get into somebody's ribs for something substantial. And the only person he could think of who was good for the sum he required – twenty quid seemed to him about the figure – was old Blicester.

It would not be an easy touch. He realized that. The third Earl of Blicester was a man who, though well blessed with the world's goods, hated loosening up. Moths had nested in his pocket-book for years and raised large families. However, one of the fundamental facts of life is that you can't pick and choose when you want twenty quid – you have to go to the man who's got twenty quid. So he went round to tackle the old boy.

There was a bit of a lull when he got to the house. Some sort of by-election, it appeared, was pending down at Bottleton in the East End, and Lord Blicester had gone off there to take the chair at a meeting in the Conservative interest. So Freddie had to wait. But eventually he appeared, a bit hoarse from addressing the proletariat but in excellent fettle. He was very bucked at the way Freddie had shaped at the luncheon-table.

'You surprised me, my boy,' he said. 'I am really beginning to think that if you continue as you have begun and are careful, when you propose, to do it in a dim light so that she can't get a good look at you, you may win that girl.'

'And you want me to win her, don't you, uncle?'

'I do, indeed.'

'Then will you give me twenty pounds?'

The sunlight died out of Lord Blicester's face.

'Twenty pounds? What do you want twenty pounds for?'

'It is vital that I acquire that sum,' said Freddie. And in a few words he explained that he had pledged himself to lush up the mothers of Notting Hill on buns and cocoa a week from that day, and that if he welshed and failed to come through the girl would never forgive him – and rightly.

Lord Blicester listened with growing gloom. He had set his heart on this union, but the overhead made him quiver. The thought of parting with twenty pounds was like a dagger in his bosom.

'It won't cost twenty pounds.'

'It will.'

'You can do it on much less than that.'

'I don't see how. There must have been fully two hundred mothers present. They will bring friends and relations. Add gate-crashers, and I can't budget for less than four hundred. At a bob a nob.'

Lord Blicester pshawed. 'Preposterous!' he cried. 'A bob a nob, forsooth! Cocoa's not expensive.'

'But the buns. You are forgetting the buns.'

'Buns aren't expensive, either.'

'Well, how about hard-boiled eggs? Have you reflected, uncle, that there may be hard-boiled eggs?'

'Hard-boiled eggs? Good God, boy, what is this thing you're planning? A Babylonian orgy? There will be no question of hard-boiled eggs.'

'Well, all right. Then let us return to the buns. Allowing twelve per person . . .'

'Don't be absurd. Twelve, indeed! These are simple, God-fearing English mothers you are entertaining – not tapeworms. I'll give you ten pounds. Ten is ample.'

And nothing that Freddie could say would shake him. It was with a brace of fivers in his pocket that he left the other's presence, and every instinct in him told him that they would not be enough. Fifteen quid, in his opinion, was the irreducible minimum. He made his way to the club in pensive mood, his brain darting this way and that in the hope of scaring up some scheme for adding to his little capital. He was still brooding on a problem which seemed to grow each moment more hopeless of solution, when he entered the smoking room and found a group of fellows there, gathered about a kid in knicker-bockers. And not only were they gathered about this kid – they were practically fawning on him.

This surprised Freddie. He knew that a chap has to have something outstanding about him to be fawned upon at the Drones, and nothing in this child's appearance suggested that he was in any way exceptional. The only outstanding thing about him was his ears.

'What's all this?' he asked of Catsmeat Potter-Pirbright, who was hovering on the outskirts of the group.

'It's Barmy Phipps's cousin Egbert from Harrow,' said Catsmeat. 'Most remarkable chap. You see that catapult he's showing those birds. Well, he puts a Brazil nut in it and whangs off at things and hits them every time. It's a great gift, and you might think it would make him conceited. But no, success has not spoiled him. He is still quite simple and unaffected. Would you like his autograph?'

Freddie frankly did not believe the story. The whole nature of a Brazil nut, it being nobbly and of a rummy semicircular shape, unfits it to act as a projectile. The thing, he felt, might be just barely credible, perhaps, of one who was receiving his education at Eton, but Catsmeat had specifically stated that this lad was at Harrow, and his reason revolted at the idea of a Harrovian being capable of such a feat.

'What rot,' he said.

'It isn't rot,' said Catsmeat Potter-Pirbright, stung. 'Only just now he picked off a passing errand-boy as clean as a whistle.'

'Pure fluke.'

'Well, what'll you bet he can't do it again?'

A thrill ran through Freddie. He had found the way.

'A fiver!' he cried.

Well, of course, Catsmeat hadn't got a fiver, but he swiftly formed a syndicate to cover Freddie's money, and the stakes were deposited with the chap behind the bar and a Brazil nut provided for the boy Egbert at the club's expense. And it was as he fitted nut to elastic that Catsmeat Potter-Pirbright said 'Look.'

'Look,' said Catsmeat Potter-Pirbright. 'There's a taxi just drawing up with a stout buffer in it. Will you make this stout buffer the test? Will you bet that Egbert here doesn't knock off his topper as he pays the cabby?'

'Certainly,' said Freddie.

The cab stopped. The buffer alighted, his top hat gleaming in the sunshine. The child Egbert with incredible nonchalance drew his bead. The Brazil nut sang through the air. And the next moment Freddie was staggering back with his hands to his eyes, a broken man. For the hat, struck squarely abaft the binnacle, had leaped heavenwards and he was down five quid.

And the worst was yet to come. About a minute later he was informed that Lord Blicester had called to see him. He went to the small smoking room and found his uncle standing on the hearth-rug. He was staring in a puzzled sort of way at a battered top hat which he held in his hand.

'Most extraordinary thing,' he said. 'As I was getting out of my cab just now, something suddenly came whizzing out of the void and knocked my hat off. I think it must have been a small meteor. I am going to write to *The Times* about it. But never mind that. What I came for was to get fifty shillings from you.'

Freddie had already tottered on discovering that it was old Blicester who had been the victim of the boy Egbert's uncanny skill. These words made him totter again. That his uncle should be touching him instead of him touching his uncle gave him a sort of goose-fleshy feeling as if he were rubbing velvet the wrong way.

'Fifty shillings?' he bleated.

'Two pounds ten,' said old Blicester, making it clear to the meanest intelligence. 'After you left me, I was dissatisfied with your figures, so I went and consulted my cook, a most capable woman, as to the market price of buns and cocoa, and what she told me convinces me that you can do the whole thing comfortably on seven pounds ten. So I hurried here to recover the fifty shillings which I overpaid you. I can give you change.'

Five minutes later, Freddie was at a writing table with pen and paper, trying to work out how he stood. Of his original capital, two pounds ten shillings remained. According to his uncle, who had it straight from the cook's mouth, buns and cocoa could be provided for four hundred at a little over fourpence a head. It seemed incredible, but he knew that his uncle's cook, a level-headed woman named Bessemer, was to be trusted implicitly on points of this kind. No doubt the explanation was that a considerable reduction was given for quantity. When you buy your buns by the ton, you get them cheaper.

Very well then. The deficit to be made up appeared still to be five pounds. And where he was to get it was more than he could say. He couldn't very well go back to old Blicester and ask for a further donation, giving as his reason the fact that he had lost a fiver betting that a kid with wind-jammer ears wouldn't knock his, old Blicester's, hat off with a Brazil nut.

Then what to do? It was all pretty complex, and I am not surprised that for the next two or three days Freddie was at a loss.

During these days he continued to haunt Notting Hill. But though he was constantly in the society of the girl Dora, and though he was treated on all sides as the young Lord Bountiful, he could not bring himself to buck up and be fizzy. Wherever he went, the talk was this forthcoming beano of his, and it filled him with a haunting dread. Notting Hill was plainly planning to go for the buns and cocoa in a big way, and who – this was what he asked himself – who was going to foot the bill?

The ironical thing, he saw now, was that his original capital would have seen him through. There had been no need whatsoever for him to go plunging like that in the endeavour to bump up the kitty. When he reflected that, but for getting his figures twisted, he would now have been striding through Notting Hill with his chin up and his chest out and not a care on his mind, he groaned in spirit. He told me so himself. 'I groaned in spirit,' he said.

And then one afternoon, after he had explored every possible avenue, as he thought, without getting a bite, he suddenly stumbled on one that promised to bring home the gravy. Other avenues had let him down with a bump, but this one really did look the goods.

For what happened was that he learned that on that very evening the East Bottleton Palace of Varieties was holding its monthly Amateur Night and that the prize of victory – he reeled as he read the words – was a handsome five-pound note.

At the moment when he made this discovery, things had been looking their darkest. Freddie, in fact, was so up against it that he had come to the conclusion that the only thing to do, if he was to fulfil his honourable obligations, was to go to his uncle, confess all, and try to tap him again.

The old boy, apprised of the facts in the matter of his ruined topper, would unquestionably want to disembowel him, but he was so keen on the wedding coming off that it might just conceivably happen that he would confine himself to harsh words and at the end of a powerful harangue spring the much-needed.

Anyway, it was his only chance. He rang up the Blicester residence and was informed that the big chief was again down at Bottleton East presiding at one of those political meetings. At the Bottleton Palace of Varieties, said the butler. So, though he would much have preferred to go to Whipsnade and try to take a mutton chop away from a tiger, Freddie had a couple of quick ones, ate a clove and set off.

I don't suppose you are familiar with Bottleton East, except by name. It is a pretty tough sort of neighbourhood, rather like Lime-house only with fewer mysterious Chinamen. The houses are small and grey, cats abound, and anyone who has a bit of old paper or a piece of orange peel throws it on the pavement. It depressed Freddie a good deal, and he was feeling pretty well down among the wines and spirits when a burst of muffled cheering came to his ears, and he found that he was approaching the Bottleton Palace of Varieties.

And he was just toddling round to send in his name to old Blicester when he saw on the wall this poster announcing the Grand Amateur Night and the glittering reward offered to the performer who clicked.

It altered the whole aspect of things in a flash. What it meant was that that distressing interview with Lord Blicester could now be pigeonholed indefinitely. Here was the five he needed, as good as in his pocket.

This gay confidence on his part may surprise you. But you must remember that it was only a day or two since he had burned up the Notting Hill mothers with his crooning. A man who could put over a socko like that had little to fear, he felt, from any opposition a place like Bottleton East could bring against him.

There was just one small initial difficulty. He would require an accompanist, and it was rather a problem to see where he was to get one. At Notting Hill, you will recall, the girl Dora had tinkled the ivories on his behalf, but he could scarcely ask her to officiate on the present occasion, for – apart from anything else – secrecy was of the essence. For the same reason he could not get anyone from the Drones. The world must never know that Frederick Widgeon had been raising the wind by performing at Amateur Nights in the East End of London.

He walked on, musing. It was an annoying little snag to crop up just as everything looked nice and smooth.

However, his luck was in. Half-way down a grubby little street he saw a card in a window announcing that Jos. Waterbury gave piano lessons on those premises: and rightly reasoning that a bloke who could teach the piano would also know how to accompany, he knocked at the door. And after he had been subjected to a keen scrutiny by a mysterious eye through the keyhole, the door opened and he found himself vis-à-vis with the greasy bird whom you saw outside there just now.

The first few minutes of the interview were given up to mutual explanations. Freddie handed the greasy bird his card. The greasy bird said that he would not have kept Freddie waiting, only something in the timbre of his knock had given him the idea that he was Ginger Murphy, a gentleman friend of his with whom he had had a slight difference and who had expressed himself desirous of seeing the colour of his insides. Freddie explained that he wanted the greasy bird to accompany him on the piano at Amateur Night. And the greasy bird said that Freddie couldn't have made a wiser move, because he was an expert accompanist and having him with you on such an occasion was half the battle.

After this, there was a bit of haggling about terms, but in the end it was arranged that Freddie should pay the greasy bird five bob – half a crown down and the rest that night, and that they should meet at the stage door at eight sharp.

'If I'm not there,' said the greasy bird, 'you'll find me in the public bar of the Green Goose round the corner.'

'Right ho,' said Freddie. 'I shall sing "When the Silver of the Moonlight Meets the Lovelight in Your Eyes".'

'Ah, well,' said the greasy bird, who seemed a bit of a philosopher, 'I expect worse things happen at sea.'

Freddie then pushed off, on the whole satisfied with the deal. He hadn't liked this Jos. Waterbury much. Not quite the accompanist of his dreams. He would have felt kindlier towards him if he had bathed more recently and had smelled less strongly of unsweetened gin. Still, he was no doubt as good as could be had at the price. Freddie was not prepared to go higher than five bob, and that ruled out the chaps who play at Queen's Hall.

Having completed the major preliminary arrangements, Freddie now gave thought to make-up and appearance. The other competitors, he presumed, would present themselves to their public more or less aziz, but their circumstances were rather different from his own. In his case, a certain caution was indicated. His uncle appeared to be making quite a stamping ground of Bottleton East just now, and it would be disastrous if he happened to come along and see him doing his stuff. So though it was not likely that Lord Blicester would attend Amateur Night at the Palace of Varieties, he thought it best to be on the safe side and adopt some rude disguise.

After some meditation, he decided to conceal his features behind a strip of velvet and have himself announced as The Masked Troubadour.

He dined lightly at the club off oysters and a pint of stout, and at eight o'clock, after an afternoon spent in gargling throat tonic and saying 'Mi-mi-mi' to limber up the larynx, he arrived at the stage door.

Jos. Waterbury was there, wearing the unmistakable air of a man who has been more or less submerged in unsweetened gin for several hours, and, half a crown having changed hands, they proceeded to the wings together to await their turn.

It was about a quarter of an hour before they were called upon, and during this quarter of an hour Freddie tells me that his spirits soared heavenwards. It was so patently absurd, he felt, as he watched the local talent perform, to suppose that there could be any question of his ability to cop the gage of victory. He didn't know how these things were decided – by popular acclamation, presumably – but whatever system of marking might prevail it must inevitably land him at the head of the poll.

These Bottleton song-birds were all well-meaning – they spared no pains and gave of their best – but they had nothing that could by the remotest stretch of the word be described as Class. Five of them preceded him, and not one of the five could have held those Notting Hill mothers for a minute – let alone have wowed them as he had wowed them. These things are a matter of personality and technique. Either you have got personality and technique or you haven't. These chaps hadn't. He had. His position, he saw, was rather that of a classic horse put up against a lot of selling-platers.

So, as I say, he stood there for a quarter of an hour, muttering 'Mi-mi-mi' and getting more and more above himself: and finally, after a cove who looked like a plumber's mate had finished singing 'Just Break the News to Mother' and had gone off to sporadic applause, he saw the announcer jerking his thumb at him and realized that the moment had come.

He was not a bit nervous, he tells me. From what he had heard of these Amateur Nights, he had rather supposed that he might for the first minute or so have to quell and dominate a pretty tough audience. But the house seemed in a friendly mood, and he walked on to the stage, adjusting his mask, with a firm and confident tread.

The first jarring note was struck when the announcer turned to inquire his name. He was a stout, puffy man with bags under his eyes and a face the colour of a damson, and on seeing Freddie he shied like a horse. He backed a step or two, throwing up his arms, as he did so, in a defensive sort of way.

'It's all right,' said Freddie.

The man seemed reassured. He gulped once or twice, but became calmer.

'What's all this?' he asked.

'It's quite all right,' said Freddie. 'Just announce me as The Masked Troubadour.'

'Coo! You gave me a nasty shock. Masked what?'

'Troubadour,' said Freddie, spacing the syllables carefully.

He walked over to the piano, where Jos. Waterbury had seated himself and was playing chords.

'Ready?' he said.

Jos. Waterbury looked up, and a slow look of horror began to spread itself over his face. He shut his eyes, and his lips moved silently. Freddie thinks he was praying.

'Buck up,' said Freddie sharply. 'We're just going to kick off.'

Jos. Waterbury opened his eyes.

'Gawd?' he said. 'Is that you?'

'Of course it's me.'

'What have you done to your face?'

This was a point which the audience, also, seemed to wish thrashed out. Interested voices made themselves heard from the gallery.

'Wot's all this, Bill?'

'It's a masked trebudder,' said the announcer.

'Wot's a trebudder?'

'This is.' The damson-faced man seemed to wash his hands of the whole unpleasant affair. 'Don't blame me, boys,' he begged. 'That's what he says he is.'

Jos. Waterbury bobbed up again. For the last few moments he had been sitting muttering to himself.

'It isn't right,' said Jos. Waterbury. 'It isn't British. It isn't fair to lead a man on and then suddenly turn round on him – '

'Shut up!' hissed Freddie. All this, he felt, was subversive. Getting the audience into a wrong mood. Already the patrons' geniality was beginning to ebb. He could sense a distinct lessening of that all-pals-together spirit. One or two children were crying.

'Laydeezun-gennelmun,' bellowed the damson-faced man, 'less blinking noise, if you please. I claim your kind indulgence for this 'ere trebudder.'

'That's all right,' said Jos. Waterbury, leaving the piano and coming downstage. 'He may be a trebudder or he may not, but I appeal to this fair-minded audience – is it just, is it ethical, for a man suddenly to pop out on a fellow who's had a couple – '

'Come on,' cried the patrons. 'Less of it.' And a voice from the gallery urged Jos. Waterbury to put his head in a bucket.

'All right,' said Jos. Waterbury, who was plainly in dark mood. 'All right. But you haven't heard the last of this by any means.'

He reseated himself at the piano, and Freddie began to sing 'When the Silver of the Moonlight Meets the Lovelight in Your Eyes'.

The instant he got going, he knew that he had never been in better voice in his life. Whether it was the oysters or the stout or the throat tonic, he didn't know, but the notes were floating out as smooth as syrup. It made him feel a better man to listen to himself.

And yet there was something wrong. He spotted it almost from the start. For some reason he was falling short of perfection. And then suddenly he got on to it. In order to make a song a smash, it is not enough for the singer to be on top of his form. The accompanist, also, must do his bit. And the primary thing a singer expects from his accompanist is that he shall play the accompaniment of the song he is singing.

This Jos. Waterbury was not doing, and it was this that was causing the sweet-bells-jangled effect which Freddie had observed. What the greasy bird was actually playing, he could not say, but it was not the twiddly-bits to 'When the Silver of the Moonlight Meets the Lovelight in Your Eyes'.

It was obviously a case for calling a conference. A bit of that inter-office communication stuff was required. He made a sideways leap to the piano, encouraging some of the audience to suppose that he was going into his dance.

'*There is silver in the moonlight* . . . What the hell are you playing?' sang Freddie.

'Eh?' said Jos. Waterbury.

'*But its silver tarnished seems* . . . You're playing the wrong song.'

'What are you singing?'

'*When it meets the golden lovelight* . . . I'm singing "When the Silver of the Moonlight Meets the Lovelight in Your Eyes", you silly ass.'

'Coo!' said Jos. Waterbury. 'I thought you told me "Top Hat, White Tie and Tails". All right, cocky, now we're off.'

He switched nimbly into the correct channels, and Freddie was able to sing '*In your eyes that softly beams*' without that set-your-teeth-on-edge feeling that he had sometimes experienced when changing gears unskilfully in his two-seater. But the mischief had been done. His grip on his audience had weakened. The better element on the lower floor were still sticking it out like men, but up in the gallery a certain liveliness had begun to manifest itself. The raspberry was not actually present, but he seemed to hear the beating of its wings.

To stave it off, he threw himself into his warbling with renewed energy. And such was his magnetism and technique that he very nearly put it over. The muttering died away. One of the crying children stopped crying. And though another was sick Freddie thinks this must have been due to something it had eaten. He sang like one inspired.

> 'Oh the moon is bright and radiant,
> But its radiance fades and dies
> When the silver of the moonlight
> Meets the lovelight in your eyes.'

It was when he had reached this point, with that sort of lingering, caressing, treacly tremolo on the 'eyes' which makes all the difference, that the mothers of Notting Hill, unable to restrain themselves any longer, had started whooping and stamping and whistling through their fingers. And there is little doubt, he tells me, that ere long these Bottletonians would have begun expressing themselves in similar fashion, had not Jos. Waterbury, who since the recent conference had been as good as gold, at this moment recognized an acquaintance in the front row of the stalls.

This was a large, red-haired man in a sweater and corduroy trousers who looked as if he might be in some way connected with the jellied eel industry. His name was Murphy, and it was he who, as Jos. Waterbury had informed Freddie at their first meeting, wished to ascertain the colour of the accompanist's insides.

What drew Jos. Waterbury's attention to this eel-jellier – if eel-jellier he was – was the circumstance of the latter, at this juncture, throwing an egg at him. It missed its mark, but it had the effect of causing the pianist to stop playing and rise and advance to the footlights. There was a cold look of dislike in his eyes. It was plain that there was imperfect communion of spirit between these two men. He bent over and asked:

'Did you throw that egg?'

To which the red-haired man's reply was:

'R.'

'You did, did you?' said Jos. Waterbury. 'Well, what price sausage and mashed?'

Freddie says he cannot understand these East End blokes. Their psychology is a sealed book to him. It is true that Jos. Waterbury had spoken in an unpleasant sneering manner, but even so he could see nothing in his words to stir the passions and cause a human being to lose his kinship with the divine. Personally, I am inclined to think that there must have been some hidden significance in them, wounding the eel-jellier's pride, so that when Jos. Waterbury said 'What price sausage and mashed?' the phrase did not mean to him what it would to you or me, but something deeper. Be that as it may, it brought the red-haired chap to his feet, howling like a gorilla.

The position of affairs was now as follows: the red-haired chap was saying wait till he got Jos. Waterbury outside. Jos. Waterbury was saying that he could eat the red-haired chap for a relish with his tea. Three more children had begun to cry, and the one who had stopped crying had begun again. Forty, perhaps – or it may have been fifty voices were shouting 'Oy!' The announcer was bellowing 'Order, please, order!' Another infant in the gallery was being sick. And Freddie was singing verse two of 'When the Silver of the Moonlight Meets the Lovelight in Your Eyes.'

Even at Queen's Hall I don't suppose this sort of thing could have gone on long. At the Bottleton Palace of Varieties the pause before

the actual outbreak of Armageddon was only of a few seconds'
duration. Bottleton East is crammed from end to end with coster-
mongers dealing in tomatoes, potatoes, Brussels sprouts and fruits in
their season, and it is a very negligent audience there that forgets to
attend a place of entertainment with full pockets.

Vegetables of all kinds now began to fill the air, and Freddie, abandoning his Art as a wash-out, sought refuge behind the piano. But
this move, though shrewd, brought him only a temporary respite. No
doubt this audience had had to deal before with singers who hid
behind pianos. It took them perhaps a minute to find the range, and
then some kind of a dried fish came dropping from the gallery and
caught him in the eye. Very much the same thing, if you remember,
happened to King Harold at the battle of Hastings.

Forty seconds later, he was in the wings, brushing a tomato off his
coat.

In circumstances like these, you might suppose that Freddie's soul
would have been a maelstrom of mixed emotions. This, however, was
not the case. One emotion only gripped him. He had never been more
single-minded in his life. He wanted to get hold of Jos. Waterbury
and twist his head off and stuff it down his throat. It is true that the
red-haired chap had started the final mix-up by throwing an egg, but
an accompanist worth his salt, felt Freddie, should have treated a
mere egg with silent disdain, not deserted his post in order to argue
about the thing. Rightly or wrongly, he considered that it was to Jos.
Waterbury that his downfall was due. But for that sozzled pianist, he
held, a triumph might have been his as outstanding as his furore at
Notting Hill.

Jos. Waterbury had disappeared, but fortunately Freddie was now
not unfamiliar with his habits. His first act, on reaching the stage
door and taking a Brussels sprout out of his hair, was to ask to be
directed to the Green Goose. And there, a few moments later, he
came upon the man he sought. He was standing at the counter
drinking an unsweetened gin.

Now, just before the tiger of the jungle springs upon its prey, I am
told by chaps who know tigers of the jungle, there is always a moment
when it pauses, flexing its muscles and rubbing its feet in the resin. It
was so with Freddie at this point. He did not immediately leap upon
Jos. Waterbury, but stood clenching and unclenching his fists, while
his protruding eyes sought out soft spots in the man. His ears were
red and he breathed heavily.

The delay was fatal. Other people were familiar with Jos. Waterbury's habits. Just as he was about to take off, the swing door flew
open violently, disclosing the red-haired man. And a moment later

the red-haired man, pausing only to spit on his hands, had gone into action.

The words we speak in our heat seldom stand the acid test. In the very first seconds of the encounter it would have become plain to the poorest judge of form that in stating that he could eat the red-haired man for a relish with his tea Jos. Waterbury had overestimated his powers. He put up the rottenest kind of show, being as chaff before the red-haired bloke's sickle. Almost before the proceedings had begun, he had stopped a stinker with his chin and was on the sawdust.

In places like Bottleton East, when you are having a scrap and your antagonist falls, you don't wait for anyone to count ten – you kick him in the slats. This is a local rule. And it was so obvious to Freddie that this was what the red-haired bird was planning to do that he did not hesitate, but with a passionate cry rushed into the fray. He isn't a chap who goes out of his way to get mixed up in bar-room brawls, but the sight of this red-haired fellow murdering the bounder he wanted to murder himself seemed to him to give him no option. He felt that his claim was being jumped, and his generous spirit resented it.

And so moved was he by the thought of being done out of his rights, that he might have put up a very pretty fight indeed had not the chucker-out attached to the premises intervened.

When the summons for his professional services reached him, the honest fellow had been enjoying a pint and a bit of bread and cheese in a back room. He now came in, wiping his mouth.

These chuckers-out are no fools. A glance showed this one that a big, beefy, dangerous-looking chap was having a spot of unpleasantness with a slim, slight, slender chap, and with swift intelligence and sturdy common sense he grabbed the slim, slender chap. To pick Freddie up like a sack of coals and carry him to the door and hurl him out into the great open spaces was with him the work of a moment.

And so it came about that Lord Blicester, who was driving home after one of his meetings in the Conservative interest, became aware of stirring doings afoot off-stage left, and the next moment perceived his nephew Frederick coming through the air like a shooting star.

He signalled to the chauffeur to stop and poked his head out of the window.

'Frederick!' he called – not, as you may well suppose, quite grasping the gist.

Freddie did not reply. Already he was re-entering the swing door in order to take up the argument at the point where it had been broken off. He was by now a bit stirred. Originally he had wanted to assassinate Jos. Waterbury, but since then his conception had broadened, if you know what I mean. He now wished to blot out the red-haired chap as well – also the chucker-out and anybody else who crossed his path.

Old Blicester emerged from the car, just in time to see his flesh and blood come popping out again.

'Frederick!' he cried. 'What is the meaning of this?' And he seized him by the arm.

Well, anybody could have told him he was asking for it. This was no time to seize Freddie by the arm. There was an arm left over which old Blicester hadn't seized, and with this Freddie smote him a snappy one in the midriff. Then, passing a weary hand over his brow, he made for the swing door again.

The catch about all this sort of thing – running amuck, I mean, and going berserk, or whatever they call it – is that there inevitably comes a morning after. The following morning found Freddie in bed, and so did old Blicester. He appeared as early as nine a.m., rousing Freddie from a troubled sleep, and what he wanted, it seemed, was a full explanation. And when Freddie, who was too weak for polished subterfuge, had given him a full explanation, not omitting the incident of the Brazil nut and the top hat, he put on the black cap.

He had changed his mind about that marriage. It was not right, he said – it was not human – to inflict a fool like Freddie on so sweet a girl, or on any girl, for that matter. After a powerful passage, in which he pointed this out, he delivered sentence. Freddie was to take the afternoon train to Blicester Regis, repair by the station cab to Blicester Towers, and at Blicester Towers to remain secluded till further notice. Only thus, in his opinion, could the world be rendered safe for the human race. So there was nothing for Freddie to do but ring up the girl, Dora, and inform her that the big binge was off.

The statement was not very well received.

'Oh, dear,' she said, and Freddie, reading between the lines, could see that what she really meant was 'Oh, hell.' 'Why?'

Freddie explained that he had got to go down to the country that afternoon till further notice. The girl's manner changed. Her voice, which had been sniffy, brightened.

'Oh, but that's all right,' she said. 'We shall all miss you, of course, but I can send you the bill.'

'Something in that,' said Freddie. 'Only the trouble is, you see, I can't pay it.'

'Why not?'

'I haven't any money.'

'Why haven't you any money?'

Freddie braced himself.

'Well, the fact is that in a mistaken moment of enthusiasm, thinking – wrongly, as it turned out – that I was on a pinch, I betted – '

And in broken accents he told her the whole story. Wasted, of course, because she had hung up with a sharp cry at the word 'betted'. And about ten minutes later, after saying 'Hullo, hullo' a good many times, he, too, hung up – sombrely, because something told him that one more girl whom he had loved had gone out of his life.

And no sooner had he left his rooms and tottered into the street, his intention – and a very sound one – being to make his way to the club and have a few before it was too late, something small and greasy nipped out from the shadows. To cut a long story short, Jos. Waterbury.

And Freddie was just about to summon up all that remained of his frail strength after last night's doings and let him have it right in the eyeball, when Jos. Waterbury began to thank him for saving his life.

Well, you can't swat a man who is thanking you for saving his life, not if your own is ruled by the noblesse oblige code of the Widgeons. And when he tells you that times are hard and moots the possibility of your being able to spare a trifle, you cannot pass on unheeding. It was a bob that time, and on Freddie's return to London some three weeks later – the very day, oddly enough, when he read in the *Morning Post* that a marriage had been arranged and would shortly take place between Percival Alexander, eldest son of Gregory Hotchkiss, Esq., and Mrs Hotchkiss, and Dora, only daughter of the late Sir Ramsworthy Pinfold and Lady Pinfold – it was two, Freddie not having anything smaller on him. And there you are.

There was a thoughtful silence.

'And so it goes on,' said the Crumpet.

'So it goes on,' said the Senior Bean.

The Junior Bean agreed that so it went on.

10

ALL'S WELL WITH BINGO

A Bean and a Crumpet were in the smoking room of the Drones Club having a quick one before lunch, when an Egg who had been seated at the writing table in the corner rose and approached them.

'How many "r's" in "intolerable"?' he asked.

'Two,' said the Crumpet. 'Why?'

'I am writing a strong letter to the Committee,' explained the Egg, 'drawing their attention to the intolerable... Great Scot!' he cried, breaking off. 'There he goes again!'

A spasm contorted his face. Outside in the passage a fresh young voice had burst into a gay song with a good deal of vo-de-o-de-o about it. The Bean cocked an attentive ear as it died away in the direction of the dining room.

'Who is this linnet?' he inquired.

'Bingo Little, blast him. He's always singing nowadays. That's what I'm writing my strong letter to the Committee about – the intolerable nuisance of this incessant heartiness of his. Because it isn't only his singing. He slaps backs. Only yesterday he came sneaking up behind me in the bar and sloshed me between the shoulder-blades, saying "Aha!" as he did so. Might have choked me. How many "s's" in "incessant"?'

'Three,' said the Crumpet.

'Thanks,' said the Egg.

He returned to the writing-table. The Bean seemed perplexed.

'Odd,' he said. 'Very odd. How do you account for young Bingo carrying on like this?'

'Just *joie de vivre*.'

'But he's married. Didn't he marry some female novelist or other?'

'That's right. Rosie M. Banks, authoress of *Only A Factory Girl*, *Mervyne Keene, Clubman*, *'Twas Once In May*, and other works. You see her name everywhere. I understand she makes a packet with the pen.'

'I didn't know married men had any *joie de vivre*.'

'Not many, of course. But Bingo's union has been an exceptionally happy one. He and the other half of the sketch have hit it off from the start like a couple of love-birds.'

'Well, he oughtn't to slap backs about it.'

'You don't know the inside facts. Bingo is no mere wanton back-slapper. What has made him that way at the moment is the fact that he recently had a most merciful escape. There was within a toucher of being very serious trouble in the home.'

'But you said they were like a couple of love-birds.'

'Quite. But even with love-birds circumstances can arise which will cause the female love-bird to get above herself and start throwing her weight about. If Mrs Bingo had got on Bingo what at one time it appeared inevitable that she must get on him, it would have kept her in conversation for the remainder of their married lives. She is a sweet little thing, one of the best, but women are women and I think that there can be no doubt that she would have continued to make passing allusions to the affair right up to the golden wedding day. The way Bingo looks at it is that he has escaped the fate that is worse than death, and I am inclined to agree with him.'

The thing started one morning when Bingo returned to the love-nest for a bite of lunch after taking the Pekinese for a saunter. He was in the hall trying to balance an umbrella on the tip of his nose, his habit when at leisure, and Mrs Bingo came out of her study with a wrinkled brow and a couple of spots of ink on her chin.

'Oh, there you are,' she said. 'Bingo, have you ever been to Monte Carlo?'

Bingo could not help wincing a little at this. Unwittingly, the woman had touched an exposed nerve. The thing he had always wanted to do most in the world was to go to Monte Carlo, for he had a system which couldn't fail to clean out the Casino; but few places, as you are probably aware, are more difficult for a married man to sneak off to.

'No,' he said with a touch of moodiness. Then, recovering his usual sunny aplomb: 'Look,' he said. 'Watch, old partner in sickness and in health. I place the umbrella so. Then, maintaining a perfect equilibrium . . .'

'I want you to go there at once,' said Mrs Bingo.

Bingo dropped the umbrella. You could have knocked him down with a toothpick. For a moment, he tells me, he thought that he must be dreaming some beautiful dream.

'It's for my book. I can't get on without some local colour.'

Bingo grasped the gist. Mrs Bingo had often discussed this business of local colour with him. Nowadays he knew, if you are providing wholesome fiction for the masses, you have simply got to get your atmosphere right. The customers have become cagey. They know too much. Chance your arm with the *mise en scène*, and before you can say 'What ho,' you've made some bloomer and people are writing you nasty letters, beginning 'Dear Madam, Are you aware – ?'

'And I can't go myself. There's the Pen and Ink dinner on Friday, and on Tuesday the Writers' Club is giving a luncheon to Mrs Carrie Melrose Bopp, the American novelist. And any moment now I shall be coming to the part where Lord Peter Shipbourne breaks the bank. So do you think you could possibly go, Bingo darling?'

Bingo was beginning to understand how the Israelites must have felt when that manna started descending in the wilderness.

'Of course I'll go, old egg,' he said heartily. 'Anything I can – '

His voice trailed away. A sudden thought had come, biting into his soul like acid. He had remembered that he hadn't a bean to his name. He had lost every penny he possessed two weeks before on a horse called Bounding Beauty which was running – if you could call it running – in the two-thirty at Haydock Park.

The trouble with old Bingo is that he will allow his cooler judgment to be warped by dreams and omens. Nobody had known better than he that by the ruling of the form-book Bounding Beauty hadn't a chance: but on the eve of the race he had a nightmare in which he saw his Uncle Wilberforce dancing the rumba in the nude on the steps of the National Liberal Club and, like a silly ass, accepted this as a bit of stable information. And bang, as I say, had gone every penny he had in the world.

For a moment he reeled a bit. Then he brightened. Rosie, he reasoned, would scarcely expect him to undertake an irksome job like sweating all the way over to Monte Carlo without financing the tedious expedition.

'Of course, of course, of course,' he said. 'Yes, rather! I'll start tomorrow. And about expenses. I suppose a hundred quid would see me through, though two would be still better, and even three wouldn't hurt...'

'Oh, no, that's all right,' said Mrs Bingo. 'You won't need any money.'

Bingo gulped like an ostrich swallowing a brass door-knob.

'Not ... need ... any ... money?'

'Except a pound or two for tips and so on. Everything is arranged. Dora Spurgeon is at Cannes, and I'm going to phone her to get you a room at the Hôtel de Paris at Monte Carlo, and all the bills will be sent to my bank.'

Bingo had to gulp a couple more times before he was able to continue holding up his end of the duologue.

'But I take it,' he said in a low voice, 'that you want me to hobnob with the international spies and veiled women and so forth and observe their habits carefully, don't you? This will run into money. You know what international spies are. It's champagne for them every time, and no half-bots, either.'

'You needn't bother about the spies. I can imagine them. All I want is the local colour. An exact description of the Rooms and the Square and all that. Besides, if you had a lot of money, you might be tempted to gamble.'

'What!' cried Bingo. 'Gamble? Me?'

'No, no,' said Mrs Bingo remorsefully. 'I'm wronging you, of course. Still, I think I'd sooner we did it in the way I've arranged.'

So there you have the position of affairs, and you will not be surprised to learn that poor old Bingo made an indifferent lunch, toying with the minced chicken and pushing the roly-poly pudding away untasted. His manner during the meal was distrait, for his brain was racing like a dynamo. Somehow he had got to get the stuff. But how? How?

Bingo, you see, is not a man who finds it easy to float a really substantial loan. People know too much about his financial outlook. He will have it in sackfuls some day, of course, but until he realizes on his Uncle Wilberforce – who is eighty-six and may quite easily go to par – the wolf, so far as he is concerned, will always be in or about the vestibule. The public is aware of this, and it makes the market sluggish.

It seemed to him, brooding over the thing, that his only prospect for the sort of sum he required was Oofy Prosser. Oofy, while not an easy parter, is a millionaire, and a millionaire was what he required. So round about cocktail time he buzzed off to the club, only to be informed that Oofy was abroad. The disappointment was so severe that he was compelled to go to the smoking room and have a restorative. I was there when he came in, and so haggard and fishlike was his demeanour that I asked him what was up, and he told me all.

'You couldn't lend me between twenty and twenty-five, or, better still, thirty quid, could you?' he said.

I said 'No, I couldn't,' and he heaved a long, low, quivering sigh.

'And so it goes on,' he said. 'That's Life. Here I am with this unique opportunity of making a stupendous fortune, and crippled for lack of essential capital. Did you ever hear of a chap called Garcia?'

'No.'

'Skinned the Monte Carlo Administration of a hundred thousand quid in his day. Even hear of a chap called Darnborough?'

'No.'

'Eighty-three thousand of the best was what he pocketed. Did you ever hear of a chap called Owers?'

'No.'

'His winning streak lasted for more than twenty years. These three birds of whom I speak simply went to Monte Carlo and lolled back in their chairs with fat cigars, and the Casino just thrust the money on them. And I don't suppose any of them had a system like mine. Oh, hell, a thousand curses,' said Bingo.

Well, there isn't much you can say when a fellow's in the depths like that. The only thing I could suggest was that he should put some little trinket up the spout temporarily. His cigarette case, for instance, I said; and it was then that I learned that that cigarette case of his is not the solid gold we have always imagined. Tin, really. And except for the cigarette case, it appeared, the only trinket he had ever possessed was a diamond brooch which, being in funds at the time as the result of a fortunate speculation at Catterick Bridge, he had bought Mrs Bingo for a birthday present.

It all seemed pretty hopeless, accordingly, so I merely offered him my heartfelt sympathy and another snootful. And next morning he steamed off on the eleven o'clock express, despair in his soul and in his pocket a notebook, four pencils, his return ticket, and about three pounds for tips and so on. And shortly before lunch on the following day he was alighting at Monte Carlo station.

I don't know if you remember a song some years ago that went 'Ti-um-ti-um-ti-um-ti-um, Ti-um-ti-um-ti-ay,' and then, after a bit more of that, finished up:

Ti-um-ti-um-ti-um-ti-UM,
The curse of an aching heart.

You don't hear it much nowadays, but at one time you were extraordinarily apt to get it shot at you by bassos at smoking concerts and entertainments in aid of the Church Organ Fund in the old village hall. They would pause for a moment after the 'UM' and take a breath that came up from their ankle bones, and then:

It's the curse of an A-ching heart.

Most unpleasant, of course, the whole thing, and I wouldn't have mentioned it, only the phrase absolutely puts in a nutshell the way poor old Bingo felt during his first two days at Monte Carlo. He had an aching heart, and he cursed like billy-o. And I'm not surprised, poor chap, for he was suffering severe torments.

All day long, though it was like twisting the knife in the wound, he would wander through the Rooms, trying out that system of his on paper; and the more he tried it out, the more iron-clad it revealed itself. Simply couldn't lose.

By bedtime on the second night he found that, if he had been playing in hundred-franc chips, he would have been no less than two hundred and fifty pounds ahead – just like that. In short, there was all that stuff – his for the picking up, as you might say – and he couldn't get it.

Garcia would have got it. Darnborough would have got it. So would Owers. But he couldn't. Simply, mark you, for lack of a trifling spot of initial capital which a fellow like Oofy Prosser could have slipped him and never felt it. Pretty bitter.

And then, on the third morning, as he sat glancing through the newspaper over the breakfast-table, he saw a news item which brought him up in his chair with a jerk, choking over his coffee.

Among the recent arrivals at the Hôtel Magnifique at Nice, it said, were Their Serene Highnesses the Prince and Princess of Graustark, His Majesty the ex-King of Ruritania, Lord Percy Poffin, the Countess of Goffin, Major-General Sir Everard Slurk, K.V.O., and Mr Prosser.

Well, of course, it might be some other brand of Prosser, but Bingo didn't think so. An hotel where Serene Highnesses were to be found was just the place for which a bally snob like Oofy would have made a bee-line. He rushed to the telephone and was presently in communication with the concierge.

'Hullo? Yes?' said the concierge. 'This is the Hôtel Magnifique. Hall porter speaking.'

'*Dites-moi*,' said Bingo. '*Esker-vous avez dans votre hôtel un monsieur nommé* Prosser?'

'Yes, sir. Quite correct. There is a Mr Prosser staying in the hotel.'

'*Est-il un oiseau avec beaucoup de* . . . Oh, hell, what's the French for "pimples"?'

'The word you are trying to find is *bouton*,' said the concierge. 'Yes, sir, Mr Prosser is liberally pimpled.'

'Then put me through to his room,' said Bingo. And pretty soon he heard a sleepy and familiar voice hullo-ing.

'Hullo, Oofy, old man,' he cried. 'This is Bingo Little.'

'Oh, my God!' said Oofy, and something in his manner warned Bingo that it would be well to proceed with snakiness and caution.

There were, he knew, two things which rendered Oofy Prosser a difficult proposition for the ear-biter. In the first place, owing to his habit of mopping it up at late parties, he nearly always had a dyspeptic headache. In the second place, his position as the official moneyed man of the Drones Club had caused him to become shy and wary, like

a bird that's been a good deal shot over. You can't touch a chap like
that on the telephone at ten in the morning. It would, he perceived, if
solid results were to be obtained, be necessary to sweeten Oofy.

'I just this minute saw in the paper that you were in these parts,
Oofy, old man. A wonderful surprise it was. "Gosh," I said. "Golly,"
I said. "Dear old Oofy," I said. "Well, well, well!"'

'Get on with it,' said Oofy. 'What do you want?'

'Why, to give you lunch, of course, old chap,' said Bingo.

Yes, he had made the great decision. That money which he had
been earmarking for tips must be diverted to another end. It might
lead to his having to sneak out of the hotel at the conclusion of his
visit with his face scarlet and his ears hanging down, but the risk had
to be taken. Nothing venture, nothing have.

At the other end of the telephone he heard a sort of choking gasp.

'There must be something wrong with this wire,' said Oofy. 'It
sounds just as if you were saying you want to give me lunch.'

'So I am.'

'*Give* me lunch?'

'That's right.'

'What, pay the bill?'

'Yes.'

There was a silence.

'I must send this to Ripley,' said Oofy.

'Ripley?'

'The Believe-it-or-not man.'

'Oh!' said Bingo. He was not quite sure that he liked Oofy's
attitude, but he remained sunny. 'Well, where and when? What
time? What place?'

'We may as well lunch here. Come fairly early, because I'm going
to the races this afternoon.'

'Right,' said Bingo. 'I'll be on the mat at one sharp.'

And at one sharp there he was, his little all in his pocket. His
emotions, he tells me, as he drove in on the Monte Carlo–Nice bus,
were mixed. One moment, he was hoping that Oofy would have his
usual dyspeptic headache, because that would blunt his, Oofy's,
appetite and enable him, Bingo, to save something out of the wreck:
the next, he was reminding himself that an Oofy with dull, shooting
pains about the temples would be less likely to come across. It was all
very complex.

Well, as it turned out, Oofy's appetite was the reverse of blunted.
The extraordinary position in which he found himself – guest and not
host to a fellow-member of the Drones – seemed to have put an edge
on it. It is not too much to say that from the very outset he ate like a

starving python. The light, casual way in which he spoke to the head waiter about hot-house grapes and asparagus froze Bingo to the marrow. And when – from force of habit, no doubt – he called for the wine list and ordered a nice, dry champagne, it began to look to Bingo as if the bill for this binge was going to resemble something submitted to Congress by President Roosevelt in aid of the American Farmer.

However, though once or twice – notably when Oofy started wading into the caviare – he had to clench his fists and summon up all his iron self-control, he did not on the whole repine. Each moment, as the feast proceeded, he could see his guest becoming more and more mellow. It seemed merely a question of time before the milk of human kindness would come gushing out of him as if the dam had burst. Feeling that a cigar and liqueur ought just about to do the trick, Bingo ordered them: and Oofy, unbuttoning the last three buttons of his waistcoat, leaned back in his chair.

'Well,' said Oofy, beaming, 'this will certainly be something to tell my grandchildren. I mean, that I once lunched with a member of the Drones Club and didn't get stuck with the bill. Listen, Bingo, I'd like to do something for you in return.'

Bingo felt like some great actor who has received his cue. He leaned forward and relighted Oofy's cigar with a loving hand. He also flicked a speck of dust off his coat-sleeve.

'And what I'm going to do is this. I'm going to give you a tip. On these races this afternoon. Back Spotted Dog for the *Prix Honoré Sauvan*. A sure winner.'

'Thanks, Oofy, old man,' said Bingo. 'That's splendid news. If you will lend me a tenner, then, Oofy, old boy, I'll put it on.'

'What do you want me to lend you a tenner for?'

'Because, after I've paid the lunch bill, Oofy, old chap, I shan't have any money.'

'You won't need any money,' said Oofy, and Bingo wondered how many more people were going to make this blithering remark to him. 'My London bookie is staying here. He will accommodate you in credit, seeing that you are a friend of mine.'

'But doesn't it seem a pity to bother him with a lot of extra book-keeping, Oofy, old fellow?' said Bingo, flicking another speck of dust off Offy's other coat-sleeve. 'Much better if you would just lend me a tenner.'

'Joking aside,' said Oofy, 'I think I'll have another kümmel.'

And it was at this moment, when the conversation appeared to have reached a deadlock and there seemed no hope of finding a formula, that a stout, benevolent-looking man approached their table. From the fact that he and Oofy at once began to talk odds and figures, Bingo deduced that this must be the bookie from London.

'And my friend, Mr Little,' said Oofy, in conclusion, 'wants a tenner on Spotted Dog for the *Prix Honoré Sauvan*.'

And Bingo was just about to shake his head and say that he didn't think his wife would like him to bet, when the glorious Riviera sunshine, streaming in through the window by which they sat, lit up Oofy's face and he saw that it was a perfect mass of spots. A moment later, he perceived that the bookie had a pink spot on his nose and the waiter, who was now bringing the bill, a bountifully spotted forehead. A thrill shot through him. These things, he knew, are sent to us for a purpose.

'Right ho,' he said. 'A tenner at the current odd.'

And then they all went off to the races. The *Prix Honoré Sauvan* was the three o'clock. A horse called Lilium won it. Kerry second, Maubourget third, Ironside fourth, Irresistible fifth, Sweet and Lovely sixth, Spotted Dog seventh. Seven ran. So there was Bingo owing ten quid to this bookie and not a chance of a happy ending unless the fellow would consent to let the settlement stand over for a bit.

So he buttonholed the bookie and suggested this, and the bookie said 'Certainly.'

'Certainly,' said the bookie. He put his hand on Bingo's shoulder and patted it. 'I like you, Mr Little,' he said.

'Do you?' said Bingo, putting his hand on the bookie's and patting that. 'Do you, old pal?'

'I do indeed,' said the bookie. 'You remind me of my little boy Percy, who took the knock the year Worcester Sauce won the Jubilee Handicap. Bronchial trouble. So when you ask me to wait for my money, I say of course I'll wait for my money. Suppose we say till next Friday?'

Bingo blenched a bit. The period he had had in mind had been something more along the lines of a year or eighteen months.

'Well,' he said, 'I'll try to brass up then ... but you know how it is ... you mustn't be disappointed if ... this world-wide money shortage ... circumstances over which I have no control...'

'You think you may not be able to settle?'

'I'm a bit doubtful.'

The bookie pursed his lips.

'I do hope you will,' he said, 'and I'll tell you why. It's silly to be superstitious, I know, but I can't help remembering that every single bloke that's ever done me down for money has had a nasty accident occur to him. Time after time, I've seen it happen.'

'Have you?' said Bingo, beginning to exhibit symptoms of

bronchial trouble, like the late Percy.

'I have, indeed,' said the bookie. 'Time after time after time. It almost seems like some kind of fate. Only the other day there was a fellow with a ginger moustache named Watherspoon. Owed me fifty for Plumpton and pleaded the Gaming Act. And would you believe it, less than a week later he was found unconscious in the street – must have got into some unpleasantness of some kind – and had to have six stitches.'

'Six!'

'Seven. I was forgetting the one over his left eye. Makes you think, that sort of thing does. Hoy, Erbut,' he called.

A frightful plugugly appeared from nowhere, as if he had been a Djinn and the bookie had rubbed a lamp.

'Erbut,' said the bookie, 'I want you to meet Mr Little, Erbut. Take a good look at him. You'll remember him again?'

Herbert drank Bingo in. His eye was cold and grey, like a parrot's.

'Yus,' he said. 'Yus, I won't forget him.'

'Good,' said the bookie. 'That will be all, Erbut. Then about that money, Mr Little, we'll say Friday without fail, shall we?'

Bingo tottered away and sought out Oofy.

'Oofy, old man,' he said, 'it is within your power to save a human life.'

'Well, I'm jolly well not going to,' said Oofy, who had now got one of his dyspeptic headaches. 'The more human lives that aren't saved, the better I shall like it. I loathe the human race. Any time it wants to go over Niagara Falls in a barrel, it will be all right with me.'

'If I don't get a tenner by Friday, a fearful bounder named Erbut is going to beat me into a pulp.'

'Good,' said Oofy, brightening a little. 'Capital. Splendid. That's fine.'

Bingo then caught the bus back to Monte Carlo.

That night he dressed for dinner moodily. He was unable to discern the bluebird. In three months from now he would be getting another quarter's allowance, but a fat lot of good that would be. In far less than three months, if he had read aright the message in Erbut's eyes, he would be in some hospital or nursing home with stitches all over him. How many stitches, time alone could tell. He fell to musing on Watherspoon. Was it, he wondered, to be his fate to lower that ginger-moustached man's melancholy record?

His thoughts were still busy with the stitch outlook, when the telephone rang.

'Hullo,' said a female voice. 'Is that Rosie?'

'No,' said Bingo, and might have added that the future was not either. 'I'm Mr Little.'

'Oh, Mr Little, this is Dora Spurgeon. Can I speak to Rosie?'

'She isn't here.'

'Well, when she comes in, will you tell her that I'm just off to Corsica in some people's yacht. We leave in an hour, so I shan't have time to come over and see her, so will you give her my love and tell her I am sending the brooch back.'

'Brooch?'

'She lent me her brooch when I left London. I think it's the one you gave her on her birthday. She told me to take special care of it, and I don't feel it's safe having it with me in Corsica – so many brigands about – so I am sending it by registered post to the Hôtel de Paris. Goodbye, Mr Little. I must rush.'

Bingo hung up the receiver and sat down on the bed to think this over. Up to a point, of course, the situation was clear. Dora Spurgeon, a muddle-headed boob if ever there was one, obviously supposed that Mrs Bingo had accompanied him to Monte Carlo. No doubt Mrs Bingo had gone to some pains in her telephone call to make it thoroughly clear that she was remaining in London, but it was no good trying to drive things into a head like Dora Spurgeon's by means of the spoken word. You needed a hammer. The result was that on the morrow that brooch which he had given Mrs Bingo would arrive at the hotel.

So far, as I say, Bingo found nothing to perplex him. But what he could not make up his mind about was this – should he, after he had pawned the brooch, send the proceeds straight to that bookie? Or should he take the money and go and have a whack at the Casino?

Far into the silent night he pondered without being able to reach a decision, but next morning everything seemed to clarify, as is so often the way after a night's sleep, and he wondered how he could ever have been in doubt. Of course he must have a whack at the Casino.

The catch about sending the money to the bookie was that, while this policy would remove from his future the dark shadow of Erbut, it would not make for contentment and happiness in the home. When Mrs Bingo discovered that he had shoved her brooch up the spout in order to pay a racing debt, friction would ensue. He unquestionably had a moral claim on the brooch – bought with his hard-earned money – the thing, you might say, was really his to do what he liked with – nevertheless, something told him that friction would ensue.

By going and playing his system he would avoid all unpleasantness. It was simply a matter of strolling into the Rooms and taking the stuff away.

And, as it turned out, he couldn't have paid off Erbut's bookie, anyway, because the local pop-shop would only give him a fiver on the brooch. He pleaded passionately for more, but the cove behind the counter was adamant. So, taking the fiver, he lunched sparingly at a pub up the hill, and shortly after two o'clock was in the arena, doing his stuff.

I have never been able to quite get the hang of that system of Bingo's. He has explained it to me a dozen times, but it remains vague. However, the basis of it, the thing that made it so frightfully ingenious, was that instead of doubling your stake when you lost, as in all these other systems, you doubled it when you won. It involved a lot of fancy work with a pencil and a bit of paper, because you had to write down figures and add figures and scratch figures out, but that, I gathered, was the nub of the thing – you doubled up when you won, thus increasing your profits by leaps and bounds and making the authorities look pretty sick.

The only snag about it was that in order to do this you first had to win, which Bingo didn't.

I don't suppose there is anything – not even Oofy Prosser – that has a nastier disposition than the wheel at Monte Carlo. It seems to take a sinister pleasure in doing down the common people. You can play mentally by the hour and never get a losing spin, but once you put real money up the whole aspect of things alters. Poor old Bingo hadn't been able to put a foot wrong so long as he stuck to paper punting, but he now found himself in the soup from the start.

There he stood, straining like a greyhound at the leash, waiting for his chance of doubling up, only to see all his little capital raked in except one solitary hundred-franc chip. And when with a weary gesture he bunged this on Black, up came Zero and it was swept away.

And scarcely had he passed through this gruelling spiritual experience, when a voice behind him said, 'Oh, there you are!' and, turning, he found himself face to face with Mrs Bingo.

He stood gaping at her, his heart bounding about inside him like an adagio dancer with nettlerash. For an instant, he tells me, he was under the impression that this was no flesh and blood creature that stood before him, but a phantasm. He thought that she must have been run over by a bus or something in London and that this was her spectre looking in to report, as spectres do.

'You!' he said, like someone in a play.

'I've just arrived,' said Mrs Bingo, very merry and bright.

'I – I didn't know you were coming.'

'I thought I would surprise you,' said Mrs Bingo, still bubbling over with joyous animation. 'You see, what happened was that I was talking to Millie Pringle about my book, and she said that it was no use getting local colour about the Rooms, because a man like Lord Peter Shipbourne would never go to the Rooms – he would do all his playing at the Sporting Club. And I was just going to wire you to go there, when Mrs Carrie Melrose Bopp trod on a banana-skin in the street and sprained her ankle, and the luncheon was postponed, so there was nothing to prevent me coming over, so I came. Oh, Bingo, darling, isn't this jolly!'

Bingo quivered from cravat to socks. The adjective 'jolly' was not the one he would have selected. And it was at this point that Mrs Bingo appeared to observe for the first time that her loved one was looking like a corpse that has been left out in the rain for a day or two.

'Bingo!' she cried. 'What's the matter?'

'Nothing,' said Bingo. 'Nothing. Matter? How do you mean?'

'You look...' A wifely suspicion shot through Mrs Bingo. She eyed him narrowly. 'You haven't been gambling?'

'No, no,' said Bingo. He is a fellow who is rather exact in his speech, and the word 'gambling', to his mind, implied that a chap had a chance of winning. All that he had done, he felt, had been to take his little bit of money and give it to the Administration. You couldn't describe that as gambling. More like making a donation to charity. 'No, no,' he said. 'Rather not.'

'I'm so glad. Oh, by the way, I found a letter from Dora Spurgeon at the hotel. She said she was sending my brooch. I suppose it will arrive this afternoon.'

Bingo's gallant spirit was broken. It seemed to him that this was the end. It was all over, he felt, except the composition of the speech in which he must confess everything. And he was just running over in his mind a few opening remarks, beginning with the words 'Listen, darling,' when his eye fell on the table, and there on Black was a pile of chips, worth in all no less than three thousand, two hundred francs – or, looking at it from another angle, about forty quid at that date. And as he gazed at them, wondering which of the lucky stiffs seated round the board had got ahead of the game to that extent, the croupier at the bottom of the table caught his eye and smirked congratulatingly, as croupiers do when somebody has won a parcel and they think that there is going to be something in it for them in the way of largess.

And Bingo, tottering on his base, suddenly realized that this piled-up wealth belonged to him. It was the increment accruing from that last hundred francs of his.

What he had forgotten, you see, was that though, when Zero turns up, those who have betted on numbers, columns, and what not get it in the neck, stakes on the even chances aren't scooped up – they are what is called put in prison. I mean, they just withdraw into the background for the moment, awaiting the result of the next spin. And, if that wins, out they come again.

Bingo's hundred francs had been on Black, so Zero had put it in prison. And then, presumably, Black must have turned up, getting it out again. And, as he hadn't taken it off, it had, of course, stayed on Black. And then, while he was immersed in conversation with Mrs Bingo about brooches, the wheel, from being a sort of mechanical Oofy Prosser, had suddenly turned into a Santa Claus.

Seven more times it had come up Black, putting Bingo in the position in which that system of his ought to have put him, viz., of doubling up when he won. And the result, as I say, was that the loot now amounted to the colossal sum of forty quid, more than double what he required in order to be able to pay off all his obligations and look the world in the eye again.

The relief was so terrific that Bingo tells me he came within a toucher of swooning. And it was only as he was about to snatch the stuff up and trouser it and live happily ever after – he had, indeed, actually poised himself for the spring – that he suddenly saw that there was a catch. To wit, that if he did, all must be discovered. Mrs Bingo would know that he had been gambling, she would speedily ascertain the source whence had proceeded the money he had been gambling with, and the home, if not actually wrecked, would unquestionably become about as hot for him as the inside of a baked potato.

And yet, if he left the doubloons where they were, the next spin might see them all go down the drain.

I expect you know the expression 'A man's cross-roads'. Those were what Bingo was at at this juncture.

There seemed just one hope – to make a face at the croupier and do it with such consummate skill that the other would see that he wanted those thirty-two hundred francs taken off the board and put on one side till he was at liberty to come and collect. So he threw his whole soul into a face, and the croupier nodded intelligently and left the money on. Bingo, he saw, was signalling to him to let the works ride for another spin, and he admired his sporting spirit. He said something to the other croupier in an undertone – no doubt '*Quel homme!*' or '*Epatant!*' or something of that kind.

And the wheel, which now appeared definitely to have accepted the role of Bingo's rich uncle from Australia, fetched up another Black.

Mrs Bingo was studying the gamesters. She didn't seem to think much of them.

'What dreadful faces these people have,' she said.

Bingo did not reply. His own face at this moment was nothing to write home about, resembling more than anything else that of an anxious fiend in Hell. He was watching the wheel revolve.

It came up Black again, bringing his total to twelve thousand, eight hundred.

And now at last it seemed that his tortured spirit was to be at rest. The croupier, having shot another smirk in his direction, was leaning forward to the pile of chips and had started scooping. Yes, all was well. At the eleventh hour the silly ass had divined the message of that face of his and was doing the needful.

Bingo drew a deep, shuddering breath. He felt like one who had passed through the furnace and, though a bit charred in spots, can once more take up the burden of life with an easy mind. Twelve thousand, eight hundred francs . . . Gosh! It was over a hundred and fifty quid, more than he had ever possessed at one time since the Christmas, three years ago, when his Uncle Wilberforce had come over all Dickensy as the result of lemon punch and had given him a cheque on which next day he had vainly tried to stop payment. There was a frowst in the Rooms which you could have cut with a knife, but he drew it into his lungs as if it had been the finest ozone. Birds seemed to be twittering from the ceiling and soft music playing everywhere.

And then the world went to pieces again. The wheel had begun to spin, and there on Black lay twelve thousand francs. The croupier, though he had scooped, hadn't scooped enough. All he had done was to remove from the board the eight hundred. On that last coup, you see, Bingo had come up against the limit. You can't have more than twelve thousand on an even chance.

And, of course, eight hundred francs was no use to him whatever. It would enable him to pay off Erbut and the bookie, but what of the brooch?

It was at this point that he was aware that Mrs Bingo was saying something to him. He came slowly out of his trance with a Where-am-I look.

'Eh?' he said.

'I said, "Don't you think so?"'

'Think so?'

'I was saying that it didn't seem much good wasting any more time in here. Millie Pringle was quite right. Lord Peter Shipbourne would never dream of coming to a place like this. He would never stand the smell, for one thing. I have drawn him as a most fastidious man. So shall I go on to the Sporting Club . . . Bingo?'

Bingo was watching the wheel, tense and rigid. He was tense and rigid, I mean, not the wheel. The wheel was spinning.

'Bingo!' •

'Hullo?'

'Shall I go on to the Sporting Club and pay our entrance fees?'

A sudden bright light came into Bingo's face, rendering it almost beautiful. His brow was bedewed with perspiration, and he rather thought his hair had turned snowy white, but the map was shining like the sun at noon, and he beamed as he had seldom beamed before.

For the returns were in. The wheel had stopped. And once again Black had come up, and even now the croupier was removing twelve thousand francs from the pile and adding them to the eight hundred before him.

'Yes, do,' said Bingo. 'Do. Yes, do. That'll be fine. Splendid. I think I'll just stick on here for a minute or two. I like watching these weird blokes. But you go on and I'll join you.'

Twenty minutes later he did so. He walked into the Sporting Club a little stiffly, for there were forty-eight thousand francs distributed about his person, some of it in his pockets, some of it in his socks, and quite a good deal tucked inside his shirt. He did not see Mrs Bingo at first: then he caught sight of her sitting over in the bar with a bottle of Vittel in front of her.

'What ho, what ho,' he said, lumbering up.

Then he paused, for it seemed to him that her manner was rummy. Her face was sad and set, her eyes dull. She gave him an odd look, and an appalling suspicion struck him amidships. Could it be, he asked himself – was it possible that somehow, by some mysterious wifely intuition . . .

'There you are,' he said. He sat down beside her, hoping that he wasn't going to crackle. 'Er – how's everything?' He paused. She was still looking rummy. 'I've got that brooch,' he said.

'Oh?'

'Yes. I – er – thought you might like to have it, so I – ah – nipped out and got it.'

'I'm glad it arrived safely . . . Bingo!' said Mrs Bingo.

She was staring sombrely before her. Bingo's apprehension increased. He now definitely feared the worst. It was as if he could feel the soup plashing about his ankles. He took her hand in his and pressed it. It might, he felt, help. You never knew.

'Bingo,' said Mrs Bingo, 'we always tell each other everything, don't we?'

'Do we? Oh yes. Yes.'

'Because when we got married, we decided that that was the only way. I remember your saying so on the honeymoon.'

'Yes,' said Bingo, licking his lips and marvelling at the depths of fatheadedness to which men can sink on their honeymoons.

'I'd hate to feel that you were concealing anything from me. It would make me wretched.'

'Yes,' said Bingo.

'So if you had been gambling, you would tell me, wouldn't you?'

Bingo drew a deep breath. It made him crackle all over, but he couldn't help that. He needed air. Besides, what did it matter now if he crackled like a forest fire? He threw his mind back to those opening sentences which he had composed.

'Listen, darling,' he began.

'So I must tell you,' said Mrs Bingo. 'I've just made the most dreadful fool of myself. When I came in here, I went over to that table over there to watch the play, and suddenly something came over me . . .'

Bingo uttered a snort which rang through the Sporting Club like a bugle.

'You didn't have a pop?'

'I lost over two hundred pounds in ten minutes – Oh, Bingo, can you ever forgive me?'

Bingo had still got hold of her hand, for he had been relying on the soothing effects of hanging on to it during the remarks which he had outlined. He squeezed it lovingly. Not immediately, however, because for perhaps half a minute he felt so boneless that he could not have squeezed a grape.

'There, there!' he said.

'Oh, Bingo!'

'There, there, there!'

'You do forgive me?'

'Of course. Of course.'

'Oh, Bingo,' cried Mrs Bingo, her eyes like twin stars, and damp ones at that, 'there's nobody like you in the world.'

'Would you say that?'

'You remind me of Sir Galahad. Most husbands – '

'Ah,' said Bingo, 'but I understand these sudden impulses. I don't have them myself, but I understand them. Not another word. Good gosh, what's a couple of hundred quid, if it gave you a moment's pleasure?'

His emotions now almost overpowered him, so strenuously did they call for an outlet. He wanted to shout, but he couldn't shout –

the croupiers would object. He wanted to give three cheers, but he couldn't give three cheers – the barman wouldn't like it. He wanted to sing, but he couldn't sing – the customers would complain.

His eye fell on the bottle of Vittel.

'Ah!' said Bingo. 'Darling!'

'Yes, darling?'

'Watch, darling,' said Bingo. 'I place the bottle so. Then, maintaining a perfect equilibrium...'

11

BINGO AND THE PEKE CRISIS

A Bean was showing his sore leg to some Eggs and Piefaces in the smoking room of the Drones Club, when a Crumpet came in. Having paused at the bar to order an Annie's Night Out, he made his way to the group.

'What,' he asked, 'is the trouble?'

It was a twice – or even more than that – told tale, but the Bean embarked upon it without hesitation.

'That ass Bingo Little. Called upon me at my residence the day before yesterday with a ravening Pekinese, and tried to land me with it.'

'Said he had brought it as a birthday present,' added one of the Eggs.

'That was his story,' assented the Bean. 'It doesn't hold water for an instant. It was not my birthday. And if it had been, he should have been well enough acquainted with my psychology to know that I wouldn't want a blasted, man-eating Peke with teeth like needles and a disposition that led it to take offence at the merest trifle. Scarcely had I started to deflect the animal to the door, when it turned like a flash and nipped me in the calf. And if I hadn't had the presence of mind to leap on to a table, the outcome might have been even more serious. Look!' said the Bean. 'A nasty flesh wound.'

The Crumpet patted his shoulder and, giving as his reason the fact that he was shortly about to lunch, asked the other to redrape the limb.

'I don't wonder that the episode has left you in something of a twitter,' he said. 'But I am in a position to give you a full explanation. I saw Bingo last night, and he told me all. And when you have heard the story, you will, I feel sure, agree with me that he is more to be pitied than censured. *Tout comprendre*,' said the Crumpet, who had taken French at school, '*c'est tout pardonner*.'

You are all, he proceeded, more or less familiar with Bingo's circumstances, and I imagine that you regard him as one of those rare birds who are absolutely on velvet. He eats well, sleeps well and is happily married to a charming girl well provided with the stuff – Rosie M. Banks, the popular female novelist, to wit – and life for him, you feel, must be one grand, sweet song.

But it seems to be the rule in this world that though you may have goose, it is never pure goose. In the most apparently Grade A ointment there is always a fly. In Bingo's case it is the fact that he seldom, if ever, has in his possession more than the merest cigarette money. Mrs Bingo seems to feel that it is best that this should be so. She is aware of his fondness for backing horses which, if they finish at all, come in modestly at the tail of the procession, and she deprecates it. A delightful girl – one of the best, and the tree, as you might say, on which the fruit of Bingo's life hangs – she is deficient in sporting blood.

So on the morning on which this story begins it was in rather sombre mood that he seated himself at the breakfast-table and speared a couple of eggs and a rasher of ham. Mrs Bingo's six Pekes frolicked about his chair, but he ignored their civilities. He was thinking how bitter it was that he should have an absolute snip for the two o'clock at Hurst Park that afternoon and no means of cashing in on it. For his bookie, a man who seemed never to have heard of the words 'Service and Cooperation', had informed him some time back that he was no longer prepared to accept mere charm of manner as a substitute for money down in advance.

He had a shot, of course, at bracing the little woman for a trifle, but without any real hope of accomplishing anything constructive. He is a chap who knows when he is chasing rainbows.

'I suppose, my dear old in-sickness-and-in-health-er,' he began diffidently, 'you wouldn't care for me to make a little cash for jam today?'

'How do you mean?' said Mrs Bingo who was opening letters behind the coffee apparatus.

'Well, it's like this. There's a horse – '

'Now, precious, you know I don't like you to bet.'

'I would hardly call this betting. Just reaching out and gathering in the stuff is more the way I would describe it. This horse, you see, is called Pimpled Charlie – '

'What an odd name.'

'Most peculiar. And when I tell you that last night I dreamed that I was rowing in a boat on the fountain in Trafalgar Square with Oofy Prosser, you will see its extraordinary significance.'

'Why?'

'Oofy's name,' said Bingo in a low, grave voice, 'is Alexander

Charles, and what we were talking about in the boat was whether he ought not to present his collection of pimples to the nation.'

Mrs Bingo laughed a silvery laugh.

'You *are* silly!' she said indulgently, and Bingo knew that hope, never robust, must now be considered dead. If this was the attitude she proposed to take towards what practically amounted to a divine revelation, there was little to be gained by pursuing the subject. He cheesed it, accordingly, and the conversation turned to the prospects of Mrs Bingo having a fine day for her journey. For this morning she was beetling off to Bognor Regis to spend a couple of weeks with her mother.

And he had just returned to his meditations after dealing with this topic, when he was jerked out of them by a squeal of ecstasy from behind the coffee-pot, so piercing in its timbre that it dislodged half an egg from his fork. He looked up and saw that Mrs Bingo was brandishing a letter, beaming the while like billy-o.

'Oh, sweetie-pie,' she cried for it is in this fashion that she often addresses him, 'I've heard from Mr Purkiss!'

'This Purkiss being who?'

'You've never met him. He's an old friend of mine. He lives quite near here. He owns a children's magazine called *Wee Tots*.'

'So what?' said Bingo, still about six parasangs from getting the gist.

'I didn't like to tell you before, darling, for fear it might not come to anything, but some time ago he happened to mention to me that he was looking out for a new editor for *Wee Tots*, and I asked him to try you. I told him you had had no experience, of course, but I said you were awfully clever, and he would be there to guide you, and so on. Well, he said he would think it over, but that his present idea was to make a nephew of his the editor. But now I've had this letter from him, saying that the nephew has been county-courted by his tailor, and this has made Mr Purkiss think his nature is too frivolous, and he wants to see you and have a talk. Oh, Bingo, I'm sure he means to give you the job.'

Bingo had to sit for a moment to let this sink in. Then he rose and kissed Mrs Bingo tenderly.

'My little helpmeet!' he said.

He was extraordinarily bucked. The appointment, he presumed, carried with it something in the nature of a regular salary, and a regular salary was what he had been wanting for years. Judiciously laid out on those tips from above which he so frequently got in the night watches, he felt, such a stipend could speedily be built up into a vast fortune. And, even apart from the sordid angle, the idea of being an editor, with all an editor's unexampled opportunities for putting on dog and throwing his weight about, enchanted him. He looked forward with a bright enthusiasm to getting fellow-members of the Drones to send in contributions to the Kiddies' Korner, and then bunging them back as not quite up to his standard.

'He has been staying with his wife with an aunt at Tunbridge Wells, and he is coming back this morning, and he wants you to meet him under the clock at Charing Cross at twelve. Can you be there?'

'I can,' said Bingo. 'And not only there, but there with my hair in a braid.'

'You will be able to recognize him, he says, because he will be wearing a grey tweed suit and a Homburg hat.'

'I,' said Bingo, with a touch of superiority, 'shall be in a morning coat and the old topper.'

Once again he kissed Mrs Bingo, even more tenderly than before. And pretty soon after that it was time for her to climb aboard the car which was to take her to Bognor Regis. He saw her off at the front door, and there were unshed tears in her eyes as she made her fare-wells. For the poignancy of departure was intensified by the fact that, her mother's house being liberally staffed with cats, she was leaving the six Pekes behind her.

'Take care of them while I'm away,' she murmured brokenly, as the animals barged into the car and got shot out again by Bagshaw, the butler. 'You will look after them, won't you, darling?'

'Like a father,' said Bingo. 'Their welfare shall be my constant concern.'

And he spoke sincerely. He liked those Pekes. His relations with them had always been based on a mutual affection and esteem. They licked his face, he scratched their stomachs. Pleasant give and take, each working for each.

'Don't forget to give them their coffee-sugar every night.'

'Trust me,' said Bingo, 'to the death.'

'And call in at Boddington and Biggs's for Ping-Poo's harness. They are mending it. Oh, and by the way,' said Mrs Bingo, opening her bag and producing currency, 'when you go to Boddington and Biggs, will you pay their bill. It will save me writing out a cheque.'

She slipped him a couple of fivers, embraced him fondly and drove off, leaving him waving on the front steps.

I mention this fact of his waving particularly, because it had so important a bearing on what followed. You cannot wave a hand with a couple of fivers in it without them crackling. And a couple of fivers cannot crackle in the hand of a man who has received direct infor-mation from an authoritative source that a seven-to-one shot is going

to win the two o'clock race at Hurst Park without starting in his mind
a certain train of thought. The car was scarcely out of sight before the
Serpent had raised its head in this Garden of Eden – the Little home
was one of those houses that stand in spacious grounds along the edge
of Wimbledon Common – and was whispering in Bingo's ear: 'How
about it, old top?'

Now at ordinary times and in normal circumstances, Bingo is, of
course, the soul of honesty and would never dream of diverting a
Bond Street firm's legitimate earnings into more private and personal
channels. But here, the Serpent pointed out, and Bingo agreed with
him, was plainly a special case.

There could be no question, argued the Serpent, of doing down
Boddington and Biggs. That could be dismissed right away. All it
meant, if Bingo deposited these fivers with his bookie, to go on
Pimpled Charlie's nose for the two o'clock, was that Boddington and
his boy-friend would collect tomorrow instead of today. For if by
some inconceivable chance Pimpled Charlie failed to click, all he,
Bingo, had to do was to ask for a small advance on his salary from Mr
Purkiss, who by that time would have become his employer.
Probably, said the Serpent, Purkiss would himself suggest some such
arrangement. He pointed out to Bingo that it was not likely that he
would have much difficulty in fascinating the man. Quite apart from
the morning coat and the sponge-bag trousers, that topper of his was
bound to exercise a spell. Once let Purkiss get a glimpse of it, and
there would be very little sales-resistance from him. The thing, in
short, was as good as in the bag.

It was with the lightest of hearts, accordingly, that Bingo proceeded
to London an hour later, lodged the necessary with his bookie, whose
office was in Oxford Street and sauntered along to Charing Cross
Station, arriving under the clock as its hands pointed to five minutes
to twelve. And promptly at the hour a stout elderly man in a grey
tweed suit and a Homburg hat rolled up.

The following conversation then took place.
'Mr Little?'
'How do you do?'
'How do you do? Lovely day.'
'Beautiful.'
'You are punctual, Mr Little.'
'I always am.'
'A very admirable trait.'
'What ho!'
And it was at this moment, just as everything was going as smooth

as syrup and Bingo could see the awe and admiration burgeoning in his companion's eyes as they glued themselves on the topper, that out of the refreshment-room, wiping froth from his lips, came B. B. Tucker, Gents' Hosier and Bespoke Shirt Maker, of Bedford Street, Strand, to whom for perhaps a year and a quarter Bingo had owed three pounds, eleven and fourpence for goods supplied.

It just shows you how mental exhilaration can destroy a man's clear, cool judgment. When this idea of meeting under the clock at Charing Cross had been mooted, Bingo, all above himself at the idea of becoming editor of a powerful organ for the chicks, had forgotten prudence and right-hoed without a second thought. It was only now that he realized what madness it had been to allow himself to be lured within a mile of Charing Cross. The locality was literally stiff with shops where in his bachelor days he had run up little accounts, and you never knew when the proprietors of these shops were not going to take it into their heads, as B. B. Tucker had plainly done, to step round to the station refreshment-room for a quick one.

He was appalled. He knew how lacking in tact and *savoir-faire* men like B. B. Tucker are. When they see an old patron chatting with a friend, they do not just nod and smile and pass by. They come right up and start talking about how a settlement would oblige, and all that sort of rot. And if Purkiss was the sort of person who shrank in horror from nephews who got county-courted by their tailors, two minutes of B. B. Tucker, Bingo felt, would undo the whole effect of the topper.

And the next moment, just as Bingo had anticipated, up he came. 'Oh, Mr Little,' he began.

It was a moment for the swiftest action. There was a porter's truck behind Bingo, and most people would have resigned themselves to the fact that retreat was cut off. But Bingo was made of sterner stuff.

'Well, goodbye, Purkiss,' he said, and, springing lightly over the truck, was gone with the wind. Setting a course for the main entrance, he passed out of the station at a good rate of speed and was presently in the Embankment gardens. There he remained until he considered that B. B. Tucker had had time to blow over, after which he returned to the old spot under the clock, in order to resume his conference with Purkiss at the point where it had been broken off.

Well, in one respect, everything was fine, because B. B. Tucker had disappeared. But in another respect the posish was not so good. Purkiss also had legged it. He had vanished like snow off a mountain-top, and after pacing up and down for half an hour Bingo was forced to the conclusion that he wasn't coming back. Purkiss had called it a day. And in what frame of mind, Bingo asked himself, had he called it a day? Now that he had leisure to think, he remembered that as he had hurdled the truck he had seen the man shoot an odd glance at him, and it occurred to him that Purkiss might have gone on thinking him a bit eccentric. He feared the worst. An aspirant to an editorial chair, he knew, does not win to success by jumping over trucks in the presence of his prospective proprietor.

Moodily, he went off and had a spot of lunch, and he was just getting outside his coffee when the result of the two o'clock came through on the tape. Pimpled Charlie had failed to finish in the first three. Providence, in other words, when urging him to put his chemise on the animal, had been pulling his leg. It was not the first time that this had happened.

And by the afternoon post next day there arrived a letter from Purkiss which proved that his intuition had not deceived him. He read it, and tore it into a hundred pieces. Or so he says. Eight, more likely. For it was the raspberry. Purkiss, wrote Purkiss, had given the matter his consideration and had decided to make other arrangements with regard to the editorship of *Wee Tots*.

To say that Bingo was distrait as he dined that night would not be to overstate the facts. There was, he could see, a lot which he was going to find it difficult to explain to Mrs Bingo on her return, and it was not, moreover, going to be any too dashed good when he had explained it. She would not be pleased about the ten quid. That alone would cast a cloud upon the home. Add the revelation that he had mucked up his chance of becoming Ye Ed., and you might say that the home would be more or less in the melting-pot.

And so, as I say, he was distrait. The six Pekes accompanied him into the library and sat waiting for their coffee-sugar, but he was too preoccupied to do the square thing by the dumb chums. His whole intellect was riveted on the problem of how to act for the best.

And then – gradually – he didn't know what first put the idea into his head – it began to steal over Bingo that there was something peculiar about these six Pekes.

It was not their appearance or behaviour. They looked the same as usual, and they behaved the same as usual. It was something subtler than that. And then, suddenly, like a wallop on the base of the skull, it came to him.

There were only five of them.

Now, to the lay mind, the fact that in a house containing six Pekes only five had rolled up at coffee-sugar-time would not have seemed so frightfully sinister. The other one is off somewhere about its domestic duties, the lay mind would have said – burying a bone, taking a refreshing nap, or something of the sort. But Bingo knew Pekes. Their psychology was an open book to him. And he was aware that if only five of them had clustered round when there was coffee-sugar going, there could be only five on the strength. The sixth must be A.W.O.L.

He had been stirring his coffee when he made the discovery, and the spoon fell from his nerveless fingers. He gazed at the Shape Of Things To Come, all of a doodah.

This was the top. He could see that. Everything else was by comparison trifling, even the trousering of Boddington and Biggs's ten quid. Mrs Bingo loved these Pekes. She had left them with him as a sacred charge. And at the thought of what would ensue when the time came for him to give an account of his stewardship and he had to confess that he was in the red, imagination boggled. There would be tears ... reproaches ... oh-how-could-you's ... Why, dash it, felt Bingo, with a sudden start that nearly jerked his eyeballs out of their sockets, it was quite possible that, taking a line through that unfortunate ten quid business, she might even go so far as to suppose that he had snitched the missing animal and sold it for gold.

Shuddering strongly, he leaped from his chair and rang the bell. He wished to confer with Bagshaw and learn if by any chance the absentee was down in the kitchen. But Bagshaw was out for the evening. A parlourmaid answered the bell, and when she had informed him that the downstairs premises were entirely free from Pekes, Bingo uttered a hollow groan, grabbed his hat and started out for a walk on Wimbledon Common. There was just a faint chance – call it a hundred to eight – that the little blighter might have heard the call of the wild and was fooling about somewhere out in the great open spaces.

How long he wandered, peering about him and uttering chirruping noises, he could not have said, but it was a goodish time, and his rambles took him far afield. He had halted for a moment in quite unfamiliar territory to light a cigarette, and was about to give up the search, and totter home, when suddenly he stiffened in every limb and stood goggling, the cigarette frozen on his lips.

For there, just ahead of him in the gathering dusk, he had perceived a bloke of butlerine aspect. And this butler, if butler he was, was leading on a leash a Peke so identical with Mrs Bingo's gang that it could have been signed up with the troupe without exciting any suspicions whatever. Pekes, as you are probably aware, are either beige and hairy or chestnut and hairy. Mrs Bingo's were chestnut and hairy.

The sight brought new life to Bingo. His razor-like intelligence had been telling him for some time that the only possible solution of the impasse was to acquire another Peke and add it to the strength, and the snag about that was, of course, that Pekes cost money – and of money at the moment he possessed but six shillings and a little bronze.

His first impulse was to leap upon this butler and choke the animal out of him with his bare hands. Wiser counsels, however, prevailed, and he contented himself with trailing the man like one of those fellows you read about who do not let a single twig snap beneath their feet. And presently the chap left the common and turned into a quiet sort of road and finished up by going through a gate into the garden of a sizable house. And Bingo, humming nonchalantly, walked on past till he came to some shops. He was looking for a grocer's and eventually he found one and, going in, invested a portion of his little capital in a piece of cheese, instructing the man behind the counter to give him the ripest and breeziest he had in stock.

For Bingo, as I said before, knew Pekes, and he was aware that, while they like chicken, are fond of suet pudding and seldom pass a piece of milk chocolate if it comes their way, what they will follow to the ends of the earth and sell their souls for is cheese. And it was his intention to conceal himself in the garden till the moment of the animal's nightly airing, and then come out and make a dicker with it by means of the slab which he had just purchased.

Ten minutes later, accordingly, he was squatting in a bush, waiting for zero hour.

It is not a vigil to which he cares to look back. The experience of sitting in a bush in a strange garden, unable to smoke and with no company but your thoughts and a niffy piece of cheese, is a testing one. Ants crawled up his legs, beetles tried to muscle in between his collar and his neck, and others of God's creatures, taking advantage of the fact that he had lost his hat, got in his hair. But eventually his resolution was rewarded. A french window was thrown open, and the Peke came trotting out into the pool of light from the lamps within, followed by a stout, elderly man. And conceive Bingo's emotion when he recognized in this stout, elderly exhibit none other than old Pop Purkiss.

The sight of him was like a tonic. Until this moment Bingo had not been altogether free from those things of Conscience ... not psalms ... yes, qualms. He had had qualms about the lay-out. From time to time there crept over him a certain commiseration for the bloke whose household pet he was about to swipe. A bit tough on the poor bounder, he had felt. These qualms now vanished. After the way he had let him down, Purkiss had forfeited all claim to pity. He was a man who deserved to be stripped of every Peke in his possession.

The question, however, that exercised Bingo a bit at this juncture was how was this stripping to be done. If it was the man's intention to follow hard on the animal's heels till closing time, it was difficult to see how he was to be de-Peked without detection.

But his luck was in. Purkiss had apparently been entertaining himself with a spot of music on the radio, for when he emerged it was playing a gay rumba. And now, as radios do, it suddenly broke off in the middle, gave a sort of squawk and began to talk German. And Purkiss turned back to fiddle with it.

It gave Bingo just the time he needed. He was out of the bush in a jiffy, like a leopard bounding from its lair. There was one anxious moment when the Peke drew back with raised eyebrows and a good deal of that To-what-am-I-indebted-for-this-visit stuff, but fortunately the scent of the cheese floated to its nostrils before it could utter more than a *sotto voce* whoofle, and from then on everything went with a swing. Half a minute later, Bingo was tooling along the road with the Peke in his arms. And eventually he reached the common, struck a spot which he recognized and pushed home.

Mrs Bingo's Pekes were all in bed when he got there, and when he went and sprang the little stranger on them he was delighted with the ready affability with which they made him one of themselves. Too often, when you introduce a ringer into a gaggle of Pekes, there ensues a scrap like New Year's Eve in Madrid; but tonight, after a certain amount of tentative sniffing, the home team issued their O.K., and he left them all curled up in their baskets like so many members of the Athenaeum. He then went off to the library, and rang the bell. He wished, if Bagshaw had returned, to take up with him the matter of a stiff whisky and soda.

Bagshaw had returned, all right. He appeared, looking much refreshed from his evening out, and biffed off and fetched the fixings. And it was as he was preparing to depart that he said: 'Oh, about the little dog, sir.'

Bingo gave a jump that nearly upset his snifter.

'Dog?' he said, in his emotion putting in above five d's at the beginning of the word. 'What dog?' he said, inserting about seven w's in the 'what'.

'Little Wing-Fu, sir. I was unable to inform you earlier, as you were not in the house when Mrs Little's message arrived. Mrs Little telephoned shortly after luncheon, instructing me to send Wing-Fu by rail to Bognor Regis Station. It appears that there is an artist gentleman residing in the vicinity who paints animals' portraits, and Mrs Little wished to have Wing-Fu's likeness done. I dispatched the

little fellow in a hamper, and on my return to the house found a
telegram announcing his safe arrival. It occurred to me that I had
better mention the matter to you, as it might have caused you some
anxiety, had you chanced to notice that one of the dogs was missing.
Good night, sir,' said Bagshaw, and popped off.

He left Bingo, as you may well suppose, chafing quite a goodish
deal. Thanks to Mrs Bingo's lack of a sense of what was fitting having
led her to conduct these operations through an underling instead of
approaching him, Bingo, in her absence the head of the house, he had
imperilled his social standing by becoming a dog-stealer. And all for
nothing.

Remembering the agonies he had gone through in that bush – not
only spiritual because of the qualms of conscience, but physical
because of the ants, the beetles and the unidentified fauna which had
got in his hair, you can't blame him for being pretty sick about the
whole thing. He had a sense of grievance. Why, he asked, had he not
been informed of what was going on? Was he a cipher? And, anyway,
where was the sense of pandering to Wing-Fu's vanity by having his
portrait painted? He was quite sidey enough already.

And the worst of it was that though he could see that everything
now pointed to some swift, statesmanlike move on his part, he was
dashed if he could think of one. It was in a pretty dark mood that he
swallowed a second snort and trudged up to bed.

But there's nothing like sleeping on a thing. He got the solution in
his bath next morning. He saw that it was all really quite simple. All
he had to do was to take Purkiss's Peke back to the Purkiss shack, slip
it in through the garden gate, and there he would be, quit of the
whole unpleasant affair.

And it was only when towelling himself after the tub that he
suddenly realized that he didn't know the name of Purkiss's house –
not even the name of the road it was in – and that he had tacked to and
fro so assiduously on his return journey that he couldn't possibly find
his way back to it.

And, what was worse, for it dished the idea of looking him up in
the telephone book, he couldn't remember Purkiss's name.

Oh, yes, he knows it now, all right. It is graven on his heart. If you
stopped him on the street today and said, 'Oh, by the way, Bingo,
what is the name of the old blister who owns *Wee Tots*?' he would
reply like a flash: 'Henry Cuthbert Purkiss.' But at that moment it
had clean gone. You know how it is with names. Well, when I tell you
that during breakfast he was convinced that it was Winterbottom and
that by lunchtime he had switched to Benjafield, you will see how far
the evil had spread.

And, as you will recall, his only documentary evidence no longer existed. With a peevishness which he now regretted, he had torn the fellow's letter into a hundred pieces. Or at least eight.

At this juncture, Bingo Little was a broken man.

Stripping the thing starkly down to its bare bones, he saw that the scenario was as follows. Mrs Bingo was a woman with six Pekes. When she returned from Bognor Regis, she would be a woman with seven Pekes. And his knowledge of human nature told him that the first thing a six-Peke woman does, on discovering that she has suddenly become a seven-Peke woman, is to ask questions. And to these questions what would be his answer?

It would, he was convinced, be perfectly useless for him to try to pretend that the extra incumbent was one which he had bought her as a surprise during her absence. Mrs Bingo was no fool. She knew that he was not a man who frittered away his slender means buying people Pekes. She would consider the story thin. She would institute inquiries. And those inquiries must in the end lead her infallibly to this Winterbottom, or Benjafield, or whatever his name was.

It seemed to Bingo that there was only one course open to him. He must find the stowaway a comfortable home elsewhere, completely out of the Benjafield-Winterbottom zone, and he must do it immediately.

So now you understand why the poor old bird called upon you that day with the animal. And, as I said, you will probably agree that he was more to be p. than c. In this connection, he has authorized me to say that he is prepared to foot all bills for sticking-plaster, arnica, the Pasteur treatment and what not.

After your refusal to hold the baby, he appears to have lost heart. I gather that the scene was a painful one, and he did not feel like repeating it. Returning home, he decided that there was nothing to be done but somehow to dig up that name. So shortly after lunch he summoned Bagshaw to his presence.

'Bagshaw,' he said, 'mention some names.'

'Names, sir?'

'Yes. You know. Like people have. I am trying to remember a man's name, and it eludes me. I have an idea,' said Bingo, who had now begun to veer towards Jellaby, 'that it begins with a J.'

Bagshaw mused.

'J, sir?'

'Yes.'

'Smith?' said the ass.

'Not Smith,' said Bingo. 'And if you mean Jones, it's not as common as that. Rather a bit on the exotic side it struck me as, when

I heard it. As it might be Jerningham or Jorkins. However, in supposing that it begins with a J, I may quite easily be mistaken. Try the A's.'

'Adams, sir? Allen? Ackworth? Anderson? Arkwright? Aarons? Abercrombie?'

'Switch to the B's.'

'Bates? Bulstrode? Burgess? Bellinger? Biggs? Bultitude?'

'Now do me a few C's.'

'Collins? Clegg? Clutterbuck? Carthew? Curley? Cabot? Cade? Cackett? Cahill? Caffrey? Cahn? Cain? Caird? Cannon? Carter? Casey? Cooley? Cuthbertson? Cope? Cork? Crowe? Cramp? Croft? Crewe? . . .'

A throbbing about the temples told Bingo that in his enfeebled state he had had about enough of this. He was just waving a hand to indicate this, when the butler, carried along by his momentum, added:

'Cruickshank? Chalmers? Cutmore? Carpenter? Cheffins? Carr? Cartwright? Cadwallader?'

And something seemed to go off in Bingo's brain like a spring.

'Cadwallader!'

'Is that the gentleman's name, sir?'

'No,' said Bingo. 'But it'll do.'

He had suddenly recalled that Cadwallader was the name of the grocer from whom he had purchased the cheese. Starting from that grocer's door, he was pretty sure that he could find his way to Chez Purkiss. His position was clear. Cadwallader ho! was the watchword.

The prudent thing, of course, would have been to postpone the expedition until darkness had fallen, for it is under cover of night that these delicate operations are best performed. But at this season of the year, what with summertime and all that, darkness fell so dashed late, and he was all keyed up for rapid action. Refreshing his memory with another look at Cadwallader's address in the telephone book he set out in the cool of the evening, hope in his heart and the Peke under his arm. And presently he found himself on familiar ground. Here was Cadwallader's grocery establishment, there was the road down which he had sauntered, and there a few moments later was the box hedge that fringed the Purkiss's domain and the gate through which he had entered.

He opened the gate, shoved the Peke in, bade it a brief farewell and legged it. And so home, arriving there shortly before six.

As he passed into the Little domain, he was feeling in some respects like a murderer who has at last succeeded in getting rid of the body and in other respects like Shadrach, Meshach and Abednego on emerging from the burning fiery furnace. It was as if a great load had been lifted from him. Once, he tells me, in the days of his boyhood, while enjoying a game of football at school, he was compelled in pursuance of his duties to fall on the ball and immediately afterwards became the base of a sort of pyramid consisting of himself and eight beefy members of the opposing team with sharp elbows and cleated boots. Even after all these years, he says, he can still recall the sense of buoyancy and relief when this mass of humanity eventually removed itself from the small of his back. He was feeling exactly the same relief and buoyancy now. I don't know if he actually sang but I shouldn't be at all surprised if he didn't attempt a roundelay or two.

Bingo, like Jonah, is one of those fellows who always come up smiling. You may crush him to earth, but he will rise again. Resilient is, I believe, the word. And he now found the future, if not actually bright, at least beginning to look for the first time more or less fit for human consumption. Mistily, but growing every moment more solid, there had begun to shape itself in his mind a story which might cover that business of the Boddington and Biggs ten quid. The details wanted a bit of polishing, but the broad, basic structure was there. As for the episode at Charing Cross Station, there he proposed to stick to stout denial. It might or might not get by. It was at least worth trying. And, in any event, he was now straight on the Peke situation.

Walking on the tips of his toes with his hat on the side of his head, Bingo drew near to the house. And it was at this point that something brushed against his leg with a cheery gurgle and, looking down, he saw that it was the Peke. Having conceived a warm regard for Bingo, and taking advantage of the fact that he had omitted to close the Purkiss's gate, it had decided to toddle along with him.

And while Bingo stood rooted to the spot, staring wanly at the adhesive animal, along came Bagshaw.

'Might I inquire, sir,' said Bagshaw, 'if you happen to know the telephone number of the house at which Mrs Little is temporarily residing?'

'Why?' asked Bingo absently, his gaze still gummed to the Peke.

'Mrs Little's friend, Mr Purkiss, called a short while back, desirous of obtaining information. He was anxious to telephone to Mrs Little.'

The wanness with which Bingo had been staring at the Peke was as nothing compared to the wanness with which he now stared at the butler. With the mention of that name, memory had returned to him, sweeping away all the Jellabys and Winterbottoms which had been clogging up his thought processes.

'Purkiss?' he cried, tottering on his base. 'Did you say Purkiss?'
'Yes, sir.'
'He has been calling here?'
'Yes, sir.'
'He wanted to telephone to Mrs Little?'
'Yes, sir.'
'Did he ... did Mr Purkiss... Had he... Had Mr Purkiss...
Did Mr Purkiss convey the impression of having something on his
mind?'
'Yes, sir.'
'He appeared agitated?'
'Yes, sir.'
'You gathered ... you inferred that he had some urgent communi-
cation to make to Mrs Little?'
'Yes, sir.'
Bingo drew a deep breath.
'Bagshaw,' he said, 'bring me a whisky and soda. A large whisky
and soda. One with not too much soda in it, but with the whisky
stressed. In fact, practically leave the soda out altogether.'
He needed the restorative badly, and when it came lost no time in
introducing it into his system. The more he contemplated Purkiss's
call, the more darkly sinister did it seem to him.
Purkiss had wanted to telephone to Mrs Bingo. He had appeared
agitated. Facts like these were capable of but one interpretation.
Bingo remembered the hat which he had left somewhere in the bush.
Obviously, Purkiss must have found that hat, observed the initials in
its band, leaped to the truth and was now trying to get hold of Mrs
Bingo to pour the whole story into her receptive ear.
There was only one thing to be done. Bingo shrank from doing it,
but he could see that he had no other alternative. He must seek
Purkiss out, explain all the circumstances and throw himself on his
mercy, begging him as a sportsman and a gentleman to keep the
whole thing under his hat. And what was worrying him was a grave
doubt as to whether Purkiss was a sportsman and a gentleman. He
had not much liked the man's looks on the occasion of their only
meeting. It seemed to him, recalling that meeting, that Purkiss had
had the appearance of an austere sort of bird, with that cold, distant
look in his eyes which he, Bingo, had so often seen in those of his
bookie when he was trying to get him to let the settlement stand over
till a week from Wednesday.
However, the thing had to be done, and he set forth to do it. He
made his way to the Purkiss's home, and the butler conducted him to
the drawing room.

'Mr Little,' he announced, and left him. And Bingo braced himself
for the ordeal before him.

He could see at a glance that Purkiss was not going to be an easy
audience. There was in his manner nothing of the genial host greeting
the welcome popper-in. He had been standing with his back turned,
looking out of the open french window, and he spun round with sickening rapidity and fixed Bingo with a frightful stare. A glare of
loathing, Bingo diagnosed it as – the natural loathing of a ratepayer
who sees before him the bloke who has recently lured away his Peke
with cheese. And he felt that it would be necessary for him, if
anything in the nature of a happy ending was to be arrived at, to be
winning and spell-binding as never before.

'Well?' said Purkiss.

Bingo started to make a manly clean breast of it without preamble.

'I've come about that Peke,' he said.

And at that moment, before he could say another word, there
barged down his windpipe, wiping speech from his lips and making
him cough like the dickens, some foreign substance which might
have been a fly – or a gnat – or possibly a small moth. And while he
was coughing he saw Purkiss give a sort of despairing gesture.

'I was expecting this,' he said.

Bingo went on coughing.

'Yes,' said Purkiss, 'I feared it. You are quite right. I stole the dog.'

Bingo had more or less dealt with the foreign substance by this
time, but he still couldn't speak. Astonishment held him dumb.
Purkiss was looking like somebody in a movie caught with the goods.
He was no longer glaring. There was a dull, hopeless agony in his
eyes.

'You are a married man, Mr Little,' he said, 'so perhaps you will
understand. My wife has gone to stay with an ailing aunt at Tunbridge Wells. Shortly before she left, she bought a Pekinese dog.
This she entrusted to my care, urging me on no account ever to allow
it out of the house except on a lead. Last night, as the animal was
merely going to step out into the garden for a few moments, I omitted
the precaution. I let it run out by itself. I never saw it again.'

He gulped a bit. Bingo breathed heavily a bit. He resumed.

'It was gone, and I saw that my only course was immediately to
secure a substitute of similar appearance. I spent the whole of today
going round the dog-shops of London, but without avail. And then I
remembered that Mrs Little owned several of these animals – all, as I
recalled, singularly like the one I had lost. I thought she might
possibly consent to sell me one of them.'

He sighed somewhat.

'This evening,' he went on, 'I called at your house, to find that she was away and that I could not reach her by telephone. And it would be useless to write to her, for my wife returns tomorrow. So I turned away, and as I reached the gate something jumped against my leg. It was a Pekinese dog, Mr Little, and the very image of the one I had lost. The temptation was too great...'

'You pinched it?' cried Bingo, shocked.

Purkiss nodded. Bingo clicked his tongue.

'A bit thick, Purkiss,' he said gravely.

'I know, I know. I am fully conscious of the heinousness of what I did. My only excuse must be that I was unaware that I was being observed.' He heaved another sigh. 'The animal is in the kitchen,' he said, 'enjoying a light supper. I will ring for the butler to bring it to you. And what my wife is going to say, I shudder to think,' said Purkiss, doing so.

'You fancy that she will be upset when she returns and finds no Peke to call her Mother?'

'I do, indeed.'

'Then, Purkiss,' said Bingo, slapping him on the shoulder, 'keep this animal.'

He likes to think of himself at that moment. He was suave, kindly, full of sweetness and light. He rather imagines that Purkiss must have thought he had run up against an angel in human shape or something.

'Keep it?'

'Definitely.'

'But Mrs Little – ?'

'Have no concern. My wife doesn't know from one day to another how many Pekes she's got. Just so long as there is a reasonable contingent messing about, she is satisfied. Besides,' said Bingo, with quiet reproach, 'she will have far too much on her mind, when she gets back, to worry about Pekes. You see, Purkiss, she had set her heart on my becoming editor of *Wee Tots*. She will be distressed when she learns of your attitude in that matter. You know what women are.'

Purkiss coughed. He looked at Bingo, and quivered a bit. Then he looked at him again, and quivered a bit more. Bingo received the impression that some sort of spiritual struggle was proceeding within him.

'Do you *want* to edit *Wee Tots*, Mr Little?' he said at length.

'I do, indeed.'

'You're sure?'

'Quite sure.'

'I should have thought that a young man in your position would have been too busy, too occupied – '

'Oh, no. I could have fitted it in.'

A touch of hope came into Purkiss's manner.

'The work is hard.'

'No doubt I should have capable assistants.'

'The salary,' said Purkiss wistfully, 'is not large.'

'I'll tell you what,' said Bingo, inspired. 'Make it larger.'

Purkiss took another look, and quivered for the third time. Then his better self triumphed.

'I shall be delighted,' he said in a low voice, 'if you will assume the editorship of *Wee Tots*.'

Bingo patted him on the shoulder once more.

'Splendid, Purkiss,' he said. 'Capital. And now, in the matter of a small advance of salary . . .'

12

THE EDITOR REGRETS

When Bingo Little's wife, the well-known female novelist Rosie M. Banks, exerted her pull and secured for Bingo the editorship of *Wee Tots*, that popular and influential organ which has done so much to mould thought in the nursery, a sort of literary renaissance swept the Drones Club. Scarcely an Egg, Bean, Pieface or Crumpet on the list of members but took pen in hand with the feeling that here was where he cashed in and got back some of the stuff that had gone down the drain at Ally Pally and Kempton Park.

It was a painful shock to the intelligentsia, accordingly, when they discovered that their old friend was not going to prove the geyser of easy money they had anticipated. In quick succession he turned down the Egg who wanted to do Racing Notes, the Bean with the inside stuff on Night Clubs, and the Pieface who suggested that he should be given a sort of roving commission to potter round the south of France and contribute gossipy articles of human interest from such centres as Cannes and Monte Carlo. Even a Crumpet who had known him since they were in sailor suits had his thoughtful piece on Some Little Known Cocktails declined with thanks.

'On the plea,' said the Crumpet, 'that his proprietor wouldn't like it.'

'That's what he told me,' said the Egg. 'Who is this bally proprietor of Bingo's?'

'A man named Purkiss. It was through her life-long friendship with Mrs Purkiss that Mrs Bingo was able to get Bingo the job.'

'Then Purkiss can have no red blood in him,' said the Egg.

'Purkiss lacks vision,' said the Bean.

'Purkiss is an ass,' said the Pieface.

The Crumpet shook his head.

'I'm not so sure,' he said. 'My belief is that Bingo merely uses Purkiss as a blind or screen. I think the man is drunk with a sense of power and definitely enjoys rejecting contributions from outside talent. And one of these days he is going to get himself into serious trouble by coming the heavy editor like this. In fact, not long ago he very nearly did so. Only the luck of the Littles saved him from taking a toss which threatened to jar his fat trouser-seat clean out of the editorial chair, never to return. I allude, of course, to the Bella Mae Jobson affair.'

The Bean asked what the Bella Mae Jobson affair was, and the Crumpet, expressing surprise that he had not heard of it, said that it was the affair of Bella Mae Jobson.

The American authoress, he explained. Scarcely known in this country, she has for some years past been holding American childhood spellbound with her tales of Willie Walrus, Charlie Chipmunk, and other fauna. Purkiss, who had been paying a visit to New York, met her on the boat coming back, and she lent him *Charlie Chipmunk Up the Orinoco*. A single glance was enough to tell him that here was the circulation-building stuff for which *Wee Tots* had been waiting, and he entered into tentative negotiations for her whole output, asking her on arriving in London to look in at the office and fix things up with his editor – viz. Bingo.

Now, unfortunately, Purkiss's absence from the centre of things had caused Bingo to get it up his nose a bit. When on the spot, the other had a way of making criticisms and suggestions, and an editor, he tells me, feels shackled when a proprietor with bronchial catarrh keeps popping in all the time, trying to dictate the policy of the 'Uncle Joe to His Chickabiddies' page. All through these last weeks of freedom, therefore, he had been getting more and more above himself, with the result that, when informed per desk telephone that a Miss Jobson waited without he just tapped his teeth with a pencil and said: 'Oh, she does, does she? Well, bung her out and tell her to write. We do not see callers without an appointment.'

He then returned to the 'What a Tiny Girlie Can Do to Help Mother' feature, and was still roughing it out when the door opened an in walked Purkiss, looking bronzed and fit. And after a bit of Well-here-I-am-back-again-ing and Oh-hullo-Mr-Purkiss-did-you-have-a-good-trip-ing, as is inevitable on these occasions, Purkiss said: 'By the way, Mr Little, a Miss Jobson will be calling shortly.'

Bingo gave a light laugh.

'Oh, jolly old Jobson?' he said airily. 'She's been and gone, leaving not a wrack behind. I gave her the air.'

'I beg your pardon?'

'Turfed her out,' explained Bingo.

Purkiss reeled.

'You mean . . . you refused to see her?'

'That's right,' said Bingo. 'Busy. Busy, busy, busy. Much too busy to talk to females. I told her to write, stating her business legibly on one side of the paper only.'

I don't know if any of you happened to see that picture, 'The Hurricane', that was on not long ago. Briefly, the plot of it was that there was a bevy of unfortunate blighters on a South Sea island and the dickens of a howling tempest came along and blew them cross-eyed. I bring it up because Bingo tells me that very much the same sort of thing happened now. For some moments, he says, all he was conscious of was a vast atmospheric disturbance, with him swaying in the middle of it, and then gradually, Purkiss's remarks becoming clearer, he gathered that he had made something of a floater, and that this bird Jobson was a bird who should have been conciliated, sucked up to, given the old oil and generally made to feel that she was among friends and admirers.

'Well, I'm sorry,' he said, feeling that something in the nature of an apology was indicated. 'I deeply regret the whole unfortunate occurrence. I was the victim of a misunderstanding. It never crossed my mind that the above was a sweet ginger specializing in chipmunks. The impression I received was of somebody trying to sell richly illustrated sets of Dumas on the easy payment plan.'

Then, seeing that Purkiss had buried his face in his hands and hearing him mutter something about 'God's gift to the nursery' and 'ruin', he stepped across and gave him a kindly pat on the shoulder.

'Cheer up,' he said. 'You still have me.'

'No, I haven't,' said Purkiss. 'You're fired.'

And in words whose meaning there was no mistaking he informed Bingo that the end of the month would see his finish as Ye Ed., and that it was his, Purkiss's, dearest hope that when he, Bingo, finally left the premises, he would trip over the doormat and break his neck.

He, Purkiss, then withdrew.

His departure gave Bingo the opportunity for some intensive thinking. And as you will readily appreciate, intensive thinking was just what the situation could do with a spot of.

It was on Mrs Bingo's reactions that he found himself brooding for the most part. There were many reasons why it cut him to the quick to be forced to relinquish his grasp on the tiller of *Wee Tots*. The salary, though small, had come under the head of manna from heaven, and the holding of the post had filled him with a spiritual pride such as he had not experienced since he won the Woolly-Mat-Tatting Prize at his first kindergarten. But what really got in amongst him was the thought of what Mrs Bingo was going to say on hearing the news.

The Bingo *ménage*, as you are no doubt aware, is one that has been

conducted from its inception on one hundred per cent Romeo and
Juliet lines. She is devoted to him, and his ingrowing love for her is
such that you would be justified in comparing them to a couple of
turtle doves. Nevertheless, he was ill at ease. Any male turtle dove
will tell you that, if conditions are right, the female turtle dove can
spit on her hands and throw her weight about like Donald Duck. And
it needed no diagram to show Bingo that conditions here were just
right. Mrs Bingo had taken a lot of trouble to get him this job, and
when she found that through sheer fatheadedness he had chucked it
away she would, something told him, have a lot of comment to make.

Little wonder, then, that the barometer of his soul pointed steadily
to 'Stormy'. Out of the night that covered him, black as the pit from
pole to pole, one solitary bit of goose presented itself – the fact that
the head of the family was away at the moment, visiting friends in the
country. This at least enabled him to postpone the springing of the
bad tidings.

But the thought that the hour of that springing must inevitably
come kept him in pretty much of a doodah, and to distract his mind
he plunged into the life of pleasure. And it was at a bottle-party a
couple of nights later that he found himself going like a breeze with a
female of considerable attractions, and with indescribable emotion
learned that her name was Jobson, Bella Mae.

It altered the whole outlook, enabling him to get an entirely new
angle on the situation.

Until this moment, he had been feeling that his only chance of
wangling a happy ending would be to put up a good, carefully constructed, plausible story. He had planned, accordingly, on Mrs
Bingo's return, to inform her quite frankly that he had been relieved
of his portfolio for giving Purkiss's girlfriend the raspberry, and then
to go on to explain why he had taken this stand. He had felt, he would
say, that he owed it to her not to allow himself to be closeted with
strange women. Too often, he would tell her, female visitors pat
editors on the knee or even straighten their ties, and his pure soul had
shrunk from the thought of anything like that happening to a sober
married man like himself. It might get by, or it might not get by. It
was a straight, sporting venture.

But now he saw that he could do much better than this. He could
obviate all necessity for such explanations by retaining his job.

When I said that he found himself going like a breeze with this
chipmunk-fancier, I used the expression in its most exact sense. I
don't know if any of you have ever seen Bingo when he was going
really well, but I can testify that at such times he does his stuff like a
master. Irresistible charm about sums it up. Think of Ronald

Colman, and you have the idea. Well, you will understand what I mean when I tell you that as early as the second cocktail B. M. Jobson was saying how lonely she felt in this big, strange city, and he was saying 'There, there' and pointing out that this was a state of things that could readily be adjusted. They parted in a flurry of telephone numbers and good wishes, and he went home feeling that the thing was in the bag.

What he proposed to do, I need scarcely explain, was to keep after this tomato and bump up their ripening friendship to a point where she would be able to refuse him nothing. He would then tear off his whiskers and reveal himself as the editor of *Wee Tots*, whereupon she would let him have her frightful bilge on easy terms and he would go to Purkiss and say: 'Well, Purkiss, and now how about it?' Upon which, of course, Purkiss would immediately fold him in a close embrace and issue a reprieve at the foot of the scaffold.

To this end, accordingly, he devoted all his energies. He took Bella Mae Jobson to the Zoo, the Tower of London, Madame Tussaud's, five matinées, seven lunches and four dinners. He also gave her a bunch of white heather, several packets of cigarettes, eleven lots of roses and a signed photograph. And came a day when she said she really must buy back. She was sailing for America on the following Wednesday, she said, and on the Tuesday she was going to give a lovely luncheon party at her hotel suite and he must be the guest of honour.

Bingo accepted effusively. The moment, he realized, had come. He had got the thing all worked out. He would stick on till the other guests had gone and then, while she was still mellowed with lunch, spring his big scene. He didn't see how it could miss.

It was only when a telegram arrived from Mrs Bingo on the Monday morning, announcing that she would be returning that evening, that he began to appreciate that there might be complications which he had not foreseen.

In normal circs., the return of the wife of his b. after a longish absence would have been enough to send Bingo singing about the house. But now he didn't emit so much as a single bar, and it was with a drawn and thoughtful face that he met her at the station round about six-thirty.

'Well, well, well,' he said heartily, or as heartily as he could manage, embracing her on the platform. 'This is fine! This is great! This is terrific! And what a surprise, what? I thought you were planning to put in rather longer in the provinces.'

Mrs Bingo registered astonishment.

'What, miss our wedding anniversary?' she cried. She paused, and he became aware that she was eyeing him fairly narrowly. 'You hadn't forgotten that tomorrow was our wedding anniversary?'

Bingo, who had given a sharp, convulsive leap like a gaffed salmon, reassembled himself.

'Me?' he cried. 'I should say not. I've been ticking off the days on the calendar.'

'So have I,' said Mrs Bingo. 'Oh, Bingo, darling, we'll have lunch tomorrow at that little place near Charing Cross, where we had our wedding breakfast. And we'll pretend we've just been married. Won't it be fun!'

Bingo swallowed a couple of times. He was having trouble with his Adam's apple.

'Stupendous,' he said.

'Only it won't be quite the same, of course, because then you hadn't an important job to hurry back to.'

'No,' said Bingo.

'How is everything at the office, by the way?'

'Oh, fine.'

'Is Mr Purkiss still pleased with your work?'

'Fascinated,' said Bingo.

But he spoke absently, and it was with a heavy heart that he rose next morning and toyed listlessly with a fried egg and bacon. Nor was he any chirpier when he reached the editorial sanctum. He could see no daylight.

It would be possible, of course, to pop in on Bella Mae in the course of the afternoon, but he saw only too clearly that that would not be the same thing at all. The way he had had it planned out, he was to have been the life and soul of the gathering all through lunch, winning all hearts with his gay wit; and then, when the last guest had tottered away, holding his sides, and his hostess was thanking him brokenly for making her party such a success, he would have given her the works. It would be very different barging in on her at four o'clock and trying to swing the deal in cold blood.

And then, after he had been sitting for a goodish time with his head in his hands, exercising every cell in his brain to its utmost capacity, he received an inspiration and saw what Napoleon would have done. A moment later, he was on the telephone, with Mrs Bingo's silvery voice are-you-there-ing at the other end.

'Hullo, darling,' he said.

'Hullo, angel,' said Mrs Bingo.

'Hullo, precious,' said Bingo.

'Hullo, sweetie-pie,' said Mrs Bingo.

'I say, moon of my delight,' said Bingo, 'listen. A rather awkward thing has happened, and I should like your advice as to how to act for the best. There's a most important *littérateuse* we are anxious to land for the old sheet, and the question has arisen of my taking her out to lunch today.'

'Oh, Bingo!'

'Now, my personal inclination is to tell her to go to blazes.'

'Oh, no, you mustn't do that.'

'Yes, I think I will. "Nuts to you, *littérateuse*," I shall say.'

'No, Bingo, please! Of course you must take her to lunch.'

'But how about our binge?'

'We can have dinner instead.'

'Dinner?'

'Yes.'

Bingo allowed himself to be persuaded.

'Now, that's an idea,' he said. 'There, I rather think, you've got something.'

'Dinner will be just as good.'

'Better. More suited to unbridled revelry.'

'You won't have to hurry off after dinner.'

'That's right.'

'We'll go to a theatre and supper afterwards.'

'We will, indeed,' said Bingo, feeling how simple these things were, if only one used a bit of tact. 'That, as I see it, is the exact programme.'

'And, as a matter of fact,' said Mrs Bingo, 'it's really rather convenient, because now I shall be able to go to Miss Jobson's luncheon party, after all.'

Bingo swayed like a jelly in a high wind.

'Miss who's luncheon party?'

'Jobson. You wouldn't know her. An American writer named Bella Mae Jobson. Mrs Purkiss rang up a little while ago, saying she was going and could I come along, because Miss Jobson has long been an admirer of my work. Of course, I refused. But now it's all right, and I shall be able to go. She sails tomorrow, so this is our last chance of meeting. Well, goodbye, my poppet, I mustn't keep you from your work any longer.'

If Mrs Bingo supposed that Bingo, having hung up the receiver, immediately returned to the task of assembling wholesome literature for the kiddies, she was gravely in error. For possibly a quarter of an hour after she had rung off, he sat motionless in his chair, using up time which Purkiss was paying him for in staring sightlessly before

him and breathing in quick jerks. His whole aspect was that of a man
who has unexpectedly been struck by lightning.

This, it seemed to him, was the end. He couldn't possibly roll up to
the Jobson lunch, if Mrs Bingo was going to be there. You see, in
order not to divert her mind from the main issue, he had avoided
informing Bella Mae that he was married. Rightly or wrongly, he had
felt that better results were to be obtained by keeping this news item
under his hat. And if she lugged Mrs Bingo up to him and said, 'Oh,
Mr Little, I wonder if you know Miss Rosie M. Banks?' and he
replied, 'Oh, rather. She's my wife,' only embarrassment could
ensue.

No, there was only one thing to be done. He must abandon all idea
of retaining his job and go back to the plan he had originally sketched
out, of explaining to Mrs Bingo why he had refused to see Bella Mae
Jobson that day when she called at the office. This, he felt with the
first stirring of optimism which so far had animated him, might go
pretty well after the former had met the latter. For Bella Mae, as I
have said, was a female of considerable personal attractions. She had
a lissome form, surmounted by a map of elfin charm and platinum-
blonde hair. Stranger things had happened than that Mrs Bingo
might approve his prudence in declining to be cooped up with all that
sex-appeal.

Feeling somewhat better, he went out and dispatched a telegram to
the Jobson, regretting his inability to be present at the festivities.
And he was about to return to the office, when a sudden thought
struck him amidships and he had to clutch at a passing lamp-post to
keep himself from falling in his tracks.

He had remembered that signed photograph.

The whole question of signed photographs is one that bulks largely
in married life. When husbands bestow them on external females,
wives want to know why. And the present case was complicated by
the fact that in doing the signing Bingo – with the best motives – had
rather spread himself. Mere cordiality would have been bad enough,
and he had gone a shade beyond the cordial. And the finished product
was probably standing on the Jobson's mantelpiece and would be the
first thing that Mrs Bingo would see on entering the other's suite.

It was not an enterprise to which he in any sense of the phrase
looked forward, but he saw that, if a major disaster was to be avoided
and the solidity of the Bingo – Mrs Bingo axis to be maintained, he
would have to get hold of that photograph well in advance of the
luncheon hour and remove it.

I don't know if you have ever called at an hotel with a view to pinching a signed photograph from one of the suites. If not, I may tell you that technical difficulties present themselves at the very outset – notably the problem of how the hell to get in. Bingo, inquiring at the desk, learned that Miss Jobson was not at home, and was for a moment encouraged by the information. It was only after he had sneaked up the stairs and was standing outside the locked door that he realized that this was not an end but a beginning.

And then, just as he was feeling that he was a mere puppet in the grip of a remorseless fate and that it wasn't any use going on struggling, he saw a maid coming along the corridor, and remembered that maids have keys.

It was a moment for exerting that charm of his to the uttermost. He switched it on and allowed it to play upon the maid like a searchlight.

'Oh, hullo, maid,' he said. 'Good morning.'

'Good morning, sir,' said the maid.

'Gosh!' said Bingo. 'You have a nice, kind, open, tender-hearted face. I wonder if you would do something for me. First, however,' he said, shoving across a ten-bob note, 'take this.'

'Thank you, sir,' said the maid.

'The facts, briefly,' said Bingo, 'are these. I am lunching today with Miss Jobson.'

'She's out,' said the maid. 'I saw her go along the passage with the little dog.'

'Exactly,' said Bingo. 'And there you have put your finger on the nub. She's out, and I want to get in. I hate waiting in hotel lobbies. You know how it is. Bores come up and tell you their troubles. Cadgers come up and try to touch you. I shall be happier in Miss Jobson's suite. Could you possibly' – here he ladled out another currency bill – 'let me in?'

'Certainly, sir,' said the maid, and did so.

'Thanks,' said Bingo. 'Heaven bless you, my dear old maid. Lovely day.'

'Beautiful,' said the maid.

He had scarcely crossed the threshold before he perceived that he had done the shrewd thing in sweetening her. He was a quid down, and he could ill spare quids, but it had been worth every penny of the money. There, as he had anticipated, was the photograph, plumb spang in the middle of the mantelpiece where it could not have failed to catch the eye of an incoming wife. To snatch it up and trouser it was with him the work of a moment, and he was just turning to the door to make the quick get away, when his attention was drawn to a row of bottles on the sideboard. There they stood, smiling up at him, and as he was feeling more than a little faint after his ordeal he decided to have one for the road before withdrawing.

So he sloshed some Italian vermouth into a glass, and sloshed some French vermouth on top of it, and was reaching for the gin, to start sloshing that, when his heart did three double somersaults and a swan-dive. There had come to his ears the rattle of a key in the door.

It is difficult to say what would really have been the right thing to do in the circumstances. Some chaps, I suppose, would just have stayed put and tried to pass it off with jovial breeziness. Others might have jumped out of the window. But he wasn't feeling equal to jovial breeziness and the suite was on the fourth floor, so he took a middle course. He cleared the sofa in a single bound, and had scarcely gone to earth behind it when the door opened.

It was not Bella Mae Jobson who entered, but his old pal the maid. She was escorting another early popper-in. Through the gap at the bottom of his zareba he could see the concluding portion of a pair of trousers and a pair of boots. And when the lips above these trousers spoke, he found that this was no stranger but a familiar acquaintance. The voice was the voice of Purkiss.

'Thank you, my dear,' said Purkiss.

'Thank you, sir,' said the maid, leading Bingo to suppose that once more money had passed into her possession. He found himself brooding on the irony of the thing. Such a big day for the maid, I mean, and such a rotten one for him.

Purkiss coughed.

'I seem to be early.'

'Yes, sir.'

'Then, perhaps, to fill in the time, I might be taking Miss Jobson's dog for a run.'

'Miss Jobson's out with the dog now, sir.'

'Oh?' said Purkiss.

There was a momentary silence, and then the maid said that that was funny, and Purkiss asked what was funny.

'There ought to be another gentleman here,' said the maid. 'But I don't see him. Oh yes,' she proceeded, as Bingo, who for some little while now had been inhaling fluff in rather large quantities, gave a hearty sneeze, 'there he is, behind the sofa.'

And the next moment Bingo was aware of an eye peering down at him from the upper regions. Purkiss's eye.

'Mr Little!' cried Purkiss.

Bingo rose, feeling that it was useless to dissemble further.

'Ah, Purkiss,' he said distantly, for they were not on good terms, and with what dignity he could muster, which was not much, he rose and made for the door.

'Hey!' cried Purkiss. 'Just a minute.'

Bingo carried on doorwards.

'If you wish to speak to me, Purkiss,' he said, 'you will find me in the bar.'

But it was not thither that he immediately proceeded. His need for a bracer was urgent, but even more than a bracer he wanted air. He had been under the sofa only about three minutes, but as nobody had swept there for nearly six years quite a lot of mixed substances had found their way into his lungs. He was, indeed, feeling more like a dustbin than a man. He passed through the lobby and stood outside the door of the hotel, drinking in great draughts of the life-giving, and after a while began to feel better.

The improvement in his condition, however, was purely physical. Spiritually, he continued in the depths. As he reviewed the position of affairs, his heart struck a new low. He had secured the photograph, yes, and that was good, as far as it went. But it did not, he perceived, go so dashed far. If Purkiss was to be one of the guests at the Jobson lunch, he was still waist-high in the soup and likely to sink without trace at any moment.

He could envisage just what would occur at the beano. His tortured mind threw the thing into a sort of dialogue scene.

The Apartment of B. M. Jobson. Afternoon. Discovered – B. M. Jobson and Purkiss. Enter Mrs Bingo.

MRS BINGO: Cheerio. I'm Rosie M. Banks.

JOBSON: Oh, what ho, Miss Banks. Do you know Mr Purkiss?

MRS BINGO: You betcher. How owns the paper my husband is editor of.

JOBSON: You're married, then?

MRS BINGO: Oh, rather. Name of Little.

JOBSON: Little? Little? Odd. I know a bird named Little. In fact, when I say 'know', that's understating it a bit. He's been giving me the rush of a lifetime. 'Bingo', mine calls himself. Some relation, perhaps.

MRS BINGO:

But he preferred not to sketch in Mrs Bingo's lines. He stood there groaning in spirit. And he had just groaned for about the fifteenth time, when a car drew up before him and through a sort of mist he saw Mrs Bingo seated at the steering-wheel.

'Oh, Bingo, darling!' cried Mrs Bingo. 'What luck finding you here. Is this where you're lunching with your writer? What an extraordinary coincidence.'

It seemed to Bingo that if he was going to put up any kind of a story, now was the time to put it up. In a few brief moments Mrs Bingo would be entering the presence of the Jobson, with results as already indicated, and her mind must be prepared.

But beyond a sort of mixed snort and gurgle he found himself unable to utter, and Mrs Bingo carried on:

'I can't stop a minute,' she said. 'I've got to rush back to Mrs Purkiss. She's in great distress. When I got to her house, to pick her up and drive her here, I found her in a terrible state. Apparently her dog has been lost. I just came here to tell Miss Jobson that we shan't be able to lunch. Will you be an angel and ring her up from the desk and explain?'

Bingo blinked. The hotel, though solidly built, seemed to be swaying above him.

'You ... what was that you said? You won't be able to lunch with – '

'No. Mrs Purkiss wants me with her. She's gone to bed with a hot-water bottle. So will you ring Miss Jobson up? Then I can hurry off.'

Bingo drew a deep breath.

'Of course, of course, of course, of course, of course,' he said. 'Oh, rather. Rather. Ring Miss Jobson up ... tell her you and Mrs Purkiss will not be among those present ... explain fully. A simple task. Leave it to me, light of my life.'

'Thank you, darling. Goodbye.'

'Goodbye,' said Bingo.

She drove off, and he stood there, his eyes closed and his lips moving silently. Only once in his life before had he been conscious of this awed sense of being the favourite son of a benevolent providence. That was at his private school, when the Rev. Aubrey Upjohn, his headmaster, in the very act of raising the cane to land him a juicy one on the old spot, had ricked his shoulder and had to postpone the ceremony indefinitely.

Presently, life returned to the rigid limbs and he tottered to the bar to have one quick, followed by another rather slower. And the first person he saw there, sucking down something pink, was Purkiss. He gave him an austere look, and settled himself at the farther end of the counter. Later on, it would presumably be his nauseous task to step across and inform the man of the tragedy which had come upon his home, but the thought of holding speech with him after the way he had behaved was so revolting that he did not propose to do it until he had fortified himself with a couple of refreshers.

And he had had the first one and was waiting for the second, when he felt something pawing at his sleeve. He glanced round, and there was Purkiss with a pleading look in his eyes, like a spaniel trying to ingratiate itself with someone whom it knows to be allergic to dogs.

'Mr Little.'

'Well, Purkiss?'

'Mr Little, it is in your power to do me a great kindness.'

Well, I don't know what you would have replied to that, if you had been in Bingo's position – addressed in this fashion, I mean, by a man who had not only given you the push but in doing so had called you at least six offensive names. Personally, I would have said 'Oh?' or possibly 'Ho!' and that may have been what Bingo was intending to say. But before he could get going, Purkiss proceeded.

'Mr Little, I am faced by a disaster so hideous that the mind reels, contemplating it, and only you can save me. At any moment now, my wife will be arriving here. We are lunching with Miss Jobson. Mr Little, I appeal to you. Will you think of some suitable story and go and stand at the door and intercept her and prevent her coming to this luncheon party? My whole future happiness depends on this.'

At this juncture, Bingo's second refresher arrived and he sat sipping it thoughtfully. He could make nothing of all this, but he is a pretty intelligent chap, and he was beginning to see that circumstances had arisen which might culminate in him doing a bit of good for himself.

'It is imperative that my wife does not enter Miss Jobson's suite.'

Bingo got outside the mixture, and laid the glass down.

'Tell me the whole story in your own words, Purkiss,' he said.

Purkiss had produced a handkerchief, and was mopping his forehead with it. With his other hand he continued to massage Bingo's arm. His whole deportment was vastly different from what it had been when he had called Bingo those six offensive names.

'It was only late this morning,' he said, 'that Miss Jobson informed me on the telephone that she had invited my wife to be a guest at this luncheon party – which, until then, I had supposed would be a *tête-à-tête* between her and myself. I may mention that I have concluded negotiations with Miss Jobson for the publication of her brilliant works. I had presumed that over the luncheon-table we would discuss such details as illustrations and general make-up.'

'Matters,' said Bingo coldly, 'more customarily left to the editor.'

'Quite, quite, but as ... yes, quite. But the point is, Mr Little, that in order to secure this material from Miss Jobson I had been compelled to – ah – how shall I put it – '

'Bring a little pressure to bear?'

'Precisely. Yes, it is exactly what I did. It seemed to me that the end justified the means. *Wee Tots*, as I saw it, was standing at the cross-roads. Let me secure the works of Bella Mae Jobson, and the dear old paper would soar beyond reach of competition. Let her, on the other hand, go to one of my trade rivals, and it would sustain a blow from which it might not recover. So I left no stone unturned.'

'And avenues?'

'Avenues, too. I explored them all.'

Bingo pursed his lips.

'I have no wish to condemn you unheard, Purkiss,' he said, 'but all this begins to look a bit French. Did you kiss Miss Jobson?'

A violent start shook Purkiss from stem to stern.

'No, no, no, no!' he protested vehemently. 'Certainly not. Most decidedly not. Nothing of that nature whatsoever. From start to finish our relations have been conducted with the utmost circumspection on my part, complete maidenly dignity on hers. But I took her to the National Gallery, the British Museum, and a matinée at Sadler's Wells. And then, seeing that she was weakening, I . . .'

His voice faltered and died away. Recovering it, he asked the barman for another of those pink ones for himself and whatever Bingo desired for Bingo. Then, when the tissue-restorers had appeared and he had drained his at a gulp, he found strength to continue.

'I gave her my wife's Pekinese.'

'What!'

'Yes. She had admired the animal when visiting my house, and I smuggled it out in a hatbox when I left home this morning and brought it to this hotel. Ten minutes later she had signed the contract. An hour later she apparently decided to include my wife in her list of guests. Two hours after that, she was informing me of this fact on the telephone, and I hastened here in the hope of being able to purloin the animal.

'But it was not to be. She had taken it for a run. Consider my position, Mr Little. What am I to do if my wife enters Miss Jobson's suite and finds her in possession of this dog? There will be explanations. And what will be the harvest when those explanations have been made?' He broke off, quivering in every limb. 'But why are we wasting time? While we sit talking here, she may be arriving. Your post is at the door. Fly, Mr Little!'

Bingo eyed him coldly.

'It's all very well to say "Fly!",' he said, 'but the question that springs to the lips is, "What is there in this for me?" Really, Purkiss, after your recent behaviour I rather fail to see why I should sweat myself to the bone, lugging you out of messes. It is true,' he went on meditatively, 'that I have just thought of a pippin of a story which cannot fail to head Mrs Purkiss off when she arrives, but why should I bother to dish it out? At the end of this week I cease to be in your employment. It would be a very different thing, of course, if I were continuing as editor of *Wee Tots* – '

'But you are, Mr Little, you are.'

'– at a considerably increased salary – '

'Your salary shall be doubled.'

Bingo reflected.

'H'm!' he said. 'And no more muscling in and trying to dictate the policy of the "Uncle Joe To His Chickabiddies" page?'

'None, none. From now on, none. You shall have a completely free hand.'

'Then, Purkiss, you may set your mind at rest. Mrs Purkiss will not be present at the luncheon party.'

'You guarantee that?'

'I guarantee it,' said Bingo. 'Just step along with me to the writing room and embody the terms of our new contract in a brief letter, and I will do the needful.'

13
SONNY BOY

On the question of whether Bingo Little was ethically justified in bringing his baby into the club and standing it a milk straight in the smoking room, opinion at the Drones was sharply divided. A Bean with dark circles under his eyes said that it was not the sort of thing a chap wanted to see suddenly when he looked in for a drop of something to correct a slight queasiness after an exacting night. A more charitable Egg argued that as the child was presumably coming up for election later on, it was as well for it to get to know the members. A Pieface thought that if Bingo did let the young thug loose on the premises, he ought at least to give the committee a personal guarantee for all hats, coats and umbrellas.

'Because if ever I saw a baby that looked like something that was one jump ahead of the police,' said the Pieface, 'it is this baby of Bingo's. Definitely the criminal type. It reminds me of Edward G. Robinson.'

A Crumpet, always well informed, was able to throw a rather interesting light on the situation.

'I agree,' he said, 'that Algernon Aubrey Little is not a child whom I personally would care to meet down a dark alley, but Bingo assures me that its heart is in the right place, and as for his bringing it here and lushing it up, that is readily explained. He is grateful to this baby and feels that the best is none too good for it. By doing the right thing at the right time, it recently pulled him out of a very nasty spot. It is not too much to say, he tells me, that but for its intervention a situation would have been precipitated in his home life which might well have staggered humanity.'

When in the second year of his marriage to Rosie M. Banks, the eminent female novelist, his union was blessed and this bouncing boy appeared on the London scene, Bingo's reactions (said the Crumpet) were, I gather, very much the same as yours. Introduced to the child in the nursing home, he recoiled with a startled 'Oi!' and as the days went by the feeling that he had run up against something red-hot in no way diminished.

The only thing that prevented a father's love from faltering was the fact that there was in his possession a photograph of himself at the same early age, in which he, too, looked like a homicidal fried egg. This proof that it was possible for a child, in spite of a rocky start, to turn eventually into a suave and polished boulevardier with finely chiselled features heartened him a good deal, causing him to hope for the best.

Meanwhile, however, there was no getting away from it that the little stranger was at the moment as pronounced a gargoyle as ever drained a bottle, and Bingo, finding that a horse of that name was running in the three o'clock at Plumpton, had no hesitation in putting ten pounds on it to cop. Always on the lookout for omens from on high, he thought that this must have been what the child had been sent for.

The failure of Gargoyle to finish in the first six left him in a position of considerable financial embarrassment. The tenner which he had placed on its nose was the last one he had, and its loss meant that he would have to go a month without cigarettes, cocktails, and those other luxuries which to the man of refinement are so much more necessary than necessities.

For there was no glittering prospect open to him of being able to touch the head of the house for a trifle to be going on with. Mrs Bingo's last words, before leaving for Worcestershire some two weeks previously to see her mother through a course of treatment at the Droitwich brine baths, had contained a strong injunction to him not to bet in her absence; and any attempt on his part to palliate his action by showing that he had supposed himself to be betting on a certainty would, he felt, be badly received.

No, the cash, if it was to be raised, must be raised from some other source, and in these circumstances his thoughts, as they had so often done before, turned to Oofy Prosser. That it was never a simple task to get into Oofy's ribs, but one always calculated to test the stoutest, he would have been the first to concede. But it so happened that in the last few days the club's tame millionaire had shown himself unexpectedly friendly. On one occasion, going into the writing room to dash off a letter to his tailor which he hoped would lead to an appeasement, Bingo had found him there, busy on what appeared to be a poem: and Oofy, after asking him if he knew any good rhymes to 'eyes of blue', had gone on to discuss the married state with him, giving it as his opinion that it was the only life.

The conclusion Bingo drew was that love had at last found Oofy Prosser, and an Oofy in love, he reasoned, might – nay, must – be an Oofy in a melting mood which would lead him to scatter the stuff in heaping handfuls. It was with bright confidence, accordingly, that he made his way to the block of flats in Park Lane where the other has his lair, and it was with a feeling that his luck was in that, reaching the front door, he met Oofy coming out.

'Oh, hullo, Oofy,' he said. 'Good morning, Oofy. I say, Oofy – '

I suppose years of being the official moneyed man of the Drones had given Oofy Prosser a sort of sixth sense. You might almost say that he is clairvoyant. Without waiting to hear more, he now made a quick sideways leap, like an antelope spotting a tiger, and was off in a cab, leaving Bingo standing there considering how to act for the best.

Taking a line through stoats and weasels, he decided that the only thing to do was to continue doggedly on the trail, so he toddled off to the Savoy Grill, whither he had heard the driver being told to drive, and arriving there some twenty minutes later found Oofy in the lobby with a girl. It was with considerable pleasure that he recognized in her an old pal, with whom in his bachelor days he had frequently trodden the measure, for this enabled him to well-well-well and horn in. And once Bingo has horned it, he is not easy to dislodge. A few minutes later, they were all seated round a table and he was telling the wine waiter to be sure to take the chill off the claret.

It didn't occur to him at the time, but, looking back, Bingo had a feeling that Oofy would have been just as pleased if he hadn't shown up. There was a sort of constraint at the meal. Bingo was all right. He prattled freely. And the girl was all right. She prattled freely, too. It was just that Oofy seemed not quite to have got the party spirit. Silent. Distrait. Absent-minded. Inclined to fidget in his chair and drum on the tablecloth with his fingers.

After the coffee, the girl said, Well, she supposed she ought to be haring to Charing Cross and catching her train – she, it appeared, being headed for a country house visit in Kent. Oofy, brightening a little, said he would come and see her off. And Bingo, faithful to his policy of not letting Oofy out of his sight, said he would come too. So they all tooled along, and after the train had pulled out Bingo, linking his arm in Oofy's, said: 'I say, Oofy, I wonder if you would do me a trifling favour?'

Even as he spoke, he tells me he seemed to notice something odd in his companion's manner. Oofy's eyes had a sort of bleak glazed look in them.

'Oh?' he said distantly. 'You do, do you? And what is it, my bright young limpet? What can I do for you, my adhesive old porous plaster?'

'Could you lend me a tenner, Oofy, old man?'

'No, I couldn't.'

'It would save my life.'

'There,' said Oofy, 'you have put your finger on the insuperable objection to the scheme. I see no percentage in your being alive. I wish you were a corpse, preferably a mangled one. I should like to dance on your remains.'

Bingo was surprised.

'Dance on my remains?'

'All over them.'

Bingo drew himself up. He had his pride.

'Oh?' he said. 'Well, in that case, tinkerty-tonk.'

The interview then terminated. Oofy hailed a cab, and Bingo returned to his Wimbledon home. And he had not been there long when he was informed that he was wanted on the telephone. He went to the instrument and heard Oofy's voice.

'Hullo,' said Oofy. 'Is that you? I say, you remember me saying I would like to dance on your mangled remains?'

'I do.'

'Well, I've been thinking it over – '

Bingo's austerity vanished. He saw what had happened. Shortly after they had separated, Oofy's better nature must have asserted itself, causing remorse to set in. And he was just about to tell him not to give it another thought, because we all say more than we mean in moments of heat, when Oofy continued:

' – thinking it over,' he said, 'and I would like to add "in hob-nailed boots". Goodbye.'

It was a tight-lipped and pensive Bingo Little who hung up the receiver and returned to the drawing room, where he had been tucking into tea and muffins. As he resumed the meal, the tea turned to wormwood and the muffins to ashes in his mouth. The thought of having to get through a solid month without cocktails and cigarettes gashed him like a knife. And he was just wondering if it might not be best, after all, to go to the last awful extreme of confessing everything to Mrs Bingo, when the afternoon post came in, and there was a letter from her. And out of it, as he tore open the envelope, tumbled a ten-pound note.

Bingo tells me that his emotions at this moment were almost indescribable. For quite a while, he says, he remained motionless in his chair with eyes closed, murmuring: 'What a pal! What a helpmeet!' Then he opened his eyes and started to read the letter.

It was a longish letter, all about the people at the hotel and a kitten she had struck up an acquaintance with and what her mother looked like when floating in the brine bath, and so on and so forth, and it wasn't till the end that the tenner got a mention. Like all women, Mrs Bingo kept the big stuff for her postscript.

P.S. (she wrote) – I am enclosing ten pounds. I want you to go to the bank and open an account for little Algy with it. Don't you think it will be too sweet, him having his own little account and his own little wee passbook?

I suppose if a fairly sinewy mule had suddenly kicked Bingo in the face, he might have felt a bit worse, but not much. The letter fell from his nerveless hands. Apart from the hideous shock of finding that he hadn't clicked, after all, he thoroughly disapproved of the whole project. Himself strongly in favour of sharing the wealth, it seemed to him that the last thing to place in the hands of an impressionable child was a little wee passbook, starting it off in life – as it infallibly must – with capitalistic ideas out of tune with the trend of modern enlightened thought. Slip a baby ten quid, he reasoned, and before you knew where you were you had got another Economic Royalist on your hands.

So uncompromising were his views on the subject that there was a moment when he found himself toying with the notion of writing back and telling Mrs Bingo – in the child's best interests – that he had received a letter from her stating that she was enclosing ten pounds, but that, owing doubtless to a momentary carelessness on her part, no ten pounds had arrived with it. However, he dismissed the idea – not because it was not good, but because something told him that it was not good enough. Mrs Bingo was a woman who wrote novels about girls who wanted to be loved for themselves alone, but she was not lacking in astuteness.

He finished his tea and muffins, and then, ordering the perambulator, had the son and heir decanted into it and started off for a saunter on Wimbledon Common. Many young fathers, I believe, shrink from this task, considering that it lowers their prestige, but Bingo had always enjoyed it.

Today, however, the jaunt was robbed of all its pleasures by the brooding melancholy into which the sight of the child, lying there dumb and aloof with a thumb in its mouth, plunged him. Hitherto, he had always accepted with equanimity the fact that it was impossible for there to be any real exchange of ideas between his offspring and himself. An occasional gurgle from the former, and on his side a few musical chirrups, had served to keep them in touch. But now the thought that they were separated by an impassable gulf which no chirrups could bridge, seemed to him poignant and tragic to a degree.

Here, he reflected, was he – penniless; and there was the infant – rolling in the stuff; and absolutely no way of getting together and adjusting things. If only he could have got through to Algernon Aubrey the facts relating to his destitute condition, he was convinced that there would have been no difficulty about arranging a temporary loan. It was the old story of frozen assets, which, as everyone knows, is the devil of a business and stifles commerce at the source.

So preoccupied was he with these moody meditations that it was not immediately that he discovered that somebody was speaking his name. Then, looking up with a start, he saw that a stout man in a frock coat and a bowler hat had come alongside, wheeling a perambulator containing a blob-faced baby.

'Good evening, Mr Little,' he said, and Bingo saw that it was his bookie, Charles ('Charlie Always Pays') Pikelet, the man who had acted as party of the second part in the recent deal over the horse Gargoyle. Having seen him before only at race meetings – where, doubtless from the best of motives, he affected chessboard tweeds and a white panama – he had not immediately recognized him.

'Why, hullo, Mr Pikelet,' he said.

He was not really feeling in the vein for conversation and would have preferred to be alone with his thoughts, but the other appeared to be desirous of chatting, and he was prepared to stretch a point to oblige him. The prudent man always endeavours to keep in with bookies.

'I didn't know you lived in these parts. Is that your baby?'

'Ah,' said Charles Pikelet, speaking despondently. He gave a quick look into the interior of the perambulator to which he was attached, and winced like one who has seen some fearful sight.

'Kitchy-kitchy,' said Bingo.

'How do you mean, kitchy-kitchy?' asked Mr Pikelet, puzzled.

'I was speaking to the baby,' explained Bingo. 'A pretty child,' he added, feeling that there was nothing to be lost by giving the man the old oil.

Charles Pikelet looked up, amazement in his eyes.

'Pretty?'

'Well, of course,' said Bingo, his native honesty compelling him to qualify the statement, 'I don't say he – if it is a he – is a Robert Taylor or – if a she – a Carole Lombard. Pretty compared with mine, I mean.'

Again Charles Pikelet appeared dumbfounded.

'Are you standing there and telling me this baby of mine isn't uglier than that baby of yours?' he cried incredulously.

It was Bingo's turn to be stunned.

'Are you standing there and telling me it is?'

'I certainly am. Why, yours looks human.'

Bingo could scarcely believe his ears.

'Human? Mine?'

'Well, practically human.'

'My poor misguided Pikelet, you're talking rot.'

'Rot, eh?' said Charles Pikelet, stung. 'Perhaps you'd care to have a bet on it? Five to one I'm offering that my little Arabella here stands alone as the ugliest baby in Wimbledon.'

A sudden thrill shot through Bingo. No one has a keener eye than he for recognizing money for pickles.

'Take a tenner?'

'Tenner it is.'

'Okay,' said Bingo.

'Kayo,' said Charles Pikelet. 'Where's your tenner?'

This introduction of a rather sordid note into the discussion caused Bingo to start uneasily.

'Oh, dash it,' he protested, 'surely elasticity of credit is the very basis of these transactions. Chalk it up on the slate.'

Mr Pikelet said he hadn't got a slate.

Bingo had to think quickly. He had a tenner on his person, of course, but he realized that it was in the nature of trust money, and he had no means of conferring with Algernon Aubrey and ascertaining whether the child would wish to slip it to him. It might be that he had inherited his mother's lack of the sporting spirit.

And then, with quick revulsion, he felt that he was misjudging the little fellow. No son of his would want to pass up a snip like this.

'All right,' he said. 'Here you are.'

He produced the note, and allowed it to crackle before Charles Pikelet's eyes.

'Right,' said Charles Pikelet, satisfied. 'Here's my fifty. And we'll put the decision up to the policeman that's coming along. Hey, officer.'

'Gents?' said the policeman, halting. He was a large, comfortable man with an honest face. Bingo liked the look of him, and was well content to place the judging in his hands.

'Officer,' said Charles Pikelet, 'to settle a bet, is this baby here uglier than that baby there?'

'Or vice versa?' said Bingo.

The policeman brooded over the two perambulators.

'They're neither of 'em to be compared with the one I've got at home,' he said, a little smugly. 'There's a baby with a face that *would* stop a clock. And the missus thinks it's a beauty. I've had many a hearty laugh over that,' said the policeman indulgently.

Both Charles Pikelet and Bingo felt that he was straying from the point.

'Never mind about your baby,' said Charles Pikelet.

'No,' said Bingo. 'Stick closely to the *res*.'

'Your baby isn't a runner,' said Charles Pikelet. 'Only the above have arrived.'

Called to order, the policeman intensified his scrutiny. He looked from the one perambulator to the other, and then from the other perambulator to the one. And it suddenly came over Bingo like a cold douche that this hesitation could mean only one thing. It was not going to be the absurdly simple walk-over which he had anticipated.

'H'm!' said the policeman.

'Ha!' said the policeman.

Bingo's heart stood still. It was now plain to him that there was to be a desperately close finish. But he tells me that he is convinced that his entry would have nosed home, had it not been for a bit of extra-ordinary bad luck in the straight. Just as the policeman stood vacillating, there peeped through the clouds a ray of sunshine. It fell on Arabella Pikelet's face, causing her to screw it up in a hideous grimace. And at the same instant, with the race neck and neck, she suddenly started blowing bubbles out of the corner of her mouth.

The policeman hesitated no longer. He took Miss Pikelet's hand and raised it.

'The winnah!' he said. 'But you ought to see the one I've got at home.'

If the muffins which Bingo had had for tea had turned to ashes in his mouth, it was as nothing compared with what happened to the chump chop and fried which he had for dinner. For by that time his numbed brain, throwing off the coma into which it had fallen, really got busy, pointing out to him the various angles of the frightful mess he had let himself into. It stripped the seven veils from the situation, and allowed him to see it in all its stark grimness.

Between Bingo and Mrs Bingo there existed an almost perfect love. From the very inception of their union, they had been like ham and eggs. But he doubted whether the most Grade A affection could stand up against the revelation of what he had done this day. Look at his story from whatever angle you pleased, it remained one that reflected little credit on a young father and at the best must inevitably lead to 'Oh, how could you's?' And the whole wheeze in married life, he had come to learn, was to give the opposite number as few opportunities of saying 'Oh, how could you?' as possible.

And that story would have to be told. The first thing Mrs Bingo would want to see on her return would be Algernon Aubrey's passbook, and from the statement that no such passbook existed to the final, stammering confession would be but a step. No wonder that as he sat musing in his chair after dinner the eyes were haggard, the face drawn and the limbs inclined to twitch.

He was just jotting down on the back of an envelope a few rough notes such as 'Pocket picked,' and 'Took the bally thing out of my pocket on a windy morning and it blew out of my hand,' and speculating on the chances of these getting by, when he was called to the telephone to take a trunk call and found Mrs Bingo on the other end of the wire.

'Hullo,' said Mrs Bingo.

'Hullo,' said Bingo.

'Oh, hullo, darling.'

'Hullo, precious.'

'Hullo, sweetie-pie.'

'Hullo, angel.'

'Are you there?' said Mrs Bingo. 'How's Algy?'

'Oh, fine.'

'As beautiful as ever?'

'Substantially, yes.'

'Have you got my letter?'

'Yes.'

'And the ten pounds?'

'Yes.'

'Don't you think it's a wonderful idea?'

'Terrific.'

'I suppose it was too late to go to the bank today?'

'Yes.'

'Well, go there tomorrow morning before you come to Paddington.'

'Paddington?'

'Yes. To meet me. We're coming home tomorrow. Mother swallowed some brine this morning, and thinks she'd rather go and take the mud baths at Pistany instead.'

At any moment less tense than the present one, the thought of Mrs Bingo's mother being as far away as Pistany would have been enough to cause Bingo's spirits to soar. But now the news hardly made an impression on him. All he could think of was that the morrow would see Mrs Bingo in his midst. And then the bitter reckoning.

'The train gets to Paddington about twelve. Mind you're there.'

'I'll be there.'

'And bring Algy.'

'Right-ho.'

'Oh, and Bingo. Most important. You know my desk?'

'Desk. Yes.'

'Look in the middle top drawer.'

'Middle top drawer. Right.'

'I left the proofs of my Christmas story for *Woman's Wonder* there, and I've had a very sniffy telegram saying that they must have them tomorrow morning. So will you be an angel and correct them and send them off by tonight's post without fail? You can't miss them. Middle top drawer of my desk, and the title is "Tiny Fingers". And now I must go back to Mother. She's still coughing. Goodbye, darling.'

'Goodbye, precious.'

'Goodbye, lambkin.'

'Goodbye, my dream rabbit.'

Bingo hung up the receiver, and made his way to the study. He found the proofs of 'Tiny Fingers', and taking pencil in hand seated himself at the desk and started in on them.

His heart was heavier than ever. Normally, the news that his mother-in-law had been swallowing brine and was still coughing would have brought a sparkle to his eyes and a happy smile to his lips, but now it left him cold. He was thinking of the conversation which had just concluded and remembering how cordial Mrs Bingo's voice had been, how cheery, how loving – so absolutely in all respects the voice of a woman who thinks her husband a king among men. How different from the flat, metallic voice which was going to say '*What!*' to him in the near future.

And then suddenly, as he brooded over the galley slips, a sharp thrill permeated his frame and he sat up in his chair as if a new, firm backbone had been inserted in place of the couple of feet of spaghetti he had been getting along with up till now. In the middle of slip two the story had started to develop, and the way in which it developed caused hope to dawn again.

I don't know if any of you are readers of Mrs Bingo's output. If not, I may inform you that she goes in pretty wholeheartedly for the fruitily sentimental. This is so even at ordinary times, and for a Christmas number, of course, she naturally makes a special effort. In 'Tiny Fingers' she had chucked off the wraps completely. Scooping up snow and holly and robin redbreasts and carol-singing villagers in both hands, she had let herself go and given her public the works.

Bingo, when I last saw him, told me the plot of 'Tiny Fingers' in pitiless detail, but all I need touch on now is its main theme. It was about a hard-hearted godfather who had given his god-daughter the air for marrying the young artist, and they came right back at him by shoving the baby under his nose on Christmas Eve – the big scene, of course, being the final one, where the old buster sits in his panelled library, steadying the child on his knee with one hand while writing a whacking big cheque with the other. And the reason it made so deep an impression on Bingo was that he had suddenly remembered that Oofy Prosser was Algernon Aubrey's godfather. And what he was asking himself was, if this ringing-in-the-baby wheeze had worked with Sir Aylmer Mauleverer, the hardest nut in the old-world village of Meadowvale, why shouldn't it work with Oofy?

It was true that the two cases were not exactly parallel, Sir Aylmer having had snow and robin redbreasts to contend against and it now being the middle of June. It was true, also, that Oofy, when guardedly consenting to hold the towel for Algernon Aubrey, had expressly stipulated that there must be no funny business and that a small silver mug was to be accepted in full settlement. Nevertheless, Bingo went to bed in optimistic mood. Indeed, his last thought before dropping off to sleep was a speculation as to whether, if the baby played its cards right, it might not be possible to work Oofy up into three figures.

He had come down a bit in his budget, of course, by the time he set out for Park Lane next morning. One always does after sleeping on these things. As he saw it now, twenty quid was about what it ought to pan out at. This, however, cut fifty-fifty between principal and manager, would be ample. He was no hog. All he wanted was to place child and self on a sound financial footing, and as he reached Oofy's flat and pressed the bell, he was convinced that the thing was in the bag.

In a less sanguine frame of mind, he might have been discouraged by the fact that the infant was looking more than ever like some mass-assassin who has been blackballed by the Devil's Island Social and Outing Club as unfit to associate with the members; but his experience with Charles Pikelet and the policeman had shown him that this was how all babies of that age looked, and he had no reason to suppose that the one in 'Tiny Fingers' had been any different. The only thing Mrs Bingo had stressed about the latter had been its pink toes, and no doubt Algernon Aubrey, if called upon to do so, could swing as pink a toe as the next child. It was with bright exuberance that he addressed Oofy's man, Corker, as he opened the door.

'Oh, hullo, Corker. Lovely morning. Mr Prosser in?'

Corker did not reply immediately. The sight of Algernon Aubrey seemed momentarily to have wiped speech from his lips. Perfectly trained valet though he was, he had started back on perceiving him, his arms raised in a rudimentary posture of self-defence.

'Yes, sir,' he replied at length. 'Mr Prosser is at home. But he is not up yet, sir. He was out late last night.'

Bingo nodded intelligently. Oofy's practice of going out on the tiles and returning with the morning milk was familiar to him.

'Ah, well,' he said tolerantly. 'Young blood, Corker, eh?'

'Yes, sir.'

'It's a poor heart that never rejoices.'

'So I have been informed, sir.'

'I'll just pop in and pip-pip.'

'Very good, sir. Shall I take your luggage?'

'Eh? Oh, no, thanks. This is Mr Prosser's godson. I want them to meet. This'll be the first time he's seen him.'

'Indeed, sir?'

'Rather make his day, what?'

'So I should be disposed to imagine, sir. If you will follow me, sir. Mr Prosser is in the sitting room.'

'In the sitting room? I thought you said he was in bed.'

'No, sir. On his return home this morning, Mr Prosser appears to have decided not to go to bed. You will find him in the fireplace.'

And so it proved. Oofy Prosser was lying with his head in the fender and his mouth open. He had on an opera hat and what would have been faultless evening dress if he had had a tie on instead of a blue ribbon of the sort which the delicately nurtured use to bind up their hair. In one hand he was clutching a pink balloon, and across his shirt front was written in lipstick the word 'Whoops.' His whole aspect was so plainly that of a man whom it would be unwise to stir that Bingo, chewing a thoughtful lip, stood pondering on what was the best policy to pursue.

It was a glance at his watch that decided him. He saw that he had been running rather behind schedule, and that if he was to meet Mrs Bingo at Paddington at twelve-five he would have to be starting at once.

'This, Corker,' he said to Corker, 'has made things a bit complex, Corker. I've got to be at Paddington in ten minutes, and everything seems to point to the fact that Mr Prosser, if roused abruptly, may wake up cross. Better, I think, to let him have his sleep out. So here is the procedure, as I see it. I will leave this baby on the floor beside him, so that they can get together in due course, and I will look in and collect it on my way back.'

'Very good, sir.'

'Now, Mr Prosser's first move, on waking and finding the place crawling with issue, will no doubt be to ring for you and ask what it's all about. You will then say: "This is your godson, sir." You couldn't manage "itsy-bitsy godson", could you?'

'No, sir.'

'I was afraid not. Still, you've got the idea of the thing? Good. Fine. Right-ho.'

The train from Droitwich was rolling in just as Bingo came on to the platform, and a moment later he spotted Mrs Bingo getting out. She was supporting her mother, who still seemed rocky on the pins, but on seeing him she detached herself from the old geezer, allowing her to navigate temporarily under her own steam, and flung herself into his arms.

'Bingo, darling!'

'Rosie, my pre-eminent old egg!'

'Well, it is nice being back with you again. I feel as if I had been away years. Where's Algy?'

'I left him at Oofy Prosser's. His godfather, you know. I had a minute or two to spare on my way here, so I looked in on Oofy. He was all over the child and just wouldn't let him go. So I arranged that I would call in for him on my way back.'

'I see. Then I had better meet you there after I've taken Mother to her flat. She's not at all well.'

'No, I noticed she seemed to be looking a bit down among the wines and spirits,' said Bingo, casting a gratified glance at the old object, who was now propping herself up against a passing porter. 'The sooner you get her off to the mud baths, the better. All right, then. See you at Oofy's.'

'Where does he live?'

'Bloxham Mansions, Park Lane.'

'I'll be there as soon as I can. Oh, Bingo, darling, did you deposit that money for Algy?'

Bingo struck his forehead.

'Well, I'm dashed! In the excitement of meeting you, my dream of joy, I clean forgot. We'll do it together after leaving Oofy.'

Brave words, of course, but as he hiked back to Bloxham Mansions there suddenly came on him for the first time an unnerving feeling of doubt as to whether he was justified in taking it for granted that Oofy would come across. At the moment when he had conceived the scheme of using Algernon Aubrey as a softening influence, he had felt that it was a cinch. It had taken only about five minutes of his godson's society to bring the milk of human kindness sloshing out of Sir Aylmer Mauleverer in bucketfuls, and he had supposed that the same thing would happen with Oofy. But now there began to burgeon within him a chilling uncertainty, which became intensified with every step he took.

It had only just occurred to him that Algernon Aubrey was up against a much stiffer proposition than the child in 'Tiny Fingers'. Sir Aylmer Mauleverer had been a healthy, outdoor man, the sort that springs from bed and makes a hearty breakfast. There had been no suggestion, so far as he could remember, of him having a morning head. Oofy on the other hand, it was only too abundantly evident, was going to have, when he awoke to face a new day, a morning head of the first water. Everything, he realized, turned on how that head would affect a godfather's outlook.

It was with tense anxiety that he demanded hot news from Corker as the door opened.

'Any developments, Corker?'

'Well, yes and no, sir.'

'How do you mean, yes and no? Has Mr Prosser rung?'

'No, sir.'

'Then he's still asleep?'

'No, sir.'

'But you said he hadn't rung.'

'No, sir. But a moment ago I heard him utter a cry.'

'A cry?'

'Yes, sir. A piercing cry, indicative of considerable distress of mind. It was in many respects similar to his ejaculation on the morning of January the first of the present year, on the occasion when he supposed – mistakenly – that he had seen a pink elephant.'

Bingo frowned.

'I don't like that.'

'Nor did Mr Prosser, sir.'

'I mean, I don't like the way things seem to have been shaping. You're a man of the world, Corker. You know as well as I do that god-fathers don't utter piercing cries on meeting their godsons, unless there is something seriously amiss. I think I'll step along and take a dekko.'

He did so, and, entering the sitting room and noting contents, halted with raised eyebrows.

Algernon Aubrey was seated on the floor, his attention riveted on the balloon which he appeared to be trying to swallow. Oofy Prosser was standing on the mantelpiece, gazing down with bulging eyes. Bingo is a pretty shrewd sort of chap, and it didn't take him long to see that there was a sense of strain in the atmosphere. He thought the tactful thing to do was to pass it off as if one hadn't noticed anything.

'Hullo, Oofy,' he said.

'Hullo, Bingo,' said Oofy.

'Nice morning,' said Bingo.

'Wonderful weather we're having,' said Oofy.

They chatted for a while about the prospects for Hurst Park and the latest mid-European political developments, and then there was a pause. It was Oofy who eventually broke it.

'Tell me, Bingo,' he said, speaking with a rather overdone carelessness. 'I wonder if by any chance you can see anything on the floor, just over there by the fireplace. I dare say it's only my imagination, but it seems to me – '

'Do you mean the baby?'

Oofy gave a long sort of whistling gasp.

'It *is* a baby? I mean, you can see it, too?'

'Oh, rather. With the naked eye,' said Bingo. 'Pipsy-wipsy,' he added, lugging the child into the conversation so that it wouldn't feel out of it. 'Dada can see you.'

Oofy started.

'Did you say "dada"?'

'"Dada" was the word.'

'Is this your baby?'

'That's right.'

'The little blighter I gave that silver mug to?'

'None other.'

'What's he doing here?'

'Oh, just paying a social call.'

'Well,' said Oofy, in an aggrieved voice, starting to climb down, 'if he had had the sense to explain that at the outset, I would have been spared a terrible experience. I came in a bit late last night and sank into a refreshing sleep on the floor, and I woke to find a frightful face glaring into mine. Naturally, I thought the strain had been too much and that I was seeing things.'

'Would you care to kiss your godson?'

Oofy shuddered strongly.

'Don't say such things, even in fun,' he begged.

He reached the floor, and stood staring at Algernon Aubrey from a safe distance.

'And to think,' he murmured, 'that I thought of getting married!'

'Marriage is all right,' argued Bingo.

'True,' Oofy conceded, 'up to a certain point. But the risk! The fearful risk! You relax your vigilance for a second, you turn your head for a single instant, and bing! something like that happens.'

'Popsy-wopsy,' said Bingo.

'It's no good saying "popsy-wopsy" – it's appalling. Bingo,' said

Oofy, speaking in a low, trembling voice, 'do you realize that, but for your muscling in on that lunch of mine, this might have happened to me? Yes,' he went on, paling beneath his pimples, 'I assure you. I was definitely planning to propose to that girl over the coffee and cigarettes. And you came along and saved me.' He drew a deep breath. 'Bingo, old chap, don't I seem to recall hearing you ask me for a fiver or something?'

'A tenner.'

Oofy shook his head.

'It's not enough,' he said. 'Would you mind if I made it fifty?'

'Not a bit.'

'You've no objection?'

'None whatever, old man.'

'Good,' said Oofy.

'Fine,' said Bingo.

'Excuse me, sir,' said Corker, appearing in the doorway, 'the hall porter has rung up to say that Mrs Little is waiting for Mr Little downstairs.'

'Tell her I'll be there in two ticks, with bells on,' said Bingo.

14

THE SHADOW PASSES

A crusty roll, whizzing like a meteor out of the unknown, shot past the Crumpet and the elderly relative whom he was entertaining to luncheon at the Drones Club and shattered itself against the wall. Noting that his guest had risen some eighteen inches into the air, the Crumpet begged him not to give the thing another thought.

'Just someone being civil,' he explained. 'Meant for me, of course. Where did it come from?'

'I think it must have been thrown by one of those two young men at the table over there.'

The Crumpet gazed in the direction indicated.

'It can't have been the tall one with the tortoiseshell-rimmed spectacles,' he said. 'That's Horace Pendlebury-Davenport, the club darts champion. If he had aimed at me, he would have hit me, for his skill is uncanny. It was Bingo Little. More cheese?'

'No, thank you.'

'Then shall we go and have our coffee in the smoking room?'

'It might be safer.'

'You must make allowances for Bingo,' said the Crumpet as they took their seats, observing that his companion's expression was still austere. 'Until a few days ago a dark shadow brooded over his life, threatening the stability of the home. This has now passed away, and he is consequently a bit above himself. The shadow to which I allude was his baby's Nannie.'

'Is that young man a father?'

'Oh, rather.'

'Good heavens.'

'Bingo married Rosie M. Banks, the celebrated female novelist, and came a day when he had this baby. Well, Mrs Bingo did most of the heavy work, of course, but you know what I mean. And naturally the baby, on being added to the strength, had to have a Nannie. They fired her last week.'

'But why should the dispensing with her services give rise to such an ebullition of animal spirits?'

'Because she had once been Bingo's Nannie, too, That is the point to keep the mind fixed on. Mrs Bingo, like so many female ink-slingers, is dripping with sentiment, and this ingrowing sentiment of hers led her to feel how sweet it would be if the same old geezer who had steered Bingo through the diaper and early sailor suit phases could also direct the private life of the younger generation. So when a photograph in a woman's paper of Miss Rosie M. Banks, author of our new serial (Mrs Richard Little), brought Sarah Byles round on the run to ascertain whether this was the Richard Little she had groomed, it was not long before she was persuaded to emerge from her retirement and once more set her hand to the plough.'

'And your friend disliked the arrangement?'

'You bet he disliked the arrangement.'

The news, broken to Bingo on his return from the office – he is Ye Ed. of a weekly organ called *Wee Tots* (P. P. Purkiss, proprietor) devoted to the interests of our better-class babes and sucklings – got (said the Crumpet) right in amongst him. Sarah Byles had always lived in his memory as a stalwart figure about eight feet high and the same across, with many of the less engaging personal attributes of the bucko mate of an old-time hell-ship, and he feared for the well-being of his son and heir. He felt that the latter would be giving away too much weight.

'Golly, queen of my soul,' he ejaculated, 'that's a bit tough on the issue, isn't it? When I served under Nannie Byles, she was a human fiend at the mention of whose name strong children shook like aspens.'

'Oh, no, sweetie-pie,' protested Mrs Bingo. 'She's an old dear. So kind and gentle.'

'Well, I'll take your word for it,' said Bingo dubiously. 'Of course, age may have softened her.'

But before dressing for dinner he looked in on young Algernon Aubrey, shook him sympathetically by the hand and gave him a bar of nut chocolate. He felt like a kind-hearted manager of prize-fighters who is sending a novice up against the champion.

Conceive his relief, therefore, when he found that Mrs Bingo had not been astray in her judgment of form. Arriving on the morrow, La Byles proved, as stated, to be an old dear. In the interval since they had last met she had shrunk to about four feet ten, the steely glitter which he had always associated with her eyes had disappeared, and she had lost the rather unpleasant suggestion she had conveyed in his formative years of being on the point of enforcing discipline with a belaying pin. Her aspect was mild and her manner cooing, and when she flung her arms about him and kissed him and asked him how his stomach was, he flung his arms about her and kissed her and said his stomach was fine. The scene was one of cordial good will.

The new régime set in smoothly, conditions appearing to be hunkydory. Mrs Bingo and Nannie Byles hit it off together like a couple of members of a barber-shop quartette. Bingo himself felt distantly benevolent towards the old dug-out. And as Algernon Aubrey took to her and seemed at his ease in her society, it would not be too much to say that for a day or two everything in the home was gas and gaiters.

For a day or two, I repeat. It was on the evening of the third day, as Bingo and Mrs Bingo sat in the drawing room after dinner all happy and peaceful, Bingo reading a mystery thriller and Mrs Bingo playing solitaire in the offing, that the former heard the latter emit a sudden giggle, and always being in the market for a good laugh inquired the reason for her mirth.

'I was only thinking,' said Mrs Bingo, now guffawing heartily, 'of the story Nannie told me when we were bathing Algy.'

'Of a nature you are able to repeat?' asked Bingo, for he knew that red-hot stuff is sometimes pulled when the girls get together.

'It was about you pinning the golliwog to your Uncle Wilberforce's coat tails when he was going to the reception at the French Embassy.'

Bingo winced a little. He recalled the episode and in particular its sequel, which had involved an association between himself, his uncle and the flat side of a slipper. The old wound had ceased to trouble him physically, but there was still a certain mental pain, and he was of the opinion that it would have been in better taste for Nannie Byles to let the dead past bury its dead.

'Ha, ha,' he said, though dully. 'Fancy her remembering that.'

'Oh, her memory's wonderful,' said Mrs Bingo.

Bingo returned to his mystery thriller, and Mrs Bingo put the black ten on the red jack, and that, you would have said, was that. But Bingo, as he rejoined Inspector Keene and resumed with him the search for the murderer of Sir Rollo Murgatroyd, who had been bumped off in his library with a blunt instrument, experienced a difficulty in concentrating on the clues.

Until this moment the signing on the dotted line of his former bottlewasher had occasioned in him, as we have seen, merely a concern for his wee tot. It had not occurred to him that he himself was in peril. But now he found himself filled with a growing uneasiness. He did not like the look of things. His had been a rather notably chequered childhood, full of incidents which it had taken him years to live down, and he trusted that it was not Nannie Byles's intention to form an I-Knew-Him-When club and read occasional papers.

He feared the worst, and next day he was given proof that his apprehensions had been well founded. He was starting to help himself to a second go of jam omelette at the dinner-table, when his hand was stayed by a quick intake of the breath on the part of Mrs Bingo.

'Oh, Bingo, darling,' said Mrs Bingo, 'ought you?'

'Eh?' said Bingo, groping for the gist.

'Your weak stomach,' explained Mrs Bingo.

Bingo was amazed.

'How do you mean, weak stomach? My stomach's terrific. Ask anyone at the Drones. It's the talk of the place.'

'Well, you know what happened at that Christmas party at the Wilkinsons when you were six. Nannie says she will never forget it.'

Bingo flushed darkly.

'Has she been telling you about that?'

'Yes. She says your stomach was always terribly weak, and you *would* overeat yourself at children's parties. She says you would stuff and stuff and stuff and go out and be sick and then come back and stuff and stuff and stuff again.'

Bingo drew himself up rather coldly. No man likes to be depicted as a sort of infant Vitellius, particularly in the presence of a parlour-maid with flapping ears who is obviously drinking it all in with a view to going off and giving the cook something juicy to include in her memoirs.

'No more jam omelette, thank you,' he said reservedly.

'Now, that's very sensible of you,' said Mrs Bingo. 'And Nannie thinks it would be ever so much safer if you gave up cigarettes and cocktails.'

Bingo sank back in his chair feeling as if he had been slapped in the eye with a wet sock.

A couple of days later things took a turn for the worse. Returning from the office and heading for the nursery for a crack with Algernon Aubrey, Bingo met Mrs Bingo in the hall. It seemed to him that her manner during the initial embracings and pip-pippings was a little strange.

'Bingo,' she said, 'do you know a girl named Valerie Twistleton?'

'Oh, rather. Pongo Twistleton's sister. Known her all my life. She's engaged to Horace Davenport.'

'Oh, is she?' Mrs Bingo seemed relieved. 'Then you don't see much of her now?'

'Not much. Why?'

'Nannie was saying that you made yourself rather conspicuous with her at that Christmas party at the Wilkinsons. She says you kept kissing her under the mistletoe. She says you used to kiss all the little girls.'

Bingo reeled. It was the last picture a husband would wish to be built up in his wife's mind's eye. Besides, a chivalrous man always shrinks from bandying a woman's name, and he was wondering what would happen if this loose talk were to come to the ears of Horace Davenport, the Drones Club's leading Othello.

'She must be thinking of someone else,' he said hoarsely. 'I was noted as a child for my aloofness and austerity. My manner towards the other sex was always scrupulously correct. Do you know what the extraordinary ramblings of this Byles suggest to me?' he went on. 'They suggest that the old blister is senile and quite unequal to the testing office of ministering to Algy. Boot her out is my advice and sign on someone younger.'

'You would prefer a young nurse?'

Bingo is no fool.

'Not a *young* nurse. A sensible, middle-aged nurse. I mean to say, Nannie Byles will never see a hundred and seven again.'

'She was fifty last birthday, she tells me.'

'She tells you. Ha!'

'Well, anyway, I wouldn't dream of letting her go. She is wonderful with Algy, and she looks after your things like a mother.'

'Oh, very well. Only don't blame me when it's too late.'

'When what's too late?'

'I don't know,' said Bingo. 'Something.'

As he went on to the nursery to pass the time of day with Algernon Aubrey, his heart was leaden. No question now of his ignoring his peril. He could not have been better informed regarding it if the facts had been broadcast on a nationwide hook-up. A few more of these revelations from this voice from the past and he would sink to the level of a fifth-rate power. Somehow, by some means, he told himself, if his prestige in the home was to be maintained, he must get rid of this Nannie.

The woman knew too much.

As a matter of fact, though he would not have cared to have the thing known, his prestige at the moment was quite rocky enough, without having any Nannies nibbling at the foundations. A very serious crisis was impending in his domestic affairs, threatening to make his name a hissing and a byword.

When Bingo receives his envelope from *Wee Tots* on the first of the month, it is too often his practice, in defiance of Mrs Bingo's expressed wishes, to place its contents on the nose of some horse of whose speed and resolution he has heard good reports, and such horses have a nasty habit of pausing half-way down the stretch to pick daisies. And this had happened now. A mistaken confidence in Sarsaparilla for the three o'clock at Ally Pally had not only cleaned him out but had left him owing his bookie ten quid. This tenner would have to be coughed up in the course of the next few days, and tenners in this iron age are hard to come by.

He had explored every avenue. He had bought a ticket for the club darts sweep with his last ten bob, but had drawn a blank. He had tried to touch P. P. Purkiss for an advance of salary, but P. P. Purkiss had said that it was foreign to the policy of *Wee Tots* to brass up in advance. It really began to look as if he would be forced to the last awful extreme of biting Mrs Bingo's ear, which would mean that he might hear the last of it somewhere round about the afternoon of their golden wedding day, but scarcely before then.

It was a pretty poignant position of affairs, and what made Bingo so frightfully sick about it all was that if he had been the merest fraction of a second slippier when the hat for the darts sweep was circulating, he would have been on velvet, for he would have secured that sweep's most glittering prize. He had started to reach out for a ticket, and just as his fingers were about to close on it Oofy Prosser had reached out ahead of him and scooped it in. And that ticket, when opened, had been found to contain the name of Horace Davenport.

Horace Davenport is a bird, who, while lacking many of the other qualities which go to make a superman, has always thrown a beautiful dart. Both at school and at the University his skill had been a byword among the sporting set, and the passage of the years had in no way diminished his accuracy. His eye was not dimmed nor his natural force abated, and anyone drawing his name in the sweep was entitled to regard the contents of the kitty as money in the bank. And this singular bit of goose, as I say, had fallen to the lot of Oofy Prosser, a bloke already stinking with the stuff. That was Oofy at the next table to us at lunch, the stout, pimpled chap. You probably noticed how rich he looked. That a fellow as oofy as Oofy should get the money seemed to Bingo a crime.

But the last thing he had anticipated was that the same reflection should have occurred to Oofy. Yet so it proved. He was in the club the morning before the darts contest, and Oofy came up to him, looking, it seemed to Bingo, pensive. Though it is always hard to read the play of expression on Oofy's face, because of the pimples.

'What ho, Bingo,' said Oofy.

'What ho, Oofy,' said Bingo.

'I wonder, Bingo,' said Oofy, perking himself beside him and stroking the third pimple from the left in a meditative sort of way, 'if you have ever reflected how weird life is.'

Bingo agreed that life was pretty weird in spots, and Oofy said that what struck him about life – and he was a man who had gone into the thing – was that there was mismanagement somewhere.

'Gross mismanagement,' said Oofy. 'Well, as an instance of what I mean, take this darts sweep. Think of all the eager, hard-up waifs who would have given their left eyeball to draw Horace Davenport. And who gets him? I do. And what ensues? Horace is bound to win, so I spear thirty-three pound ten. What's the use of thirty-three pound ten to me? Do you know what my annual income is? No, I won't tell you, it would make you sick. It isn't right, Bingo,' said Oofy warmly. 'All wrong, Bingo. I shall give this ticket away. Would you like it, Bingo?'

Bingo, leaping in the air like a rising trout, said he would, and Oofy seemed to ponder. Then he said that giving Bingo the ticket might destroy Bingo's self-respect, and when Bingo urged very strongly that in his opinion the risk ought to be taken he pondered again.

'No,' he said at length, 'I should hate to have it on my mind that I had sapped a friend's self-respect. I will sell you this ticket, Bingo, for the nominal price of a fiver.'

A sharp cry of agony escaped Bingo. He had sufficient capital for the club luncheon at four-and-sixpence, but no more. Then an idea struck him.

'Will you hold it open for a couple of hours?'

'Certainly,' said Oofy. 'I shall be here till a quarter past one. Slip me the money then, and the ticket is yours.'

The idea that had struck Bingo was this. In his bedroom at home there was a set of diamond cuff links, a present from Mrs Bingo on his last birthday, worth, he estimated, five pounds of any pawnbroker's money. What simpler than to secure these, thrust them up the spout, snaffle the Horace Davenport ticket, get his hooks on the thirty-three pounds ten, rush back to the pawnbroker's, de-spout the links and return to Position One? It would afford a masterly solution of the whole difficulty.

The Bingo residence, being one of those houses off Wimbledon Common, takes a bit of getting to, but he made good time there and sneaking in unobserved was able to present himself at the club at ten minutes past one. Oofy was still there. The fiver changed hands. And Bingo, who had stuck out for eight pounds ten at the pawnbroker's so as to have a bit of spending money, went off to the Savoy grill to revel. There are moments in a man's life when the club luncheon at four-and-sixpence is not enough.

And he had just got back to the office after the repast and was about to settle down to the composition of a thoughtful editorial on What

Tiny Hands Can Do For Nannie, wishing that his own tiny hands could take her by the scruff of the neck and heave her out on her left ear, when Mrs Bingo rang up to say that, her mother having had one of her spells at her South Kensington abode, she was buzzing along there and would not be able to get home tonight.

Bingo said he would miss her sorely, and Mrs Bingo said she knew he would, and Bingo was preparing to toodle-oo and ring off, when Mrs Bingo uttered a sudden yip.

'Oh, Bingo, I knew there was something else. All this excitement about Mother put it out of my head. Your diamond links have been stolen!'

It was a pure illusion, of course, but Bingo tells me that as he heard these words it seemed to him that P. P. Purkiss, who was visible through the doorway of the inner office, suddenly started doing an Ouled Nail Stomach dance. His heart leaped sharply and became entangled with his tonsils. It was a matter of some moments before he was able to disengage it and reply.

'My links? Stolen? Absurd!'

'Well, Nannie says she was tidying your room just now and couldn't find them anywhere.'

Bingo was himself again.

'Nannie Byles,' he said sternly, 'is temperamentally incapable of finding a brass drum in a telephone booth. You are familiar with my views on that gibbering old fathead. Don't listen to a word she says.'

'Then you wouldn't advise sending for the police?'

'Certainly not. The police are busy men. It is not fair to waste their time.'

'Nannie says they would go round and make inquiries at all the pawnshops.'

'Exactly. And while they were doing it, what would happen? About fifty murders would be taking place and not a rozzer on duty to attend to them. One wishes sometimes that these Nannies had the rudiments of a civic conscience. Don't you worry about those links. I can tell you just where they are. They are . . . no, I've forgotten. But it'll come back. Well, pip-pip, light of my life,' said Bingo, and rang off.

His first act on replacing the receiver was, you will scarcely be surprised to learn, to grab his hat and nip round to the Drones for a quick one; for despite the intrepid front he had put up the news that the A.W.O.L.ness of those links had been discovered had shaken him to his foundations, and he was feeling a little like some Eliza who, crossing the ice, heard the baying of the pursuing bloodhounds.

But with the first sip of the restorative Reason returned to its throne, assuring him that there was absolutely no cause for alarm. The darts tourney, Reason pointed out, was to take place tomorrow morning. He had the Horace Davenport ticket on his person. It followed then as doth the night the day, concluded Reason, that he would be able to restore the missing trinkets the moment he got home tomorrow afternoon.

He was just musing affectionately on Horace Davenport and feeling how fortunate he was in holding all rights to a dart hurler of his incomparable skill, when his attention was attracted by a deep sigh in his vicinity, and looking up he saw Horace approaching. And with a sudden sharp alarm he noted that something seemed to have gone wrong with the Davenport works. The other's face was pale and drawn and the eyes behind their tortoiseshell-rimmed glasses were like those of a dead fish.

'Stap my vitals, Horace,' he cried, deeply concerned, for naturally what he would have liked to see on the eve of the darts tournament was a rosy-cheeked, bright-eyed Horace Davenport, full of pep, ginger and the will to win. 'You look a bit down among the wines and spirits. What's the matter?'

'Well, I'll tell you,' said Horace Davenport. 'You know Valerie Twistleton.'

'Yes.'

'You know I'm engaged to her.'

'Yes.'

'Well, that is where you make your ruddy error,' said Horace Davenport. 'I'm not. We have parted brass rags.'

'Why on earth?'

'Well, if you ask me, I think she loves another.'

'What rot!'

'I don't agree with you. We quarrelled about a mere trifle, and I maintain that no girl would have handed a man his hat for a trifle as mere as that, unless she had already decided to hitch on elsewhere and was looking out for a chance of giving him the gate.'

Bingo's tender heart was touched, of course, but he could not forget Horace's great mission.

'Too bad,' he said. 'But you mustn't brood on it, old man, or you'll go putting yourself off your stroke.'

'My stroke?'

'For the darts binge tomorrow.'

'Oh, that? I shall not be competing,' said Horace dully. 'I'm going to scratch.'

Bingo uttered a quick howl like that of a Labrador timber wolf which has stubbed its toe on a jagged rock.

'Sker-ratch?'

'Exactly what Oofy Prosser said when I told him, in the same agitated voice. But I'm dashed if I can see why you're all so surprised,' said Horace. 'Is it likely, after what has happened, that I would be in any mood for bunging darts?'

A blinding light had flashed upon Bingo. I doubt if there are half-a-dozen fellows in the club, or ten at the outside, more capable than he of detecting funny business when such is afoot. He remembered now, what he ought to have remembered before, that Oofy, despite his colossal wealth, had always been a man who would walk ten miles in tight shoes to pick up even the meanest sum that was lying around loose.

At the thought of how the subtle schemer had chiselled him out of that fiver his soul blazed in revolt, and it was with an eloquence of which he had not supposed himself capable that he now began to plead with Horace Davenport to revise his intention of scratching for the darts tournament. And so moving were the words in which he pictured the ruin which must befall him, should the other remove his name from the list of competitors, that Horace's better self awakened.

'This opens up a new line of thought,' said Horace. 'I didn't know Oofy had sold you that ticket. Well, to oblige you, Bingo, I will go through the hollow formality of entering the arena. But build no hopes on that. You can't aim darts when your heart is broken. My eyes will be so dim with unshed tears that I doubt if I'll be able to get a single double.'

As if the word 'double' had touched a chord in his mind, he moved off in the direction of the bar, and Bingo, clutching his head in both hands, started to think more tensely than he had ever thought in his puff.

There is no gainsaying the truth of Horace's parting words. If there is one thing calculated to take the edge off a fellow's form in an athletic contest, it is unrequited love. He recalled the time in his own bachelor days when a hopeless yearning for a girl whose name he had forgotten had ruined his putting touch for several weeks. What was needed here first and foremost, therefore, was some scheme for reconciling these two sundered hearts. The reinsertion of the love light in Valerie Twistleton's eyes would put Horace Davenport right back in mid-season form and the ticket bearing his name would once more be worth thirty-three quid of the best and brightest.

And it ought not, he felt, to be so dashed difficult to get that love light resuming work at the old stand. What Horace had said about

Valerie having given him the air because she loved another he regarded as the purest apple-sauce. Honoured from time to time with the girl's confidence, he knew that she looked on the darts wizard as a king among men. Obviously what had occurred was what is technically known as a lovers' tiff, and this he was convinced could be set right by a few well-chosen words from a polished man of the world.

Why, then, should he not get Valerie on the phone, ask her out for a bite of supper, and having lushed her up as far as his modest resources would permit plead with her to forgive and forget?

Bingo is a chap who knows a ball of fire when he sees one, and that this idea was a ball of fire he had no doubts whatever. He sped to the telephone booth, established communication, and a few minutes later the deal had been clinched. The girl checked up immediately on his proposition of a slab of supper, and suggested Mario's popular restaurant as the *mise en scène*.

'Okay, Valerie, old crumpet,' said Bingo, infinitely relieved. 'Eleven-fifteen at Mario's then.'

So far so good. A smooth bit of work. But it did not take Bingo long to realize that before the revels could begin there was one rather tricky hurdle to be surmounted. Nannie Byles, like the night, had a thousand eyes, and some pretty adroit manoeuvring would be required if he was to get out of the house without her spotting him. He had no desire to be called upon to explain to Mrs Bingo on her return what he had been doing oozing off the premises in the soup and fish at half-past ten p.m. The statement that he had been on his way to give Valerie Twistleton a morsel of supper in her absence would, he felt, not go any too well.

Thinking quick, he saw the policy to pursue. Immediately upon arrival he touched the bell and desired the parlourmaid to inform La Byles that he would be glad of a word with her. And when the latter hove alongside, she found him lying on the sofa, a limp, interesting figure.

'Oh, Nannie,' he said, speaking faintly, 'I think I had better not come and hobnob with Algernon Aubrey tonight. I have a strange all-overish feeling, accompanied by floating spots before the eyes, and it may be catching. Explain the circumstances to him, give him my best and say I shall hope to see him tomorrow. I, meanwhile, will be popping straight up to bed and turning in.'

Well, of course, the Byles wanted to phone Mrs Bingo and summon medical aid and all that, but he managed to head her off and they eventually settled for a basin of gruel and a hot-water bottle.

When these had been delivered at the bedside, Bingo said, still speaking faintly, that he didn't want to be disturbed again as his aim was to get a refreshing sleep.

After that everything was pretty smooth. At about ten-thirty he got up, hopped out of the window, eased himself down the water-pipe, was fortunate enough after waiting a short while at the garden gate to grab a passing taxi, and precisely at eleven-fifteen he alighted at the door of Mario's. And a few minutes later along blew Valerie Twistleton looking charming in some soft, clinging substance which revealed the slender lines of her figure, and the show was on.

Since the days when he had kissed her under the mistletoe at the Wilkinsons' Christmas party there had come to exist between Bingo and this girl one of those calm, platonic friendships which so often occur when the blood has cooled and passion waned. Their relations now were such that he would be able to talk to her like a kindly elder brother. And as soon as he had headed her off from ordering champagne by persuading her that this wine is better avoided, causing as it does acidity and often culminating in spots, it was like a kindly elder brother that he jolly well intended to talk to her.

On his way to the restaurant he had debated whether to lead up to the subject of Horace by easy stages, but when they were seated at their table with a bottle of sound and inexpensive hock between them he decided to skip preliminaries and snap straight into the agenda.

'Well, I met your future bread-winner at the Drones this morning,' he said. 'We might drink a toast to him, what, with a hey nonny nonny and a hot cha-cha. Horace Davenport,' said Bingo, raising his glass.

A quick frown disfigured Valerie Twistleton's delicate brow. The state of Bingo's finances had precluded the serving of oysters, but had these been on the bill of fare you would have supposed from her expression and manner that the girl had bitten into a bad one.

'Don't mention that sub-human gargoyle's name in my presence,' she replied with considerable evidence of feeling. 'And don't allude to him as my future bread-winner. The wedding is off. I am through with Horace Pendlebury-by-golly-Davenport, and if he trips on a banana skin and breaks his bally neck, it will be all right with me.'

Bingo nodded. With subtle skill he had got the conversation just where he wanted it.

'Yes, he rather gave me to understand that there had been a certain modicum of rift-within-the-lute-ing, but he did not go into details. What seemed to be the trouble?'

A brooding look came into Valerie Twistleton's eyes. She gnashed her teeth slightly.

'I'll tell you,' she said. 'He had come round to our house and we were in the drawing room chatting of this and that, and I happened to ask him to lie down on the floor and let Cyril, my cocker spaniel, nibble his nose, which the little angel loves. He said he wouldn't, and I said, "Oh, come on. Be a sport", and he said "No, he was blowed if he was going to be a stooge for a cocker spaniel". It ended with my digging out his letters and presents and handing them to him, together with the ring and his hat.'

Bingo t'ck-t'ck-t'ck-ed, and the girl asked him what he was t'ck-t'ck-t'ck-ing about.

'Wasn't I right?' she demanded passionately. 'Wasn't I ethically justified?'

Bingo started to be the kindly elder brother.

'We must always strive,' he urged, 'to look at these things from the other chap's point of view. Horace's, you must remember, is a sensitive, high strung nature. Many sensitive, high strung natures dislike being the supporting cast for cocker spaniels. Consider for a moment what his position would have been, had he agreed to your proposal. The spaniel would have hogged all the comedy, leaving him to all intents and purposes painted on the back drop. Not a pleasant situation for a proud man.'

If Valerie Twistleton had been a shade less pretty, one would say that she snorted.

'As if that was the trouble! Do you think I can't read between the lines? He just grabbed at that spaniel sequence as a pretext for severing diplomatic relations. Obviously what has happened is that he has gone and fallen in love with another girl and has been dying for an excuse to get rid of me. I wish you wouldn't laugh like a pie-eyed hyæna.'

Bingo explained that his reason for laughing like a pie-eyed hyæna was that he had been tickled by an amusing coincidence. Horace Davenport, he said, had made precisely the same charge against her.

'His view is that your affections are engaged elsewhere and that your giving him the bum's rush on account of his civil disobedience *in re* the cocker spaniel was simply a subterfuge. I happened to jot down his words, if you would care to hear them. "I maintain," said Horace, "that no girl would have handed a man his hat for a trifle as mere as that, unless she had already decided to hitch on elsewhere and was looking out for a chance of giving him the gate".'

The girl stared, wide-eyed.

'He must be crazy. "Decided to hitch on elsewhere", forsooth. If I live a million years, I shall never love anyone but Horace. From the very moment we met I knew he was what the doctor had ordered. I don't chop and change. When I give my heart, it stays given. But he's not like me. He is a flitting butterfly and a two-timing Casanova. I'm sure there's another girl.'

'Your view, then, is that he is tickled pink to be freed from his obligations?'

'Yes, it is.'

'Then why,' said Bingo, whipping the ace of trumps from his sleeve, 'was he looking this morning when I met him at the Drones like a living corpse out of Edgar Allan Poe?'

Valerie Twistleton started.

'Was he?'

'You bet he was. And talking about his heart being broken. Have you ever seen those "before taking" pictures in the patent medicine advertisements?'

'Yes.'

'Horace,' said Bingo. 'He looked like a stretcher case in the last stages of lumbago, leprosy, galloping consumption and the botts.'

He paused, and noted that a misty film had dimmed the incandescence of his companion's eyes. Valerie Twistleton's lips were trembling, and the bit of chicken which she had been raising to her mouth fell from her listless fork.

'The poor old slob,' she murmured.

Bingo saw that the moment had come to sew up the contract. Striking while the iron is hot is, I believe, the expression.

'Then you will forgive him?'

'Of course.'

'All will be as it was before?'

'If anything, more so.'

'Fine,' said Bingo. 'I'll go and call him up and tell him. No doubt he will be round here with his foot in his hand within ten minutes of getting the glad news.'

He had sprung to his feet and was about to dash to the telephone but the girl stopped him.

'No,' she said.

Bingo goggled.

'No?' he repeated. 'How do you mean, no?'

She explained.

'He must have at least a couple of days in which to brood and yearn. So that the lesson can sink in, if you see what I mean. What one aims at is to get it firmly into his nut that he can't go chucking his weight about whenever he feels like it. I love him more than words can tell, but we must have discipline.'

Bingo was now stepping around like a cat on hot bricks. His agony was, as you may imagine, considerable.

'But the darts tournament is tomorrow morning.'

'What darts tournament?'

'The Drones Club's annual fixture. For a Horace with his mind at rest it is a sitter, but for a heartbroken Horace not a hope. If you don't believe me, let me quote his own words. "You can't aim darts when your heart is broken," he said, and I wish you could have heard the pain and anguish in his voice. "My eyes will be so dim with unshed tears", he said, "that I doubt if I'll be able to get a single double".'

'Well, what does a potty darts tournament matter?'

And Bingo was just drawing a deep breath before starting in to explain to her in moving words just how much this darts tournament mattered to him, when the top of his head suddenly came off and shot up to the ceiling.

That is to say, he felt as if it had done so. For at this moment there came to his ears, speaking loudly and authoritatively from the direction of the door, a voice.

'Don't talk to me, young man,' it was saying. 'I keep telling you that Master Richard is in here somewhere, and I insist on seeing him. He has a nasty feverish cold and I have brought him his woolly muffler.'

And there on the threshold stood Nannie Byles. She was holding in her hand a woolly muffler bearing the colours of the Drones Club and looking in an unfriendly way at some sort of assistant head waiter who was endeavouring to bar her progress into the restaurant.

I don't know if you ever came across a play of Shakespeare's called Macbeth? If you did, you may remember that this bird Macbeth bumps off another bird named Banquo and gives a big dinner to celebrate, and picture his embarrassment when about the first of the gay throng to show up is Banquo's ghost, all merry and bright, covered in blood. It gave him a pretty nasty start, Shakespeare does not attempt to conceal.

But it was nothing to the start Bingo got on observing Nannie Byles in his midst. He felt as if he had been lolling in the electric chair at Sing-Sing and some practical joker had suddenly turned on the juice. How the dickens she had tracked him here he was at a loss to imagine. It could scarcely have been by the sense of smell, and yet there didn't seem any other explanation.

However, he didn't waste much time musing on that. This, he perceived, was a moment for rapid action. There was a door just behind where he had been sitting, which from the fact that waiters had been going in and out he took to be the entrance to the service quarters. To press a couple of quid into Valerie Twistleton's hand to pay the bill with and leave her flat and do a swan dive backwards and shoot through this emergency exit and slip a friendly native half a crown to show him the way to the street was with him the work of an instant.

Five minutes later he was in a taxi, bowling off to The Nook, Wimbledon Common. Forty minutes later he was shinning up the water-pipe. Ten minutes later, clad in pyjamas and a dressing-gown, he was at the telephone trying to get Horace.

But Horace's number was the silent tomb. The girl at the exchange said she had rung and rung and rung, and Bingo said Well, ring and ring and ring again. So she rang and rang and rang again, but there was still no answer, and eventually Bingo had to give it up and go to bed.

But it was by no means immediately that he fell into a dreamless sleep. The irony of the thing was like ants in the pants, causing him to toss restlessly on the pillow.

I mean to say, he had so nearly clicked. That was the bitter thought. He had achieved the object which he had set out to achieve – viz. the bringing together of the sundered hearts of V. Twistleton and H. Davenport, but unless he could get Horace on the phone in the morning and put him abreast before the darts tourney began, all would be lost. It was a fat lot of consolation to feel that a couple of days from now Horace Davenport would be going about with his hat on the side of his head, slapping people on the back and standing them drinks. What was of the essence was to have him in that condition tomorrow morning.

He brooded on what might have been. If only he had been able to give Valerie Twistleton the heart-melting talk he had been planning. If only Nannie Byles had postponed her appearance for another quarter of an hour. Bingo is a pretty chivalrous chap and one who, wind and weather permitting, would never lay a hand upon a woman save in the way of kindness, but if somebody at that moment had given him a blunt knife and asked him to skin Nannie Byles with it and drop her into a vat of boiling oil, he would have sprung to the task with his hair in a braid.

The vital thing, he was feeling, as he at last dozed off, was to be up bright and early next day, so as to connect with Horace in good time.

Which being so, you as a man who knows life will not be surprised to hear that what happened was that he overslept himself. When he finally came out of the ether and hared to the telephone, it was the same old story. The girl at the exchange rang and rang and rang, but there was no answer. Bingo tried the Drones, but was informed that Horace had not yet arrived. There seemed nothing for it but to get dressed and go to the club.

By the time he got there the darts tourney would, of course, be in full swing, and he could picture the sort of Horace Davenport that would be competing. A limp, listless Horace Davenport, looking like a filleted sole.

It was hardly worth going in, he felt, when he reached the club, but something seemed to force him through the doorway: and he was approaching the smoking room on leaden feet, when the door opened and out came Barmy Fotheringay-Phipps and Catsmeat Potter-Pirbright.

'A walkover,' Barmy was saying.

A sudden irrational hope stirred in Bingo's bosom like a jumping bean. It was silly, of course, to think that Barmy had been speaking about Horace, but the level of form at the Drones, except for that pre-eminent expert, is so steady that he could not picture any of the other competitors having a walkover. He clutched Barmy's coat sleeve in a feverish grip.

'Who for?' he gasped.

'Oh, hullo, Bingo,' said Barmy. 'The very chap we wanted to see. Catsmeat and I have collaborated in an article for that paper of yours entitled "Some Little-Known Cocktails." We were just going round to the office to give it to you.'

Bingo accepted the typewritten sheets absently. In his editorial capacity he was always glad to consider unsolicited contributions (though these, he was careful to point out, must be submitted at their authors' risk), and a thesis on such a subject by two such acknowledged authorities could scarcely fail to be fraught with interest, but at the moment his mind was far removed from the conduct of *Wee Tots*.

'Who's it a walkover for?' he said hoarsely.

'Horace Davenport, of course,' said Catsmeat Potter-Pirbright. 'He has been playing inspired darts. If you go in quick, you may be able to catch a glimpse of his artistry.'

But Bingo was too late. When he entered the smoking room, the contest was over and Horace Davenport, the centre of an eager group of friends and admirers, was receiving congratulations, a popular winner – except with Oofy Prosser, who was sitting in a corner pale and haggard beneath his pimples. Seeing Bingo, the champion detached himself and came over to him.

'Oh, hullo, Bingo,' said Horace, 'I was hoping you would look in. I wanted a word with you. You remember that broken heart of mine? Well, it's all right. Not broken, after all. A complete reconciliation was effected shortly before midnight last night at Mario's.'

Bingo was amazed.

'You came to Mario's?'

'Thanks to you,' said Horace Davenport, massaging his arm grate-
fully. 'I must mention, Bingo, that after I had told you about my
broken heart yesterday, I suddenly remembered that there were one
or two things about it which I had forgotten to touch on. So I came
back. They said you had been seen going to the phone booth, so I
pushed along there. You had left the door ajar, and picture my horror
on hearing you talking to Valerie and making an assignation with her
at Mario's.'

'I simply wanted – ' began Bingo, but Horace continued.

'I reeled away blindly. I was distraught. I had been telling myself
that Valerie was being false to me with another, but I had never for an
instant suspected that this snake in the grass was my old friend
Richard Little, a chap with whom when at school I had frequently
shared my last acid drop.'

'But listen. I simply wanted – '

'Well, I said to myself "I'll give them about half an hour, and then
I'll go to Mario's and stride in and confront them. This," I said to
myself, "will make them feel pretty silly." So I did. But when I got
there, you had legged it and were not there to be confronted. So I confronted Valerie.'

'Listen, Horace, old egg,' said Bingo, insisting on being heard, 'I
simply wanted to shoot a bit of nourishment into her for mellowing
purposes and then plead your cause.'

'I know. She told me. She said you had talked to her like a kindly
elder brother. What arguments you used I cannot say, but they
dragged home the gravy plenteously. I found her in melting mood.
We came together with a click, and the wedding is fixed for the
twenty-third *prox*. And now, Bingo,' said Horace, looking at his
watch, 'I shall have to be leaving you. I promised Valerie I would
drop in directly the darts contest was over and let her cocker spaniel
nibble my nose. The animal seems to wish it, and I think we all ought
to do our best to spread sweetness and light, even at some slight
personal inconvenience. Goodbye, Bingo, and a thousand thanks. I
can give you a lift, if you are coming my way.'

'Thanks,' said Bingo, 'but I must collect that thirty-three pound
ten. After that I have one or two little things to do, and then I must be
nipping home.'

Bingo reached The Nook in good time. And he had replaced the links
in their box and was about to leave his bedroom, when Mrs Bingo
shoved her head in the door.

'Why, Bingo darling,' she said, 'aren't you at the office?'

'I just popped back to see you,' explained Bingo. 'How's your mother?'

'Much better,' said Mrs Bingo. She seemed distrait. 'Bingo, darling,' she said after a bit of a pause, revealing the seat of the trouble, 'I'm a little worried. About Nannie.'

'About Nannie?'

'Yes. When you were a child, do you remember her as being at all ... eccentric?'

'Eccentric?'

'Well, the most extraordinary thing happened last night. Where were you last night, Bingo?'

'I went to bed early.'

'You didn't go out?'

Bingo stared.

'Go *out*?'

'No, of course you didn't,' said Mrs Bingo. 'But Nannie declares that at half past ten she was walking in the garden getting a breath of fresh air, and she saw you jump into a cab – '

Bingo looked grave. He gave a low whistle.

'Started seeing things, eh? Bad. Bad.'

'– and she says she heard you tell the driver to go to Mario's.'

'Hearing voices, too? Worse. Worse.'

'And she followed you with your woolly muffler. She had to wait a long time before she could get a cab, and when she got to the restaurant they wouldn't let her in, and there was a lot of trouble about that, and then she found she had no money to pay the cab, and she must have lost her temper a little or she would never have boxed the cabman's ears and bitten that waiter.'

'Bit a waiter, did she?'

'She said she didn't like his manner. And after that they sent for the police and she was taken to Vine Street, and she telephoned to me to come and bail her out. So I went round to the police station and bailed her out, and she told me this extraordinary story about you. I hurried home and peeped in at your door, and there you were, fast asleep of course.'

'Of course.'

Mrs Bingo chewed the lower lip.

'It's all very disturbing.'

'Now there, with all due deference to you, my talented old scrivener,' said Bingo, 'I think you have missed the *mot juste*. I would call it appalling. Let me tell you something else that will make you think a bit. You remember all that song and dance she made about my links having been stolen. Well, I've just been taking a look, and they're in their usual box in the usual place on the dressing-table, just where they've always been.'

'Really?'

'I assure you. Well,' said Bingo, 'suit yourself, of course, but I should have thought we were taking a big chance entrusting our first-born to the care of a Nannie who is loopy to the eyebrows and constantly seeing visions and what not, to make no mention of hearing voices and not being able to see a set of diamond cuff-links when they're staring her in the face. I threw out the suggestion once before, and it was not well received, but I will make it again. Give her the push, moon of my delight. Pension her off. Slip her a few quid per and a set of your books and let her retire to some honeysuckle-covered cottage where she can't do any harm.'

'I believe you're right.'

'I know I'm right,' said Bingo. 'You don't want her suddenly getting the idea that Algernon Aubrey is a pink hippopotamus and loosing off at him with her elephant rifle, do you? Very well, then.'

15

BRAMLEY IS SO BRACING

A general meeting had been called at the Drones to decide on the venue for the club's annual golf rally, and the school of thought that favoured Bramley-on-Sea was beginning to make headway when Freddie Widgeon took the floor. In a speech of impassioned eloquence he warned his hearers not to go within fifty miles of the beastly place. And so vivid was the impression he conveyed of Bramley-on-Sea as a spot where the law of the jungle prevailed and anything could happen to anybody that the voters were swayed like reeds and the counter proposal of Cooden Beach was accepted almost unanimously.

His warmth excited comment at the bar.

'Freddie doesn't like Bramley,' said an acute Egg, who had been thinking it over with the assistance of a pink gin.

'Possibly,' suggested a Bean, 'because he was at school there when he was a kid.'

The Crumpet who had joined the group shook his head.

'No, it wasn't that,' he said. 'Poor old Freddie had a very painful experience at Bramley recently, culminating in his getting the raspberry from the girl he loved.'

'What, again?'

'Yes. It's curious about Freddie,' said the Crumpet, sipping a thoughtful martini. 'He rarely fails to click, but he never seems able to go on clicking. A whale at the Boy Meets Girl stuff, he is unfortunately equally unerring at the Boy Loses Girl.'

'Which of the troupe was it who gave him the air this time?' asked an interested Pieface.

'Mavis Peasmarch. Lord Bodsham's daughter.'

'But, dash it,' protested the Pieface, 'that can't be right. She returned him to store ages ago. You told us about it yourself. That time in New York when he got mixed up with the female in the pink négligée picked out with ultramarine lovebirds.'

The Crumpet nodded.

'Quite true. He was, as you say, handed his portfolio on that occasion. But Freddie is a pretty gifted explainer, if you give him

248   TALES FROM THE DRONES CLUB

time to mould and shape his story, and on their return to England he
appears to have squared himself somehow. She took him on again –
on appro., as it were. The idea was that if he proved himself steady
and serious, those wedding bells would ring out. If not, not a tinkle.

'Such was the position of affairs when he learned from this Peasmarch that she and her father were proposing to park themselves for
the summer months at the Hotel Magnifique at Bramley-on-Sea.'

Freddie's instant reaction to this news was, of course (said the
Crumpet), an urge to wangle a visit there himself, and he devoted the
whole force of his intellect to trying to think how this could be done.
He shrank from spending good money on a hotel, but on the other
hand his proud soul scorned a boarding-house, and what they call an
impasse might have resulted, had he not discovered that Bingo Little
and Mrs Bingo had taken a shack at Bramley in order that the Bingo
baby should get its whack of ozone. Bramley, as I dare say you have
seen mentioned on the posters, is so bracing, and if you are a parent
you have to think of these things. Brace the baby, and you are that
much ahead of the game.

To cadge an invitation was with Freddie the work of a moment,
and a few days later he arrived with suitcase and two-seater, deposited the former, garaged the latter, kissed the baby and settled in.

Many fellows might have objected to the presence on the premises
of a bib-and-bottle juvenile, but Freddie has always been a good
mixer, and he and this infant hit it off from the start like a couple of
sailors on shore leave. It became a regular thing with him to take the
half-portion down to the beach and stand by while it mucked about
with its spade and bucket. And it was as he was acting as master of the
revels one sunny day that there came ambling along a well-nourished
girl with golden hair, who paused and scrutinized the Bingo issue
with a genial smile.

'Is the baby building a sand castle?' she said.

'Well, yes and no,' replied Freddie civilly. 'It thinks it is, but if you
ask me, little of a constructive nature will result.'

'Still, so long as it's happy.'

'Oh, quite.'

'Nice day.'

'Beautiful.'

'Could you tell me the correct time?'

'Precisely eleven.'

'Coo!' said the girl. 'I must hurry, or I shall be late. I'm meeting a
gentleman friend of mine on the pier at half past ten.'

And that was that. I mean, just one of those casual encounters which are so common at the seashore, with not a word spoken on either side that could bring the blush of shame to the cheek of modesty. I stress this, because this substantial blonde was to become entangled in Freddie's affairs and I want to make it clear at the outset that from start to finish he was as pure as the driven snow. Sir Galahad could have taken his correspondence course.

It was about a couple of days after this that a picture postcard, forwarded from his London address, informed him that Mavis and her father were already in residence at the Magnifique, and he dashed into the two-seater and drove round there with a beating heart. It was his intention to take the loved one for a spin, followed by a spot of tea at some wayside shoppe.

This project, however, was rendered null and void by the fact that she was out. Old Bodsham, receiving Freddie in the suite, told him that she had gone to take her little brother Wilfred back to his school.

'We had him for lunch,' said the Bod.

'No, did you?' said Freddie. 'A bit indigestible, what?' He laughed heartily for some moments at his ready wit; then, seeing that the gag had not got across, cheesed it. He remembered now that there had always been something a bit Wednesday-matineeish about the fifth Earl of Bodsham. An austere man, known to his circle of acquaintances as The Curse of the Eastern Counties. 'He's at school here, is he?'

'At St Asaph's. An establishment conducted by an old college friend of mine, the Rev. Aubrey Upjohn.'

'Good Lord!' said Freddie, feeling what a small world it was. 'I used to be at St Asaph's.'

'Indeed?'

'Absolutely. I served a three years' sentence there before going on to Eton. Well, I'll be pushing along, then. Give Mavis my love, will you, and say I'll be round bright and early in the morning.'

He buzzed off and hopped into the car again, and for the space of half an hour or so drove about Bramley, feeling a bit at a loose end. And he was passing through a spot called Marina Crescent, a sort of jungle of boarding-houses, when he became aware that stirring things were happening in his immediate vicinity.

Along the road towards him there had been approaching a well-nourished girl with golden hair. I don't suppose he had noticed her – or, if he had, it was merely to say to himself 'Ah, the substantial blonde I met on the beach the other morning' and dismiss her from his thoughts. But at this moment she suddenly thrust herself on his attention by breaking into a rapid gallop, and at the same time a hoarse cry rent the air, not unlike that of the lion of the desert scenting its prey, and Freddie perceived charging out of a side street an elderly man with whiskers, who looked as if he might be a retired sea captain or a drysalter or something.

The spectacle perplexed him. He had always known that Bramley was bracing, but he had never supposed that it was as bracing as all this. And he had pulled up in order to get a better view, when the substantial blonde, putting on a burst of speed in the straight, reached the car and hurled herself into it.

'Quick!' she said.

'Quick?' said Freddie. He was puzzled. 'In what sense do you use the word "Quick"?' he asked, and was about to go further into the thing when the whiskered bird came dashing up and scooped the girl out of the car as if she had been a winkle and his hand a pin.

The girl grabbed hold of Freddie, and Freddie grabbed hold of the steering wheel, and the whiskered bird continued to freeze on to the girl, and for a while the human chain carried on along these lines. Then there was a rending sound, and the girl and Freddie came apart.

The whiskered bozo regarded him balefully.

'If we weren't in a public place,' he said, 'I would horsewhip you. If I had a horsewhip.'

And with these words he dragged the well-nourished girl from the scene, leaving Freddie, as you may well suppose, quite a bit perturbed and a long way from grasping the inner meaning.

The recent fracas had left him half in and half out of the car, and he completed the process by alighting. He had an idea that the whiskered ancient might have scratched his paint. But fortunately everything was all right, and he was leaning against the bonnet, smoking a soothing cigarette, when Mavis Peasmarch spoke behind him.

'Frederick!' she said.

Freddie tells me that at the sound of that loved voice he sprang six feet straight up in the air, but I imagine this to be an exaggeration. About eighteen inches, probably. Still, he sprang quite high enough to cause those leaning out of the windows of Marina Crescent to fall into the error of supposing him to be an adagio dancer practising a new step.

'Oh, hullo, darling!' he said.

He tried to speak in a gay and debonair manner, but he could not but recognize that he had missed his objective by a mile. Gazing at Mavis Peasmarch, he noted about her a sort of rigidity which he didn't like. Her eyes were stern and cold, and her lips tightly set. Marvis had inherited from her father that austere Puritanism which makes the old boy so avoided by the County, and this she was now exuding at every pore.

'So there you are!' he said, still having a stab at the gay and debonair.

'Yes,' said Mavis Peasmarch.

'I'm here, too,' said Freddie.

'So I see,' said Mavis Peasmarch.

'I'm staying with a pal. I thought I'd come here and surprise you.'

'You have,' said Mavis Peasmarch. She gave a sniff that sounded like a nor'easter ripping the sails of a stricken vessel. 'Frederick, what does this mean?'

'Eh?'

'That girl.'

'Oh, that *girl*?' said Freddie. 'Yes, I see what you mean. You are speaking of that girl. Most extraordinary, wasn't it?'

'Most.'

'She jumped into my car, did you notice?'

'I did. An old friend?'

'No, no. A stranger, and practically total, at that.'

'Oh?' said Mavis Peasmarch, and let go another sniff that went echoing down the street. 'Who was the old man?'

'I don't know. Another stranger, even more total.'

'He said he wanted to horsewhip you.'

'Yes, I heard him. Dashed familiar.'

'Why did he want to horsewhip you?'

'Ah, there you've got me. The man's thought processes are a sealed book to me.'

'The impression I received was that he resented your having made his daughter the plaything of an idle hour.'

'But I didn't. As a matter of fact, I haven't had much spare time since I got here.'

'Oh?'

'The solution that suggests itself to me is that we have stumbled up against one of those E. Phillips Oppenheim situations. Yes, that would explain the whole thing. Here's how I figure it out. The girl is an international spy. She got hold of the plans of the fortifications and was taking them to an accomplice, when along came the whiskered bird, a secret service man. You could see those whiskers were a disguise. He thought I was the accomplice.'

'Oh?'

'How's your brother Wilfred?' asked Freddie, changing the subject.

'Will you please drive me to my hotel?' said Mavis, changing it again.

'Oh, right,' said Freddie. 'Right.'

That night, Freddie lay awake, ill at ease. There had been something in the adored object's manner, when he dropped her at the hotel, which made him speculate as to whether that explanation of his had got over quite so solidly as he had hoped. He had suggested coming in and having a cosy chat, and she had said No, please, I have a headache. He had said how well she was looking, and she had said Oh? And when he had asked her if she loved her little Freddie, she had made no audible response.

All in all, it looked to Freddie as if what is technically called a lover's tiff had set in with a good deal of severity, and as he lay tossing on his pillow he pondered quite a bit on how this could be adjusted.

What was needed here, he felt, was a gesture – some spectacular performance on his part which would prove that his heart was in the right place.

But what spectacular performance?

He toyed with the idea of saving Mavis from drowning, only to dismiss it when he remembered that on the rare occasions when she took a dip in the salty she never went in above the waist.

He thought of rescuing old Bodsham from a burning building. But how to procure that burning building? He couldn't just set a match to the Hotel Magnifique and expect it to go up in flames.

And then, working through the family, he came to little Wilfred, and immediately got a Grade-A inspiration. It was via Wilfred that he must oil back into Mavis's esteem. And it could be done, he saw, by going to St Asaph's and asking the Rev. Aubrey Upjohn to give the school a half-holiday. This kindly act would put him right back in the money.

He could picture the scene. Wilfred would come bounding in to tea one afternoon. 'Coo!' Mavis would exclaim. 'What on earth are you doing here? Have you run away from school?' 'No,' Wilfred would reply, 'the school has run away from me. In other words, thanks to Freddie Widgeon, that prince of square-shooters, we have been given a half-holiday.' 'Well, I'm blowed!' Mavis would ejaculate. 'Heaven bless Freddie Widgeon! I had a feeling all along that I'd been misjudging that bird.'

At this point, Freddie fell asleep.

Often, when you come to important decisions overnight, you find after sleeping on them that they are a bit blue around the edges. But morning, when it came, found Freddie still resolved to go through with his day's good deed. If, however, I were to tell you that he liked the prospect, I should be deceiving you. It is not too much to say that he quailed at it. Years had passed since his knickerbocker days, but the Rev. Aubrey Upjohn was still green in his memory. A man spiritually akin to Simon Legree and the late Captain Bligh of the *Bounty*, with whose disciplinary methods his own had much in common, he had made a deep impression on Freddie's plastic mind, and the thought of breezing in and trying to sting him for a half-holiday was one that froze the blood more than a bit.

But two things bore him on: (a) his great love, and (b) the fact that it suddenly occurred to him that he could obtain a powerful talking point by borrowing Bingo's baby and taking it along with him.

Schoolmasters, he knew, are always anxious to build for the future. To them, the infant of today is the pupil at so much per of tomorrow. It would strengthen his strategic position enormously if he dangled Bingo's baby before the man's eyes and said: 'Upjohn, I can swing a bit of custom your way. My influence with the parents of this child is stupendous. Treat me right, and down it goes on your waiting list.' It would make all the difference.

So, waiting till Bingo's back and Mrs Bingo's back were turned, he scooped up Junior and started out. And presently he was ringing the front door bell of St Asaph's, the younger generation over his arm, concealed beneath a light overcoat. The parlourmaid showed him into the study, and he was left there to drink in the details of the well-remembered room which he had not seen for so many years.

Now, it so happened that he had hit the place at the moment when the Rev. Aubrey was taking the senior class in Bible history, and when a headmaster has got his teeth into a senior class he does not readily sheathe the sword. There was consequently a longish stage wait, and as the minutes passed Freddie began to find the atmosphere of the study distinctly oppressive.

The last time he had been in this room, you see, the set-up had been a bit embarrassing. He had been bending over a chair, while the Rev. Aubrey Upjohn, strongly posted in his rear, stood measuring the distance with half-closed eyes, preparatory to bringing the old malacca down on his upturned trousers seat. And memories like this bring with them a touch of sadness.

Outside the French window the sun was shining, and it seemed to Freddie that what was needed to dissipate the feeling of depression from which he had begun to suffer was a stroll in the garden with a cigarette. He sauntered out, accordingly, and had paced the length of the grounds and was gazing idly over the fence at the end of them, when he perceived that beyond this fence a certain liveliness was in progress.

He was looking into a small garden, at the back of which was a house. And at an upper window of this house was a girl. She was waving her arms at him.

It is never easy to convey every shade of your meaning by waving your arms at a distance of forty yards, and Freddie not unnaturally missed quite a good deal of the gist. Actually, what the girl was trying to tell him was that she had recently met at the bandstand on the pier a man called George Perkins, employed in a London firm of book-makers doing business under the trade name of Joe Sprockett; that a mutual fondness for the Overture to *Zampa* had drawn them together; that she had become deeply enamoured of him; that her tender sentiments had been fully reciprocated; that her father, who belonged to a religious sect which disapproved of bookmakers, had refused to sanction the match or even to be introduced to the above Perkins; that he – her father – had intercepted a note from the devout lover, arranging for a meeting at the latter's boarding-house (10, Marina Crescent) and a quick wedding at the local registrar's; and that he – she was still alluding to her father – had now locked her in her room until, in his phrase, she should come to her senses. And what she wanted Freddie to do was let her out. Because good old George was waiting at 10, Marina Crescent with the licence, and if she could only link up with him they could put the thing through promptly.

Freddie, as I say, did not get quite all of this, but he got enough of it to show him that here was a damsel in distress, and he was stirred to his foundations. He had not thought that this sort of thing happened outside the thrillers, and even there he had supposed it to be confined to moated castles. And this wasn't a moated castle by any means. It was a two-storey desirable residence with a slate roof, standing in park-like grounds extending to upwards of a quarter of an acre. It looked the sort of place that might belong to a retired sea captain or possibly a drysalter.

Full of the old knight-errant spirit, for he has always been a pushover for damsels in distress, he leaped the fence with sparkling eyes. And it was only when he was standing beneath the window that he recognized in the girl who was goggling at him through the glass like some rare fish in an aquarium his old acquaintance, the substan-tial blonde.

The sight cooled him off considerably. He is rather a superstitious sort of chap, and he had begun to feel that this billowy curver wasn't lucky for him. He remembered now that a gipsy had once warned him to beware of a fair woman, and for a moment it was touch and go whether he wouldn't turn away and ignore the whole unpleasant affair. However, the old knight-errant spirit was doing its stuff, and he decided to carry on as planned. Gathering from a quick twist of her eyebrows that the key was in the outside of the door, he nipped in through the sitting room window, raced upstairs and did the needful. And a moment later she was emerging like a cork out of a bottle and shooting down the stairs. She whizzed into the sitting room and whizzed through the window, and he whizzed after her. And the first thing he saw as he came skimming over the sill was her galloping round the lawn, closely attended by the whiskered bloke who had scooped her out of the car in Marina Crescent. He had a three-pronged fork in his possession and was whacking at her with the handle, getting a bull's-eye at about every second shot.

It came as a great surprise to Freddie, for he had distinctly understood from the way the girl had twiddled her fingers that her father was at the croquet club, and for a moment he paused, uncertain what to do.

He decided to withdraw. No chivalrous man likes to see a woman in receipt of a series of juicy ones with a fork handle, but the thing seemed to him one of those purely family disputes which can only be threshed out between father and daughter. He had started to edge away, accordingly, when the whiskered bloke observed him and came charging in his direction, shouting the old drysalters' battle cry. One can follow his train of thought, of course. He supposed Freddie to be George Perkins, the lovelorn bookie, and wished to see the colour of his insides. With a good deal of emotion, Freddie saw that he was now holding the fork by the handle.

Exactly what the harvest would have been, had nothing occurred to interfere with the old gentleman's plans, it is hard to say. But by great good fortune he tripped over a flower-pot while he was still out of jabbing distance and came an impressive purler. And before he could get right side up again, Freddie had seized the girl, hurled her over the fence, leaped the fence himself and started lugging her across the grounds of St Asaph's to his car, which he had left at the front door.

The going had been so good, and the substantial blonde was in such indifferent condition, that even when they were in the car and bowling off little came through in the way of conversation. The substantial blonde, having gasped out a request that he drive her to 10, Marina Crescent, lay back panting, and was still panting when they reached journey's end. He decanted her and drove off. And it was as he drove off that he became aware of something missing. Something he should have had on his person was not on his person.

He mused.

His cigarette case?

No, he had his cigarette case.

His hat?

No, he had his hat.

His small change? . . .

And then he remembered. Bingo's baby. He had left it chewing a bit of indiarubber in the Rev. Aubrey Upjohn's study.

Well, with his nervous system still all churned up by his recent experiences, an interview with his old preceptor was not a thing to which he looked forward with anything in the nature of ecstasy, but he's a pretty clear-thinking chap, and he realized that you can't go strewing babies all over the place and just leave them. So he went back to St Asaph's and trotted round to the study window. And there inside was the Rev. Aubrey, pacing the floor in a manner which the most vapid and irreflective observer would have recognized as distraught.

I suppose practically the last thing an unmarried schoolmaster wants to find in his sanctum is an unexplained baby, apparently come for an extended visit; and the Rev. Aubrey Upjohn, on entering the study shortly after Freddie had left it and noting contents, had sustained a shock of no slight order. He viewed the situation with frank concern.

And he was turning to pace the floor again, when he got another shock. He had hoped to be alone, to think this thing over from every angle, and there was a young man watching him from the window. On this young man's face there was what seemed to him a sneering grin. It was really an ingratiating smile, of course, but you couldn't expect a man in the Rev. Aubrey's frame of mind to know that.

'Oh, hullo,' said Freddie. 'You remember me, don't you?'

'No, I do not remember you,' cried the Rev. Aubrey. 'Go away.'

Freddie broadened the ingratiating smile an inch or two.

'Former pupil. Name of Widgeon.'

The Rev. Aubrey passed a weary hand over his brow. One can understand how he must have felt. First this frightful blow, I mean to say, and on top of that the re-entry into his life of a chap he hoped he'd seen the last of years and years ago.

'Yes,' he said, in a low, toneless voice. 'Yes, I remember you. Widgeon.'

'F. F.'

'F., as you say, F. What do you want?'

'I came back for my baby,' said Freddie, like an apologetic plumber.

The Rev. Aubrey started.

'Is this your baby?'

'Well, technically, no. On loan, merely. Some time ago, my pal Bingo Little married Rosie M. Banks, the well-known female novelist. This is what you might call the upshot.'

The Rev. Aubrey seemed to be struggling with some powerful emotion.

'Then it was you who left this baby in my study?'

'Yes. You see – '

'Ha!' said the Rev. Aubrey, and went off with a pop, as if suffering from spontaneous combustion.

Freddie tells me that few things have impressed him more than the address to which he now listened. He didn't like it, but it extorted a grudging admiration. Here was this man, he meant to say, unable as a clerk in Holy Orders to use any of the words which would have been at the disposal of a layman, and yet by sheer force of character rising triumphantly over the handicap. Without saying a thing that couldn't have been said in the strictest drawing room, the Rev. Aubrey Upjohn contrived to produce in Freddie the illusion that he had had a falling out with the bucko mate of a tramp steamer. And every word he uttered made it more difficult to work the conversation round to the subject of half-holidays.

Long before he had reached his 'thirdly,' Freddie was feeling as if he had been chewed up by powerful machinery, and when he was at length permitted to back out, he felt that he had had a merciful escape. For quite a while it had seemed more than likely that he was going to be requested to bend over that chair again. And such was the Rev. Aubrey's magnetic personality that he would have done it, he tells me, like a shot.

Much shaken, he drove back to the Bingo residence, and the first thing he saw on arriving there was Bingo standing on the steps, looking bereaved to the gills.

'Freddie,' yipped Bingo, 'have you seen Algernon?'

Freddie's mind was not at its clearest.

'No,' he said. 'I don't think I've run across him. Algernon who? Pal of yours? Nice chap?'

Bingo hopped like the high hills.

'My baby, you ass.'

'Oh, the good old baby? Yes, I've got him.'

'Six hundred and fifty-seven curses!' said Bingo. 'What the devil did you want to go dashing off with him for? Do you realize we've been hunting for him all the morning?'

'You wanted him for something special?'

'I was just going to notify the police and have dragnets spread.'

Freddie could see that an apology was in order.

'I'm sorry,' he said. 'Still, all's well that ends well. Here he is. Oh no, he isn't,' he added, having made a quick inspection of the interior of the car. 'I say, this is most unfortunate. I seem to have left him again.'

'Left him?'

'What with all the talk that was going on, he slipped my mind. But I can give you his address. Care of the Rev. Aubrey Upjohn, St Asaph's, Mafeking Road, Bramley-on-Sea. All you have to do is step round at your leisure and collect him. I say, is lunch ready?'

'Lunch?' Bingo laughed a hideous, mirthless laugh. At least, that's what Freddie thinks it was. It sounded like a bursting tyre. 'A fat lot of lunch you're going to get. The cook's got hysterics, the kitchen-maid's got hysterics, and so have the parlourmaid and the housemaid. Rosie started having hysterics as early as eleven-thirty, and is now in bed with an ice pack. When she finds out about this, I wouldn't be in your shoes for a million quid. Two million,' added Bingo. 'Or, rather, three.'

This was an aspect of the matter which had not occurred to Freddie. He saw that there was a good deal in it.

'Do you know, Bingo,' he said, 'I believe I ought to be getting back to London today.'

'I would.'

'Several things I've got to do there, several most important things. I dare say, if I whipped back to town, you could send my luggage after me?'

'A pleasure.'

'Thanks,' said Freddie. 'You won't forget the address, will you? St Asaph's, Mafeking Road. Mention my name, and say you've come for the baby I inadvertently left in the study. And now, I think, I ought to be getting round to see Mavis. She'll be wondering what has become of me.'

He tooled off, and a few minutes later was entering the lobby of the Hotel Magnifique. The first thing he saw was Mavis and her father standing by a potted palm.

'Hullo, hullo,' he said, toddling up.

'Ah, Frederick,' said old Bodsham.

I don't know if you remember, when I was telling you about that time in New York, my mentioning that at a rather sticky point in the proceedings Freddie had noticed that old Bodsham was looking like a codfish with something on its mind. The same conditions prevailed now.

'Frederick,' proceeded the Bod, 'Mavis has been telling me a most unpleasant story.'

Freddie hardly knew what to say to this. He was just throwing a few sentences together in his mind about the modern girl being sound at heart despite her freedom of speech, and how there isn't really any harm in it if she occasionally gets off one from the smoking room – tolerant, broad-minded stuff, if you know what I mean – when old Bodsham resumed.

'She tells me you have become entangled with a young woman with golden hair.'

'A fat young woman with golden hair,' added Mavis, specifying more exactly.

Freddie waved his arms passionately, like a semaphore.

'Nothing in it,' he cried. 'Nothing whatever. The whole thing greatly exaggerated. Mavis,' he said, 'I am surprised and considerably pained. I should have thought that you would have had more trust in me. Kind hearts are more than coronets and simple faith than Norman blood,' he went on, for he had always remembered that gag after having to write it out two hundred times at school for loosing off a stink bomb in the form-room. 'I told you she was a total stranger.'

'Then how does it happen that you were driving her through the streets of Bramley in your car this morning?' said old Bodsham.

'Yes,' said Mavis. 'That is what I want to know.'

'It is a point,' said old Bodsham, 'upon which we would both be glad to receive information.'

Catch Freddie at a moment like this, and you catch him at his best. His heart, leaping from its moorings, had loosened one of his front teeth, but there was absolutely nothing in his manner to indicate it. His eyes, as he stared at them, were those of a spotless bimbo cruelly wronged by a monstrous accusation.

'Me?' he said incredulously.

'You,' said old Bodsham.

'I saw you myself,' said Mavis.

I doubt if there is another member of this club who could have uttered at this juncture the light, careless laugh that Freddie did.

'What an extraordinary thing,' he said. 'One can only suppose that there must be somebody in this resort who resembles me so closely in appearance that the keenest eye is deceived. I assure you, Bod – I mean, Lord Bodsham – and you, Mavis – that my morning has been far too full to permit of my giving joy rides to blondes, even if the mere thought of doing so wouldn't have sickened me to the very soul. The idea having crossed my mind that little Wilfred would appreciate it, I went to St Asaph's to ask the Rev. Aubrey Upjohn to give the school a half-holiday. I want no thanks, of course. I merely mention the matter to show how ridiculous this idea of yours is that I was buzzing about with blondes in my two-seater. The Rev. Aubrey will tell you that I was in conference with him for the dickens of a time. After which, I was in conference with my friend, Bingo Little. And after that I came here.'

There was a silence.

'Odd,' said the Bod.

'Very odd,' said Mavis.

They were plainly rattled. And Freddie was just beginning to have that feeling, than which few are pleasanter, of having got away with it in the teeth of fearful odds, when the revolving door of the hotel moved as if impelled by some irresistible force, and through it came a bulging figure in mauve, surmounted by golden hair. Reading from left to right, the substantial blonde.

'Coo!' she exclaimed, sighting Freddie. 'There you are, ducky! Excuse me half a jiff,' she added to Mavis and the Bod, who had rocked back on their heels at the sight of her, and she linked her arm in Freddie's and drew him aside.

'I hadn't time to thank you before,' she said. 'Besides being too out of breath. Papa is very nippy on his feet, and it takes it out of a girl, trying to dodge a fork handle. What luck finding you here like this. My gentleman friend and I were married at the registrar's just after I left you, and we're having the wedding breakfast here. And if it hadn't been for you, there wouldn't have been a wedding breakfast. I can't tell you how grateful I am.'

And, as if feeling that actions speak louder than words, she flung her arms about Freddie and kissed him heartily. She then buzzed off to the ladies' room to powder her nose, leaving Freddie rooted to the spot.

He didn't, however, remain rooted long. After one quick glance at Mavis and old Bodsham, he was off like a streak to the nearest exit. That glance, quick though it had been, had shown him that this was the end. The Bod was looking at Mavis, and Mavis was looking at the Bod. And then they both turned and looked at him, and there was that in their eyes which told him, as I say, that it was the finish. Good explainer though he is, there were some things which he knew he could not explain, and this was one of them.

That is why, if our annual tournament had been held this year at Bramley-on-Sea, you would not have found Frederick Widgeon in the ranks, playing to his handicap of twenty-four. He makes no secret of the fact that he is permanently through with Bramley-on-Sea. If it wants to brace anybody, let it jolly well brace somebody else, about sums up what he feels.

16

THE FAT OF THE LAND

Although he had never mentioned it to anybody, feeling that it was but an idle daydream and not within the sphere of practical politics, the idea of having a Fat Uncles sweepstake at the Drones Club had long been in Freddie Widgeon's mind, such as it was. Himself the possessor of one of the fattest uncles in London – Rodney, Lord Blicester – he had noticed how many of his fellow members had fat uncles, too, and he felt it a sad waste of good material not to make these the basis of a sporting contest similar, though on a smaller scale, to those in operation in Ireland and Calcutta.

Perfectly simple, the mechanics of the thing. Put the names of the uncles in a hat, put the names of the punters in another hat, draw a name from the first hat, draw a name from the second hat, and the holder of the fattest uncle scooped the jackpot. No difficulty there.

But there was a catch, and a very serious one – to wit, the problem of how to do the weighing. He could not, for instance, go to Lord Blicester and say 'Would you mind just stepping on this try-your-weight machine for a moment, Uncle Rodney? It is essential to satisfy the judges that you are fatter than the Duke of Dunstable.' At least, he could, but there would be questions asked, and explanations would lead to pique, bad feeling and possibly the stopping of a much-needed allowance. It was, in short, an impasse, and he had come to look on the scheme as just another of those things which, though good, cannot be pushed along, when, coming into the bar one morning, he found an animated group assembled there and as he entered heard McGarry, the man behind the counter, say 'Ten stone three'. Upon which, there was a burst of hearty cheering and, inquiring the reason for this enthusiasm, he was informed that McGarry had revealed an unsuspected talent. He was able to tell the weight of anything from a vegetable marrow to a Covent Garden tenor just by looking at it.

'Never misses by more than half an ounce,' said an Egg. 'In his circle of friends he is known as the Human Scales. A great gift, don't you think?'

'I'll say it is,' said Freddie. 'It removes the one obstacle to this project of mine.'

And in a few well-chosen words he placed his proposition before the meeting.

It caught on immediately, as he had been confident that it would, and a committee, with a prominent Crumpet at its head, was formed to rough out the details of the venture. It was decided that the deadline should be one o'clock on the opening day of the Eton and Harrow match, when all the uncles would be rolling up and having lunch at the Drones with their nephews. To parade them before McGarry, his decision to be final, would be a simple task, for the first thing they always did was to head for the bar like bison for a water-hole. The price of tickets was put up at a somewhat higher figure than suited the purse of many members, but it was pointed out to these that they could club together and form syndicates, and so few had failed to chip in by the time the day of the drawing arrived that the Crumpet was able to announce that the contents of the kitty amounted to well over a hundred pounds. And it was generally recognized that this impressive sum must inevitably go to the lucky stiff who drew the name of Lord Blicester, for while all the starters were portly, having long let their waist-lines go, not one of them could be con-sidered in the class of Freddie's outsize uncle. Others, as a well-read Bean put it, abided their question, he was free.

And, of course, as always seemed to happen on these occasions, it was Oofy Prosser, the club millionaire, the one human soul, if you could call him a human soul, not in need of the money, who drew the Blicester ticket. Freddie himself got Oofy's Uncle Horace. He had not been aware till then that Oofy had an Uncle Horace, and at the conclusion of the drawing he went over to where the plutocrat was sitting reading his morning's mail, to make inquiries.

'Who is this uncle of yours I've drawn, Oofy?' he asked. 'I didn't know you had an uncle.'

'Nor did I,' said Oofy, 'till I got a letter from him the other day, signed "Uncle Horace". It's rather odd. I could have sworn that my only uncles were Hildebrand, who had an apoplectic stroke in 1947, and Stanley, who died of cirrhosis of the liver in 1949, but apparently this is one I overlooked, no doubt because he has been in the Argen-tine for the last twenty years. He returned to England last week and is staying at a place called Hollrock Manor in Hertfordshire. I haven't seen him yet, but he will be lunching with me here on the big day.'

'I wonder if he's fat.'

'I shouldn't think so. Warm climate, the Argentine. Keeps the weight down. And isn't that the place where you spend your whole time riding over pampas? No, I wouldn't build any hopes, Freddie. Not a chance of him nosing out your Uncle Rodney. But excuse me,

THE FAT OF THE LAND

old man, I must be catching up with my reading.'

Freddie drifted away disconsolately, and Oofy returned to his letters. One of these bore the address of Hollrock Manor. He read it without any great interest, but was mildly intrigued by the postscript.

'P.S.,' his uncle wrote. 'You must be wondering what I look like these days, not having seen me since you were a child. I enclose a snapshot, taken in the garden the other morning.'

Oofy examined the envelope, but could find no snapshot. Then, looking down, he saw that it had fallen to the floor. He picked it up, and the next moment had sagged back in his chair with a stifled cry.

It was the photograph of an elderly man in a bathing suit; an elderly man who, a glance was enough to tell, had been overdoing it on the starchy foods since early childhood; an elderly man so rotund, so obese, so bulging in every direction that Shakespeare, had he beheld him, would have muttered to himself 'Upon what meat doth this our Horace feed that he is grown so great?' One wondered how any bathing suit built by human hands could contain so stupendous an amount of uncle without parting at the seams. In the letter he had written to Oofy announcing his arrival in England, Horace Prosser had spoken of coming home to lay his bones in the old country. There was nothing in the snapshot to suggest that he had any bones.

Little wonder, then, that as he ran his eye over the man, reading from left to right, Oofy should have been feeling the same sort of stunned breathless feeling he would have felt had this uncle fallen on him from the top of a high building. With pitiless clarity it was borne in on him that the Blicester ticket over which he had been gloating was not worth the paper it was written on. Compared with this mastodon, Lord Blicester was slim to the point of emaciation and hadn't a hope, and the thought that Freddie Widgeon and not he would win all that lovely money was like a dagger in Oofy's bosom. We said earlier that he did not need the cash, but it was we who said it, not Oofy. His views on the matter were sharply divergent. Whenever there was cash around, he wanted to get it. It was well said of him at the Drones that despite his revolting wealth he would always willingly walk ten miles in tight boots to pick up twopence. Many put the figure even lower.

How long he sat there motionless, he could not have said, but after a while his subtle and scheming brain, temporarily numbed, began to function again, and he perceived that all was not yet lost. There was, he saw, a way of achieving the happy ending. It called for the cooperation of a party of the second part of an innocent and unsuspicious nature, and no one could have filled the bill more adequately than Frederick Widgeon, a man whose trust in his fellow-men was a byword. Frederick Widgeon, he knew for a fact, believed everything he read in *Time*. He sought him out and laid a gentle hand on his sleeve.

'Freddie, old man,' he said, 'can you spare me a moment of your valuable time?'

Freddie said he could.

'I don't know,' said Oofy, 'if you were glancing in my direction just now?'

Freddie said he wasn't.

'Well, if you had been, you would have noticed that I was plunged in meditation, and I'll tell you why. Have you ever been a Boy Scout?'

Freddie said he hadn't.

'I was one at one time, and I have never forgotten the lessons I learned in those knickerbocker and spooring days.'

'Tying knots, do you mean, and lighting fires by rubbing sticks together?'

'Not so much that as the doing-one's-daily-good-deed routine. Boy Scouts, as you probably know, are supposed to perform at least one act of kindness every twenty-four hours, and a very good thing, too. Keeps them up on their toes.'

'Yes, I can see that. It would, of course.'

'Now, one rather tends, as one grows older, to give the daily good deed a miss, and it's all wrong, one shouldn't. There is no reason whatever why, just because one no longer goes about in a khaki shirt with a whistle attached to it, one should omit those little acts of kindness which sweeten life for all and sundry. One ought to keep plugging away. This came to me very forcibly just now, as I sat thinking about this sweepstake thing we're having. Is it right, is it fair, I asked myself, that I, to whom money means nothing, should have drawn the favourite, while somebody who really needs the stuff, like my old friend Freddie Widgeon, gets stuck with a rank outsider? There could be but one answer. It was not right. It was not fair. It was something that had to be adjusted.'

'How do you mean, adjusted?'

'Quite simple. We must swap tickets, I taking my uncle's and you yours. Yes, yes,' said Oofy, seeing that his old friend was gaping at him like a bewildered codfish, 'you are naturally surprised. It seems to you bizarre that I should be doing myself out of a hundred quid or whatever it is. But what you overlook is that I shall be getting the glow that comes from feeling that one has done an act of kindness and helped a fellow-human being on the road to happiness. What is a hundred quid compared with that?'

'But – '

'Don't say "But", Freddie. I insist on this. No, no, don't thank me. My motives are purely selfish. I want to glow.'

And Oofy went off to tell the Crumpet to record the change of tickets in the official notebook in which the names of the ticket holders were listed. He was glowing.

It is a very incurious and phlegmatic nephew who, when he has an uncle whose adiposity is going to net him more than a hundred pounds, does not hasten to go and take a look at that uncle, if only to assure himself that the latter is wading into the mashed potatoes in a satisfactory manner and getting his full supply of bread, butter, beer, roly-poly pudding and pastries. On the following morning, preceded by a telegram saying that he was coming to lunch, Oofy started out in his car for Hollrock Manor. He pictured a fine old house with spacious grounds, and found on arrival that his imagination had not led him astray. Hollrock Manor was plainly a place where the moneyed did themselves well and, always of a greedy nature, he found his mouth watering at the prospect of the lavish luncheon of which he would shortly be partaking. His drive had given him a rare appetite.

He inquired for Mr Horace Prosser and presently the other came wheezing along, and after a certain amount of Well-well-well-ing and So-here-you-are-at-last-ing, inevitable in the circumstances, they went into the dining room and seated themselves at a table. It gratified Oofy to note that as his relative lowered himself into his chair, the chair visibly quivered beneath him and gave out a protesting squeal. On his journey down he had from time to time an uneasy feeling that that snapshot might have exaggerated the other's proportions, but one glance had been enough to tell him that these were idle fears. Now that he saw the man in the flesh, he felt, like the Queen of Sheba, that the half had not been told unto him.

The only thing that disturbed him was that, no doubt in a moment of absentmindedness, his host had not suggested the pre-luncheon martini, in anticipation of which he had been licking his lips for the last hour. And as the waiter presented the bill of fare, it seemed to occur to Mr Prosser that he had been remiss. He hastened to explain his eccentric behaviour.

'Sorry I couldn't offer you a cocktail, my boy. We don't have them here. But they serve an excellent glass of parsnip juice, if you would care for it. No? Then suppose we order. Will you have stewed lettuce, or would you prefer an orange? Ah, but wait, I see we are in luck. This is grated carrot day. How about starting with potassium broth, going on to grated carrots and winding up with a refreshing cup of dandelion coffee?'

At an early point in these remarks Oofy's lower jaw had drooped like a tired lily. He hitched it up in order to ask a question.

'I say, what *is* this place?'

'It used to belong to Lord Somebody or Sir Somebody Something, I forget which. Like so many landowners, he had to sell after the war. Impossible to keep the old home up. Sad, very sad.'

'Sadder than potassium broth?'

'Don't you like potassium broth? You can have seaweed soup, if you wish.'

'But I don't understand. Is this a hotel?'

'Well, more a clinic, I suppose you would call it. We come here to reduce.'

It is not easy to totter when seated in a chair, but Oofy managed it. He goggled at his companion, the potassium broth falling from his nerveless spoon.

'Did you say "reduce"?'

'That's right. Doctor Hailsham, who runs the place, guarantees to take a pound a day off you, if you follow his regimen faithfully. I expect to lose three stone before I leave.'

Oofy tottered again, and the room seemed to swim about him. He scarcely recognized the hollow croak that proceeded from his lips as his own voice.

'Three *stone*?'

'If not more.'

'You're crazy!'

'Who's crazy?'

'You are. What do you want to lose three stone for?'

'You don't think I'm a little overweight?'

'Certainly not. Just pleasantly plump.'

Horace Prosser gave a rich chuckle, seeming entertained by some amusing recollection.

'Pleasantly plump, eh? You are more flattering than Loretta was.'

'Than who was?'

'A Mrs Delancy I met on the boat, coming over. She called me a hippopotamus.'

'A vulgar ill-bred female bounder!'

'Please! You are speaking of the woman I love.'

'I'm what-ing of the what you *what*?'

It was impossible to ascertain whether a blush mantled Horace Prosser's cheek, for in its normal state it was ruddier than a cherry, but he unquestionably looked coy. It would not be too much to say that he simpered. He murmured something about Ah, those moon-light nights, and when Oofy said Ah, what moonlight nights? explained that he was alluding to the moonlight nights when he and this Mrs Delancy – a widow of some years standing – had walked together on the boat deck. It was at the conclusion of one of these pro-menades, he added, that he had asked her to be his wife, and she had replied that the only obstacle standing in the way of the suggested merger was his adipose deposit. She refused, she said, to walk up the aisle with a human hippopotamus.

Horace Prosser chuckled again.

'The whimsical way she put it was that a woman who married a man my size ran a serious risk of being arrested for bigamy. She con-fessed that she had often yearned for someone like me, but was opposed to the idea of getting twice as much as she had yearned for. Very bright, amusing woman. She comes from Pittsburgh.'

Oofy choked on a spoonful of the yellow mess which had been placed before him.

'I consider her a cad and a bounder.'

'So we left it that I would go off somewhere and diet, and if some day I came to her with thirty pounds or so removed from my holdings, our talks would be resumed in what politicians call an atmosphere of the utmost cordiality. She is coming to see me soon, and I don't think she will be disappointed. Have some more of these carrots, my boy. Apart from acting directly on the fatty corpuscles, they are rich in Vitamins A, B, C, D, E, G and K.'

Mr Prosser went off to have a massage after he had digested his lunch, and Oofy, as he drove back to London, was still shuddering at the recollection of what the other had said about the *effleurage*, stroking, friction, kneading, *pétrissage*, *tapotement* and vibration which massage at Hollrock Manor involved. He was appalled. With that sort of thing going on in conjunction with the potassium broth and dandelion coffee, it was plain that the man would come to the post a mere shadow. Lord Blicester, if in anything like mid-season form, would make rings round him.

Many young men in such a situation would have thrown in the towel and admitted defeat, but Oofy kept his head.

'I must be calm, calm,' he was saying to himself as he went to the Drones next day, and it was with outward calmness that he approached Freddie Widgeon, who was having a ham sandwich at the bar.

'Gosh, Freddie,' he said, after they had pip-pipped, 'I'm glad I ran into you. Do you notice that I am quivering like an aspen?'

'No,' said Freddie. 'Are you quivering like an aspen?'

'You bet I'm quivering like an aspen.'

'Why are you quivering like an aspen?'

'Well, wouldn't any man of good will be quivering like an aspen if he had had the narrowest of escapes from letting an old friend down? Here are the facts in a nutshell. With the best of motives, if you remember, I persuaded you to exchange your Lord Blicester ticket for my Uncle Horace. You recall that?'

'Oh, rather. You wanted to do your Boy Scout act of kindness for the day.'

'Exactly. And now what do I find?'

'What do you find?'

'I'll tell you what I find. I find that in comparison with my Uncle your Uncle is slender. I had a letter from Uncle Horace this morning, enclosing a snapshot of himself. Take a look at it.'

Freddie examined the snapshot, and such was his emotion that the ham sandwich flew from his grasp.

'Crumbs!'

'You may well say Crumbs!'

'Golly!'

'And also Golly! I said the same thing myself. It is pretty obvious, I think you will agree with me, that Blicester hasn't a chance. A good selling-plater, I admit, but this time he has come up against a classic yearling.'

'You told me your uncle had been perspiring for years in the hot sun of the Argentine.'

'No doubt the sun was not as hot as I have always supposed, or possibly his pores do not work freely. I also said, I recall, that he did a lot of riding over pampas. I was wrong. On the evidence of his photograph he can't have ridden over a pampa in his life. Well, fortunately I discovered this in time. There is only one thing to do, Freddie. We must change tickets again.'

Freddie gaped.

'You really . . . Oh, thanks,' he said, as a passing Bean picked up the ham sandwich and returned it to him. 'You really mean that?'

'I certainly do.'

'I call it pretty noble of you.'

'Oh, well, you know how it is. Once a Boy Scout, always a Boy Scout,' said Oofy, and a few moments later he was informing the Crumpet that the list in his notebook must once more be revised.

It was Oofy's practice, whenever life in London seemed to him to be losing its savour and the conversation of his fellow members of the Drones to be devoid of its customary sparkle, to pop over to Paris and get a nice change, and shortly after his chat with Freddie he made another of his trips to the French capital. And as he sat sipping an aperitif one morning at a café on the Champs Élysées, his thoughts turned to his Uncle Horace, and not for the first time he found himself marvelling that the love of a woman could have made that dedicated man mortify the flesh as he was doing. Himself, Oofy would not have forgone the simplest pat of butter to win the hand of Helen of Troy, and had marriage with Cleopatra involved the daily drinking of potassium broth and seaweed soup, there would have been no question of proceeding with the ceremony. 'I am sorry,' he would have said to Egypt's queen, 'but if those are your ideas, I have no option but to cancel the order for the wedding cake and see that work is stopped on the bridesmaids' dresses.'

He looked at his watch. About now his uncle, in Hollrock Manor's picturesque little bar, would be ordering his glass of parsnip juice preparatory to tackling whatever garbage the bill of fare was offering that day, perfectly contented because love conquered all and so forth. Ah, well, he felt, it takes all sorts to make a world.

At this point in his reverie his meditations were interrupted by a splintering crash in his rear and, turning, he perceived that a chair at a nearby table had disintegrated beneath the weight of a very stout man in a tweed suit. And he was just chuckling heartily at the amusing incident, when the laughter died on his lips. The well-nourished body extricating itself from the debris was that of his Uncle Horace – that selfsame Uncle Horace whom he had just been picturing among the parsnip juices and seaweed soups of Hollrock Manor, Herts.

'Uncle!' he cried, hastening to the spot.

'Oh, hullo, my boy,' said Mr Prosser, starting to dust himself off. 'You here? They seem to make these chairs very flimsy nowadays,' he muttered with a touch of peevishness. 'Or it may be,' he went on in more charitable vein, 'that I have put on a little weight these last few weeks. This French cooking. Difficult always to resist those sauces. What are you doing in La Ville Lumière?'

'What are *you* doing in La Ville Lumière?' demanded Oofy. 'Why aren't you at that frightful place in Hertfordshire?'

'I left there ages ago.'

'But how about the woman you love?'

'What woman I love?'

'The one who called you a hippopotamus.'

'Oh, Loretta Delancy. That's all over. It turned out to be just one of those fleeting shipboard romances. You know how they all look good to you at sea and fade out with a pop when you get ashore. She came to Hollrock Manor one afternoon, and the scales fell from my eyes. Couldn't imagine what I had ever seen in the woman. The idea of going through all that dieting and massage for her sake seemed so damn silly that next day I wrote her a civil note telling her to take a running jump into the nearest lake and packed up and left. Well, it's nice to run into you like this, my dear boy. We must have some big dinners together. Are you staying long in Paris?'

'I'm leaving today,' said Oofy. 'I have to see a man named Widgeon on business.'

But he did not see Freddie. Though he haunted the club day and night, yearning for a sight of that familiar face, not a glimpse of it did he get. He saw Bingo Little, he saw Catsmeat Potter-Pirbright, he saw Barmy Phipps, Percy Wimbush, Nelson Cork, Archibald Mulliner and all the other pillars of the Drones who lunched there daily, but always there was this extraordinary shortage of Widgeons. It was as though the young man had vanished from human ken like the captain and crew of the *Marie Celeste*.

It was only when he happened to be having a quick one with an Egg who was Freddie's closest friend that the mystery of his disappearance was explained. At the mention of the absent one's name, the Egg sighed a little.

'Oh, Freddie,' he said. 'Yes, I can tell you about him. At the moment he is rather unfortunately situated. He owes a bookie fifty quid, and is temporarily unable to settle.'

'Silly ass.'

'Silly, unquestionably, ass, but there it is. What happened was that he drew an uncle in this sweep whom nobody had ever heard of, and blow me tight if he hadn't unexpectedly hit the jackpot. He showed me a snapshot of the man, and I was amazed. I could see at a glance that here was the winner, so far ahead of the field that there could be no competition. Blicester would be an honourable runner-up, but nothing more. Extraordinary how often in these big events you find a dark horse popping up and upsetting all calculations. Well, with the sweepstake money as good as in his pocket, as you might say, poor old Freddie lost his head and put his shirt on a horse at Kempton Park which finished fourth, with the result, as I have indicated, that he owes this bookie fifty quid, and no means of paying him till he collects on the sweep. And the bookie, when informed that he wasn't going to collect, advised him in a fatherly way to be very careful of himself from now on, for though he knew that it was silly to be superstitious, he – the bookie – couldn't help remembering that every time people did him down for money some unpleasant accident always happened to them. Time after time he had noticed it, and it could not

THE FAT OF THE LAND

be mere coincidence. More like some sort of fate, the bookie said. So Freddie is lying low, disguised in a beard by Clarkson.'

'Where?'

'In East Dulwich.'

'Whereabouts in East Dulwich?'

'Ah,' said the Egg, 'that's what the bookie would like to know.'

The trouble about East Dulwich, from the point of view of a clean-shaven man trying to find a bearded man there, is that it is rather densely populated, rendering his chances of success slim. Right up to the day before the Eton and Harrow match Oofy prowled to and fro in its streets, hoping for the best, but East Dulwich held its secret well. The opening day of the match found him on the steps of the Drones Club, scanning the horizon like Sister Anne in the Bluebeard story. Surely, he felt, Freddie could not stay away from the premises on this morning of mornings.

Member after member entered the building as he stood there, accompanied by uncles of varying stoutness, but not one of those members was Freddie Widgeon, and Oofy's blood pressure had just reached a new high and looked like going to par, when a cab drew up and something bearded, shooting from its interior, shot past him, shot through the entrance hall and disappeared down the steps leading to the washroom. The eleventh hour had produced the man.

Freddie, when Oofy burst into the washroom some moments later with a 'Tally-ho' on his lips, was staring at himself in the mirror, a thing not many would have cared to do when looking as he did. A weaker man than Oofy would have recoiled at the frightful sight that met his eyes. Freddie, when making his purchase at Clarkson's, had evidently preferred quantity to quality. The salesman, no doubt, had recommended something in neat Vandykes as worn by the better class of ambassadors, but Freddie was a hunted stag, and when hunted stags buy beards, they want something big and bushy as worn by Victorian novelists. The man whom Oofy had been seeking so long could at this moment of their meeting have stepped into the Garrick Club of the Sixties, and Wilkie Collins and the rest of the boys would have welcomed him as a brother, supposing him to be Walt Whitman.

'Freddie!' cried Oofy.

'Oh, hullo, Oofy,' said Freddie. He was pulling at the beard in a gingerly manner, as if the process hurt him. 'You are doubtless surprised – '

'No, I'm not. I was warned of this. Why don't you take that damned thing off?'

'I can't.'

'Give it a tug.'

'I have given it a tug, and the agony was excruciating. It's stuck on with spirit gum or something.'

'Well, never mind your beard. We have no time to talk of beards. Freddie, thank heaven I have found you. Another quarter of an hour, and it would have been too late.'

'What would have been too late?'

'It. We've got to change those tickets.'

'What, again?'

'Immediately. You remember me saying that my Uncle Horace was staying at a place called Hollrock Manor in Hertfordshire? Well, naturally I supposed that it was one of those luxury country hotels where he would be having twice of everything and filling up with beer, champagne, liqueurs and what not. But was it?'

'Wasn't it? What was it if it wasn't?'

'It was what they call a clinic, run by some foul doctor, where the superfatted go to reduce. He had gone there to please a woman who had told him he looked like a hippopotamus.'

'He does look rather like a hippopotamus.'

'He does in that snapshot, I grant you, but that was taken weeks and weeks ago, and during those weeks he has been living on apple juice, tomato juice, orange juice, pineapple juice, parsnip juice, grated carrots, potassium broth and seaweed soup. He has also been having daily massage, the term massage embracing *effleurage*, stroking, kneading, *pétrissage*, *tapotement* and vibration.'

'Lord love a duck!'

'Lord love a duck is right. I needn't tell you what happens when that sort of thing is going on. Something has to give. By now he must have lost at least a couple of stone and be utterly incapable of giving old Blicester a race. So slip me the Uncle Horace ticket, and I will slip you the Blicester, and the situation will be stabilized once more. Gosh, Freddie, old man, when I think how near I came to letting you down, thinking I was acting in your best interests, I shudder.'

Freddie stroked his beard. To Oofy's dismay, he seemed hesitant, dubious.

'Well, I'm not so sure about this,' he said. 'You say your Uncle Horace has lost a couple of stone. I am strongly of the opinion that he could lose three and still be fatter than my Uncle Rodney, and I'm wondering if I ought to take a chance. You see, a great deal hangs on my winning this tourney. I owe fifty quid to a clairvoyant bookie, who, looking in his crystal ball, has predicted that if I don't brass up, some nasty accident will happen to me, and from what he tells me that crystal ball of his is to be relied on. I should feel an awful ass if I

gave up the Uncle Horace ticket and took the Uncle Rodney ticket
and Uncle Horace won and I found myself in a hospital with surgeons
doing crochet work all over me.'

'I only want to help.'

'I know you do, but the question is, are you helping?'

Oofy was unable to stroke his beard, for he had not got one, but he
fingered his chin. He was thinking with the rapidity with which he
always thought when there was money floating around to be picked
up. It did not take him long to reach a decision. Agony though it was
to part with fifty pounds, winning the sweep would leave him with a
nice profit. There was nothing for it but to make the great sacrifice. If
you do not speculate, you cannot accumulate.

'I'll tell you what I'll do,' he said, producing his wallet and extract-
ing the bank notes with which it always bulged. 'I'll give you fifty
quid. That will take care of the bookie, and you'll be all right,
whatever happens.'

As much as was visible of Freddie's face between the crevices of the
beard lit up. He looked like someone staring incredulously at
someone through a haystack.

'Golly, Oofy! Will you really do that?'

'It's not much to do for an old friend.'

'But what is there in it for you?'

'Just that glow, old man, just that glow,' said Oofy.

Going upstairs, he found the Crumpet in the hall, studying the
list in his notebook, and broke the news that a little further
pencil-work would be required of him. It brought a frown to the
other's face.

'I disapprove of all this chopping and changing,' he said, though
agreeing that there was nothing in the rules against it. 'Let's get this
straight. Freddie Widgeon now has the Blicester ticket and you have
the Horace Prosser ticket. Right?'

'Yes, that's right.'

'Not vice versa?'

'No, not vice versa.'

'Good. I'm glad that's settled. I've worn out one piece of india-
rubber already.'

It was at this moment that the hall porter, who for some little time
had been trying to attract Oofy's attention, spoke.

'There's a gentleman asking for you, Mr Prosser. Name of Prosser,
same as yours.'

'Ah, yes, my uncle. Where is he?'

'He stepped into the bar.'

'He would. Will you go and give him a cocktail,' said Oofy to the

Crumpet. 'I'll be with you in a minute, after I've booked a table in the dining room.'

It was with the feeling that all was for the best in this best of all possible worlds that he entered the dining room. Like the Battle of Waterloo, it had been a devilish close-run thing, but he had won through, and his morale was high. He did not actually say 'Tra-la' as he ordered his table, but the ejaculation was implicit in the sunniness of his smile and the sparkle in his eyes. Coming out again into the hall with a gay air on his lips, he was surprised to find the Crumpet there.

'Hullo,' he said. 'Didn't you go to the bar?'

'I went.'

'Didn't you find the old boy?'

'I found him.' The Crumpet's manner seemed strange to Oofy. He was looking grave and reproachful, like a Crumpet who considers that he has been played fast and loose with. 'Oofy,' he said, 'fun's fun, and no one's fonder of a joke than I am, but there are limits. I can see no excuse for a fellow pulling a gag in connection with a race meeting as important as this one. You knew the rules governing the sweep perfectly well. Only genuine uncles were eligible. I suppose you thought it would be humorous to ring in a non-uncle.'

'Do what?'

'It's as bad as entering a greyhound for the Grand National.'

Oofy could make nothing of this. The thought flitted through his mind that the other had been lunching.

'What on earth are you talking about?'

'I'm talking about that bloke in there with the billowy curves. You said he was your uncle.'

'He is my uncle.'

'He is nothing of the bally sort.'

'His name's Prosser.'

'No doubt.'

'He signed his letter "Uncle Horace".'

'Very possibly. But that doesn't alter the stark fact that he's a sort of distant cousin. He was telling me about it while we quaffed. It appears that as a child you used to call him Uncle Horace but, stripped of his mask, he is, as I say, merely a distant cousin. If you didn't know this and were not just trying to be funny when you entered him, I apologize for my recent remarks. You are more to be pitied than censured, it would seem, for the blighter is of course disqualified and the stakes go to Frederick Fortescue Widgeon, holder of the Blicester ticket.'

To think simultaneously of what might have been and what is going to be is not an easy task, but Oofy, as he heard these words of doom, found himself doing it. For even as his mind dwelled on the thought that he had paid Freddie Widgeon fifty pounds to deprive himself of the sweepstake money, he was also vividly aware that in a brace of shakes he would be standing his distant cousin Horace a lunch which, Horace being the man he was, could scarcely put him in the hole for less than a fiver. His whole soul seethed like a cistern struck by a thunderbolt, and everything seemed to go black.

The Crumpet was regarding him with concern.

'Don't gulp like that, Oofy,' he said. 'You can't be sick here.'

Oofy was not so sure. He was feeling as if he could be sick anywhere.

17

THE WORD IN SEASON

Among the names on the list of candidates up for election at the Drones Club there appeared, proposed by R. P. Little and seconded by an influential Crumpet, that of

LITTLE, ALGERNON AUBREY

and several of the Eggs, Beans and Piefaces who had gathered about the notice board were viewing it with concern. In every club you will find an austere conservative element that looks askance at the unusual and irregular.

'He can't do that there here,' said an Egg, putting into words the sentiment of this *bloc*. 'Hoy!' he went on, addressing the Crumpet, who had entered as he spoke. 'What about this nominee of Bingo Little's?'

'Yes,' said a Bean. 'He can try as much as he likes to cloud the issue by calling him "Algernon Aubrey", as if he were a brother or cousin or something, but the stark fact remains that the above is his baby. We don't want infants mewling and puking about the Drones.'

'Keep it clean,' urged a Pieface.

'Shakespeare,' explained the Bean.

'Oh, Shakespeare? Sorry. No,' said the Pieface, 'we don't want any bally babies here.'

A grave look came into the Crumpet's face.

'You want this one,' he said. 'You can't afford to do without him. Recent events have convinced Bingo that this offspring of his is a Grade A mascot, and he feels that the club should have the benefit of his services. Having heard his story, I agree with him. This half-portion's knack of doing the right thing at the right time is uncanny. I believe the child is almost human.'

His eloquence was not without its effect. But though some of the malcontents wavered, the Egg remained firm.

'That's all very well, but the question that presents itself is – Where will this stop? What guarantee have we that if we elect this juvenile, Bingo won't start trying to ring in his old nurse or his Uncle Wilberforce, or the proprietor of that children's paper he's editor of – what's his name – Purkiss?'

'I don't know about the nurse or his Uncle Wilberforce,' said the Crumpet, 'but you need have no anxiety concerning Henry Cuthbert Purkiss. Bingo's relations with his overlord are at the moment formal, even distant. Owing to Purkiss, he recently had to undergo a mental strain almost without parallel in his experience. And though, thanks to this beneficent baby's faultless sense of timing, he was enabled to emerge from the soup which was lashing angrily about his ankles, he finds it difficult to forgive. He expressly stated to me that if Henry Cuthbert Purkiss were to step on a banana skin and strain a ligament, it would be all right with him.'

'What did Purkiss do?'

'It was what he didn't do. He refused to pay ten quid for Bingo's story, and this at a crisis in Bingo's affairs when only ten quid could save him from the fate that is worse than death – viz. having the wife of his bosom draw in her breath sharply and look squiggle-eyed at him. He had been relying on Purkiss to do the square thing, and Purkiss let him down.'

Here briefly (said the Crumpet) are the facts. As most of you are probably aware, Bingo buzzed off a couple of years ago and went and married the eminent female novelist Rosie M. Banks, authoress of *Only A Factory Girl*, *Mervyn Keene, Clubman*, *'Twas Once in May* and other stearine works of fiction, and came a day when there burst on the London scene a bouncing baby of the name of Algernon Aubrey. Very pleasant for all concerned, of course, but the catch is that this sort of thing puts ideas in the heads of female novelists. As they sat at dinner one night, Mrs Bingo looked up from her portion of steak and French fried, and said:

'Oh, sweetie-pie,' for it is thus that she habitually addresses the other half of the sketch, 'you haven't forgotten it's Algy's birthday on the twenty-third? Just think! He'll be one year old.'

'Pretty senile, pretty senile,' said Bingo. 'Silver threads among the gold, what? We must give him a rattle or something.'

'We can do better than rattles. Shall I tell you the wonderful thing I've thought of?'

'Say on, old partner in sickness and in health.'

And Mrs Bingo said that she had decided to start a wee little deposit account for Algernon Aubrey at the local bank. She was going to pay in ten pounds, and her mother was going to pay in ten pounds, and so was the child's maternal aunt Isabel, and what a lovely surprise it would be for the young buster, when he got older, to find that all unknown his dear ones had been working on his behalf, bumping up his holdings like billy-o. And Bingo, mellowed by a

father's love, got the party spirit and said that if that was the trend
affairs were taking, blow him tight if he didn't chip in and add to the
kitty his own personal tenner.

Upon which, Mrs Bingo said, 'Oh, sweet-ie-*pie!*' And kissed him
with a good deal of fervour, and the curtain of Act One falls on a
happy and united home.

Now, though at the moment when he made this fine gesture Bingo
actually had ten quid in his possession, having touched Purkiss for an
advance on his salary, one would have expected him, thinking things
over in the cold grey light of the morning after, to kick himself
soundly for having been such an ass as to utter those unguarded
words, committing him as they did to a course of conduct which
would strip him of his last bean. But such was not the case. Still
mellowed by a father's love, all he thought next day was that as a gift
to a superchild like Algernon Aubrey a tenner was a bit on the cheese-
paring side. Surely twenty would be far more suitable. And he could
pick that up by slapping his ten on Hot Potato in the two-thirty at
Haydock Park. At dinner on the previous night he had burned his
mouth by incautiously placing in it a fried spud about ninety degrees
Fahrenheit warmer than he had supposed it to be, and he is always far
too inclined to accept omens like this as stable information. He made
the investment, accordingly, and at two-forty-five was informed by
the club tape that he was now penniless.

Well, as you can readily imagine, it did not take him long to
perceive that a crisis of the first magnitude had been precipitated.
Mrs Bingo, a charming woman but deficient in sporting blood, had
strictly forbidden him ever to venture money on the speed and endur-
ance of racehorses, and the discovery that he had once more been
chancing his arm would be bound to lead to an unpleasant scene,
from which he shrank. As every young husband knows, there is
nothing less agreeable than having the little woman bring her teeth
together with a sharp click and after saying 'Oh, how *could* you?'
follow it up with about two thousand words of the kind that go
through the soul like a bullet through butter.

And discovery, unless he could somehow balance the budget, was
of course inevitable. Sooner or later Mrs Bingo would be taking a
look at the infant's wee little passbook, and when she did would immediately spot something wrong with the wee little figures. 'Hoy!'
she would cry. 'Where's that ten-spot you said you were depositing?'
and from this to the bleak show-down would be but a short step.

It was a situation in which many fellows would just have turned
their faces to the wall and waited for the end. But there is good stuff in
Bingo. A sudden inspiration showed him the way out. He sat right

down and wrote a story about a little girl called Gwendoline and her cat Tibby. The idea of course being to publish it in *Wee Tots* and clean up.

It was no easy task. Until he started on it he had had no notion what blood, sweat and tears are demanded from the poor sap who takes a pop at the life literary, and a new admiration for Mrs Bingo awoke in him. Mrs Bingo, he knew, did her three thousand words a day without ricking a muscle, and to complete this Tibby number, though it ran only to about fifteen hundred, took him over a week, during which period he on several occasions as near as a toucher went off his onion.

However, he finished it at last, copied it out neatly, submitted it to himself, read it with considerable interest and accepted it, putting it down on the charge sheet for ten of the best. And when pay day arrived and no tenner, he sought audience of Purkiss.

'Oh, Mr Purkiss,' he said. 'Sorry to come butting in at a moment when you were probably meditating, but it's about the story.'

Purkiss looked at him fishily. Nature having made it impossible for him to look at anyone otherwise, he being a man with a face like a halibut.

'Story?'

Bingo explained the circumstances. He said that he was the author of 'Tibby's Wonderful Adventure' in the current issue, and Purkiss Oh-yes-ed and said he had read it with considerable interest, and Bingo oh-thanks-ed and simpered coyly, and then there was a rather long silence.

'Well, how about the emolument?' said Bingo at length, getting down to the *res*.

Purkiss started. The fishy glitter in his eye became intensified. He looked like a halibut which has just been asked by another halibut to lend it a couple of quid till next Wednesday.

'There should be a tenner coming to me,' said Bingo.

'Oh, no, no, no,' said Purkiss. 'Oh, no, no, no, no, no. All contributions which you may make to the paper are of course covered by your salary.'

'What!' cried Bingo. 'You mean I don't touch?'

Purkiss assured him that he did not, and Bingo tottered from the room and went off to the club to pull himself together with a couple of quick ones. And he was just finishing the second when Oofy Prosser came in. One glance at him told Bingo that here was the fountainhead to which he must go. He needed someone to lend him a tenner, and Oofy, he felt, was the People's Choice.

Now I need scarcely tell you that a fellow who is going to lend you a tenner must have two prime qualifications. He must be good for the amount and he must be willing to part with it. Oofy unquestionably filled the bill in the first particular, but experience had taught Bingo that he was apt to fall down on the second. Nevertheless it was in optimistic mood that he beetled over to his old friend. Oofy, he reminded himself, was Algernon Aubrey's godfather, and it was only natural to suppose that he could be delighted to come through with a birthday present for the little chap. Well, not delighted, perhaps. Still, a bit of persevering excavating work would probably dig up the needful.

'Oh, hullo, Oofy old man,' he said. 'Oofy, old man, do you know what? It's Algy's birthday very shortly.'

'Algy who?'

'Algy A. Little. The good old baby. Your godson.'

A quick shudder ran through Oofy. He was thinking of the occasion when he had had a severe morning head and Bingo had brought the stripling to his flat and introduced them.

'Oh, my Aunt!' he said. 'That frightful little gumboil!'

His tone was not encouraging, but Bingo carried on.

'Presents are now pouring in, and I knew you would be hurt if you were not given the opportunity of contributing some little trifle. Ten quid was what suggested itself to me. The simplest thing,' said Bingo, 'would be if you were to slip me the money now. Then it would be off your mind.'

Oofy flushed darkly beneath his pimples.

'Now listen,' he said, and there was no mistaking the ring of determination in his voice. 'When you talked me – against my better judgment – into becoming godfather to a child who looks like a ventriloquist's dummy, I expressly stipulated that a silver mug was to be accepted in full settlement, and we had a gentleman's agreement to that effect. It still holds good.'

'Ten quid isn't much.'

'It's ten quid more than you're going to get out of me.'

Bingo was reluctantly compelled to come clean.

'As a matter of fact, Oofy, old man, it's not the baby who wants the stuff, it's me – your old friend, the fellow you've known since he was so high. Unless I get a tenner immediately, disaster stares me in the eyeball. So give of your plenty, Oofy, like the splendid chap you are.'

'No!' cried Oofy. 'No, no, a thousand times – '

The words died on his lips. It was as though a thought had come, flushing his brow.

'Listen,' he said. 'Are you doing anything this evening?'

'No. Unless I decide to end it all in the river.'

'Can you slip away from home?'

'Yes, I could do that all right. As it happens, I'm all alone at the moment. My wife and Mrs Purkiss, the moon of my boss's delight, have legged it to Brighton to attend some sort of Old Girls binge at their late school, and won't be back till tomorrow.'

'Good. I want you to dine at the Ritz.'

'Fine. Nothing I should like better. I meet you there, do I?'

'You do not. I'm leaving for Paris this afternoon. What you meet is a girl named Mabel Murgatroyd with red hair, a vivacious manner and a dimple on the left side of the chin. You give her dinner.'

Bingo drew himself up. He was deeply shocked at the other's loose ideas of how married men behave when their wives are away.

'Do this, and you get your tenner.'

Bingo lowered himself.

'Listen,' said Oofy. 'I will tell you all.'

It was a dubious and discreditable story that he related. For some time past, it appeared, he had been flitting round this girl like a pimpled butterfly, and it had suddenly come to him with a sickening shock that his emotional nature had brought him to the very verge of matrimony. Another step and he would be over the precipice. It was the dimple that did it principally, he said. Confronted with it at short range, he tended to say things which in sober retrospect he regretted.

'I asked her to dine with me tonight,' he concluded, 'and if I go, I'm sunk. Only instant flight can save me. But that's not all. I want you not only to give her dinner, but finally and definitely to choke her off me. You must roast me roundly. Pretend you think I'm the world's leading louse.'

The verb 'pretend' did not seem to Bingo very happily chosen, but he nodded intelligently.

'Here's your tenner,' said Oofy, 'and here's the money for the dinner. Don't get carried away by that dimple and forget to roast me.'

'I won't.'

'Pitch it strong. I'll tell you some things to say.'

'No, no, don't bother,' said Bingo. 'I'll think of them.'

Bingo had not been waiting long in the lobby of the Ritz that night when a girl appeared, so vermilion in the upper storey and so dimpled on the left side of the chin that he had no hesitation in ambling up and establishing contact.

'Miss Murgatroyd?'

'You never spoke a truer word.'

'My name is Little, R. P. Oofy Prosser, having been unexpectedly called away to the Continent, asked me to roll up and deputize for him.'

'Well, I must say it's a bit thick, asking a girl to dinner and then buzzing off to Continents.'

'Not for Oofy,' said Bingo, starting the treatment. 'His work is generally infinitely thicker than that. I don't know how well you know him?'

'Fairly well.'

'When you know him really well you will realize that you are up against something quite exceptional. Take a wart hog, add a few slugs and some of those things you see under flat stones, sprinkle liberally with pimples and you will have something which, while of course less loathsome than Alexander Prosser, will give you the general idea.'

And so saying, he led her into the dining salon and the meal started.

It went with a swing from start to finish. The girl's views on Oofy proved to be as sound as his own. She told him that she had gone around with this Prosser because he had made such a point of it, but, left to herself, she would not have touched him with a ten-foot pole. And as Bingo would not willingly have touched Oofy with an eleven-foot pole, a perfect harmony prevailed.

It was some two hours later that the girl rose.

'Oh, don't go yet,' pleaded Bingo, for it seemed to him that they had not nearly exhausted the topic of Oofy, but she was firm.

'I must,' she said. 'I promised to meet a man I know at one of these private gambling places.'

The words stirred Bingo like a bugle. He had heard much of these establishments, but had never had the opportunity of visiting one, and the tenner Oofy had given him seemed to leap in his pocket. Technically, of course, it belonged to Algernon Aubrey, but he knew no son of his would object to him borrowing it for the evening for such a worthy purpose.

'Gosh!' he said. 'You couldn't take me along, could you?'

'Why, of course, if you want to come. It's out in the wilds of St John's Wood somewhere.'

'Really? Then it's on my way home. I live in St John's Wood.'

'I've got the address written down. Forty-Three Magnolia Road.'

Bingo, always on the lookout for omens and portents, leaped in his seat. Any lingering doubts he may have entertained as to the advisability of arranging that loan with Algernon Aubrey vanished. Obviously this was going to be his lucky night, and he would be vastly surprised if on the morrow he would not be able to pay twenty or thirty pounds into the other's wee little deposit account.

'Of all the coincidences!' he exclaimed. 'That's next door but one to my little nest.'

The girl said Well, fancy that, adding that it was a small world, and Bingo agreed that he had seldom met a smaller.

The police raid on Number Forty-Three Magnolia Road took place, oddly enough, just as Bingo was preparing to leave. He had lost the last of his borrowed capital at the roulette board owing to a mistaken supposition that Red was going to turn up, and was standing at an open window, trying by means of some breaths of fresh air to alleviate that Death-where-is-thy-sting feeling that comes to gamesters at such times, when suddenly bells began to ring all over the place and a number of those present, jostling him to one side, proceeded to pour out of the window in a foaming stream.

Always a quick thinker, it took him but an instant to appreciate that the minds of these persons were working along the right lines. He knew what happened to those who dallied and loitered on occasions like this. They appeared next day before the awful majesty of the Law, charged with being found on enclosed premises, entered by virtue of a warrant in writing signed by the Commissioner of Police and alleged to be a common gaming house, contrary to Section 6 of the Gaming Act of 1845, – the last thing a young husband, whose wife disapproved of gaming-houses, would wish to occur.

With the utmost promptitude he added himself to the torrent. A quick dash, and he was in the garden of the house next door to his own, hiding in a convenient water barrel that stood against the potting shed, where some moments later he was joined by Mabel Murgatroyd, who seemed in petulant mood.

'This is the fourth or fifth time this has happened to me,' she said peevishly, as she slid into the barrel's interior. 'Why can't these rozzers have a heart and not be for ever interfering with private enterprise? Do you know what? I had a quid on sixteen, and sixteen came up, but before I could collect the bells began to ring and it was Ho for the open spaces. Thirty-seven pounds sterling gone with the wind. Shift over a bit, will you.'

Bingo shifted over a bit.

'These water barrels are always rather cramped,' he said. 'Still, this one hasn't any water in it,' he added, pointing out the bright side.

'No, there's that, of course. But last time I hid in a cucumber frame. Solid comfort, that was. Ease away, you're crowding me. I wish you wouldn't suddenly expand like that.'

'I was only breathing.'

'Well, don't breathe. Is this your water barrel, by the way?'

'No, I'm just a lodger. What gave you that idea?'

'I thought you told me you lived next door to the recent Casino.'

'Next door but one. We are at the moment enjoying the hospitality of an artist of the name of Quintin.'

'Nice fellow?'

'Not particularly.'

'Ah well, who is? Hullo, am I wrong, or have things quieted down somewhat? I believe the All Clear's been blown.'

And so it proved. They emerged, paused for a moment on the lawn to take a cordial farewell, and then she went her way and he his. With something of the emotions of one who has been tried in the furnace, he hopped over the fence, sneaked into the house and so to bed.

He slept late next morning, and was about to set out for the office of *Wee Tots*, though feeling ill attuned to the task of providing wholesome reading matter for the juvenile public, when Mrs Bingo came in, back from Brighton.

'Oh, hullo, my precious dream-rabbit,' said Bingo with as much animation as he could dig up. 'Welcome to Meadowsweet Hall. I've missed you, angel.'

'Me, too, you, sweetie-pie. And I seem to have missed all sorts of excitement. Mrs Simmons across the way was telling me about it. Apparently those people at Number Forty-Three have been running one of those gambling places, and last night it was raided by the police.'

'Good heavens!'

'I don't wonder you're shocked. We don't want that sort of thing going on in Magnolia Road.'

'I should say not. Disgraceful.'

'But how curious that you should have heard nothing.'

'I sleep very soundly.'

'You must, because Mrs Simmons says there was a great deal of whistling and shouting going on. I expect Mr Quintin was furious. People were running about his garden half the night, and you know how fussy he is. He complained about Algy crying, and your ukelele and everything. He's always complaining. Are you off to the office?'

'Just leaving.'

'Won't you be very late? I hope Mr Purkiss won't be annoyed.'

'Oh, that's all right. I have a thorough understanding with Purkiss, who knows a good man when he sees one. "Be sure always to get a good night's rest," he has often said to me.'

'You don't look as if you had had a good night's rest. You're a sort of funny yellow colour.'

'Intellectual pallor,' said Bingo, and withdrew.

Arrived at the office, he listlessly tried to bring his mind to bear on the letters which had come in for the Correspondence page 'Uncle Percy's Post-Bag', but he found it difficult to concentrate. The standard of pure reason reached by the little subscribers who wrote to the editor of *Wee Tots* about their domestic pets was never a high one, but today it seemed to him that either he or they must have got water on the brain. There was one communication about a tortoise called Rupert which, in his opinion, would have served as a passport for its young author to any padded cell in the kingdom.

The only thing that enabled him to win through to closing time was the fact that Purkiss was absent. He had telephoned to say that he was nursing a sick headache. Purkiss at this juncture would have been more than he could have coped with.

It was with a feeling of relief that he started homeward at the end of the long day, and he had just unlatched the front door with his latchkey, and was standing his hat on the hatstand, when Mrs Bingo spoke from the drawing room.

'Will you come here a moment, please, Bingo.'

His heart, already low, sank lower. He had a sensitive ear, and he did not like the timbre of her voice. Usually Mrs Bingo's voice seemed to him like the tinkling of silver bells across a scented meadow at sunset, but now it was on the flat side, and he fancied that he detected in it that metallic note which married men dislike so much.

She was standing in mid-carpet, looking cold and stern. She had a paper of some kind in her hand.

'Bingo,' she said, 'where were you last night?'

Bingo passed a finger round the inside of his collar. His brow was wet with honest sweat. But he told himself that he must be calm ... cool ... nonchalant.

'Last night?' he said, frowning thoughtfully. 'Let me see, that would be the night of June the fifteenth, would it not? H'm. Ha. The night of – '

'I see you have forgotten,' said Mrs Bingo. 'Let me refresh your memory. You were fleeing from the police because they had caught you gambling at Number Forty-Three.'

'Who me? You're sure you mean me?'

'Read this,' said Mrs Bingo, and thrust at him the document she was holding.

It was a letter, and ran as follows:

Picasso Lodge
41 Magnolia Road
St John's Wood
London, N.8
Madam:

While sympathizing with your husband's desire to avoid being arrested by the police for gambling on enclosed premises, I would be glad if you would ask him next time not to take refuge in my water barrel, as he and some unidentified female did last night.

I remain,
Yours faithfully,
Dante Gabriel Quintin.

'Well?' said Mrs Bingo.

Bingo's spine had turned to gelatine. It seemed useless to struggle further. His gallant spirit was broken. And he was about to throw in the towel and confess all, when there was a sound outside like a mighty rushing wind and Algernon Aubrey's nanny came tottering in. Her eyes were wide and glassy, she breathed stertorously, and it was obvious that she was in the grip of some powerful emotion.

'Oh, ma'am!' she cried. 'The baby!'

All the Mother in Mrs Bingo awoke. She forgot Bingo and police and water barrels and everything else. She gasped. Bingo gasped. The nanny was already gasping. A stranger, entering the room, would have supposed himself to have strayed into a convention of asthma patients.

'Is he ill?'

'No, ma'am, but he just said "Cat".'

'Cat?'

'Yes, ma'am, as plain as I'm standing here now. I was showing him his little picture book, and we'd come to the rhinoceros, and he pointed his finger at it and looked up at me and said "Cat".'

A footnote is required here for the benefit of those who are not family men. 'Cat', they are probably feeling, is not such a tremendously brilliant and epigrammatic thing to say. But what made Algernon Aubrey's utterance of the word so sensational was that it was his first shot at saying anything. Up till now he had been one of those strong silent babies, content merely to dribble at the side of the mouth and emit an occasional gurgle. It can readily be understood, therefore, that the effect of this piece of hot news on Mrs Bingo was about the same as that of the arrival of Talkies on the magnates of Hollywood. She left the room as if shot out of a gun. The nanny hurried after her. And Bingo was alone.

His first emotion, of course, was one of stunned awe at having been saved from the scaffold at the eleventh hour, but he soon saw that he had been accorded but a brief respite and that on Mrs Bingo's return he would have to have some good, watertight story in readiness for her: and, try as he might, he could think of nothing that would satisfy her rather exacting taste. He toyed with the idea of saying that he had been in conference with Purkiss last night, discussing matters of office policy, but was forced to dismiss it.

For one thing, Purkiss would never abet his innocent deception. All that Bingo had seen of the man told him that the proprietor of *Wee Tots* was one of those rigidly upright blisters who, though possibly the backbone of England, are no earthly use to a chap in an emergency. Purkiss was the sort of fellow who, if approached on the matter of bumping up a pal's alibi, would stare fishily and say 'Am I to understand, Mr Little, that you are suggesting that I sponsor a lie?'

Besides, Purkiss was at his home nursing a sick headache, which meant that negotiations would have to be conducted over the telephone, and you cannot swing a thing like that by remote control. You want the pleading eye and the little pats on the arm.

No, that was no good, and there appeared nothing to be done except groan hollowly, and he was doing this when the door opened and the maid announced 'Mr and Mrs Purkiss'.

As they entered, Bingo, who was pacing the room with unseeing eyes, knocked over a table with a vase, three photograph frames and a bowl of potpourri on it. It crashed to the floor with a noise like a bursting shell, and Purkiss soared silently to the ceiling. As he returned to position one, Bingo saw that his face was Nile green in colour and that there were dark circles beneath his eyes.

'Ah, Mr Little,' said Purkiss.

'Oh, hullo,' said Bingo.

Mrs Purkiss did not speak. She seemed to be brooding on something.

Purkiss proceeded. He winced as he spoke, as if articulation hurt him.

'We are not disturbing you, I hope, Mr Little?'

'Not at all,' said Bingo courteously. 'But I thought you were at home with a sick headache.'

'I was at home with a sick headache,' said Purkiss, 'the result, I think, of sitting in a draught and contracting some form of tic or migraine. But my wife was anxious that you should confirm my statement that I was in your company last night. You have not forgotten that we sat up till a late hour at my club? No doubt you will recall that we were both surprised when we looked at our watches and found how the time had gone?'

There came to Bingo, listening to these words, the illusion that a hidden orchestra had begun to play soft music, while somewhere in the room he seemed to smell the scent of violets and mignonette. His eye, which had been duller than that of Purkiss, suddenly began to sparkle, and what he had supposed to be a piece of spaghetti in the neighbourhood of his back revealed itself as a spine, and a good spine, too.

'Yes,' he said, drawing a deep breath, 'that's right. We were at your club.'

'How the time flew!'

'Didn't it! But then, of course, we were carried away by the topics we were discussing.'

'Quite. We were deep in a discussion of office policy.'

'Absorbing subject.'

'Intensely gripping.'

'You said so-and-so, and I said such-and-such.'

'Precisely.'

'One of the points that came up,' said Bingo, 'was, if you recollect, the question of payment for that story of mine.'

'Was it?' said Purkiss doubtfully.

'Surely you haven't forgotten that?' said Bingo. 'You told me you had been thinking it over and were now prepared to pay me ten quid for it. Or,' he went on, his gaze fixed on the other with a peculiar intensity, 'am I wrong?'

'No, no. It all comes back to me.'

'I may as well take it now,' said Bingo. 'Save a lot of book-keeping.'

Purkiss groaned, perhaps not quite so hollowly as Bingo had been doing before his entrance, but distinctly hollowly.

'Very well,' he said, and as the money changed hands, Mrs Bingo came in.

'Oh, how do you do, Mr Purkiss,' she said. 'Julia,' she cried, turning to Mrs Purkiss, 'you'll never believe! Algy has just said "Cat".'

It was plain that Mrs Purkiss was deeply moved.

'Cat?'

'Yes, isn't it wonderful! Come on up to the nursery, quick. We may be able to get him to say it again.'

Bingo spoke. He made a strangely dignified figure as he stood there looking rather like King Arthur about to reproach Guinevere.

'I wonder, Rosie, if I might have a moment of your valuable time?'

'Well?'

'I shall not detain you long. I merely wish to say what I was about to say just now when you dashed off like a jack rabbit of the western prairies. If you ask Mr Purkiss, he will tell you that, so far from eluding the constabulary by hiding in water barrels, I was closeted with him at his club till an advanced hour. We were discussing certain problems of interest which had arisen in connection with the conduct of *Wee Tots*. For Mr Purkiss and I are not clock-watchers. We put in overtime. We work while others sleep!'

There was a long silence. Mrs Bingo seemed to sag at the knees, as if some unseen hand had goosed her. Tears welled up in her eyes. Remorse was written on every feature.

'Oh, Bingo!'

'I thought I would just mention it.'

'Oh, sweetie-pie, what can I say? I'm sorry.'

'Quite all right, quite all right. I am not angry. Merely a little hurt.'

Mrs Bingo flung herself into his arms.

'I'm going to sue Mr Quintin for libel!'

'Oh, I wouldn't bother to do that. Just treat him with silent contempt. I doubt if you would get as much as a tenner out of a man like that. Oh, by the way, talking of tenners, here is the one I have been meaning to pay in to Algy's account. You had better take it. I keep forgetting these things. Overwork at the office, no doubt. But I must not detain you, Mrs Purkiss. You will be wishing to go to the nursery.'

Mrs Bingo and Mrs Purkiss passed from the room. Bingo turned to Purkiss, and his eye was stern.

'Purkiss,' he said, 'where *were* you on the night of June the fifteenth?'

'I was with you,' said Purkiss. 'Where were you?'

'I was with you,' said Bingo, 'and a most entertaining companion you were, if you will allow me to say so. But come, let us go and listen to Algernon Aubrey on the subject of Cats. They tell me he is well worth hearing.'

18

LEAVE IT TO ALGY

As so often happened in August when the citizenry was taking its annual vacation, that popular resort, Bramley-on-Sea, had filled up with ozone-breathers till there was barely standing room. Henry Cuthbert Purkiss, proprietor of the widely read journal for children, *Wee Tots*, was there with Mrs Purkiss. Oofy Prosser, the Drones Club millionaire, was there, staying at the Hotel Magnifique and looking perfectly foul in a panama hat with a scarlet ribbon. A distinguished visitor from the United States – Wally Judd the cartoonist, the man behind the Dauntless Desmond comic strip which is syndicated in sixteen hundred American papers – was weekending there. And on the beach in front of the Magnifique an observer, scanning the throng, would have noticed among those present Bingo Little, the able young editor of *Wee Tots*, and his wife Mrs Bingo, better known as the novelist Rosie M. Banks. They were watching their infant son, Algernon Aubrey, build a sand castle.

The day was a bright, beautiful, balmy day, with an anticyclone doing its stuff and all nature smiling, but it too frequently occurs in this disturbed postwar world that, when all nature smiles, there are a whole lot of unfortunate toads beneath the harrow who cannot raise so much as a simper, and Bingo was one of them. The sun was shining, but there was no sunshine in his heart. The sky was blue, but he was bluer. It was not the fact that Mrs Bingo was off to London to attend the annual dinner of the Pen and Ink Club that had caused melancholy to mark him for its own, sorely though he always missed her when she went away: what had so lowered his spirits and given the sleeve across the windpipe to his morale was a remark that had just fallen from her lips.

Speaking of the mysterious disappearance of his gold cuff-links on the previous day, she was convinced, she said, that a professional cuff-link thief must have been at work, and Bingo was to place the matter immediately in the hands of the police.

'They will go round,' she explained, 'and make inquiries at all the pawn shops.'

It was this that had blotted out the sunshine for Bingo and made him feel, warm though the day was, that centipedes with icy feet were walking up and down his spine. If there was one thing more than another which would be foreign to his policy, it was to have the police making inquiries at these establishments, particularly at the one in Seaview Road. For it was there that yesterday, in order to obtain five pounds with which to back a horse that had come in seventh, he had personally put those cuff-links up the spout. And Mrs Bingo's views on that sort of thing were rigid.

'You really think that would be advisable?' he faltered.

'Of course. It's the only thing to do.'

'Throws a lot of extra work on the poor chaps.'

'They are paid for it, and I think they really enjoy the excitement of the chase. Good gracious,' said Mrs Bingo, looking at her watch, 'is that the time? I must be rushing. Goodbye, angel. Take care of Algy.'

'His welfare shall be my constant concern.'

'Don't let him out of your sight for a minute. I'll be back tomorrow night. Goodbye, my precious.'

'Goodbye, tree on which the fruit of my life hangs,' said Bingo, and a moment later was alone with his thoughts.

He was still deep in sombre meditation when a voice at his side said 'Ah, Mr Little. Good morning,' and, emerging from his reverie with a start, he saw that he had with him the Purkisses, Mr and Mrs.

'Kitchy kitchy,' observed the female Purkiss, addressing Algernon Aubrey.

The child treated the remark with silent disdain, and Mrs Purkiss, discouraged, said she must be getting along to keep an appointment with her hairdresser. As she withdrew, a stifled groan burst from Purkiss's lips, and Bingo saw that he was gazing with bulging eyes at the son and heir.

'Ugh!' said Purkiss, shuddering strongly.

'I beg your pardon?' said Bingo. He spoke coldly. He had no illusions about his first-born's appearance, being well aware that though Time, the great healer, would eventually turn Algernon Aubrey into a suave boulevardier like his father, he presented to the eye as of even date, like so many infants of tender years, the aspect of a mass murderer suffering from an ingrowing toenail. Nevertheless he resented this exhibition of naked horror. Purkiss, himself far from being an oil-painting, was, he felt, in no position to criticize.

Purkiss hastened to explain.

'I am sorry,' he said. 'I should not have let my feelings get the better of me. It is just that, situated as I am, the mere sight of the younger generation chills me to the marrow. Mr Little,' said Purkiss, avoiding Algernon Aubrey's eye, for the child was giving him the sort of cold, hard look which Jack Dempsey used to give his opponents in the ring, 'there is to be a Bonny Babies contest here tomorrow, and I have got to act as judge.'

Bingo's hauteur vanished. He could understand the other's emotion, for he knew what an assignment like that involved. Freddie Widgeon of the Drones had once got let in for judging a similar competition in the south of France, and his story of what he had gone through on that occasion had held the club smoking room spellbound.

'Golly!' he said. 'How did that happen?'

'Mrs Purkiss arranged it. She felt that the appearance of its proprietor in the public eye would stimulate the circulation of *Wee Tots*, bringing in new subscribers. Subscribers!' said Purkiss, waving a passionate hand. 'I don't want subscribers. All I want is to be allowed to enjoy a quiet and peaceful holiday completely free from bonny babies of every description. To be relieved of this hideous burden that has been laid upon me I would give untold gold.'

It was as though an electric shock had passed through Bingo. He leaped perhaps six inches.

'You would?' he said. 'Untold gold?'

'Untold gold.'

'When you say untold gold, would you go as high as a fiver?'

'Certainly, and consider the money well spent.'

'Then hand it over,' said Bingo, 'and in return I will take your place on the judge's rostrum. It will stimulate the circulation of *Wee Tots* just as much as if its editor appears in the public eye.'

For an instant ecstasy caused Purkiss to quiver from stem to stern. The word 'Whoopee!' seemed to be trembling on his lips. Then the light died out of his face.

'But what of Mrs Purkiss? She has issued her orders. How can I disobey them?'

'My dear Purkiss, use the loaf. All you have to do is sprain your ankle or dislocate your spine or something. Fall out of a window. Get run over by a lorry. Any lorry driver will be glad to run over you, if you slip him a couple of bob. Then you will be set. Obviously the old geezer ... I should say Mrs Purkiss ... can't expect you to go bounding about judging bonny babies if you are lying crippled on a chesterfield of pain. You were saying something about a fiver, Purkiss. I should be glad to see the colour of your money.'

As in a dream, Purkiss produced a five-pound note. As in a dream, he handed it over. As in a dream, Bingo took it.

'Mr Little – ' Purkiss began. Then words failed him, and with a defiant look at Algernon Aubrey such as an Indian coolie, safe up a tree, might have given the baffled crocodile at the foot of it, he strode away humming a gay air, his hat on the side of his head. And Bingo was gazing lovingly at the bank note and on the point of giving it a hearty kiss, when a nippy little breeze, springing up from the sea, blew it out of his hand and it went fluttering away in the direction of the esplanade as if equipped with wings.

It was a situation well calculated to nonplus the keenest-witted. It nonplussed Bingo completely. His primary impulse, of course, was to follow his lost treasure as it flew, it taking the high road and himself the low road, but even as he braced his muscles for the quick cross-country run there flashed into his mind those parting words of Mrs Bingo's about not letting Algernon Aubrey out of his sight. He knew what had been the thought behind them. Let out of sight, the child might well wander into the sea and go down for the third time or get on the wrong side of the law by hitting some holiday-maker on the head with his spade. None knew better than he how prone the little fellow was to cleave the casques of men, as the poet said, if you put a spade in his hands. There was a certain type of Homburg hat which had always proved irresistible to him.

It was borne in upon Bingo that he was on what is generally called the horns of a dilemma. He stood there, like Hamlet, moody and ir-resolute, and while he hesitated the issue was taken out of his hands. The five-pound note fluttered down into a car which was on the point of starting, and its driver, gathering it up with a look on his face that suggested a sudden conviction that the age of miracles was still with us, drove off.

It was some ten minutes later that Bingo, who had spent most of those ten minutes with his head buried in his hands, tottered on to the esplanade with Algernon Aubrey in his arms and was passing the door of the Hotel Magnifique, when Oofy Prosser came out.

The poet Wordsworth has told us that his heart was accustomed to leap up when he beheld a rainbow in the sky, and this was how Bingo's heart behaved when he beheld Oofy Prosser. It was not that Oofy was a thing of beauty ... his pimples alone would have kept him out of the rainbow class ... but he had that quality which so many disgustingly rich men have of looking disgustingly rich. And in addition to being disgustingly rich, he was Algernon Aubrey's god-father. It was with hope dawning in his soul that Bingo bounded forward.

'Oofy, old man!'

Observing what it was that Bingo was carrying, Oofy backed hastily.

'Hey!' he exclaimed. 'Don't point that thing at me!'

'It's only my baby.'

'I dare say. But point it the other way.'

'I think he wants to kiss you.'

'Stand back!' cried Oofy, brandishing his panama hat. 'I am armed!'

It seemed to Bingo that the conversation was straying from the right lines. He hastened to change the subject.

'I wonder if you have noticed, Oofy, that I am pale and haggard?' he said.

'You look all right to me. At least,' said Oofy, qualifying this statement, 'as right as you ever do.'

'Ah, then, it doesn't show. I'm surprised. I should have thought it would have done. For I am in desperate straits, Oofy. If I don't get hold of someone who will lend me a fiver – '

'Very hard to find, that type of man. Why do you want a fiver?'

Bingo was only too ready to explain. He knew Oofy Prosser to be a man allergic to sharing the wealth, but his, he felt, was a story calculated to break down the toughest sales resistance. In accents broken with emotion he told it from its earliest beginnings to this final ghastly tragedy that had befallen him. When he had finished, Oofy remained for some moments plunged in thought. Then his eyes, generally rather dull, lit up, as if the thought into which he had been plunged had produced an inspiration.

'You say you're judging this Bonny Babies thing?'

'Yes, but that doesn't get me anywhere. I can't ask Purkiss for another fiver.'

'You don't have to. As I see it, the matter is quite simple. Your primary object is to divert your wife's mind from gold cuff-links and pawn shops – to give her, in other words, something else to think about. Very well. Enter that little gargoyle of yours and award him the first prize, and she will be so delighted that gold cuff-links will fade out of her mind. I guarantee this. I am not a mother myself, but I understand a mother's heart from soup to nuts. In her pride at the young plugugly's triumph everything else will be forgotten.'

Bingo stared. It seemed to him that the other's brain, that brain whose subtle scheming had so often chiselled fellow members of the Drones out of half-crowns and even larger sums, must have blown a fuse.

'But, Oofy, old man, reflect. If I judge a Bonny Babies contest and raise the hand of my personal baby with the words "The winnah!", I shall be roughly handled, if not lynched. These mothers are tough stuff. You were there when Freddie Widgeon was telling us about what happened to him at Cannes.'

Oofy clicked his tongue impatiently.

'Naturally I had not overlooked an obvious point like that. The child will not be entered as whatever-its-ghastly-name-is Little, but as whatever-its-ghastly-name-is Prosser. Putting it in words of one syllable, I will bring the young thug to the trysting place, affecting to be its uncle. You will then, after careful consideration, award it the first prize. And if you're worrying about whether such a scheme is strictly honest, forget it. The prize will only be an all-day sucker or a woolly muffler or something. It isn't as if money were involved.'

'Something in that.'

'There is everything in that. If money entered into it, I would never dream of suggesting such a ruse,' said Oofy virtuously. 'But who cares who wins a woolly muffler? Well, there it is. Take it or leave it. I'm simply trying to do the friendly thing and keep your home from being in the melting pot. I take it I am right in assuming that if this business of the cuff-links comes out, your home will be in the melting pot?'

'Yes, right in the melting pot.'

'Then I would certainly advise you to adopt my plan. You will? Fine. Excuse me a moment,' said Oofy. 'I have to make a telephone call.'

He went into the hotel, rang up his bookmaker in London, and the following conversation ensued.

'Mr McAlpin?'

'Speaking.'

'This is Mr Prosser.'

'Oh, yes?'

'Listen, Mr McAlpin, I'm down at Bramley-on-Sea, and they are having a Bonny Babies contest tomorrow. I'm entering my little nephew.'

'Oh, yes?'

'And I thought it would add to the interest of the proceedings if I had a small bet on. Do your activities as a turf accountant extend to accepting wagers on seaside Bonny Baby competitions?'

'Certainly. We cover all sporting events.'

'What odds will you give against the Prosser colt?'

'Your nephew, you say?'

'That's right.'

'Does he look like you?'

'There is quite a resemblance.'

'Then you can have fifty to one.'

'Right. In tenners.'

Oofy returned to Bingo.

LEAVE IT TO ALGY 297

'The only thing I'm afraid of,' he said, 'is that when it comes to the acid test, you may lose your nerve.'

'Oh, I won't.'

'You might, if there were no added inducement. So I'll tell you what I'll do. The moment you have given your decision, I will slip you five pounds and you will be able to take the cuff-links out of pawn, thus avoiding all unpleasantness in the unlikely event of your wife continuing to bear them in mind despite her child's triumph. May as well be on the safe side.'

Bingo could not speak. His heart was too full for words. The only thing that kept his happiness from being perfect was a sudden fear lest, before the event could take place, Oofy might be snatched up to heaven in a fiery chariot.

Nevertheless, as he made his way to the arena on the following afternoon, he was conscious of distinct qualms and flutterings. And his apprehensions were not relieved by the sight of the assembled competitors.

True, the great majority of the entrants had that indefinable something in their appearance that suggested that if the police were not spreading dragnets for them, they were being very negligent in their duties, but fully a dozen were so comparatively human that he could see that it was going to cause comment when he passed them over in favour of Algernon Aubrey. Questions would be asked, investigations made. Quite possibly he would be had up before the Jockey Club and warned off the turf.

However, with the vast issues at stake there was nothing to do but stiffen the sinews, summon up the blood and have a go at it, so proceeding to the platform he bowed to the applause of what looked to him like about three hundred and forty-seven mothers, all ferocious, raised a hand to check – if possible – the howling of their offspring, and embarked on the speech which he had been at pains to prepare in the watches of the night.

He spoke of England's future, which, he pointed out, must rest on these babies and others like them, adding that he scarcely need remind them that the England to which he alluded had been described by the poet Shakespeare as this royal throne of kings, this sceptred isle, this earth of majesty, this seat of Mars, this other Eden, demi-Paradise, this fortress built by nature for herself against infection and the hand of war. Than which, he thought they would all agree with him, nothing could be fairer.

He spoke of *Wee Tots*, putting in a powerful build-up for the dear old sheet and urging one and all to take advantage of the easy subscription terms now in operation.

He spoke – and here his manner took on a new earnestness – of the good, clean spirit of fair play which has made England what it is – the spirit which, he was confident, would lead all the mothers present to accept the judge's decision, even should it go against their own nominees, with that quiet British sportsmanship which other nations envy so much. He had a friend, he said, who, acting as judge of a Baby Contest in the south of France, had been chased for a quarter of a mile along the waterfront by indignant mothers of Hon. Mentions armed with knives and hat pins. That sort of thing could never happen at Bramley-on-Sea. No, no. English mothers were not like that. And while on this subject, he said, striking a lighter note, he was reminded of a little story of two Irishmen who were walking up Broadway, which may be new to some of you present here this afternoon.

The story went well. A studio television audience could hardly have laughed more heartily. But though he acknowledged the guffaws with a bright smile, inwardly his soul had begun to shrink like a salted snail. Time was passing, and there were no signs of Oofy and his precious burden. Long ere this he should have rolled up with the makings.

He resumed his speech. He told another story about two Scotsmen who were walking down Sauchiehall Street in Glasgow. But now his comedy had lost its magic and failed to grip. A peevish voice said 'Get on with it', and the sentiment plainly pleased the gathering. As he began a third story about two Cockneys who were standing on a street corner in Whitechapel, possibly a hundred peevish voices said 'Get on with it', and shortly after that perhaps a hundred and fifty.

And still no Oofy.

Five minutes later, the popular clamour for a showdown having taken on a resemblance to the howling of timber wolves in a Canadian forest, he was compelled to act. With ashen face he awarded the handsome knitted woolly jacket to a child selected at random from the sea of faces beneath him and sank into a chair, a broken man.

And as he sat there, trying not to let his mind dwell on the shape of things to come, a finger tapped him on the shoulder and he looked up and saw standing beside him a policeman.

'Mr Little?' said the policeman.

Bingo, still dazed, said Yes, he thought so.

'I shall have to ask you to come along with me,' said the policeman.

Other policemen on other occasions, notably on the night of the annual aquatic encounter on the River Thames between the rival crews of the Universities of Oxford and Cambridge, had made the same observation to Bingo, and on such occasions he had always found it best to go quietly. He rose and accompanied the officer to the door, and with a curiosity perhaps natural in the circumstances asked why he was being pinched.

'Not pinched, sir,' said the policeman, as they walked off. 'You're wanted at the station to identify an accused ... if you *can* identify him. His statement is that he's a friend of yours and was acting with your cognisance and approval.'

'I don't follow you, officer,' said Bingo, who did not follow the officer. 'Acting how?'

'Taking your baby for an airing, sir. He claims that you instructed him to do so. It transpired this way. Accused was observed by a Mrs Purkiss with your baby on his person slinking along the public thoroughfare. He was a man of furtive aspect in a panama hat with a scarlet ribbon, and Mrs Purkiss, recognizing the baby, said to herself "Cor lumme, stone the crows!".'

'She said ... what was that line of Mrs Purkiss's again?'

'"Cor lumme, stone the crows!" sir. The lady's suspicions having been aroused, she summoned a constable and gave accused in charge as a kidnapper, and after a certain amount of fuss and unpleasantness he was conducted to the station and deposited in a cell. Prosser he said his name was. Is the name Prosser familiar to you, sir?'

The officer's statement that there had been a certain amount of fuss and unpleasantness involved in the process of getting the accused Prosser to the police station was borne out by the latter's appearance when he was led into Bingo's presence. He had a black eye and his collar had been torn from the parent stud. The other eye, the one that was still open, gleamed with fury and what was patently a loathing for the human species.

The sergeant who was seated at the desk invited Bingo to inspect the exhibit.

'This man says he knows you.'

'That's right.'

'Friend of yours?'

'Bosom.'

'And you gave him your baby?'

'Well, you could put it that way. More on loan, of course.'

'Ho!' said the sergeant, speaking like a tiger of the jungle deprived of its prey, if tigers of the jungle in those circumstances do say 'Ho!' 'You're quite sure?'

'Oh, rather.'

'So sucks to you, sergeant!' said Oofy. 'And now,' he went on haughtily, 'I presume that I am at liberty to go.'

'You do, do you? Then you pre-blinking-well-sume wrong,' said the sergeant, brightening at the thought that he was at least going to save something from the wreck of his hopes and dreams. 'Not by any manner of means you aren't at liberty to go. There's this matter of obstructing the police in the execution of their duty. You punched Constable Wilks in the abdomen.'

'And I'd do it again.'

'Not for a fortnight or fourteen days you won't,' said the sergeant, now quite his cheerful self once more. 'The Bench is going to take a serious view of that, a very serious view. All right, constable, remove the prisoner.'

'Just a second,' said Bingo, though something seemed to tell him that this was not quite the moment. 'Could I have that fiver, Oofy?'

His suspicions were proved correct. It was not the moment. Oofy did not reply. He gave Bingo a long, lingering look from the eye which was still functioning, and the arm of the law led him out. And Bingo had started to totter off, when the sergeant reminded him that there was something he was forgetting.

'Your baby, sir.'

'Oh, ah, yes.'

'Shall we send it, or do you want to take it with you?'

'Oh, with me. Yes, certainly with me.'

'Very good,' said the sergeant. 'I'll have it wrapped up.'

Referring back to the beginning of this chronicle, we see that we compared Bingo Little, when conversing with his wife Rosie on the subject of police and pawn shops, to a toad beneath the harrow. As he sat with Algernon Aubrey on the beach some quarter of an hour after parting from the sergeant, the illusion that he was what Webster's Dictionary describes as a terrestrial member of the frog family and that somebody was driving spikes through his sensitive soul had become intensified. He viewed the future with concern, and would greatly have preferred not to be compelled to view it at all. Already he could hear the sharp intake of the wifely breath and the spate of wifely words which must inevitably follow the stammering confession of his guilt. He and Rosie had always been like a couple of turtle-doves, but he knew only too well that when the conditions are right, a female turtle-dove can express herself with a vigour which a Caribbean hurricane might envy.

Emerging with a shudder from this unpleasant reverie, he found that Algernon Aubrey had strayed from his side and, looking to the south-east, observed him some little distance away along the beach. The child was hitting a man in a Homburg hat over the head with his spade, using, it seemed to Bingo, a good deal of wristy follow-through. (In hitting men in Homburg hats over the head with spades, the follow-through is everything.)

He rose, and hurried across to where the party of the second part sat rubbing his occipital bone. In his capacity of Algernon Aubrey's social sponsor he felt that an apology was due from him.

'I say,' he said, 'I'm most frightfully sorry about my baby socking you like that. Wouldn't have had it happen for the world. But I'm afraid he never can resist a Homburg hat. They seem to draw him like a magnet.'

The man, who was long and thin and horn-rimmed-spectacled, did not reply for a moment. He was staring at Algernon Aubrey like one who sees visions.

'Is this your baby?' he said.

Bingo said Yes, sir, that was his baby, and the man muttered something about this being his lucky day.

'What a find!' he said. 'Talk about manna from heaven! I'd like to draw him, if I may. We must put the thing on a business basis, of course. I take it that you are empowered to act as his agent. Shall we say five pounds?'

Bingo shook his head sadly.

'I'm afraid it's off,' he said. 'I haven't any money. I can't pay you.'

'You don't pay me. I pay you,' said the man. 'So if five pounds is all right with you...' He broke off, directed another searching glance at Algernon Aubrey and seemed to change his mind. 'No, not five. It would be a steal. Let's make it ten.'

Bingo gasped. Bramley-on-Sea was flickering before his eyes like a Western on the television screen. For an instant the thought crossed his mind that this must be his guardian angel buckling down to work after a prolonged period of loafing on his job. Then, his vision clearing, he saw that the other had no wings. He had spoken, moreover, with an American intonation, and the guardian angel of a member of the Drones Club would have had an Oxford accent.

'Ten pounds?' he gurgled. 'Did I understand you to say that you would give me ten pounds?'

'I meant twenty, and it's worth every cent of the money. Here you are,' said the man, producing notes from an inside pocket.

Bingo took them reverently and, taught by experience, held on to them like a barnacle attaching itself to the hull of a ship.

'When would you like to start painting Algy's portrait?'

The man's horn-rimmed spectacles flashed fire.

'Good God!' he cried, revolted. 'You don't think I'm a portrait painter, do you? I'm Wally Judd.'

'Wally who?'

'Judd. The Dauntless Desmond man.'

'The what man?'

'Don't you know Dauntless Desmond?'

'I'm afraid I don't.'

The other drew a deep breath.

'I never thought to hear those words in a civilized country. Dauntless Desmond, my comic strip. It's running in the *Mirror* and in sixteen hundred papers in America. Dauntless Desmond, the crooks' despair.'

'He is a detective, this D. Desmond?'

'A private eye or shamus,' corrected the other. 'And he's always up against the creatures of the underworld. He's as brave as a lion."

"Sounds like a nice chap."

"He is. One of the best. But there's a snag. Desmond is impulsive. He will go bumping off these creatures of the underworld. He shoots them in the stomach. Well, I needn't tell you what that sort of thing leads to.'

'The supply of creatures of the underworld is beginning to give out?'

'Exactly. There is a constant need for fresh faces, and the moment I saw your baby I knew I had found one. That lowering look! Those hard eyes which could be grafted on the head of a man-eating shark and no questions asked. He's a natural. Could you bring him around to the Hôtel Splendide right away, so that I can do some preliminary sketches?'

A sigh of ecstasy escaped Bingo. It set the bank notes in his pocket crackling musically, and for a moment he stood there listening as to the strains of some great anthem.

'Make it half an hour from now,' he said. 'I have to look in first on a fellow I know in Seaview Road.'

19

OOFY, FREDDIE AND THE BEEF TRUST

Conversations were in progress in the smoking room of the Drones with a view to making up a party to go and see the Wrestling Championship at the Albert Hall, and a Bean suggested that Oofy Prosser be invited to join the expedition. Oofy, he put it to the meeting, had more pimples than the man of taste liked to be seen about with and was perhaps the nearest approach to a piece of cheese which the human race had so far produced, but he possessed one outstanding merit which went far to counter-balance these defects – viz. a stupendous bank account, and it was quite conceivable that, if handled right, he might loosen up and stand supper after the performance.

The proposal was well received, and when Oofy entered a few moments later the Bean issued his invitation. To the general surprise, instead of seeming gratified by this demand for his society, the club millionaire recoiled with every evidence of loathing and horror. At the mention of the word 'wrestling' a look of intense malevolence passed over his face.

'Wrestling?' he cried. 'You ask me to spend good money on a wrestling match? You want me to pay out cash to witness the obscene gyrations of a couple of pot-bellied nitwits who fritter away their time wallowing on mats and behaving like lunatic osteopaths? Wrestlers, forsooth! The scum of the earth! I'd like to dig a hole in the ground and collect all the wrestlers in the world and dump them into it, having previously skinned them with a blunt knife and cooked them over a slow fire. Wrestlers, indeed. Bah! Pah! Faugh! Tchah!' said Oofy Prosser, and turned on his heel and left the room.

An Egg was the first to break the puzzled silence.

'Do you know what I think?' he said. 'I don't believe Oofy likes wrestlers.'

'Exactly the thought that occurred to me, reading between the lines,' agreed the Bean.

'You are perfectly right,' said a Crumpet. 'Your intuition has not deceived you. I was about to warn you, when he came in. He was recently interested in a venture connected with wrestlers and lost quite a bit of money. And you know how Oofy feels about parting with money.'

His hearers nodded. In matters of finance their clubmate's dogged adhesiveness was a byword. Not one of those present but in his time had endeavoured to dip into the Prosser millions, always without success.

'That's why he isn't speaking to Freddie Widgeon now. It was through him that he got mixed up in the thing. Owing to Freddie, Jos. Waterbury entered Oofy's life. And once Jos. Waterbury enters your life, Freddie tells me, you can kiss at least a portion of your holdings goodbye.'

'I wonder if I have happened to mention this Jos. Waterbury to you before. Did I tell you about the time when Freddie sang at that Amateur Night binge down in Bottleton East and was accompanied on the piano by a greasy bird whom he had picked up in the neighbourhood? I did? Well, that was Jos. Waterbury. In a brawl in a pub later on in the evening, Freddie happened to save his life, and on the strength of this he has been rolling up to the club and touching his brave preserver ever since for sums ranging from sixpence to as much as half a crown.

'You would think that if Bloke A saves Bloke B's life, it ought to be the former who touches the latter and not vice versa, but the noblesse oblige of the Widgeons does not permit Freddie to see it that way. He recognizes Jos. Waterbury's claim and continues to brass up.'

The chain of events with which my narrative deals (proceeded the Crumpet) started to uncoil itself, or whatever chains do, about a month ago. It was on a breezy morning towards the middle of May that Freddie, emerging from the club, found Jos. Waterbury lurking on the steps. A couple of bob changed hands, and Freddie was about to shift on, when the other froze on to his coat sleeve and detained him.

'Half a mo, cocky,' said Jos. Waterbury. 'Do you want to make a packet?' And Freddie, who has been hoping to make a packet since he was sacked from his first kindergarten, replied that Jos. Waterbury interested him strangely.

'That's the way to talk,' said the greasy bird. 'That's the spirit I like to see. Well, I can ease you in on the ground floor of the biggest thing since the Mint. Just slip me a couple of hundred quid for working expenses and we're off.'

Freddie laughed a hollow, mirthless laugh. The only time he had ever had money like that in his possession was when his uncle, Lord Blicester, had given him his wallet to hold while he brushed his topper.

'A couple of hundred quid?' he said. 'Gosh, Jos. Waterbury, from the light-hearted way you speak of such sums one would think you thought I was Oofy Prosser.'

'Oofy how much?'

'Prosser. The wealthiest bimbo in the Drones. Silk underwear, shoes by Lobb, never without a flower in the buttonhole, covered with pimples, each pimple produced by gallons of vintage champagne, and always with an unsightly bulge in his breast pocket, where he keeps his roll. Ask him for your couple of hundred quids, my misguided old chunk of grease, not a poor deadbeat who is pretty shortly going to find a difficulty in getting his three square a day, unless the ravens do their stuff.'

And he was starting to biff off, with another sardonic laugh at the idea of anyone mistaking him for a plutocrat, when Jos. Waterbury uttered these momentous words.

'Well, why don't you slip me an intro to this gentleman friend of yours? Then, if he puts up the splosh, you get a commish.'

Freddie stared at him with bulging eyes. If you had told him half an hour before that the moment would come when he would look upon Jos. Waterbury and find him almost beautiful, he would have scouted the idea. But this was what was happening now.

'A commish?' he whispered. 'Golly, now you're talking. We'll go round and see him now. What's the time? Half past eleven? We ought to catch him at breakfast.'

Their mission proved a complete success. I was at the bar next morning, having one for the tonsils, when Oofy blew in, and from the fact that his eyes were aglow and his pimples gleaming, I deduced that he had spotted a chance of making money. In repose, as you know, Oofy's eyes are like those of a dead fish, but if he thinks he sees a way of adding to his disgustingly large bank balance, they glitter with a strange light.

'I say,' he said, 'do you know anything about wrestling? Professional wrestling, I mean. The all-in stuff. Good box-office value, isn't it?'

I said that I had always understood so, especially up North.

'So this chap Waterbury says. Yesterday,' explained Oofy, 'Freddie Widgeon brought a fellow named Waterbury to see me, and he placed a proposition before me which looks dashed good. It seems that he knows a couple of all-in wrestlers, and he wants me to advance two hundred quid for working capital, the scheme being that we hire a hall in one of these Northern manufacturing towns and put these birds on and clean up. He says we can safely bill the thing as a European championship, because nobody up there is going to know if a wrestler is a champion or not. Then we have a return match, and after that the rubber match, and then we start all over again somewhere else. There ought to be a pot of money in it.'

My heart was heavy at the thought of Oofy making more money, but I had to agree. Such a series of contests, I felt, could scarcely fail to bring home the bacon. Blood in these Northern manufacturing towns is always very rich and sporting, and it was practically a certainty that the inhabitants would amble up in their thousands.

'I'm going down to a pub at Barnes this afternoon to have a look at the fellows. From what Waterbury tells me, there seems no doubt that they are the goods. I shall probably make a fortune. There is the purse, of course, and Waterbury's cut, and I'm paying Freddie a ten per cent commission, but even so the profits ought to be enormous.'

He licked his lips, and feeling that this might possibly be my moment, I asked him if he could lend me a fiver till Wednesday. He said No, he ruddy well could not, and the episode closed.

At two o'clock that afternoon, Oofy bowled down in his princely sports model two-seater to the White Stag, Barnes, and at twenty-to-three, Jos. Waterbury, looking greasier than ever, was introducing him to the two catch-as-catch-canners.

It was a breath-taking experience. His first emotion, he tells me, was one of surprise that so much human tonnage could have been assembled in one spot. A cannibal king, beholding them, would have whooped with joy and reached for his knife and fork with the feeling that for once the catering department had not failed him; and if you could have boiled them down for tallow, you would have had enough ha'penny dips to light the homes of all the residents of Barnes for about a year and a quarter.

Reading from left to right, the pair consisted of an obese bounder who looked like a gorilla which has been doing itself too well on the bananas and a second obese bounder who would have made a hippopotamus seem streamlined. They had small, glittering eyes, no foreheads and more hair all over than you would have believed possible.

Jos. Waterbury did the honours.

'Mr Porky Jupp and Mr Plug Bosher.'

The Messrs Jupp and Bosher said they were pleased to meet Oofy, but Oofy wasn't so sure he could look at the thing from the same kindly angle. The thought crossed his mind that if, when walking down a lonely alley on a moonless night, he had had to meet two of his fellow men, these were the two he would have picked last. Their whole personalities gave him the impression that neither was safe off the chain.

This conviction grew as he watched the exhibition bout which they put on for his benefit. It was like witnessing a turn-up between two pluguglies of the Stone Age. They snorted and gurgled and groaned and grunted and rolled on each other and jumped on each other and clutched each other's throats and bashed each other's faces and did the most extraordinary things to each other's stomachs. The mystery to Oofy was that they didn't come unstuck.

When the orgy scene was over, he was pale beneath his pimples and panting like a stag at bay, but convinced beyond the possibility of doubt that this was the stuff to give the rugged dwellers up North. As soon as he could get his breath back, he informed Jos. Waterbury that he would write out a cheque immediately: and this having been done, they parted; Jos. Waterbury and the almost humans leaving for a cottage in the country, where the latter could conduct their training out of reach of the temptations of the great city, and Oofy tooling home in the two-seater with the comfortable feeling that in the not distant future his current account would be swelling up as if it had got dropsy.

It had been Oofy's original intention, partly in order to keep a fatherly eye on his investment and partly because he wanted to watch the mass murderers pirouetting on each other's stomachs again, to look in at the training camp pretty shortly. But what with one thing and another, he didn't seem able to get around to it, and a couple of weeks passed with him still infesting the metrop.

However, he presumed Jos. Waterbury was carrying on all right. He pictured Jos. sweating away in and around the cottage, not sparing himself, a permanent blot on the rural scene. It surprised him, accordingly, when one morning Freddie Widgeon came into the Club and told him that the blighter was waiting in the hall.

'Looking dashed solemn and sinister,' said Freddie. 'His manner, as he touched me for two bob, was strange and absent. I say, you don't think anything's gone wrong with the works, do you?'

This was precisely what Oofy was thinking. The presence of this greasy bird in Dover Street, W., when he should have been slithering about in the depths of the country, put him into a twitter. He legged it to the hall, followed by Freddie, and found Jos. Waterbury chewing a dead cigar and giving the club appointments an approving once over.

'Nice little place you've got here. Pip, pip,' said Jos. Waterbury.

Oofy was in no mood for chit-chat.

'Never mind about my nice little place. What about your nice little place? Why aren't you at the cottage with the thugs?'

'Exactly,' said Freddie. 'Your place is at their side.'

'Well, the fact is, cockies,' said Jos. Waterbury, 'an awkward situation has arisen, and I thought we ought to have a conference. They've gone and had a quarrel. There's been a rift within the lute, if you understand the expression, and it looks as if it was spreading.'

Oofy could make nothing of this. Nor could Freddie. Oofy asked what the dickens that mattered, and Freddie asked what the dickens that mattered, too.

'I'll tell you what it matters, cockies,' said Jos. Waterbury, putting his cigar gravely behind his ear and looking like a chunk of margarine with a secret sorrow. 'Unless we can heal the rift, ruin stares us in the eyeball.' And in a few crisp words he explained the inwardness of the situation.

Professional wrestling, it seems, is a highly delicate and scientific business which you can't just bung into in a haphazard spirit, relying for your effects on the inspiration of the moment. Aggravated acts of mayhem like those perpetrated by Porky Jupp and Plug Bosher come to flower only after constant rehearsal, each move, down to the merest gnashing of the teeth, being carefully thought out in the quiet seclusion of the study and polished to the last button with unremitting patience. Otherwise the thing doesn't look right, and audiences complain.

Obviously, then, what you require first and foremost in a couple of wrestlers whom you are readying for the arena, is a mutual sympathy and a cordial willingness to collaborate. And until recently such a sympathy had existed between Porky Jupp and Plug Bosher in abundant measure, each helping each and working unselfishly together for the good of the show.

To give them an instance of what he meant, said Jos. Waterbury, Porky would come along one day, after musing apart for a while, and suggest that Plug should sock him on the nose, because it would be a swell effect and he never felt anything when socked on the nose except a rather agreeable tickling sensation. Upon which, Plug, not to be outdone in the courtesies, would place his stomach unreservedly at the other's disposal, inviting him to jump up and down on it to his heart's content; he having so much stomach that he scarcely noticed it if people did buck-and-wings on the outskirts.

'Just a couple of real good pals,' said Jos. Waterbury, 'like what's-his-name and who-was-it in the Bible. It was beautiful to see their team work. But now they've come over all nasty, and what's to be what I might call the upshot is more than I can tell you. If there hadn't been this rift within the lute, we'd have had a fine, stirring performance full of entertainment value and one long thrill from start to finish, but if they're going to be cross with each other, it won't look like anything. It'll all be over in a couple of minutes, because Plug can always clean up Porky with one hand if he wants to. And then what? People throwing pop bottles and yelling "Fake!"'

'Well, that won't matter,' said Oofy, pointing out the bright side. 'They'll already have paid for their seats.'

'And what about the return match? And the rubber match? If the first show's a flop, it'll get around and we'll be playing to empty benches.'

They saw what he was driving at now, and Freddie, all of a doodah at the prospect of losing his commish, uttered a low cry and sucked feverishly at the knob of his umbrella. As for Oofy, a look of anguish passed over his face, leaping from pimple to pimple like the chamois of the Alps from crag to crag and he asked how far the breach had widened. Were relations between these two garrotters really so very strained?'

'Well, they're still speaking to each other.'

'That's good.'

'No, that's bad,' corrected Jos. Waterbury. 'Because every time they open their mouths, it's to make a dirty crack. I tell you, if you want to see your money back, you'd better come and try and reason with them.'

Oofy said his two-seater was at the door, and they would start at once. Freddie wanted to come, too, but Oofy wouldn't let him. When you're all in a dither, with ruin staring you in the eyeball, you don't want to be hampered by Freddie Widgeon. Jos. Waterbury asked Freddie if he could lend him a couple of bob, and Freddie said he had lent him a couple of bob, and Jos. Waterbury said Oh sorry, he had forgotten, and didn't that just show what a state of mind he was in? He and Oofy popped off.

To say that Oofy was all in a dither is really to give too feeble a picture of his emotions. They were such that only a top-notcher like Shakespeare could have slapped them down on paper, and he would have had to go all out.

What made his head swim was the mystery of the thing. Here were a couple of birds who for years had apparently been two minds with but a single thought, and their ancient friendship had suddenly taken the knock. Why? For what reason? He sought in vain for a reply.

It seemed hours before they got to journey's end. When they did, a single glance was enough to show Oofy that Jos. Waterbury knew a rift within the lute when he saw one. The two gorillas were plainly on the chilliest of terms. And when he watched them wrestle, he saw exactly what Jos. had meant.

All the spirit had gone out of the thing. Plug Bosher still socked Porky Jupp on the nose, but coldly and formally, and when Porky jumped on Plug's stomach it was with a frigid aloofness which, if exhibited before a paying audience, must inevitably have brought out the pop bottles like hailstones.

Oofy stayed on to dinner, and when it was over and Plug and Porky had gone off to bed without saying goodnight to one another, Jos. Waterbury looked at him with despondency written all over his greasy face. It was obvious that only the fact of his having no soul prevented the iron entering into it.

'You see. Not a hope.'

But Oofy had perked up amazingly. His quick intelligence had enabled him by now to spot the root of the trouble. When there is money in the offing, Oofy thinks like lightning.

'Not at all,' he replied. 'Tails up, Jos. Waterbury. The sun is still shining.'

Jos. Waterbury said he didn't see any ruddy sun, and Oofy said, 'possibly not, but it was there all right and would shortly come smiling through.'

'The thing is quite simple, I was on to it in a second directly we started dinner, if you can call it dinner. All that has happened is that these two bounders have got dyspepsia.'

His companion's eyebrows rose, and he uttered a sharp 'Gorblimey!' Whoever heard of wrestlers getting dyspepsia, he asked incredulously, adding that he had once known one who lived on pickled pig's trotters and ice cream, washing the mixture down with sparkling limado, a beverage to which he was greatly attached.

'And, what's more, throve on it. Blossomed like a rose in June.'

'Quite,' said Oofy. 'No doubt wrestlers can eat almost anything. Nevertheless, there is a point beyond which the human stomach, be it even that of a wrestler, cannot be pushed, and that point has been reached – nay, passed – in this establishment. The meal of which we have just partaken was the sort of meal an inexperienced young female buzzard might have prepared for her newly married buzzard husband. When I was a boy, I had a goat that ate brass door knobs. That goat would have passed up tonight's steak with a dainty shudder of distaste. Who does the cooking in this joint? Lucrezia Borgia?'

'A woman comes from the village.'

'Then tell her to go back to the village and jolly well stay there, and I'll look in at a good agency tomorrow and get somebody who knows how to cook. You'll soon see the difference. Porky Jupp will become all smiles, and Plug Bosher will skip like the high hills. A week from now I confidently expect to find them chewing each other's ears and bashing each other's noses with all the old mateyness and camara-derie.'

Jos. Waterbury said he believed Oofy was right, and Oofy said he bally well knew he was right.

'Cor! Chase my Aunt Fanny up a gum tree!' cried Jos., infected with his enthusiasm. 'You knew something when you said the blinking sun would soon be shining through the blinking clouds, because there it is, all alive-o. But you needn't go to any agencies and be skinned for fees. I'll send for my niece.'

'Have you a niece?' said Oofy, sorry for the unfortunate girl.

'I have three nieces,' said Jos. Waterbury, with a touch of the smugness of the man of property. 'This one's in service as kitchen maid in Green Street, Mayfair. She does for the family when the cook's out, and never fails to give satisfaction.'

Oofy, thinking it over, could see no objection to engaging this Myrtle Cootes, for such, it appeared, was her name. Mayfair kitchen maids, he knew, were always red-hot stuff with the roasts and boileds, and he shared his companion's dislike for paying fees. So it was arranged that on his return to the metrop. he should call on her with a letter of introduction explaining the circs. and bright and early on the following morning he did so.

Myrtle Cootes proved to be very much the sort of niece you would have expected a man like Jos. Waterbury to have. In features and expression she resembled a dead codfish on a slab. She wore steel-rimmed spectacles, topping them off with ginger hair and adenoids. But Oofy wasn't looking for a Venus de Milo or a Helen of Troy: what he wanted was a Grade A skillet wielder, and a private word with the cook assured him that the culinary arrangements of the training camp could safely be placed in this gargoyle's hands. The cook said she had taught Myrtle Cootes all she knew, and produced testimonials from former employers to show that what she knew was practically the whole art of dinner-dishing from soup to toothpicks.

So Myrtle was instructed to get in touch with the front office and explain that she was obliged to leave immediately owing to sickness at home, and next day Oofy drove her down to the cottage with her corded box and her adenoids and left her there. He stayed on to lunch to get a flash of her form, and was more than satisfied with the girl's virtuosity. She gave them a nourishing soup of the type that sticks to the ribs and puts hair on the chest, followed by a steak and kidney pie with two veg. and a rolypoly pudding with raisins in it, and the stuff fairly melted in their mouths.

The effect of these improved browsing conditions on the two mastodons was instantaneous and gratifying. They downed their soup as if in a roseate dream, and scarcely had the echoes died away when there was another sloshing sound as the milk of human kindness came surging back into them.

By the time the rolypoly pudding with raisins in it had gone down the hatch, all disagreement and unpleasantness had been forgotten. They beamed at each other with the old cordiality. Plug Bosher's voice, as he asked Porky Jupp to reach him the bread, would have passed anywhere for that of a turtle-dove cooing to its mate, and so would Porky Jupp's when he said, 'Right ho, cully, here she comes.' Oofy was so enchanted that he actually went into the kitchen and gave Myrtle Cootes a treasury note for ten bob. And when Oofy voluntarily separates himself from ten bob, you can be pretty sure that his whole being has been stirred to its foundations.

It was on his way home that it suddenly occurred to him that he could set the seal on the day's good work by easing Freddie Widgeon out of the deal and so relieving the venture of the burden of that ten per cent commish of his. Right from the start the thought of having to slip Freddie ten per cent of the profits had been like a dagger in his heart. So when he met him in the club that night and Freddie began bleating for the lowdown on conditions at the front, he shoved on a look of alarm and despondency and told him that the whole thing was a wash-out. The rift between the two principals, he said, had got such a toe-hold that it was hopeless to attempt a reconciliation, and so, seeing no sense in going ahead and getting the bird from a slavering mob of infuriated Yorkshiremen, he had decided to cancel the whole project.

And when, as was natural, this caused Freddie to Oh-death-where-is-thy-sting a goodish bit, Oofy laid an affectionate hand on his shoulder and said he knew exactly how he felt.

'It's the thought of you that's been worrying me into a fever, Freddie old man. I know how you were looking forward to cleaning up with that ten per of yours. The first thing I said to myself was, "I mustn't let good old Freddie down." Well, it's a trifle, of course, to what you would have made, but I'm going to give you a tenner. Yes, yes, I insist. Just scribble me a line as a matter of form, saying that you accept this in full settlement of all claims, and we'll be straight.'

Freddie did so with a tear of gratitude in his eye, and that was that.

In the days that followed I doubt if you could have met a chirpier millionaire than Oofy Prosser. He came into the club whistling, he hummed as he sauntered to and fro, and once, when at the bar, actually burst into song. And when Freddie, who happened to be in the bar at the time, expressed surprise at this jauntiness, he explained that he was merely wearing the mask.

'One must be British. The stiff upper lip, what?'

'Oh, rather,' said Freddie.

Nor did Jos. Waterbury's bulletins from the training camp do anything to diminish his exuberance. Jos. Waterbury wrote that everything was going like a breeze. Brotherly love was getting stronger on the wing daily. Porky Jupp had suggested that when he jumped on Plug Bosher's stomach Plug Bosher should bite him in the ankle, and Plug Bosher had said he would be charmed to do so, only Porky Jupp must bite him on the nose. Jos. Waterbury said that Oofy was missing something in not being there to taste Myrtle's Irish stew, and added that Plug Bosher had put on another inch around the waist.

So rosy was the picture he drew that Oofy, after singing in the bar, went and sang in the hall, and those who were present said that they had never heard anything more carefree. Catsmeat Potter-Pirbright, in particular, compared it to the trilling of a nightingale. There is no question that at this juncture Oofy Prosser was sitting on top of the world.

It was consequently a shattering shock to him when Jos. Waterbury's telegram arrived. Strolling into the club one afternoon with a song on his lips and finding a telegram for him in the 'P' box, he opened it idly, with no premonition of an impending doom, and a moment later was feeling as if Porky Jupp had jumped on his stomach.

'Come running, cocky,' wired his business associate, careful even in the stress of what was evidently a powerful emotion to keep it down to twelve words. 'Another rift within lute. Ruin stares eyeball. Regards. Waterbury.'

I described Oofy's state of mind on his previous visit to the camp, if you remember, as dithery. It would be difficult to find an adjective capable of handling his emotions now. That telegram had got right in amongst him and churned him up good and proper.

He had been so sure that there would be no more unfortunate incidents and that he would soon be beaming through the grill at his receiving teller and drinking in the man's low whistle of respectful astonishment as he noted the figures on the cheque he was depositing. And now... It began to look to him as though there were a curse on this enterprise of his.

It was getting on for the quiet evenfall when he fetched up at the cottage. The air was cool and fragrant, and the declining sun, doing its stuff in and about the garden, lit up the trees and the little lawn. On the lawn he observed Porky Jupp plucking the petals from a daisy and heard, as he hurried past, his muttered, 'She loves me, she loves

me not'; while a short distance away, Plug Bosher, armed with a
pocket knife, was carving on a tree a heart with an arrow through it.
Neither appeared aware of the other's existence.

In the doorway stood Jos. Waterbury, moodily regarding the pair.
His sombre face lightened a little as he perceived Oofy, and he drew
him into the house.

'You saw them, cocky?' he said. 'You took a good gander at them?
Then there's no need for me to explain. That picture tells the story.'

Oofy, recoiling, for the other was breathing heavily in his face and
the first thing the man of sensibility does when Jos. Waterbury
breathes in his face is to recoil as far as possible, replied with some
asperity that there was every need for him to explain. And Jos.
Waterbury said had he observed the daisy? Had he noticed the heart
with the arrow through it? He had? Well, there you are, then.

'They're rivals in love, cocky, that's what's happened. They've
both of 'em gone and got mushy on Myrtle.'

You could have knocked Oofy down with a feather. The thing
didn't seem to him to make sense. With a strong effort he succeeded
in steadying his brain, which was going round in circles like a performing mouse. He stared at Jos. Waterbury.'

'With Myrtle?'

'That's right.'

Oofy still found himself unable to grasp the gist. He stared harder
than ever.

'With Myrtle?' he repeated. 'Here, let's get this straight. You say
these two blisters love Myrtle? The Cootes disaster, you mean? You
are not speaking of some other Myrtle? Your reference is to the slab-
faced human codfish in the kitchen?'

Jos. Waterbury drew himself up with a touch of pique.

'I'd call Myrtle a nice-looking girl.'

'I wouldn't.'

'She's supposed to look like me.'

'That's what I mean,' said Oofy. 'You must have got your facts
twisted. Why would anyone fall in love with Myrtle?'

'Well, there's her cooking.'

For the first time Oofy began to find the thing credible. Himself a
greedy hog, he could appreciate the terrific force of the impact of
Myrtle Cootes's cooking on two men whose meals had previously
been prepared by the woman who came in from the village. Fellows
like Porky Jupp and Plug Bosher, he reminded himself, are practical.
They do not seek for the softer feminine graces. Overlooking codfish
faces and adenoids, they allow their affections to be ensnared by the
succulent steak, the cunningly handled veg., the firm, white, satisfy-

ing rolypoly pudding with raisins in it. Beauty fades, but these things remain.

'But this is frightful!' he yipped.

'Bad enough for me,' assented Jos. Waterbury. 'They've got the idea that she thinks wrestling ungentlemanly, and they're considering chucking it and going in for something else. I heard Plug ask her yesterday if she could love a copper's nark, and I've seen Porky reading a correspondence course advertisement about how to make a large fortune breeding Angora rabbits. If you ask me if the outlook's black, I reply, "Yes, cocky, blacker than Plug Bosher's nails." I see no future in the racket.'

At these words of doom, Oofy tottered to the window. He needed air. Looking out, he saw that Porky Jupp had finished plucking the petals of his daisy. He had crossed the lawn to where Plug Bosher was carving the heart on the tree and was gazing on his handiwork with an unpleasant sneer. He said nothing, but there was a quiet contempt in his manner which was plainly affecting the other like a bad notice in the Art section of the *Spectator*. With a sullen scowl Plug Bosher closed his pocket knife and walked away.

'See?' said Jos. Waterbury. 'That's the way they go on all the time now. Rivals in love.'

'Which one of them does she like?' asked Oofy dully.

'She doesn't like either of 'em. I keep telling them that, but they won't believe me. You can't drive reason into a wrestler's nut. Porky says there's something in the way she looks at him which convinces him that he could put it over if only Plug wasn't always messing around; and Plug says you've only got to listen to the girl's quick breathing when he comes along to see that the thing's in the bag; only every time he's just going to pour out his heart, he steps on something and it's Porky. They're vain. That's what's the trouble with them. I've never met an all-in wrestler who didn't think he was Clark Gable. But listen, cocky, I've got an idea.'

'I'll bet it's rotten.'

'It isn't any such thing. It's a pip. It came to me like a flash while we were talking. Suppose somebody was to come along and cut both of 'em out. See what I mean? The handsome man about town from the city.'

Oofy had not expected to be impressed by any suggestion of this greasy bird's, but he had to admit that he had spoken what looked very like a mouthful. He said he believed that Jos. Waterbury had got something there, and Jos. Waterbury said he was convinced of it.

'You get two blokes that's rivals in love,' he went on, elaborating his point, 'and another bloke comes along and makes monkeys out of both of 'em, and what happens? It draws them together. They're so sore on the other bloke that they forget their little tiff. That's human nature.'

In a cooler moment Oofy would probably have pointed out that the snag about that was that Porky Jupp and Plug Bosher weren't human, but he was too stirred to think of that now. He slapped Jos. Waterbury on the back and said he was a genius, and Jos. Waterbury said he had been from a child.

Then Oofy's joyous enthusiasm started to sag a bit. The thought that had sprung into his mind had been that here was a job right up Freddie Widgeon's street, Freddie being the sort of chap who can make love to anything. But he couldn't approach Freddie. And, failing Freddie, who could handle the assignment? You couldn't just go to anyone and ask him to sit in. It would mean tedious explaining, and of course, one didn't want to let the whole world into the secrets of professional wrestling.

He put this to Jos. Waterbury, who seemed surprised.

'I was thinking of you,' he said.

'Me?'

'That's right.'

Oofy goggled.

'You expect me to make love to that – '

He paused, and Jos. Waterbury in a rather cold voice said, 'That what?' Oofy, loathe to wound an uncle's feelings, substituted the word 'girl' for the 'gargoyle' which he had been about to employ, and Jos. Waterbury said that it seemed the only way.

'You want to protect your investment, don't you? You don't want all that lovely splosh to slip through your hands, do you? Well, then.'

He had struck the right note. The last thing in the world Oofy wanted was to lose any lovely splosh. It was true that the last thing but one was to make advances to Myrtle Cootes, but, as his colleague had pointed out, it was the only way.

'Right ho,' he said in a low voice, like a premier basso with tonsillitis. 'How do I start?'

'Take her for a nice little spin in your car,' suggested Jos. Waterbury.

So Myrtle Cootes was summoned and told to put on her hat, coat and scent, and Oofy took her out for a nice little spin in his car.

When he returned, a good deal shaken and breathing rather heavily through the nostrils, Jos. Waterbury informed him that the treatment had begun to work already. The green-eyed monster, running up their legs and biting them, had caused Porky Jupp and Plug Bosher to watch the expedition set out with smouldering eyes and grinding teeth; and scarcely had Myrtle Cootes's patchouli faded away on the evening breeze before they were speaking to each other for the first time in days and, what is more, speaking in a friendly and cordial spirit.

The spirit of their conversation, as Jos. Waterbury had predicted that it would be, was Oofy and the many things they found in him to dislike. Porky had criticized his pimples, Plug his little side-whiskers, and each had agreed unreservedly with the other's findings. On several occasions Plug had said that Porky had taken the very words out of his mouth, and when Plug described Oofy as a la-di-da Gawd-help-us, Porky said Plug put these things so well. It has been a treat, Jos. Waterbury asserted, to listen to them.

'It looked to me,' he said, 'as though the rift and breach was pretty near healed. Twice I heard Plug call Porky "cully", and there was an affectionate look in Porky's eye when Plug said you reminded him of a licentious clubman in the films which it would have done you good to see. I helped the thing along by telling them that you'd been hanging around Myrtle for weeks, bringing her bouquets and taking her to the pictures, so one more push, cocky, and we're home. What you do now is kiss her.'

Oofy rocked on his base.

'Kiss her?'

'It's the strategic move.'

'But dash it – '

'Come, come, come,' said Jos. Waterbury reprovingly, 'you don't want to spoil the ship for a ha'p'orth of tar. Think of that crowded hall at Huddersfield,' he urged, for it was in that thriving town that they were billed to open. 'Think of those rows and rows of seats, crammed to bursting. Think of the splosh that'll have been handed in at the box office to pay for those seats. Run your eye over the standees at the back. And when you've done that, think of the return match and the rubber match and all the other matches at Leeds, Wigan, Middlesbrough, Sheffield, Sunderland, Newcastle, Hull and what not.'

Oofy shut his eyes and did so. The result was immediate. He ceased to hesitate, and got the do-or-die spirit. It was true that many of the seats alluded to would be merely shilling ones, but Jos. Waterbury had spoken freely of a ten-bob top and once you start thinking in tens the total soon mounts up. When he opened his eyes again, there was a gleam of courage and resolution in them. A faint feeling lingered that he would much rather go over Niagara Falls in a barrel than kiss Myrtle Cootes, but nobody was asking him to go over Niagara Falls in a barrel.

'She'll be bringing in the dinner in a minute,' said Jos. Waterbury. 'If you look slippy, you can catch her in the passage.'

So Oofy looked slippy and caught Myrtle Cootes in the passage. As his eyes fell on that ginger hair and that fishlike face, there swept over him once more a feeling of regret that Freddie Widgeon was not available. There is probably not a girl in the world, not even Myrtle Cootes, whom Freddie couldn't kiss with relish. It seemed hard that with a specialist like that to hand, he couldn't utilize his services. Then he thought of Freddie's ten per cent commish, and was strong again.

Myrtle Cootes was looking so like her uncle, that kissing her was practically tantamount to kissing Jos. Waterbury, but Oofy had at it. Shutting his eyes, for he felt happier that way, he commended his soul to God and folded her in a close embrace. And scarcely had he done so when the air was rent by a couple of hoarse cries and a massive hand descended on his right shoulder. At the same moment another, equally massive, descended on his left shoulder, and he opened his eyes to find the two gorillas regarding him with all the aversion which good men feel towards licentious members of clubs.

His heart did three somersaults and dashed itself against his front teeth. He had not foreseen this angle.

'Coo!' said Porky Jupp.

'Cor!' said Plug Bosher.

They both then said, 'Lor-love-a-duck!'

'Ho!' said Porky. 'Making her the plaything of an idle hour, are you? Well, stand still while we break you in half.'

'Into little pieces,' said Plug Bosher.

'Into little pieces,' said Porky Jupp, accepting his friend's suggestion. 'When we've done with you, your mother won't know you.'

Oofy, contriving to disentangle his heart from his front teeth, said he didn't have a mother, and the two gorillas said that that was immaterial. What they had meant was, supposing for the purpose of argument Oofy had had a mother, that mother wouldn't know him, and the conversation was threatening to get a bit abstruse, when Jos. Waterbury took the floor.

'Boys, boys,' he said soothingly, 'you've got the wrong slant. You misjudge Mr Prosser. There's no harm in a gentleman cuddling the lady he's engaged to be married to, is there?'

Porky Jupp looked at Plug Bosher. His eyes were so small that you could hardly see them, but Oofy could spot the agony. Plug Bosher looked back at Porky Jupp and it was plain that if he had had a forehead, it would have been seamed with lines of anguish.

'Coo!' said Porky. 'Is that straight?'

'Cor!' said Plug. 'Is it?'

'Certainly,' said Jos. Waterbury. 'That's right, isn't it, Mr Prosser?'

Oofy, who from the very inception of these proceedings had started to turn a pretty green, hastened to say that Jos. Waterbury was perfectly correct. He had never liked the man, but he was conscious now of a positive reverence for his sterling qualities. A fellow who thought on his feet in an emergency and said the right thing. I believe if Jos. Waterbury had tried to touch Oofy for half a crown at that moment, Oofy would have disgorged without a murmur.

At this point Myrtle Cootes announced dinner, and they all pushed in.

Dinner was a silent meal. It always checks the flow of small talk if fifty per cent of the company have broken hearts, and it was plain that those of Porky Jupp and Plug Bosher were smashed into hash. When they wiped their gravy up with bread, they did it dully, and there was a listlessness in the way they chivvied bits of rolypoly pudding about the plate with their fingers which told its own story. At the conclusion of the meal they went sadly off to the garden, Jos. Waterbury following, no doubt to comfort and console. Oofy remained where he was, smoking a dazed cigarette and feeling like Daniel after he had shaken off the lions and had a moment to himself.

Still, though he had passed through the furnace and would have to absorb at least a quart of champagne before he could really be himself again, he was happy. Porky Jupp and Plug Bosher were reconciled, and would give of their best before the discriminating residents of Huddersfield, and that was all that mattered. He took out his pencil and paper, and started to work out the probable takings, assuming that at least the first six rows were ten-bobbers.

He was still at this task when Jos Waterbury returned. And the greasy bird's first words sent a black frost buzzing through his garden of dreams.

'Cocky,' said Jos. Waterbury briefly, with no attempt to break the bad news, 'we're sunk. Everything's off.'

'Whark?' cried Oofy. He meant to say 'What?' but in the agitation of the moment he had swallowed his cigarette, and this prevented bell-like clarity.

'Off,' repeated Jos. Waterbury. 'O-r-ruddy-double-f. The thing's gone and worked out all wrong.'

'What do you mean? They're like a couple of brothers.'

'Ah,' said Jos. Waterbury, 'but they've decided to chuck wrestling and go out to Africa together, where might is right and the strong man comes into his own. They say that after what's happened, they just wouldn't have the heart to wrestle. What's that word that begins with a Z?'

'What word that begins with a Z?'

'That's what I'm asking you. I've got it. Zest. They say the zest has gone. Porky says he never wants to be hit on the nose again, and Plug says the idea of having anyone jump on his stomach simply revolts him. Purged in the holocaust of a mighty love, they're going to wander out into the African sunset and become finer, deeper men. So there it is, cocky. Too bad, too bad.'

They sat in silence for a while. Oofy, thinking of that tenner he had given Freddie, writhed like an electric fan, but from the look on his face it seemed that Jos. Waterbury had spotted some sort of silver lining. A moment later he told Oofy what this was.

'Well, there's one good thing come out of it all,' he said. 'It's nice to think that Myrtle's going to be happy. I could wish her no better husband. You must start calling me "Uncle Jos."', said Jos. Waterbury, with a kindly smile.

Oofy stared at him.

'You don't seriously imagine I'm going to marry your blasted niece?'

'I haven't got a blasted niece. I've got three nieces who are all good, sweet girls and the apple of my eye, and the applest of the lot is Myrtle. Aren't you going to marry her?'

'I wouldn't marry her with a barge pole.'

'What, not after announcing the betrothal before witnesses?' Jos. Waterbury pursed his lips. 'Haven't you ever heard of breach of promise? And there's another thing,' he went on. 'I don't know how the boys are going to take this, I tell you straight I don't. They won't like it. I'm afraid they'll want to start breaking you into little pieces again. Still, we can settle the point by having them in and asking them. Boys,' he called, going to the window, 'just come here a minute, will you, boys?'

It took Oofy perhaps thirty seconds to find a formula. He looked Jos. Waterbury in the eye and said:

'How much?'

'How much?' Jos. Waterbury seemed puzzled. Then his face cleared. 'Ah, now I get you. You mean you want to break the engagement, and you feel it's your duty as a gentleman to see that Myrtle gets her bit of heart-balm. Well, that would be one way of doing it, of course. It'ud have to be something pretty big, because there's her despair and desolation to be considered. She'll cry buckets.'

'How much?'

'I'd put it at a thousand quid.'

'A thousand quid!'

'Two thousand,' said Jos. Waterbury, correcting himself.

'Right,' said Oofy. 'I'll give you a cheque.'

You may think it strange that a chap like Oofy, who loves money more than his right eye, should have acquiesced so readily in the suggestion that he pay out two thousand of the best and brightest. You are feeling, possibly, that this part of my story does not ring true. But you must remember that the two pluguglies were even now entering the room, each with small, glittering eyes, hands like hams and muscles like iron bands. Besides, a thought had floated into his mind like drifting thistledown.

This thought was that he could nip back to London in his car tonight and be at the bank first thing next morning, stopping the cheque. By these means all unpleasantness could be averted. The loss of the twopenny stamp he was prepared to accept in view of the urgency of the crisis.

So he wrote out the cheque, and Jos. Waterbury, who had asked him to make it open, trousered it.

'Well, boys,' he said, 'all I wanted to tell you was that I'll have to leave you tonight. I've a little business to do in town.'

'Me, too,' said Oofy. 'I might as well be starting now. Goodnight, everybody, goodnight, goodnight.'

Jos. Waterbury was regarding him with incredulous amazement.

'Here, half a mo'. You're going back to London?'

'Yes.'

'Tonight?'

'Yes.'

'But how about Myrtle's birthday? Have you forgotten it's tomorrow? You can't possibly leave tonight, cocky. She's been looking forward for weeks to having you kiss her in the morning and give her the diamond sunburst or whatever it is you're giving her.'

Oofy slapped his forehead.

'I clean forgot the diamond sunburst. I must be in London first thing tomorrow, to buy it.'

'I could get it for you.'

'No. I want to choose it myself.'

'I see a way out,' said Jos. Waterbury. 'Give her a posy of wild flowers instead. After all, it's the spirit behind the gift that counts. Plug and Porky will help you gather them. Eh, boys?'

The two gorillas said they would.

'He's simply got to be here for Myrtle's birthday, hasn't he, boys?'

'R,' said the two gorillas.

'You mustn't let him leave, boys.'

They both said they wouldn't, and they didn't. When Jos. Waterbury got up to go, saying that he would have to hurry or he would
miss his train, Oofy tried to accompany him and make a quick dash
for the two-seater; but those massive hands descended on his
shoulders again and he fell bonelessly back into his chair. And Jos.
made a clean getaway.

It was about a week later that Freddie Widgeon, leaving the club,
found Jos. Waterbury on the steps and was stunned by the spectacle
he presented. From head to foot the fellow was pure What The Well-
Dressed Man Is Wearing. His shoes glittered in the sunshine like
yellow diamonds, and the hat alone couldn't have set him back much
less than thirty bob. He explained that he had been fortunate in his
investments of late, and what he wanted to see Freddie about was
being put up for the Drones. He liked the place, he said, what he had
seen of it, and would willingly become a member.
   He was just saying that he would leave all the arrangements in
Freddie's hands, when Oofy came out of the door. And at the sight of
Jos. Waterbury there escaped his lips so animal a snarl that Freddie
says that if you had shut your eyes you might have supposed yourself
in the Large Cats house at the Zoo at feeding time. The next moment
he had hurled himself at the greasy bird and was trying to pull his
head off at the roots.
   Well, Freddie isn't particularly fond of Jos. Waterbury and would
be the first to applaud if he stepped on a banana skin and sprained his
ankle, but a human life is a human life. He detached Oofy's clutching
fingers from the blighter's throat, and Oofy, after having a shot at
kicking Jos. Waterbury on the shin, went reeling down the street and
was lost to view.
   Jos. Waterbury recovered his hat, which had been knocked off in a
sou'-sou'-westerly direction, and straightened out the kinks. He put
a hand to his head, and seemed surprised that it was still there.
   'Coo!' he said. 'That was a close call. My whole past life flashed
before me.'
   'Tough luck,' said Freddie sympathetically. 'That must have been
rotten.'
   Jos. Waterbury brooded for a moment. He seemed to be thinking
something out.
   'So you've gone and saved my life *again*, cocky,' he said at length.
'Do you realize that if we were in China you would have to hand over
all your property to me, give me all you've got, if you take my
meaning?'
   'Would I?'

OOFY, FREDDIE AND THE BEEF TRUST   323

'You certainly would. That's the law in China, when you save a man's life.'

'What asses these Chinese are!'

'Not at all,' said Jos. Waterbury warmly. 'I call it a very good rule. You can't expect to go about saving people's lives and not suffer for it. However, I won't be hard on you. Let's call it a tenner.'

'Right,' said Freddie. 'After all, noblesse oblige, doesn't it?'

'You betcher,' said Jos. Waterbury.

'Absolutely,' said Freddie.

20
BINGO BANS THE BOMB

As Bingo Little left the offices of *Wee Tots,* the weekly journal which has done so much to mould thought in the nurseries of Great Britain, his brow was furrowed and his heart heavy. The evening was one of those fine evenings which come to London perhaps twice in the course of an English summer, but its beauty struck no answering chord in his soul. The skies were blue, but he was bluer. The sun was smiling, but he could not raise so much as a simper.

When his wife and helpmeet, Rosie M. Banks the popular novelist, had exerted her pull and secured for him the *Wee Tots* editorship, she had said it would be best not to haggle about salary but to take what Henry Cuthbert Purkiss, its proprietor, offered, and he had done so, glad to have even the smallest bit of loose change to rattle in his pocket. But recently there had been unforeseen demands on his purse. Misled by a dream in which he had seen his Aunt Myrtle (relict of the late J. G. Beenstock) dancing the Twist in a bikini bathing suit outside Buckingham Palace, he had planked his month's stipend on Merry Widow for the two-thirty at Catterick Bridge, and it had come in fifth in a field of seven. This disaster had left him with a capital of four shillings and threepence, so he had gone to Mr Purkiss and asked for a raise, and Mr Purkiss had stared at him incredulously.

'A *what?*' he cried, wincing as if some unfriendly tooth had bitten him in the fleshy part of the leg.

'Just to show your confidence in me and encourage me to rise to new heights of achievement,' said Bingo. 'It would be money well spent,' he pointed out, tenderly picking a piece of fluff off Mr Purkiss's coat sleeve, for everything helps on these occasions.

No business resulted. There were, it seemed, many reasons why Mr Purkiss found himself unable to accede to the request. He placed these one by one before his right-hand man, and an hour or so later, his daily task completed, the right-hand man went on his way, feeling like a left-hand man.

He told himself that he had not really hoped, for Mr Purkiss notoriously belonged to – indeed, was the perpetual president of – the slow-with-a-buck school of thought and no one had ever found it easy

to induce him to loosen up, but nevertheless the disappointment was
substantial. And what put the seal on his depression was that Mrs
Bingo was not available to console him. In normal circumstances he
would have hastened to her and cried on her shoulder, but she was
unfortunately not among those present. She had gone with Mrs
Purkiss to attend the Founder's Day celebrations at the Brighton
seminary where they had been educated and would not be back till
tomorrow.

It looked like being a bleak evening. He was in no mood for
revelry, but even if he had been, he would have found small scope for
it on four shillings and threepence. It seemed to him that his only
course was to go to the Drones for a bite of dinner and then return to
his lonely home and so to bed, and he was passing through Trafalgar
Square en route for Dover Street, where the club was situated, when
a sharp exclamation or cry at his side caused him to halt, and looking
up he saw that what had interrupted his reverie was a redhaired girl of
singular beauty who had that indefinable air of being ready to start
something at the drop of a hat which redhaired girls in these
disturbed times so often have.

'Oh, hullo,' he said, speaking with the touch of awkwardness customary in young husbands accosted by beautiful girls when their
wives are away. He had had no difficulty in recognizing her. Her
name was Mabel Murgatroyd, and they had met during a police raid
on the gambling club they were attending in the days before modern
enlightened thought made these resorts legal, and had subsequently
spent an agreeable half hour together in a water barrel in somebody's
garden. He had not forgotten the incident, and it was plain that it
remained green in Miss Murgatroyd's memory also, for she said:

'Well, lord love a duck, if it isn't my old room-mate Bingo Little!
Fancy meeting you again. How's tricks? Been in any interesting
water barrels lately?'

Bingo said No, not lately.

'Nor me. I don't know how it is with you, but I've sort of lost my
taste for them. The zest has gone. When you've seen one, I often say,
you've seen them all. But there's always something to fill the long
hours. I'm going in more for politics these days.'

'What, standing for Parliament?'

'No, banning the bomb and all that.'

'What bomb would that be?'

'The one that's going to blow us all cross-eyed unless steps are
taken through the proper channels.'

'Ah yes, I know the bomb you mean. No good to man or beast.'

'That's what we feel. When I say "we", I allude to certain of the younger set, of whom I am one. We're protesting against it. Every now and then we march from Aldermaston, protesting like a ton of bricks.'

'Hard on the feet.'

'But very satisfying to the soul. And then we sit a good deal.'

'Sit?'

'That's right.'

'Sit where?'

'Wherever we happen to be. Here, to take an instance at random.'

'What, in the middle of Trafalgar Square? Don't the gendarmerie object?'

'You bet they do. They scoop us up in handfuls.'

'Is that good?'

'Couldn't be better. The papers feature it next morning, and that helps the cause. Ah, here comes a rozzer now, just when we need him. Down with you,' said Mabel Murgatroyd, and seizing Bingo by the wrist she drew him with her to the ground, causing sixteen taxi cabs, three omnibuses and eleven private cars to halt in their tracks, their drivers what-the-hell-ing in no uncertain terms.

It was a moment fraught with discomfort for Bingo. Apart from the fact that all this was doing his trousers no good, he had the feeling that he was making himself conspicuous, a thing he particularly disliked, and in this assumption he was perfectly correct. The suddenness of his descent, too, had made him bite his tongue rather painfully.

But these were, after all, minor inconveniences. What was really disturbing him was the approach of the Government employee to whom his companion had alluded. He was coming alongside at the rate of knots, and his aspect was intimidating to the last degree. His height Bingo estimated at about eight feet seven, and his mood was plainly not sunny.

Nor was this a thing to occasion surprise. For weeks he had been straining the muscles of his back lifting debutantes off London's roadways, and the routine had long since begun to afflict him with ennui. His hearty dislike of debutantes was equalled only by his distaste for their escorts. So now without even saying 'Ho' or 'What's all this?' he attached himself to the persons of Bingo and Miss Murgatroyd and led them from the scene. And in next to no time Bingo found himself in one of Bosher Street's cosy prison cells, due to face the awful majesty of the law on the following morning.

It was not, of course, an entirely novel experience for him. In his bachelor days he had generally found himself in custody on Boat Race night. But he was now a respectable married man and had said goodbye to all that, and it is not too much to say that he burned with shame and remorse. He was also extremely apprehensive. He knew the drill on these occasions. If you wished to escape seven days in the jug, you had to pay a fine of five pounds, and he doubted very much if the M.C. next morning would be satisfied with four shillings and threepence down and an IOU for the remainder. And what Mrs Bingo would have to say when informed on her return that he was in stir, he did not care to contemplate. She would unquestionably explode with as loud a report as the bomb which he had been engaged in banning.

It was consequently with a surge of relief that nearly caused him to swoon that on facing the magistrate at Bosher Street Police Court he found him to be one of those likeable magistrates who know how to temper justice with mercy. Possibly because it was his birthday but more probably because he was influenced by Miss Murgatroyd's radiant beauty, he contented himself with a mere reprimand, and the erring couple were allowed to depart without undergoing the extreme penalty of the law.

Joy, in short, had come in the morning, precisely as the psalmist said it always did, and it surprised Bingo that his fellow-lag seemed not to be elated. Her lovely face was pensive, as if there was something on her mind. In answer to his query as to why she was not skipping like the high hills she explained that she was thinking of her white-haired old father, George Francis Augustus Delamere, fifth Earl of Ippleton, whose existence at the time when she was making her Trafalgar Square protest had temporarily slipped her mind.

'When he learns of this, he'll be fit to be tied,' she said.

'But why should he learn of it?'

'He learns of everything. It's a sort of sixth sense. Have you any loved ones who will have criticisms to make?'

'Only my wife, and she's away.'

'You're in luck,' said Mabel Murgatroyd.

Bingo could not have agreed with her more wholeheartedly. He and Mrs Bingo had always conducted their domestic life on strictly turtle-dove lines, but he was a shrewd enough student of the sex to know that you can push a turtle-dove just so far. Rosie was the sweetest girl in a world where sweet girls are rather rare, but experience had taught him that, given the right conditions, she was capable of making her presence felt as perceptibly as one of those hurricanes which become so emotional on reaching Cape Hatteras. It was agreeable to think that there was no chance of her discovering that in her absence he had been hobnobbing in the dock at Bosher Street Police

Court with red-haired girls of singular beauty.

It was, accordingly, with the feeling that if this was not the best of all possible worlds, it would do till another came along that he made his way to the office of *Wee Tots* and lowered his trouser-seat into the editorial chair. He had slept only fitfully on the plank bed with which the authorities had provided him and he had had practically no breakfast, but he felt that the vicissitudes through which he had passed had made him a deeper, graver man, which is always a good thing. With a light heart he addressed himself to the morning's correspondence, collecting material for the Uncle Joe To His Chickabiddies page which was such a popular feature of the paper, and he was reading a communication from Tommy Bootle (aged twelve) about his angora rabbit Kenneth, when the telephone rang and Mrs Bingo's voice floated over the wire.

'Bingo?'

'Oh, hullo, light of my life. When did you get back?'

'Just now.'

'How did everything go?'

'Quite satisfactorily.'

'Did Ma Purkiss make a speech?'

'Yes, Mrs Purkiss spoke.'

'Lots of the old college chums there, I suppose?'

'Quite a number.'

'Must have been nice for you meeting them. No doubt you got together and swopped reminiscences of midnight feeds in the dormitory and what the games mistress said when she found Maud and Angela smoking cigars behind the gymnasium.'

'Quite. Bingo, have you seen the *Mirror* this morning?'

'I have it on my desk, but I haven't looked at it yet.'

'Turn to page eight,' said Mrs Bingo, and there was a click as she rang off.

Bingo did as directed, somewhat puzzled by her anxiety to have him catch up with his reading and also by a certain oddness he had seemed to detect in her voice. Usually it was soft and melodious, easily mistaken for silver bells ringing across a sunlit meadow in Springtime, but in the recent exchanges he thought he had sensed in it a metallic note, and it perplexed him.

But not for long. Scarcely had his eyes rested on the page she had indicated when all was made clear to him and the offices of *Wee Tots* did one of those *entrechats* which Nijinsky used to do in the Russian ballet. It was as if the bomb Miss Murgatroyd disliked so much had been touched off beneath his swivel chair.

Page eight was mostly pictures. There was one of the Prime

Minister opening a bazaar, another of a resident of Chipping Norton who had just celebrated his hundredth birthday, a third of students rioting in Pernambuco or Mozambique or somewhere. But the one that interested him was the one at the foot of the page. It depicted a large policeman with a girl of singular beauty in one hand and in the other a young man whose features, though somewhat distorted, he was immediately able to recognize. Newspaper photographs tend occasionally to be blurred, but this one was a credit to the artist behind the camera.

It was captioned

THE HON. MABEL MURGATROYD AND FRIENDS

and he sat gazing at it with his eyes protruding in the manner popularized by snails, looking like something stuffed by a taxidermist who had learned his job from a correspondence course and had only got as far as Lesson Three. He had had nasty jars before in his time, for he was one of those unfortunate young men whom Fate seems to enjoy kicking in the seat of the pants, but never one so devastating as this.

Eventually life returned to the rigid limbs, and there swept over him an intense desire for a couple of quick ones. He had got, he realized, to do some very quick thinking and he had long ago learned the lesson that nothing so stimulates the thought processes as a drop of the right stuff. To grab his hat and hasten to the Drones Club was with him the work of an instant. It was not that the stuff was any righter at the Drones than at a dozen other resorts that sprang to the mind, but at these ready money had to pass from hand to hand before the pouring started and at the Drones there were no such tedious formalities. You just signed your name.

It occurred to him, moreover, that at the Drones he might find someone who would have something to suggest. And as luck would have it the first person he ran into in the bar was Freddie Widgeon, not only one of the finest minds in the club but a man who all his adult life had been thinking up ingenious ways of getting himself out of trouble with the other sex.

He related his story, and Freddie, listening sympathetically, said he had frequently been in the same sort of jam himself. There was, he said, only one thing to do, and Bingo said that one would be ample.

'I am assuming,' said Freddie, 'that you haven't the nerve to come the heavy he-man over the little woman?'

'The what?'

'You know. Looking her in the eye and making her wilt. Shoving your chin out and saying "Oh, yeah?" and "So what?" '

Bingo assured him that he was not in error. The suggested

procedure was not within the range of practical politics.

'I thought not,' said Freddie. 'I have seldom been able to function along those lines myself. It's never easy for the man of sensibility and refinement. Then what you must do is have an accident.'

Bingo said he did not grasp the gist, and Freddie explained.

'You know the old gag about women being tough babies in the ordinary run of things but becoming ministering angels when pain and anguish wring the brow. There's a lot in it. Arrange a meeting with Mrs Bingo in your normal robust state with not even a cold in the head to help you out, and she will unquestionably reduce you to a spot of grease. But go to her all bunged up with splints and bandages, and her heart will melt. All will be forgiven and forgotten. She will cry "Oh, Bingo darling!" and weep buckets.'

Bingo passed a thoughtful finger over his chin.

'Splints?'

'That's right.'

'Bandages?'

'Bandages is correct. If possible, bloodstained. The best thing to do would be to go and get knocked over by a taxi cab.'

'What's the next best thing?'

'I have sometimes obtained excellent results by falling down a coal hole and spraining an ankle, but it's not easy to find a good coal hole these days, so I think you should settle for the taxi.'

'I'm not sure I like the idea of being knocked over by a taxi.'

'You would prefer a lorry?'

'A lorry would be worse.'

'Then I'll tell you what. Go back to the office and drop a typewriter on your foot.'

'But I should break a toe.'

'Exactly. You couldn't do better. Break two or even three. No sense in spoiling the ship for a ha'porth of tar.'

A shudder passed through Bingo.

'I couldn't do it, Freddie old man,' he said, and Freddie clicked his tongue censoriously.

'You're a difficult fellow to help. Then the only thing I can suggest is that you have a double.'

'I've already had one.'

'I don't mean that sort of double. Tell Mrs Bingo that there must be someone going about the place so like you that the keenest eye is deceived.'

Bingo blossomed like a flower in June. Almost anything that did not involve getting mixed up with taxi cabs and typewriters would have seemed good to him, and this seemed particularly good.

'This business of doubles,' Freddie continued, 'is happening every day. You read books about it. I remember one by Phillips Oppenheim where there was an English bloke who looked just like a German bloke, and the English bloke posed as the German bloke or vice versa, I've forgotten which.'

'And got away with it?'

'With his hair in a braid.'

'Freddie,' said Bingo, 'I believe you've hit it. Gosh, it was a stroke of luck for me running into you.'

But, back at the office, he found his enthusiasm waning. Doubts began to creep in, and what he had supposed to be the scheme of a lifetime lost some of its pristine attractiveness. Mrs Bingo wrote stories about girls who wanted to be loved for themselves alone and strong silent men who went out into the sunset with stiff upper lips, but she was not without a certain rude intelligence and it was more than possible, he felt, that she might fail to swallow an explanation which he could now see was difficult of ingestion. In its broad general principles Freddie's idea was good, but his story, he could see, would need propping up. It wanted someone to stiffen it with a bit of verisimilitude, and who better for this purpose than Miss Murgatroyd? Her word would be believed. If he could induce her to go to Mrs Bingo and tell her that she had never set eyes on him in her life and that her Trafalgar Square crony was a cousin of hers of the name – say – of Ernest Maltravers or Eustace Finch-Finch – he was not fussy about details – the home might yet be saved from the melting pot. He looked up George Francis Augustus Delamere, fifth Earl of Ippleton, in the telephone book and was presently in communication with him.

'Lord Ippleton?'

'Speaking.'

'Good morning.'

'Who says so?'

'My name is Little.'

'And mine,' said the peer, who seemed to be deeply moved, 'is mud.'

'I beg your pardon?'

'Mud.'

'Mud?'

'Yes, mud, after what that ass of a daughter of mine got up to yesterday. I shan't be able to show my face at the club. The boys at the Athenaeum will kid the pants off me. Sitting on her fanny in the middle of Trafalgar Square and getting hauled in by the flatties. I don't know what girls are coming to these days. If my mother had behaved like that, my old governor would have spanked her with the butt end of a slipper, and that's what some responsible person ought to do to young Mabel. "See what you've done, you blighted female," I said to her when she rolled in from the police court. "Blotted the escutcheon, that's what you've done. There hasn't been such a scandal in the family since our ancestress Lady Evangeline forgot to say No to Charles the Second!" I let her have it straight from the shoulder.'

'Girls will be girls,' said Bingo, hoping to soothe.

'Not while I have my health and strength they won't,' said Lord Ippleton.

Bingo saw that nothing was to be gained by pursuing this line of thought. Mabel Murgatroyd's parent was plainly in no mood for abstract discussion of the modern girl. Even at this distance he could hear him gnashing his teeth. Unless it was an electric drill working in the street. He changed the subject.

'I wonder if I could speak to Miss Murgatroyd?'

'Stop wondering.'

'I can't.'

'No.'

'Why not?'

'Because I've shipped her off to her aunt in Edinburgh with strict instructions to stay there till she's got some sense into her fat little head.'

'Oh, gosh!'

'Oh what?'

'Gosh.'

'Why do you say "Gosh"?'

'I couldn't help it.'

'Don't be an ass. Anybody can help saying "Gosh". It only requires willpower. What are you, a reporter?'

'No, just a friend.'

Bingo had never heard the howl of a timber wolf which had stubbed its toe on a rock while hurrying through a Canadian forest, but he thought it must closely resemble the sound that nearly cracked his ear drum.

'A friend, eh? You are, are you? No doubt one of the friends who have led the ivory-skulled little moron astray and started her off on all this escutcheon-blotting. I'd like to skin the lot of you with a blunt knife and dance on your remains. Bounders with beards! You have a beard, of course?'

'No, no beard.'

'Don't try to fool me. All you ghastly outsiders are festooned with

the fungus. You flaunt it. Why the devil don't you shave?'
    'I shave every day.'
    'Is that so? Did you shave today?'
    'As a matter of fact, no. I hadn't time. I had rather a busy morning.'
    'Then will you do me a personal favour?'
    'Certainly, certainly.'
    'Go back to whatever germ-ridden den you inhabit and do it now. And don't use a safety razor, use one of the old fashioned kind, because then there's a sporting chance that you may sever your carotid artery, which would be what some writer fellow whose name I can't recall described as a consummation devoutly to be wished. Goodbye.'
    It was in thoughtful mood that Bingo replaced the receiver. He fancied that he had noticed an animosity in Lord Ippleton's manner – guarded, perhaps, but nevertheless unmistakably animosity – and he was conscious of that feeling of frustration which comes to those who have failed to make friends and influence people. But this was not the main cause of his despondency. What really made the iron enter into his soul was the realization that with Mabel Murgatroyd in Edinburgh, not to return till the distant date when she had got some sense into her fat little head, he had lost his only chance of putting across that double thing and making it stick. It was, he now saw more clearly than ever, not at all the sort of story a young husband could hope to make convincing without the cooperation of a strong supporting cast. Phillips Oppenheim might have got away with it, but that sort of luck does not happen twice.
    It really began to seem as if Freddie Widgeon's typewriter-on-toe sequence was his only resource, and he stood for some time eyeing the substantial machine on which he was wont to turn out wholesome reading matter for the chicks. He even lifted it and held it for a moment poised. But he could not bring himself to let it fall. He hesitated and delayed. If Shakespeare had happened to come by with Ben Jonson, he would have nudged the latter in the ribs and whispered 'See that fellow, rare Ben? He illustrates exactly what I was driving at when I wrote that stuff about letting "I dare not" wait upon "I would" like the poor cat in the adage.'
    Finally he gave up the struggle. Replacing the machine, he flung himself into his chair and with his head in his hands uttered a hollow groan. And as he did so, he got the impression that there was a curious echo in the room, but looking up he saw that he had been in error in attributing this to the acoustics. There had been two groans in all, and the second one had proceeded from the lips of H. C.

Purkiss. The proprietor of *Wee Tots* was standing in the doorway of his private office, propping himself against the woodwork with an outstretched hand, and it was obvious at a glance that he was not the suave dapper H. C. Purkiss of yesterday. There were dark circles under his eyes, and those eyes could have stepped straight on to any breakfast plate and passed without comment as poached eggs. His nervous system, too, was plainly far from being in midseason form, for when one of the local sparrows, perching on the window sill, uttered a sudden *cheep*, he quivered in every limb and made what looked to Bingo like a spirited attempt to lower the European record for the standing high jump.

'Ah, Mr Little,' he said huskily. 'Busy at work, I see. Good, good. Is there anything of interest in the morning post bag?'

'Mostly the usual gibbering,' said Bingo. 'Amazing how many of our young subscribers seem to have softening of the brain. There is a letter from Wilfred Waterson (aged seven) about his parrot Percy which would serve him as a passport into any but the most choosy lunatic asylum. He seems to think it miraculous that the bird should invite visitors to have a nut, as if that wasn't the first conversational opening every parrot makes.'

Mr Purkiss took a more tolerant view.

'I see your point, Mr Little, but we must not expect old heads on young shoulders. And speaking of heads,' he went on, quivering like an Ouled Nail stomach dancer, 'I wonder if you could oblige me with a couple of aspirins? Or a glass of tomato juice with a drop of Worcester sauce in it would do. You have none? Too bad. It might have brought a certain relief.'

Illumination flashed upon Bingo. If an editor's respect for his proprietor had been less firmly established, it might have flashed sooner.

'Good Lord!' he cried. 'Were you on a toot last night?'

Mr Purkiss waved a deprecating hand, nearly overbalancing in the process.

'Toot is a harsh word, Mr Little. I confess that in Mrs Purkiss's absence I attempted to alleviate my loneliness by joining a group of friends who wished to play poker. It was a lengthy session, concluding only an hour ago, and it is possible that in the course of the evening I may have exceeded – slightly – my customary intake of alcoholic refreshment. It seemed to be expected of me, and I did not like to refuse. But when you use the word "toot" . . .'

Bingo had no wish to be severe, but except when throwing together stories to tell Mrs Bingo he liked accuracy.

'It sounds like a toot to me,' he said. 'The facts all go to show that . . .'

He broke off. An idea of amazing brilliance had struck him. Twenty-four hours ago he would never have had the moral courage to suggest such a thing, but now that H. C. Purkiss had shown himself to be one of the boys – poker parties in the home and all that – he was convinced that if he, Bingo, begged him, Purkiss, to say that he, Bingo, had been with him, Purkiss, last night, he, Purkiss, would not have the inhumanity to deny him, Bingo, a little favour which would cost him, Purkiss, nothing and would put him, Bingo, on velvet. For Mrs Bingo would not dream of disbelieving a statement from such a source. And he had just opened his lips to speak, when Mr Purkiss resumed his remarks.

'Perhaps you are right, Mr Little. Quite possibly toot may be the *mot juste*. But however we describe the episode, one thing is certain, it has placed me in a position of the gravest peril. The party – "party" is surely a nicer word – took place at the house of one of the friends I was mentioning, and I am informed by my maidservant that Mrs Purkiss made no fewer than five attempts to reach me on the telephone last night – at 10.30 p.m., at 11.15 p.m., shortly after midnight, at 2 a.m. and again at 4.20 p.m., and I greatly fear...'

'You mean you were away from home all *night*?'

'Alas, Mr Little, I was.'

Bingo's heart sank. He would have reeled beneath the shock, had he not been seated. This was the end. This put the frosting on the cake. Impossible now to assure Mrs Bingo that he had been with Mr Purkiss during the hours he had spent in his Bosher Street cell. So poignant was his anguish that he uttered a piercing cry, and Mr Purkiss rose into the air, dislodging some plaster from the ceiling with the top of his head.

'So,' the stricken man went on, having returned to terra firma, 'I should be infinitely grateful to you, Mr Little, if you would vouch for it that I was with you till an advanced hour at your home. It would, indeed, do no harm if you were to tell Mrs Purkiss that we sat up so long discussing matters of office policy that you allowed me to spend the night in your spare room.'

Bingo drew a deep breath. It has been sufficiently established that the proprietor of *Wee Tots* was not as of even date easy on the eye, but to him he seemed a lovely spectacle. He could not have gazed on him with more appreciation if he had been the Taj Mahal by moonlight.

His manner, however, was austere. A voice had seemed to whisper in his ear that this was where, if he played his cards right, he could do himself a bit of good. There was, so he had learned from a reliable source, a tide in the affairs of men which, taken at the flood, leads on to fortune.

He frowned, at the same time pursing his lips.

'Am I to understand, Purkiss, that you are asking me to tell a deliberate falsehood?'

'You would be doing me a great kindness.'

In order to speak Bingo had been obliged to unpurse his lips, but he still frowned.

'I'm not sure,' he said coldly, 'that I feel like doing you kindnesses. Yesterday I asked you for a raise of salary and you curtly refused.'

'Not curtly. Surely not curtly, Mr Little.'

'Well, fairly curtly.'

'Yes, I remember. But I have given the matter thought, and I am now prepared to increase your stipend by – shall we say ten pounds a month?'

'Make it fifty.'

'Fifty!'

'Well, call it forty.'

'You would not consider thirty?'

'Certainly not.'

'Very well.'

'You agree?'

'I do.'

The telephone rang.

'Ah,' said Bingo. 'That is probably my wife again. Hullo?'

'Bingo?'

'Oh, hullo, moon of my delight. What became of you when we were talking before? Why did you buzz off like a jack rabbit?'

'I had to go and look after Mrs Purkiss.'

'Something wrong with her?'

'She was distracted because Mr Purkiss was not at home all night.'

Bingo laughed a jolly laugh.

'Of course he wasn't. He was with me.'

'What!'

'Certainly. We had office matters to discuss, and I took him home with me. We sat up so long that I put him up in the spare room. He spent the night there.'

There was a long silence at the other end of the wire. Then Mrs Bingo spoke.

'But that photograph!'

'Which photograph? Oh, you mean the one in the paper, and I think I know what's in your mind. It looked rather like me, didn't it? I was quite surprised. I've often heard of this thing of fellows having doubles, but I've never come across an instance of it before. Except in books, of course. I remember one by Phillips Oppenheim where there was an English bloke who looked just like a German bloke, and the English bloke posed with complete success as the German bloke or vice versa. I've forgotten which. I believe it caused quite a bit of confusion. But, getting back to that photograph, obviously if I spent the night with Mr Purkiss I couldn't have spent it in a dungeon cell, as my double presumably did. But perhaps you would care to have a word with Mr Purkiss, who is here at my side. For you, Purkiss,' said Bingo, handing him the telephone.

21

STYLISH STOUTS

'Ah, there you are, Mr Little,' said H. C. Purkiss. 'Are you engaged for dinner tonight?'

Bingo replied...

But before recording Bingo's reply it is necessary to go back a step or two and do what is known to lawyers as laying the proper foundation.

It was the practice of H. C. Purkiss, proprietor of *Wee Tots*, the journal for the nursery and the home, to take his annual holiday in July. This meant that Bingo, the paper's up-and-coming young editor, had to take his in June or August. This year, as in the previous year, he had done so towards the middle of the former month, and he rejoined the human herd, looking bronzed and fit, a few days before the Eton and Harrow match. And he was strolling along Piccadilly, thinking of this and that, when he ran into his fellow clubman Catsmeat Potter-Pirbright (Claude Cattermole, the popular actor of juvenile roles) and after a conversation of great brilliance but too long to be given in detail Catsmeat asked him if he would care to have a couple of seats next week for the dramatic entertainment in which he was appearing. And Bingo, enchanted at the prospect of getting into a theatre on the nod, jumped at the offer like a rising trout. He looked forward with bright enthusiasm to seeing Catsmeat bound on with a racquet at the beginning of act one shouting 'Tennis, anyone?' as he presumed he would do.

There remained the problem of choosing a partner for the round of pleasure. His wife, Rosie M. Banks the widely read author of novels of sentiment, was at Droitwich with her mother and Algernon Aubrey, the bouncing baby who had recently appeared on the London scene. He thought of Mr Purkiss, but rejected the idea. Eventually he decided to go and ask his Aunt Myrtle, Mrs J. G. Beenstock, if she would like to come along. It would mean an uncomfortable evening. She would overflow into his seat, for she was as stout a woman as ever paled at the sight of a diet sheet and, had she been in Parliament, would have counted two on a division, but she was a lonely, or fairly lonely, widow and he felt it would be a kindly act to bring a little sunshine into her life. He ankled round, accordingly, to her house and his ring at the bell was answered by Wilberforce, her butler, who regretted to say that Madam was not in residence, being on one of those Mediterranean cruises. He was anticipating her return, said Wilberforce, either tomorrow or the day after, and Bingo was about to push off when the butler, putting a hand over his mouth and speaking from the side of it, said in a hushed whisper:

'Do you want to make a packet, Mr Richard?'

A packet being what above all things Bingo was always desirous of making, his reply in the affirmative was both immediate and eager.

'Put your shirt on Whistler's Mother for the two o'clock at Hurst Park tomorrow,' whispered Wilberforce, and having added that prompt action would enable him to get odds of eight to one he went about his butlerine duties, leaving Bingo in a frame of mind which someone like the late Gustave Flaubert, who was fussy about the right word, would have described as chaotic.

What to do, what to do, he was asking himself, this way and that dividing the swift mind. On the one hand, Wilberforce was a knowledgeable man who enjoyed a wide acquaintance with jockeys, race course touts, stable cats and others who knew a bit. His judgment of form could surely be trusted. On the other hand, Mrs Bingo, who like so many wives was deficient in sporting blood, had specifically forbidden him to wager on racehorses, and he shrank from the scene which must inevitably ensue, should the good thing come unstuck and she found out about it. The situation was unquestionably one that provided food for thought.

And then he realized that his problem was after all only an academic one, for he was down to his last five bob with nothing coming in till pay day and with bookies money has to change hands before a deal can be consummated. If a dozen Whistler's Mothers were entered for a dozen two o'clock races, he was in no position to do anything about it.

It was quite a relief really to have the thing settled for him, and he was in excellent spirits when he got home. He took off his shoes, mixed himself a mild gin and tonic, and was about to curl up on the sofa with a good book, when the telephone rang.

A well-remembered voice came over the wire.

'Sweetie?'

'Oh, hullo, sweetie.'

'When did you get back?'

'Just clocked in.'

'How are you?'

'I'm fine, though missing you sorely. And you?'

'I'm fine.'

'And Algy?'

'He's fine.'

'And your mother?'

'Only pretty good. She swallowed some water at the brine baths this morning. She's better now, but she still makes a funny whistling sound when she breathes.'

The receiver shook in Bingo's right hand. The good book with which he had been about to curl up fell limply from his left. He had always been a great believer in signs and omens, and if this wasn't a sign and omen he didn't know a sign and omen when he saw one.

'Did you say your mother was a Whistler's – or rather a whistling mother?' he gasped at length.

'Yes, it sounds just like gas escaping from a pipe.'

Bingo tottered to a chair, taking the telephone with him. He was feeling bitter, and he had every excuse for feeling bitter. Here he was with a sure thing at his disposal, barred from cashing in on it for lack of funds. Affluence had been offered to him on a plate with watercress round it, and he must let it go because he did not possess the necessary entrance fee. He could not have had a more vivid appreciation of the irony of life if he had been Thomas Hardy.

'Oh, by the way,' said Mrs Bingo, 'what I really rang up about. You know it's Algy's birthday next week. I've bought him a rattle and some sort of woolly animal, but I think we ought to put something in his little wee bank account, as we did last year. So I'm sending you ten pounds. Goodbye, sweetie, I must rush. I'm having a perm and I'm late already.'

She rang off, and Bingo sat tingling in every limb. He continued to tingle not only till bedtime but later. Far into the silent night he tossed on his pillow, a prey to the hopes and fears he had experienced when Wilberforce had mooted the idea of his making a packet. Once more the question 'What to do?' raced through his fevered mind. It was not qualms about touching his offspring for a temporary loan that made him waver and hesitate. That end of it was all right. Any son of his, he knew, would be only too glad to finance a father's sporting venture, particularly when that sporting venture was in the deepest and fullest sense of the words money for jam. And he did not need to tell the child that when the bookie brassed up on settling day he would get his cut and find his little wee bank account augmented not by one tenner but by two.

No, it was the thought of Mrs Bingo that made him irresolute.

Wilberforce was confident that Whistler's Mother would defy all competition, giving the impression that having a bit on her was virtually tantamount to finding money in the street, but these good things sometimes go wrong. The poet Burns has pointed this out to his public. 'Gang agley' was how he put it, for he did not spell very well, but it meant the same thing. And if this one went agley, what would the harvest be? He fell asleep still wondering if he dared risk it.

But the next morning he was his courageous self again. The luncheon hour found him in the offices of Charles ('Charlie Always Pays') Pikelet, the well-known turf accountant, handing over the cash, and at 2.13 sharp he was in a chair in the Drones Club smoking room with his face buried in his hands. The result of the two o'clock race at Hurst Park had just come over the tape, and the following horses had reached journey's end ahead of Whistler's Mother – Harbour Lights, Sweet Pea, Scotch Mist, Parson's Pleasure, Brian Boru, Ariadne and Christopher Columbus. Eight ran. Unlike Wilberforce, the poet Burns had known what he was talking about.

How long he sat there, a broken man, he could not have said. When he did emerge from his coma, it was to become aware that a good deal of activity was in progress in the smoking room. A Crumpet was sitting at a table near the door with a pencil in his hand and a sheet of paper before him, and there was a constant flowing of members to this table. He could make nothing of it, and he turned for an explanation to Catsmeat Potter-Pirbright, who had just taken the chair next to him.

'What's going on?' he asked.

'It is the Fat Uncles Sweep,' Catsmeat said.

'The what?'

Catsmeat was amazed.

'Do you mean to say you don't know about the Fat Uncles Sweep? Weren't you here last year when it started?'

'I must have been away.'

'The race is run on the first day of the Eton and Harrow match.'

'Ah, then I was away. I always have to take my holiday early, and don't get back for the Eton and Harrow match. I did this time, but not as a rule. What is it?'

Catsmeat explained. An intelligent Drone, he said, himself the possessor of one of the fattest uncles in London, had noticed how many of his fellow members had fat uncles, too, and had felt it a waste of good material not to make these the basis of a sporting contest similar, though on a smaller scale, to those in operation in Ireland and Calcutta. The mechanics of the thing were simple. You entered your uncle, others entered theirs, the names were shaken up in a hat and the judging was done by McGarry, the club bartender, who had the uncanny gift of being able to estimate to an ounce the weight of anything, from a Pekinese to a Covent Garden soprano, just by looking at it.

'And the fellow who draws the winning ticket,' Catsmeat concluded, 'scoops the jackpot. Except, of course, for the fifty pounds allotted to the winning uncle's owner as prize money.'

A loud gasp escaped Bingo. A passer-by would have noticed that his eyes were shining with a strange light.

'Fifty pounds?'

'That's right.'

Bingo shot from his chair and gazed wildly about the room.

'Where's Oofy?' he cried, alluding to Oofy Prosser, the club's millionaire.

'In the bar, I believe. What do you want him for?'

'I want to enter my Aunt Myrtle and sell him a piece of her to enable me to meet current expenses.'

'But – '

'Don't sit there saying "But". When's the drawing?'

'Three days from now.'

'Plenty of time. I'll approach him at once.'

'But – '

'That word again! What's bothering you? If you think Oofy won't make a deal, you're wrong. He's a business man. He'll know he'll be on a sure thing. You've seen my Aunt Myrtle and you can testify to her stoutness. There can't possibly be an uncle fatter than her. Let's go and find Oofy now and have him draw up an agreement.'

'But aunts aren't eligible. Only uncles.'

Bingo stared at him, aghast.

'What ... what did you say?'

Catsmeat repeated his statement, and Bingo quivered in every limb.

'You mean to tell me that if a man has the stoutest aunt in the West End of London, an aunt who, if she were not independently wealthy, could be making a good living as the Fat Woman in a circus, he can't cash in on her?'

'I'm afraid not.'

'What a monstrous thing! Are you sure?'

'Quite sure. It's all in the book of rules.'

It was a Bingo with heart bowed down and feeling more like a toad beneath a harrow than the editor of a journal for the nursery and the

home who returned to the offices of *Wee Tots* and endeavoured to concentrate on the letters which had come in from subscribers for the
Correspondence page. He took up a communication from Edwin
Waters (aged seven) about his Siamese cat Miggles, but he found his
attention wandering. He found the same difficulty in becoming
engrossed in four pages from Alexander Allbright (aged six) about his
tortoise, Shelley, and he had started on a lengthy screed from Anita
Ellsworth (aged eight) which seemed to have to do with a canary of
the name of Birdie, when the door of the inner office opened and Mr
Purkiss appeared.

'Ah, there you are, Mr Little,' said H. C. Purkiss. 'Are you
engaged for dinner tonight?'

Which, if you remember, is where we came in.

Bingo replied hollowly that he was not, and might have added that
if his employer was about to invite him to share the evening meal, he
was prepared to defend himself with tooth and claw.

'I thought that Mrs Little might be having guests.'

'She's at Droitwich with her mother. Her mother is taking the
brine baths. She has rheumatism.'

'Splendid. Excellent. Capital,' said Mr Purkiss, hastening to
explain that it was not the fact of Bingo's mother-in-law having
trouble with her joints that exhilarated him. 'Then you are free. I am
delighted to hear it. Tell me, Mr Little, are you familiar with the
work of an American author of juvenile fiction named Kirk
Rockaway? No? I am not surprised. He is almost unknown on this
side of the Atlantic, but his Peter the Pup, Kootchy the Kitten and
Hilda the Hen are, I understand, required reading for the children of
his native country. I have glanced at some of his works and they are
superb. He is just the circulation-builder *Wee Tots* needs. He is here
in London on a visit.'

Bingo was a conscientious editor. His personal affairs might be in a
state of extreme disorder, but he was always able to shelve his private
worries when it was a matter of doing his paper a bit of good.

'We'd better go after him before those blighters at *Small Fry* get
ahead of us,' he said.

Mr Purkiss smiled triumphantly.

'I have already done so. I met him at a tea party given in his honour
yesterday, and he has accepted an invitation to dine with me tonight
at Barribault's Hotel.'

'That's good.'

'And this,' said Mr Purkiss, 'is better. At that tea party a most significant thing happened. Somebody mentioned Mrs Little's books,

and he turned out to be a warm admirer of them. He spoke of them with unbounded enthusiasm. You see what I am about to say, Mr Little?'

'He wants her autograph?'

'That, of course, and I assured him that he could rely on her. But obviously tonight's arrangements must be changed. You, not I, must be his host. As Mrs Little's husband, you are the one he will want to meet. I will ring him up now.'

Mr Purkiss went back to his room, to return a few moments later, beaming.

'All is settled, Mr Little. I had, I am afraid, to stoop to a slight prevarication. I told him I was subject to a bronchial affection which rendered it inadvisable for me to venture out at night, but that my editor, the husband of Rosie M. Banks, would be there in my place. He was all enthusiasm and is looking forward keenly to meeting you. I will, of course, defray your expenses. Here are ten pounds. That will amply cover the cost of dinner, for Mrs Rockaway tells me he is a lifelong teetotaller, so there will be no wine bill. You can bring me the change tomorrow.'

To say that Bingo was elated at the prospect of an evening out with a man who wrote about hens and kittens and drank only lemonade would be incorrect. Nor did he fail to writhe at the thought that Life had sprung another of its ironies on him by putting ten pounds in his trouser pocket but making it impossible for him to divert the sum into Algernon Aubrey's little wee bank account. For one mad moment he toyed with the idea of not giving Kirk Rockaway dinner and holding on to Mr Purkiss's tenner, but he discarded it. If he stood Kirk Rockaway up, the hen and kitten specialist would be bound to contact Mr Purkiss and ask him what the hell, and Mr Purkiss, informed of the circumstances, would instantly relieve his young assistant of his editorial post. And if he suddenly ceased to occupy the editorial chair Mrs Bingo would want to know why, and ... but here Bingo preferred to abandon this train of thought. Shortly before eight o'clock he was in the lobby of Barribault's Hotel, and in due course Kirk Rockaway appeared.

One says 'appeared', but the word would not have satisfied Gustave Flaubert. He would have suggested some such alternative as 'loomed up' or 'came waddling along' as being more exact, for the author of Kootchy the Kitten and Peter the Pup was one of the fattest men that ever broke a try-your-weight machine. He looked as if he had been eating nothing but starchy foods since early boyhood, and it saddened Bingo to think of all this wonderful material going to waste. If only this man could have been his uncle, he felt wistfully. Oofy Prosser would have paid twenty pounds for a mere third of him.

'Mr Little?' said this human hippopotamus. He grasped Bingo's hand and subjected him to a pop-eyed but reverent gaze. 'Well, well, well!' he said. 'This is certainly a great moment for me. Mrs Little's books have been an inspiration to me for years. I read them incessantly and I am not ashamed to say with tears in my eyes. She seems to make the world a better, sweeter place. I am looking forward to having the privilege of meeting her. How is she? Well, I hope?'

'Oh, fine.'

'That's good,' said Kirk Rockaway, and then he uttered these astounding words: 'Let's get one thing straight, Mr Little. The money of Rosie M. Banks's husband is no good in this hotel. Dismiss all thought of picking up the tab tonight. This dinner is on me.'

'What!'

'Yes, sir. I wouldn't be able to look Mrs Little in the face if I let you pay for it.'

The lobby of Barribault's Hotel is solidly constructed and the last thing in the world to break suddenly into the old fashioned buck-and-wing dance, but to Bingo it seemed that it was forgetting itself in this manner. There were two pillars in its centre, and he distinctly saw them do a kick upwards and another kick sideways. Ecstasy for a moment kept him dumb. Then he was able to murmur that this was awfully kind of Mr Rockaway.

'Don't give it a thought,' said Kirk Rockaway. 'Let's go in, shall we?'

Over the smoked salmon what conversation took place was confined to Bingo's host. Bingo himself still felt incapable of speech. The realization that by this miracle at the eleventh hour he had been saved from the fate that is worse than death – viz. having to confess the awful truth to Mrs Bingo and listen to her comments on his recent activities, seemed to have paralysed his vocal cords. He was still dazed and silent when the soup arrived.

The evening was warm and it had been quite a walk through the lobby and into the restaurant and across the restaurant to their table, and Kirk Rockaway, evidently unused to exercise, had felt the strain. By the time the soup came, beads of perspiration had begun to form on his forehead, and after about the fifth spoonful he reached in his breast pocket for a handkerchief. He pulled it out and with it came a cabinet size photograph which shot through the air and fell into Bingo's plate. And as Bingo fished it from the purée and started to dry it with his napkin, something familiar about it struck his attention. It portrayed a woman of ample dimensions looking over her shoulder in an arch sort of way, and with a good deal of surprise he recognized her as Mrs J. G. Beenstock, the last person he would have expected to find in his soup.

'Well, well,' he said. 'So you know my aunt?'

'Your what?'

'My aunt.'

Kirk Rockaway stared at him, astounded.

'Is that divine woman your aunt?'

'That's just what she is.'

'You amaze me!'

'I'm amazed, too. What are you doing going about with her photograph next to your heart?'

Kirk Rockaway hesitated for a moment. He seemed to be blushing, though it was hard to say for certain, his face from the start having been tomatoesque. Finally he spoke.

'Shall I tell you something?' he said.

'Do.'

'I've come all the way from Oakland, San Francisco, to marry her.'

It was Bingo's turn to stare, astounded.

'You mean you and Aunt Myrtle are engaged?'

So great was his emotion that he could hardly frame the words. It seemed to him too good to be true, too like a beautiful dream, that this obese bimbo was about to become his uncle and so eligible for the Drones Club contest.

An embarrassed look had come into Kirk Rockaway's face. Again he hesitated before he spoke.

'No, we're not engaged.'

'You aren't?'

'Not yet. It's like this. She came to San Francisco a year or so ago.'

'Yes, I remember she went over to America. She's very fond of travelling.'

'We met at a dinner party. It was a Thanksgiving dinner with turkey, sweet potatoes, mince pie – the customary Thanksgiving menu. She sat opposite me, and the way she sailed into the turkey – enjoying it, *understanding* it, not pecking at it as the other women were doing – hit me right here,' said Kirk Rockaway, touching the left side of his bulging waistcoat. 'And when I watched her handle the mince pie, I knew my fate was sealed. But I haven't actually proposed yet.'

'Why not?'

'I haven't the nerve.'

'What!'

'No, sir, I haven't the nerve.'

'Why not?'

'I don't know. I just haven't.'

A blinding light flashed upon Bingo. Mr Purkiss's words rang in his ears. 'He is a lifelong teetotaller', Mr Purkiss had said, and the whole thing became clear to him.

'Have you tried having a drink?' he asked.

'I've drunk a good deal of barley water.'

'Barley water!'

'But it seems to have no effect.'

'I'm not surprised. Barley water!' Bingo's voice was vibrant with scorn. 'What on earth's the good of barley water? How can you expect to be the masterful wooer on stuff like that? I should be a bachelor today if I hadn't had the prudence to fill myself to the brim with about a quart of mixed champagne and stout before asking Rosie to come registrar's-officing with me. That's what you want, champagne and stout. It'll make a new man of you.'

Kirk Rockaway looked dubious.

'But that's alcohol, and I promised my late mother I would never drink alcohol.'

'Well, I think if you could get in touch with her on the ouija board and explain the situation, making it clear that you needed the stuff for a good cause, she would skip the red tape and tell you to go to it. But that would take time. It might be hours before you got a connection. What you want is a noggin of it now, and then when you are nicely primed, we will go and drop in on my aunt. She has been away on a Mediterranean cruise, but she may be back by now. Waiter, bring us a bottle of Bollinger and all the stout you can carry.'

It was some half hour later that Kirk Rockaway looked across the table with a new light in his eyes. They had become reddish in colour and bulged a good deal. His diction, when he spoke, was a little slurred.

'Old man,' he said. 'I like your face.'

'Do you, old man?' said Bingo.

'Yes, old man, I do. And do you know why I like your face?'

'No, old man, I don't. Why do you like my face?'

'Because it is so different in every respect from Mortimer Frisby's.'

'Who is Mortimer Frisby?'

'You may well ask. He conducts the Children's Page on the San

Francisco Herald, and calls himself a critic. Do you know what he
said about my last book, old man?'

'No, what did he say, old man?'

'I'll tell you what he said. His words are graven on my heart and I
quote verbatim. "We think," he said, "that Mr Rockaway should not
too lightly assume that all the children he writes for have water on the
brain". How about that?'

'Monstrous!'

'Monstrous is right.'

'Abominable!'

'Abominable is correct.'

'The man must be mad.'

'Of course he is. But if he thinks he'll get off on a plea of insanity,
he's very much mistaken. I propose to poke him in the snoot. We'll
have just one more bottle for the road, and then I'll go and attend to
it.'

'Where is he?'

'San Francisco.'

'You can't go to San Francisco.'

'Why not? I believe,' said Kirk Rockaway a little stiffly, 'that San
Francisco is open for being gone to at about this time.'

'But it's such a long way. Besides, you were going to propose to my
aunt.'

'Was I? Yes, by jove, you're right. It had slipped my mind.'

'Do it now, if you're feeling up to it.'

'I'm feeling great. I'm feeling strong, forceful, dominant. Do you
know what I shall do to that woman?'

'Bend her to your will?'

'Precisely. I shall stand no nonsense from her. Women are apt to
want long engagements and wedding services with full choral effects,
but none of that for me. We shall be married ... where was it you
said you were married?'

'At the registrar's.'

'They give you quick service there?'

'Very quick. Over in a flash.'

'Then that's the place that gets my custom. And if I hear a yip out
of her to the contrary, I shall poke her in the snoot. Come on, pay the
check and let's go.'

Bingo's jaw fell.

'You mean pay the bill?'

'If that's what you like to call it.'

'But I thought you were standing me this dinner.'

'What ever gave you that silly idea?'

'You said you would because I was Rosie M. Banks's husband.'

'Whose husband?'

'Rosie M. Banks's.'

'Never heard of her,' said Kirk Rockaway. 'It's your treat, so come across. Or would you prefer that I gave you a poke in the snoot?'

And his physique was so robust and his manner so intimidating that it seemed to Bingo that he had no alternative. With a groan that came up from the soles of his feet he felt in his pocket for Mr Purkiss's ten pounds and with trembling finger beckoned to the waiter.

Bingo's aunt's house was in the Kensington neighbourhood, and thither they repaired in a taxi cab. It was a longish journey, but Kirk Rockaway enlivened it with college yells remembered from earlier days. As they alighted, he was in the middle of one and he finished it while ringing the door bell.

The door opened. Willoughby appeared. Kirk Rockaway tapped him authoritatively on the chest and said: 'Take me to your leader!'

'Sir!'

'The Beenstock broad. I want a word with her.'

'Mrs Beenstock is not at home, and I would be greatly obliged, sir, if you would pop off.'

'I will not pop off. I demand to see the woman I love instantly,' thundered Kirk Rockaway, continuing to tap the butler like a woodpecker. 'There is a plot to keep her from me, and I may mention that I happen to know the ringleaders. If you do not immediately – '

He broke off, not because he had said his say but because he overbalanced and fell down the steps. Bingo, who had entered the hall, thought he saw him bounce twice, but he was in a state of great mental perturbation and may have been mistaken. Willoughby closed the front door, and Bingo wiped his forehead. His own forehead, not Willoughby's.

'Isn't my aunt at home?'

'No, sir. She returns tomorrow.'

'Why didn't you tell the gentleman that?'

'The gentleman was pie-eyed, Mr Richard. Hark at him now.'

He was alluding to the fact that Kirk Rockaway was now banging on the door with the knocker, at the same time shouting in a stentorian voice that the woman he loved was being held incommunicado by a gang in the pay of Mortimer Frisby. Then abruptly the noise ceased and Bingo, peering through the little window at the side of the door, saw that the sweet singer of Oakland, San Francisco, was in

conversation with a member of the police force. He was too far away
to catch the gist of their talk, but it must have been acrimonious, for it
had been in progress only a few moments when Kirk Rockaway, sub-
stituting action for words, hit the constable on the tip of the nose.
The hand of the law then attached itself to his elbow and he was led
away into the night.

The magistrate at Bow Street next morning took a serious view of the
case. The tidal wave of lawlessness which was engulfing London, he
said, must be checked and those who added fuel to its flames by
punching policemen must be taught that they could not escape the
penalty of their misdeeds.

'Fourteen days,' he said, coming to the point, and Bingo, who had
attended the proceedings, tottered from the court feeling that this
was the end. No hope now of that well nourished man marrying his
Aunt Myrtle in time to be entered for the Fat Uncles stakes. When
the judging was done, he would still be in his prison cell – gnawed,
Bingo hoped, for he was in bitter mood, by rats. The future looked
dark to him. He recalled a poem in which there had occurred the line
'The night that covers me, black as the Pit from pole to pole', and he
felt that if he had been asked to describe his general position at the
moment, he could not have put the thing better himself. The words
fitted his situation like the paper on the wall.

Only one ray of hope, and that a faint one, lightened his darkness.
Willoughby had said that his aunt would be back from her Mediterranean cruise today, and he had sometimes found her responsive to
the touch, if tactfully approached. It was a chance which Charles
('Charlie Always Pays') Pikelet would have estimated at perhaps 100
to 8, but it was a chance. He hastened to her house and pressed the
front door bell.

'Good morning, Willoughby.'

'Good morning, Mr Richard.'

'You and your Whistler's Mothers!'

'I would prefer not to dwell on that topic, sir.'

'So would I. Is my aunt in?'

'No, sir. They have gone out to do some shopping.'

'They?' said Bingo, surprised that the butler should have spoken of
his employer, stout though she was, in the plural.

'Madam and Sir Hercules, Mr Richard.'

'Who on earth is Sir Hercules?'

'Madam's husband, sir. Sir Hercules Foliot-Foljambe.'

'What!'

'Yes, sir. It appears that they were shipmates on the cruise from which Madam has just returned. I understand that the wedding took place in Naples.'

'Well, I'll be blowed. You never know what's going to happen next in these disturbed times, do you?'

'No, sir.'

'Of all the bizarre occurrences! What sort of a chap is he?'

'Bald, about the colour of tomato ketchup, and stout.'

Bingo started.

'Stout?'

'Yes, sir.'

'How stout?'

'There is a photograph of the gentleman in Madam's boudoir, if you care to see it.'

'Let's go,' said Bingo. He was conscious of a strange thrill, but at the same time he was telling himself that he must not raise his hopes too high. Probably judged by Drones standards, this new uncle of his would prove to be nothing special.

A minute later, he had reeled and a sharp cry had escaped his lips. He was looking, spellbound, at the photograph of a man so vast, so like a captive balloon, that Kirk Rockaway seemed merely pleasantly plump in comparison. A woman, he felt, even one as globular as his Aunt Myrtle, would have been well advised before linking her lot with his to consult her legal adviser to make sure that she was not committing bigamy.

A long sigh of ecstasy proceeded from him.

'Up from the depths!' he murmured. 'Up from the depths!'

'Sir?'

'Nothing, nothing. Just a random thought. I'm going to borrow this photograph, Willoughby.'

'Madam may be annoyed on discovering its absence.'

'Tell her she'll have it back this afternoon. I only want to show it to a man at the Drones,' said Bingo.

He was thinking of his coming interview with Oofy Prosser. If Oofy was prepared to meet his terms, he would let him have – say – twenty per cent of this certain winner, but he meant to drive a hard bargain.

PELHAM GRENVILLE WODEHOUSE (his brothers were Ernest Armine, Philip Peverel and Richard Lancelot, so he got off fairly lightly) was born in England in 1881 while his mother was on a visit from Hong Kong, to which she shortly returned with the infant Plum. Like many youths of the time, quite a number of whom became writers, he was sent back to England for schooling and raised by aunts, shadows of whom haunt much of his later work.

At his public school, Dulwich, he developed a lifelong passion for cricket and discovered that he could get paid for writing. Two years of working for a London bank persuaded him and the world of finance that they were irreconcilably incompatable, and he never worked again, except to write 130 books and hundreds of short stories, articles, and song lyrics, and to people the literary universe with such immortals as Jeeves, Bertie Wooster, the Hon. Galahad Threepwood, Lord Emsworth, Mr. Mulliner, Aunt Agatha, and Roberta (Bobbie) Wickham.

Because British copyright law protects works for a period of 50 years after the author's death, Wodehouse's first book, The Pothunters, published in 1902, will be in copyright for a total of 123 years, which must be a record or close to it.

A resident of the United States since 1947, Wodehouse became a citizen in 1955, but all the same was knighted by the Queen a few weeks before his death in 1975. As on most days, Wodehouse's last day began with work on his next book.

—D. R. Bensen

THE LIBRARY OF CRIME CLASSICS®

CHARLOTTE ARMSTRONG
The Balloon Man
The Chocolate Cobweb
A Dram of Poison
Lemon in the Basket
A Little Less Than Kind
Mischief
The Unsuspected
The Witch's House

JACQUELINE BABBIN
Bloody Soaps
Bloody Special

GEORGE BAXT
The Affair at Royalties
The Alfred Hitchcock Murder Case
The Dorothy Parker Murder Case
I! Said the Demon
The Neon Graveyard
A Parade of Cockeyed Creatures
A Queer Kind of Death
Satan Is a Woman
Swing Low Sweet Harriet
The Talullah Bankhead Murder Case
Topsy and Evil
Who's Next?

KYRIL BONFIGLIOLI
After You With the Pistol
Don't Point That Thing At Me
Something Nasty in the Woodshed

ANTHONY BOUCHER
Nine Times Nine
Rocket to the Morgue

CARYL BRAHMS & S.J. SIMON
A Bullet in the Ballet
Murder a la Stroganoff
Six Curtains for Stroganova

CHRISTIANNA BRAND
Cat and Mouse

MAX BRAND
The Night Flower

HERBERT BREAN
The Traces of Brillhart
Wilders Walk Away

JOHN DICKSON CARR
Below Suspicion
The Burning Court
Death Turns the Tables
The Door to Doom
Fell and Foul Play
Hag's Nook
He Who Whispers
The House at Satan's Elbow
Merrivale, March and Murder
The Murder of Sir Edmund Godfrey
The Problem of the Green Capsule
The Sleeping Sphinx
The Three Coffins
Till Death Do Us Part
Writing as Carter Dickson
Death In Five Boxes
The Gilded Man
He Wouldn't Kill Patience
The Judas Window
Nine—and Death Makes Ten
The Peacock Feather Murders
The Plague Court Murders
The Punch and Judy Murders
The Reader Is Warned
The Red Widow Murders

The Skeleton In the Clock
The Unicorn Murders
The White Priory Murders

HENRY CECIL
Daughter's In Law
Settled Out of Court
Without Fear or Favour

LESLIE CHARTERIS
Angels Of Doom
The First Saint Omnibus
Getaway
Knight Templar
The Last Hero
The Saint In New York

EDMUND CRISPIN
The Case of the Gilded Fly
Holy Disorders

CARROLL JOHN DALY
Murder from the East

LILLIAN DE LA TORRE
Dr. Sam: Johnson, Detector
The Detections of Dr. Sam: Johnson
The Return of Dr. Sam: Johnson, Detector
The Exploits of Dr. Sam: Johnson, Detector

PETER DICKINSON
Perfect Gallows
The Glass Sided Ants' Nest
Lizard In the Cup
The Sinful Stones

PAUL GALLICO
The Abandoned
Love of Seven Dolls
Mrs.'Arris Goes To Paris
Farewell To Sport

Too Many Ghosts
Thomasina

J. H. H. GAUTE AND ROBIN ODELL
The New Murderers Who's Who

JAMES GOLLIN
Eliza's Galliardo
The Philomel Foundation

DOUGLAS GREENE & ROBERT ADEY
Death Locked In

JONATHAN GOODMAN
The Passing of Starr Faithfull

DASHIELL HAMMETT & ALEX RAYMOND
Secret Agent X-9

A.P. HERBERT
Uncommon Law

REGINALD HILL
A Killing Kindness

RICHARD HULL
The Murder of My Aunt

E. RICHARD JOHNSON
Cage 5 Is Going To Break
Case Load Maximum
Dead Flowers
The God Keepers
The Inside Man
The Judas
Mongo's Back in Town
Silver Street

JONATHAN LATIMER
The Dead Don't Care
Headed for a Hearse

The Lady in the Morgue
Murder In the Madhouse
The Search for My Great Uncle's Head
Red Gardenias
Solomon's Vineyard

VICTORIA LINCOLN
A Private Disgrace—Lizzie Borden by Daylight

BARRY MALZBERG
Underlay

CYNTHIA MANSON & CHARLES ARDAI
New England Crime Chowder

NGAIO MARSH
The Collected Short Fiction of Ngaio Marsh

MARGARET MILLAR
An Air That Kills
Ask for Me Tomorrow
Banshee
Beast in View
Beyond This Point Are Monsters
The Cannibal Heart
The Fiend
Fire Will Freeze
How Like An Angel
The Iron Gates
The Listening Walls
Mermaid
The Murder of Miranda
Rose's Last Summer
Spider Webs
A Stranger in My Grave
Vanish In An Instant
Wall of Eyes

WILLIAM F. NOLAN
Look Out for Space
Space for Hire

WILLIAM O'FARRELL
Repeat Performance

STUART PALMER
The Penguin Pool Murder
Murder On The Blackboard
Murder On Wheels

STUART PALMER & CRAIG RICE
People VS Withers and Malone

BARBARA PAUL
Liars & Tyrants & People Who Turn Blue
Your Eyelids Are Growing Heavy

ELLERY QUEEN
Cat of Many Tails
Drury Lane's Last Case
The Ellery Queen Omnibus
The Tragedy of X
The Tragedy of Y
The Tragedy of Z

PATRICK QUENTIN
Black Widow
Puzzle for Players
Puzzle for Puppets
Puzzle for Wantons
Run To Death

S.S. RAFFERTY
Cork of the Colonies
Die Laughing

CLAYTON RAWSON
Death from a Top Hat
Footprints on the Ceiling
The Headless Lady
No Coffin for the Corpse

CRAIG RICE
The Big Midget Murders
The Corpse Steps Out
8 Faces at 3
Having Wonderful Crime
The Right Murder
Trial By Fury
The Wrong Murder

DAMON RUNYON
Trials and Tribulations

GEORGE SANDERS
Crime On My Hands

WALTER SATTERTHWAIT
Miss Lizzie

HAKE TALBOT
Rim of the Pit

ROBERT TAYLOR
Fred Allen—His Life and Wit

DARWIN L. TEILHET
The Talking Sparrow Murders

P.G. WODEHOUSE
Full Moon
If I Were You
Plum's Peaches
Service with a Smile
Tales From the Drones Club
The Uncollected Wodehouse
Who's Who In Wodehouse
Wodehouse On Crime

Write For Our Free Catalog:
International Polygonics, Ltd.
Madison Square, P.O. Box 1563
New York, NY 10159